The Amazing Adventures of Stick Daring

Sailing around Britain in a £50 boat

Part 1 - Just To Jeff's

&

Part 2 - Laugh? I Nearly Died

The Amazing Adventures of Stick Daring Part 1 and Part 2

Copyright © 2019, 2020, text and pictures. Neil Peters. Cover design and map illustrations. Guy Noble.

Front cover background image Jen Kneale.

All rights reserved. No part of this publication may be reproduced or used in any form or by any means – photographic, electronic or mechanical, including photocopying, recording taping or information storage and retrieval systems – without permission of the author.

Published by Smartdial Limited

Printed by Book Printing UK www.bookprintinguk.com
Remus House, Coltsfoot Drive, Peterborough, PE2 9BF
Printed in Great Britain

Although every precaution has been taken in the preparation of this book, the publisher and author assume no responsibility for errors or omissions. Neither is any liability assumed for damages resulting from the use of information contained herein.

ISBN 978-1-3999-7498-1

A Stick Daring production

Find videos and pictures on

www.stickdaring.com
Facebook: stickdaringarounduk

Foreword

Why would someone set off in a tiny plastic boat and sail around one of the most dangerous coastlines? A landmass with the second largest tidal range in the world and the cause of more than 40,000 shipwrecks.

Does this decision really matter? Can it affect anything? What could be achieved and would it be of any relevance? These are questions that I didn't even consider before I left. But ones I have pondered upon since.

One of my friends compared my trip around the UK to being a bit like the lunar landing of Neil Armstrong. I couldn't really see that at the time except for the fact that I'd sprayed my boat safety orange and grey like the lunar module. In every other way my trip was different.

It was an ill-conceived idea fuelled by beer and implemented because peer pressure from fellow sailors made it happen. A loss of face was the initial driver. Very quickly the euphoria from the thrill of adventure turned into a hangover of reality. A long, relentless, often desperate slog ensued. There were highs and lows throughout the journey, most frequently all of life's emotions crammed into one day. Every day was different. Every day was testing. There were very few easy miles.

I'm often asked what were the worst and what were the hardest moments. The ones I was least expecting is my best reply.

There were numerous events when I conveniently ignored advice because it wasn't what I wanted to hear which in turn led to thoughts like "OMG it's actually worse than they said". At this point, fear is a useful emotion to have. It makes you grip more tightly to stop yourself being catapulted out of the boat as she's tossed into the air and comes crashing down. All you can think is. I want to go home!

My account of a journey around the UK in a £50 singlehanded Laser sailing dinghy is true. I do confess that on occasion it may appear that I've not let the truth get in the way of a good story. Believe it all or don't, I just hope you enjoy this adventure as much as I did. I'm also proud to say that, in the process, I helped raise awareness of and contributions to an incredible worthwhile charity.

Ron Pattenden introduced me to Prostate Cancer UK at an inspirational talk he gave at Pevensey Bay Sailing Club back in March of 2019. I decided I would use my Laser circumnavigation to support this cause because when I researched it, I was very surprised to learn that prostate cancer kills one person every 45 minutes. It's the most common cancer in men in the UK, many men have it and never even know they do. Early detection can significantly increase survival so awareness is one of the key weapons in the battle against this terrible disease that kills more than 11,500 people a year.

The day before I set off, I set up a Just Giving page in the hope that my trip might raise £1000 for Prostate Cancer UK. At the time I think I hadn't quite decided in my heart whether Inverness would be my final destination or I'd carry on but, in the end, with Gift Aid my voyage round Britain raised over £20,000 for this truly worthy cause and I am grateful to every single person who contributed.

Thank you.

The Amazing Adventures of Stick Daring

Contents

The Amazing Adventures of Stick Daring

Contents
Part 1 - Just To Jeff's

Chapter 1
Whose Idea Was This Anyway? 1

Chapter 2
Bexhill or Bust 9

Chapter 3
100 Things 17

Chapter 4
Mad May 21

Chapter 5
Countdown From Roses, A Place of Rest 28

Chapter 6
The First Day 45

Chapter 7
The White Cliffs of Dover 50

Chapter 8
First Crossing: Thames Estuary 64

Chapter 9
It's a Blast – East Coast 78

Chapter 10
Southwold Ahoy! 91

Chapter 11
Humber Crossing 116

Chapter 12
The Slow Route North 126

Chapter 13
Climbing Out of a Big Hole 130

Chapter 14
Beat the North East 138

Chapter 15
Geordie Shore 155

Chapter 16
Impossible Task! 160

Chapter 17
The God Effect 166

Chapter 18
Last English Stronghold then Scotland 174

Chapter 19
Écosse de bas 176

Chapter 20
Oil Country 186

Chapter 21
Peterhead "Blood Draining!" 193

Chapter 22
Take Rosehearty 203

Chapter 23
Keep on Trouping 206

Chapter 24
Just to Jeff's 212

Dedication 219

Special Thanks 220

The Amazing Adventures of Stick Daring

Contents
Part 2 - Laugh?I Nearly Died

Chapter 25
    Monsters and Madness 1

Chapter 26
    Fun and Games at Helmsdale 6

Chapter 27
    Moine Schists at Duncansby Head 13

Chapter 28
    Ivor and the Merry Men 31

Chapter 29
    Radioactive... Oh Betty! 41

Chapter 30
    Flattened at Sango Sands 50

Chapter 31
    Dive for Cover – Kinlochbervie 63

Chapter 32
    Wet Wet Wet – Clachtoll 71

Chapter 33
    Leopard's Place 81

Chapter 34
    Magic Carpet to Portnadoran 89

Chapter 35
    Western Most Point Latitude 56°43.619'N/Longitude 006°13.567'W 97

Chapter 36
Josh n' Craigy Fish 104

Chapter 37
Carsaig Caravan 111

Chapter 38
Madness at the Mull 120

Chapter 39
Meltdown at Portpatrick 134

Chapter 40
Across to Man to Meet a Poole 142

Chapter 41
Aground at Port St Mary 151

Chapter 42
Holyhead Whip 163

Chapter 43
Friday 13th, Whistling Sands 168

Chapter 44
Commodore's Reception 175

Chapter 45
Torpedoes at Fishguard 182

Chapter 46
Put the Bentley Back in the Garage, Uncle Francis 195

Chapter 47
Julie Seaweed and Friends 202

Chapter 48
Dr Bottom 207

Chapter 49
Hiding in a Mousehole **214**

Chapter 50
At Last, The Lizard **223**

Chapter 51
Salcombe Salute **229**

Chapter 52
The Way to Weymouth **235**

Chapter 53
"Double Dinner" **247**

Chapter 54
Red Zone! **255**

Chapter 55
Flying Cowes **260**

Chapter 56
Watch Out for Bill **269**

Chapter 57
Five Day Finale **278**

Appendix
Three Years on **286**

Dedication **291**

Glossary of Terms **292**

Special Thanks **298**

The Amazing Adventures of Stick Daring

Part 1
Just To Jeff's

Chapter 1

Whose Idea Was This Anyway?

You're probably thinking how did I get to this stage in the first place? The insane idea of circumnavigating Britain in a 1970s built, 13-foot Laser sailing dinghy made of thin fibreglass; a single-handed sailing dinghy a little longer than your bath. One that is nearly 50 years old which, in Laser years is equivalent to about 150. That then is a really good question and one that I'm not entirely sure I know the full answer to, even now.

People I've known for many years told me subsequent to my trip that I'd mentioned this idea at least 20 years ago. I can't recall that but I can confess to having a wanderlust. My thirst for adventure and desire to meet different people and explore new places has been in me ever since I can remember.

Blame Jeff. Yes, I think it was really Jeff's fault. Back in the winter of 2016, Jeff, a cycling friend and well-known Eastbourne decorator and personality, had come to help me in the Historic Doors empire that I owned; an empire consisting of myself and usually one or two other semi- permanent contractors. Jeff had been brought in as a materials coating expert; painter and decorator to you and me. We'd had a big run on the sale of front doors so Jeff was clearing the order backlog, mostly preparing and painting. We'd had a lot of doors on the go in the workshop so Jeff was with me for a many of the cold winter months, happy to have some inside work.

Jeff liked to talk. He worked and lived on his own and apart from Leo, his totally soppy English Bull Terrier, Jeff was currently between girlfriends and had no one else to vent to. No air was usually spared. He talked about everything from remote control model aeroplanes to remote model aeroplanes, model planes, more model planes, oh and did I mention model planes? This was interlaced with stories of the disastrous romances in his life. Jeff often recited tales of the Shetland Isles. Unst, Britain's northernmost isles on the Shetlands, usually got a mention most days. He would tell me how he'd catch the ferry across from Inverness and take his bike all the way up to the tip of Britain and watch the sky. He'd go on his own with a bottle of whisky for company and enjoy the Highlands.

At the time I'd no idea what he was talking about. It just seemed like a lonely, pretty saddo thing to do. Go on your own to a place with only a handful of people in the entire village, climb up the side of the mountain and neck a bottle of whisky.

Over time, Jeff's stories started to infect me. I increasingly found myself looking up place names on maps and on one occasion I even researched house prices and places for sale on the Shetland Islands. One particularly conversationally active day resulted in Jeff and I looking into the possibility of jointly investing in the remote island of Lingua. We explored the idea of making it into a yacht haven during the summer months. The entire island was cheaper than my back garden in the south of England. This island project took up a few weeks of my time. I made calls and looked into grants. Lingua was very close to the mainland but had no running water, power or indeed any services. It did have planning consent for a crofting village and museum though. It also had the benefit of a few derelict buildings still standing. The idea soon wore off when we found out we needed at least a million pounds to install the essential services and set up the required buildings and infrastructure for a tiny harbour but in the process, I studied rainfall, of which there was lots, and wind, of which there was also lots; both more often than not. The people we talked to about our ideas on Shetland were lovely, really excited and super helpful. When we finally came to our senses and binned the plan, they were probably quite disappointed. We'd virtually doubled the Shetland Isles tourism trade by the time we'd exhausted our fantasy island project. I'm sure they'd heard it all before from other fantasists like myself. They may have even been disappointed at not being able to witness at first hand the certain project failure of those southerners!

Jeff and I carried on renovating historic doors throughout the winter of 2016. We undertook many beautiful resuscitation projects as I'd call them, beating off the plastic fantastic brigade from ripping out England's finest old wooden doors and stuffing in some draught proof plastic monstrosity. I was a purist. I loved old wood. My desire to renovate often clouded my commercial judgement. The doors we worked on usually turned into labours of love. We never seemed to make any money but they always looked sensational by the time we'd finished.

If we weren't sanding, painting or fixing doors we were out cycling across the beautiful rolling hills of the South Downs of England; usually ending up rehydrating from our journeys at our favourite watering hole, The Eight Bells. We'd meet other likeminded loons on their bikes here, clad in mud covered lycra and often smelling like they'd just been extracted from a pile of rotting fish. We, the mountain bikers, regarded it as our duty to keep The Eight Bells authentic for all the tourists visiting the quaint village of Jevington. I'd always get my best ideas in The Eight Bells, bouncing up and down on the edge of my bar stool, extolling the virtues of something that had just entered my head, describing it as if it were reality and usually ending up wondering why everyone else didn't want to instantly join in with the latest hare-brained scheme, something PY, later to be one of my Safety Channel team, politely used to point out was another 'brain fart'.

Well, sailing round Britain in a Laser came about after one of these high-energy, alcohol fuelled moments. I can't recall the exact day or time or even who was in the pub at the time. I remember applying one of my maximum excitement plans to this idea. Every time I went into the pub I'd try to persuade any of my unsuspecting, and mostly very suspecting, drinking or biking mates to join in with me.

I tried to convince Jason to do it with me on a kite surfer and Neil on a paddleboard. I then tried to persuade Jeff to race me round the entire British coastline on his bike, on account that he couldn't swim but at least he'd still be involved. Jay, I even suggested, might try to drive it in his Bentley but if you'd seen his Bentley, you'd probably safely stake your house on my Laser beating him round the UK. Mostly it ended up with roars of laughter and a million reasons why we couldn't do it. Do you like the way I slipped in 'We'? I always tried to build a movement using 'we' as if it was a more inclusive statement.

My main protagonist, PY, saw through the bluff and puff very quickly. He had this annoying habit of being super boring; almost autistic in his outlook on life but expertly insightful when one of my brain farts was turned up to max volume. PY was the ultimate sales prevention officer. His opening technique was usually to drive a Tomahawk missile straight through the middle of anything I proposed. Nuke it before it got off the ground. His normal retort, after my anti sales prevention defence systems were deployed was,

"For God's sake man! Let the air breathe."

I'd see this as the ultimate moment to double the enthusiasm and triple the energy, turn on max volume about the latest madcap scheme. PY, facing certain intellectual defeat or just simply exhausted with the pointlessness of it all, would usually retire to bed or excuse himself but, if he did get the upper hand in one of these exchanges, he became unbearably obnoxious and rude to such an extent that jaws often gaped at the breathless, directness of his acerbically blunt insults being launched at me.

PY pointed out to me once that he thought the reason why I spouted every idea I ever had out loud first was because it was the only way my left-side brain could figure out what my right-side brain was thinking. I think he's right. In fact, I know he's right. I was tested with my youngest son, Fred, a few years earlier. We were both assessed for ADHD or whatever they want to label 'can't sit still long enough before moving onto the next great moment in life'. Well as it turns out, they identified a few areas of Fred's brain that needed some attention and training but when it came to mine, they were slightly more concerned. I told them not to worry as I'd lived with this brain for enough years now to know how it operated. They didn't look convinced. PY could have given them a documentary report longer than the Hillsborough Investigation if they'd asked him. I didn't volunteer him the opportunity to do so.

Somehow, the round Britain idea in the Laser started to gain some traction. I even started getting people I bumped into on the sailing circuit saying,

"Thought you were supposed to be going round Britain this summer."

I felt a bit feeble when this was levelled at me and mumbled something about it wasn't the right year, work commitments were getting in the way, it's an El Nino year or something similarly weak and pathetic. This one wasn't going away now, I used to think. I might even actually have to do this. The more this happened, the harder I tried to find some other willing victims to join in.

It didn't get any easier when Rupert Bedell, one of my 'G7' sailing gang and future Safety Channel officer, decided to set up a Facebook page in 2016 entitled stickdaringrounduk. The G7 are a bunch of my closest laser sailing mates and we often meet up at events both in the UK and at international opens overseas. The G7 included Neil Peters, Pete Young, Rupert Bedell, Organic Gareth (no-one ever knew his surname), Roger O'Gorman, Dave Freeman and a wonderful man called Chris Fyans.

Anyway, Rupert drew a large map, plotted a line around the UK and actually added some of the words I'd been spouting on the Facebook page. This really was the catalyst I needed to start looking into the proposed voyage properly.

I began researching online, studying places, looking regularly at sea and wind forecasts. I tried to imagine how my day would have gone had I been sailing that day. I even jumped in my van one day and drove down to somewhere in the West Country in order to meet up with Jeremy Warren. At the time, Jeremy and Phil, his crew, held the record for being the fastest to circumnavigate the UK in a sailing dinghy. The boat they did it in was a Wayfarer class dinghy which, to those unfamiliar with this craft, is a 15-foot long, two person sailing dinghy, designed for cruising but not necessarily the first choice of boat to sail around Britain in. A great achievement!

Jeremy was suitably helpful and furnished me with extensive notes of their journey. They'd analysed their trip for a year before departing, working on numerous and various passage plan scenarios. Phil, whom I'd never met, was some kind of maths expert and had concluded that mathematically it really didn't matter which way round you sailed as it all depended on the wind direction. They went clockwise. Knowing what I now know, I'm not convinced Phil was right.

When I arrived at Jeremy's, his wife didn't seem so keen to meet me as I was ushered into their sitting room. Maybe I'd rekindled bad memories of Jeremy's and Phil's adventure for her because, reading between the lines, I think she found the whole experience quite stressful and deeply worrying. They'd both encountered numerous life-threatening moments during their circumnavigation of the UK. I'd already mentally devised a danger scale to assess the risks involved. When I quizzed Jeremy and asked him to score the most dangerous moment of his trip, his highest score was a nine. I think this was crossing the Bristol Channel when they got caught out in a big storm but I could be completely wrong about this. On my danger scale, 10 is dead and one is fantastically alive. Jeremy then suggested I meet Ron and quiz him.

"Who's Ron?"

Ron Pattenden is probably the most insane person I've ever met and I include myself in this assessment. Ron sailed clockwise round Britain in his Laser called Oops in 2004. It took him the best part of half a year to do so. He also managed to break almost half a dozen masts in the process! When he set off, Ron was better known for his extreme land based athletic prowess. From what I learned, Ron has virtually licked his way across the finish line of some of his super marathon runs where he has competed all across the world. Runs where you do 150 miles straight without stopping or sleeping. How do people do that? Runs where you are shown a desert and you've got to get to the other side, only there is a mere 20,000 foot mountain range you have to ascend on the way.

Ron happened to believe all these adventuring skills could be transferred to sailing a Laser. Fitness for sure is one skill you need to sail a Laser round Britain, survival and roughing it another. Some degree of sailing technique is also helpful. Ron was certainly very brave, very, very brave in my view. Clearly fit and quite good at planning, although instead of the techno navigation plotter favoured by Jeremy and Phil, Ron opted for an AA road atlas! However, on the planning scale, he sat somewhere in the middle of Jeremy and Phil and myself. I concluded that I occupied the extreme low end of the planning class reserved for those of us who utilise a fag paper to record their conclusions on!

Ron had and still has a fantastically optimistic outlook on life. An example of this was his utilisation of the AA road atlas to plan his sea passage around Britain. Those of a less optimistic disposition might conclude that locating any roads at sea might be a somewhat unlikely prospect! He'd regularly rolled up, often quite literally rolled in the surf on the way in to shore, and frequently had to ask the local inhabitants where he was. Back in 2004 when he did it, he was afforded none of the luxuries of modern-day portable navigation aids such as satelite navigation, apps like Navionics or even GPS. His was what I'd call an adventure in the RAW. He made it round alive. He loved doing it. Or so he remembers. He proved to be an extremely positive ally in my preparation stage; that is until he mentioned a week before leaving that he thought I was cutting it a bit fine on the preparation.

Chapter 2

Bexhill or Bust

It was a freezing cold day in March 2016. Jeff stood by my boat as I rigged the sail. There wasn't a lot of wind so it was always going to be a bit of a mismatch; Jeff cycling on the flat tarmac roads to Bexhill, me sailing against the tide from Pevensey Bay. My route was obviously more direct than Jeff's, but not by a lot. I felt mine to be safer than his. He thought otherwise. I loaded two Tesco five litre water bottles into the back of my cockpit and lashed them to the toe strap. I also hung one 20 litre dry bag round the mast at the front of the boat. My idea was to simulate carrying the same weight of kit as I'd need to take with me round the UK. Jeff couldn't stop laughing at me struggling down the beach with my boat.

The air temperature was about five degrees and the water temperature was seven degrees on the Celsius. The sea is usually at its coldest point in March after the winter has cooled it down. Unlike air, sea water temperatures take a long time to change even when the air temperature is hot. My hands felt numb from cold just sorting the rigging out and as soon as they got wet, the wind chill factor would make them feel even colder. I braced myself and pushed off the beach. On this occasion, Jeff had agreed to retrieve my boat's galvanised steel and pneumatic wheeled launching trolley from the water's edge back up the beach. Going round Britain, I wouldn't be able to have the luxury of a launching trolley.

I still hadn't figured out how I was going to launch and recover the boat yet. Thirteen foot long and perhaps 130 kilos with kit, the boat wouldn't be an easy launch and recovery task especially when low tides might leave hundreds of yards of beach to negotiate. I wasted several days before the test run with Jeff messing about trying to modify an old golf trolley which I thought might be light enough to carry with me. When I tested my contraption in the car park of my workshop, a flat concrete base, the wheels snapped off almost immediately. What a waste of time that was! I started looking around for old Laser plastic trolleys, the obsolete type supplied with the very early manufactured Laser dinghy. These were lightweight plastic tubes roped together and attached to a thin metal axle with hollow plastic wheels. They nearly always broke because they were too light. I had this bizarre idea that I could strap one of these to the deck of my boat and sail around Britain. I hadn't met Ron Pattenden then so hadn't been privy to his simple master plan on launching and recovery. He used a pneumatic tubular yacht fender which was placed under the boat and acted as a roller. Each time it reached the back of the boat it was taken out and put back at the front which is broadly the same historic technique used to launch fishing boats on shingle beaches when wooden planks were utilised. Why hadn't I thought of this? So much for my research and strategic planning!

When I launched the boat for this test, I used a standard Laser sail. I'd previously been experimenting with a three-piece mast, the idea being it would be possible to make the rig larger or smaller depending on the weather conditions. When the wind was light, I'd run with the maximum sail size and when it was strong, I'd run with the minimum sail size and remove the central sleeve. I'd taken a standard two-piece mast and added a middle extension section to make it longer. My sail making friend, Gary Smith, then kindly modified my Rooster 8.1m sail (an extra-large sail) so it could be reefed.

The reefing modifications weren't quite as simple as I'd first thought. Gary added a zip along the whole width of the sail so I could fold the sail into smaller segments. It was quite a neat solution except it needed to have a sail that could slide down the mast. A standard Laser sail has a tube that slides over the mast and is fixed at the top so is deliberately designed not to slide down the mast. To be able to lower the sail from inside the boat, the top of the sail tube had to be open but normally there's a webbing strap to prevent the sail sliding down whilst sailing. In order to keep the sail up the mast, I needed a further modification so I had to add a halyard which, to the average layman, is a piece of string. The string is attached to a pulley fixed to the top of the sail passing through it and dropping to the deck so the sail can be hauled up and down. The halyard is secured fast at the bottom using a cleat attached to the mast or deck. For the uneducated, reefing is merely a way of reducing the overall size of the sail in an effort to make a sailing vessel more manageable in strong winds.

There was a further problem. The mast becomes wider at the bottom and the sail tube is a tight fit at the top of the sail so the sail gets stuck after only a few feet. That was enough although I decided to make some difference to reduce the sail area in an emergency. Before my test sail with Jeff, I tried out the sail. I reduced the sail height using the halyard to lower it. I zipped up the sail, reduced the extra sail cloth using Gary's new reefing system and launched the boat. This manufacturing process had been a lengthy one that I concluded would be brilliant and I excitedly embarked on sea trials of this newly devised system. Sadly, and to my bitter disappointment, as soon as the sail filled with wind the zip instantly failed and split wide open, creating a parachute shaped sail. Another failure, so back to the proverbial drawing board or in my case, fag paper!

Back to my race against Jeff to Bexhill. The breeze was blowing from the north east about 12 knots and the tide was against me. It was a tight fetch, sailing almost on the slowest point of sailing into the wind. As I passed the Cooden Beach Hotel, I kept looking up to the cliff top road to see if Jeff was visible. No sign of him. We were both carrying a VHF radio and a mobile so I tried calling him on the VHF. No reply. I concluded that he probably had his head down on the bike blasting along at full speed towards Bexhill. I was fully hiked. This is where you sit out of the boat using your feet to stop you falling backwards by hooking them under the central toe strap. Your body weight is stretched as far out over one side to keep the boat flat. Usually, the flatter the boat, the faster you go. If you do this properly it's quite tiring and after an hour of doing it, I was starting to fade. I was freezing too. Every few seconds the water kept splashing over my lower back each time I hit a wave. I thought I could make out the De La Warr Pavilion but wasn't certain as I was quite a way offshore. As I started closing in, I was sure I was right. The thing I realised on this test run is that even though I was only half a mile offshore, buildings you're familiar with driving around in your car look totally different from the sea and become much more difficult to identify. I wasn't very familiar with the buildings down here anyway.

I decided I needed to sail in closer to shore. Close enough to use the VHF radio. I sailed in towards the shore hoping I might spot Jeff. No sign, so I pulled out the radio and gave it a quick blast. Nothing. Jeff wasn't responding. I decided I'd use my mobile phone now. I was in my good boat and didn't want to scratch the underside of the hull landing on the rocky beach at Bexhill. If I could find Jeff, he could help lift the boat up the beach to avoid damaging it. I stood up squinting along the shoreline for any clues as to Jeff's whereabouts. I had to remove the phone from the waterproof case to call him as I couldn't get the screen to work. Just as I finally got the mobile to connect and start ringing, I got caught off balance standing up in the boat. A larger than normal wave broke over the bow and I fell overboard, arms and legs clutching at thin air as I entered the freezing water head first. I was clutching the phone in one hand and trying to hang onto the boat with the other. I missed as the boat capsized, now dangerously close to the beach in the breaking waves of the shore dump. My foot had got twisted around the mainsheet – the rope used to pull in the sail. The mainsheet got caught around the two five litre water bottles strapped in the cockpit. The effect of this was that the boat had capsized but the sail was jammed so it was still pointing in the air while the boat was on its side.

Now I was in trouble. With the sail in the air, it effectively meant the boat was still powered up, a bit like leaving the accelerator depressed in an accident. Being blown inshore into the worst of the breaking waves, I was really struggling to free my foot but kept being pulled under each wave as it broke over me. The mainsheet got tighter and tighter around my ankle as the wind now seemed to be blowing much harder. Usually, the sail of an upturned Laser dinghy flops lifelessly into the water, making getting the boat back upright relatively easy. In this instance, the sail was still pointing up in the air because the rope looped around my foot was continuing to pull it in, powering the partially upturned boat along the surf whilst still on its side. My body was going into cold shock. I had a wet suit on but my hands just weren't working properly and I was getting breathless. I struggled to get back into the boat. Every time I nearly made it into the cockpit, a gust of wind and a new set of waves smashed into me, tightening the noose around my foot, pulling my head under water.

This was ridiculous I thought to myself. I'm only a few yards offshore. Surely I can't drown before I've even started. It took a radical decision to escape. I must have been capsized for 10 minutes or more before I decided to dive under the water and reach for my boot and try to remove it. I was wearing my expensive Aigle sailing boots. These are lace up ankle length boots, very popular in the late 1980s. They are quite bulky by today's standards and usually incredibly difficult to get off as they're tight around the ankles. Originally these laced up the front but in my case all the lacing eyes had been ripped out so I'd wrapped duct tape around the top to keep them on. I'm not noted as a fashion guru on the sailing circuit!

I wrestled with the trapped boot for ages before finally it came off but not before I'd unpicked the duct tape. Now that my foot was free, I swung my body onto the centreboard; this is the long fibreglass blade that sticks two feet out of the bottom of the boat and stops the boat sliding sideways in the water when it's sailing. When the boat is on her side it can be climbed onto. It looks a bit like a diving board and can be used to lever the sail out of the water by standing on the tip furthest from the bottom of the boat until the boat returns back upright. I managed to get both hands on the centreboard. This took all my strength as it was floating a good foot above my head. Timing it to catch a wave which lifted me out of the water, I heaved myself up onto my chest so that I was now lying on my stomach across the board. I clung on for a few moments catching my breath. Now I had to try to swing a leg up so I could kneel and then get myself into a standing up position, keeping my balance while the boat crashed around in the breaking waves. As soon as I was in position it was obvious there was no way I could right the boat. I was now on the wrong side of the sail for the wind direction. If I pulled her up now, she'd just fall on top of my head and flop over the other way, trapping me underneath the sail. I decided to improvise and surfy-swooshed the boat along, still lying half on her side until it was shallow enough for me to just stand up. I couldn't right her fully as the waves were breaking over me so I just let her wash ashore, keeping the mast tip just clear of the sand and rocks so it didn't stick in and snap.

Phew I was ashore! The boat looked a total mess, covered in seaweed with sand, rocks and stones everywhere. However, amazingly when I did my checks afterwards, nothing seemed to have broken. I removed my bag and emptied the two five litre water bottles. I was shivering badly when Jeff appeared laughing hysterically. He helped me to drag then carry the boat up the beach. The mobile phone was dead but the VHF was still working. More importantly, I'd not lost my treasured 1980s Aigle sailing boot. Man, what a day! I concluded that sailing round Britain alone might not be as easy as it seemed after all!

Jeff and I headed for the warmth of the cafe on the De La Warr Pavilion. Cake and a cappuccino later and I'd stopped shivering. It turns out Jeff had been waiting nearly an hour. He'd stopped along the way at the pub and even found time to down a pint of beer. Some locals asked Jeff what he was up to so Jeff explained he was in a race. The locals quizzed him as to who with then commented on how relaxed he looked. Jeff pointed out to me, a speck on the sea and said,

"Against him."

The locals looked out to sea and saw me slowly creeping along against the tide and said,

"Against him!"

They started laughing then the whole pub came over and they all joined in the mirth.

My return sail back to Pevensey Bay was uneventful and slow as the tide had turned against me. Jeff managed two more pints on the way back and still comfortably beat me by over an hour.

The following evening, we agreed to have a debrief in The Eight Bells. We rode the five mile off-road trip we regularly made over the South Downs on our bikes. A few beers were consumed that night. Most of The Eight Bells bar crew thought the account of the race was hilarious. Jeff fell off his stool laughing and I was the butt of the jokes. I joined in but realised...

It had started!

Chapter 3

100 Things

After the sea trial with Jeff, I felt surprisingly motivated for a few months. I sourced an old Laser sailing boat that had been painted bright yellow to add to my collection. In fact, I already owned two nearly new identical Lasers but these were immaculate and expensively set up for racing. Both were parked up at Pevensey Bay Sailing Club, two miles from Eastbourne.

The old yellow boat had no mast or sail nor any of the required hull fittings to enable her to be rigged or indeed sailed. She had been abandoned and therefore was now a useful experimental boat. I started cutting holes in her, adding hatches, trying to figure out how to store everything I'd need to take with me, experimenting with places to sit, inventing storage areas, thinking about navigation devices, solar panels, oars, tent, sleeping bag, food, cooker, pots and pans; then what about the safety kit and would I need clothes for every eventuality?

I really had no idea what I'd need to take with me so one rainy day I sat down at my work desk in the second-hand door emporium that was all my own and scribbled down a list. I got to three pages of A4 paper – 100 things – easily. How much would this lot weigh? More to the point, where would I put it all? After scratching my head for several days, pondering on where I could store it all, I abandoned the idea again. It was just impossible. How on earth was I going to fit me and all the gear in?

A few more weeks passed, then a few months and the kit I'd initially assembled on the yellow boat was gathering dust. I'd see-sawed mentally, swaying between sailing round Britain in my speedos carrying only a credit card or loading up with the full monty from my list of 100 things. I mused that speedos may be a tad chilly and probably lacked a pocket to hold a credit card but equally the list of 100 things would be too heavy and unwieldy. I'd struggle to get the boat up the beach with no gear on board and I'd never get her up the beach loaded. And, even if I did, she'd probably float so low in the water, it would be impossible to sail. Another logistics dilemma!

I parked the whole idea. I was getting bored with this now. 2016 turned into a year of racing Lasers for me. I entered numerous events on the Masters circuit for competitors over 35 years, politely referred to as Apprentice Masters. The youngsters call us the Geriatrics. Sad to think you are considered old at 35! I raced at Hayling Island, Parkstone in Poole Harbour, the Queen Mary Sailing Club on a reservoir in Ashford near Heathrow Airport and Felpham Sailing Club near Bognor on the south coast where I managed a win. During the following years, 2017 and 2018, a similar set of events ensued with my usual mixed results. I helped to arrange for Pevensey Bay Sailing Club, my home club, to host one of the World Championship qualifying events in September 2016 through to 2019, attracting over 100 boats each time. I visited various other UK and European Laser racing events including Fousenant in France for the Laser Europeans in 2017 and large international races at Ostend in Belgium and the European Championships with close to 300 boats in Roses, Spain in 2019. In fact,

I competed in that event three weeks before setting off to sail around the UK.

I travelled a lot with PY and the rest of the G7, making sporadic appearances, all of them being somewhat younger than me and somehow attending most events while juggling childcare and family duties with their number one passion, sailing together with drinking and generally acting like juveniles which also came closely behind in the passion stakes.

I travelled around in my 'half-arse' camper, appropriately named by our late G7 gang member, Chris Fyans. Chris, a great friend and mentor to me, sadly died aged just 70 just a week before Christmas 2017 after setting off on a bike for a local ride and being found on the grass a few hours later. I still miss him greatly. Chris called my van this because it was really just a beaten-up Transit panel van converted by Network Rail as a welfare or surveillance van. I'd always argue the hidden qualities of the half-arse claiming it could offer a million assets: central heating, a hot shower, chemical toilet, microwave oven, gas cooker, sink, tool store, fold out bed, dining chair and table, surround sound hi-fi and, yes, cinema, pull-out awning with safari canvas surround, external lights, rear tool store and sink. Nothing half-arsed about it!

I used to load the boat onto the roof which was no small achievement as the van was a high-top Transit. To get her up the three metres onto the top of the van, I'd devised and built a special solution I called the 'easy loader'. Search YouTube for the Brian Bathroyd Easy Loader. Don't ask, why Brian Bathroyd? – that's a whole new story but the easy loader was really not even a not so easy loader but more of a 'just possible to load a Laser boat alone if absolutely necessary (and there was an odd tyre or grassy bank to stand on) loader'.

Usually I'd park the half-arse anywhere other than on an official campsite. Stealth camping was the way to go. PY would usually accompany me on these extreme stealth camping escapades though his van was not as well-stealthed as mine. He'd helpfully correct me by referring to it as 'not as shite'.

PY had a proper OCD van. His VW camper was 100% prissy. Very shiny. Nothing was out of place and everything was on a miniature scale to mine. We'd regularly have 'van off' conversations. Although not pretty, my van clearly was more suited to living in than his for these sailing events but he never saw it that way. He always refused to sample any cuisine I created in my ocean-sized galley, usually on the grounds of hygiene. The fact the cooker unfolded directly above the toilet was irrelevant in my eyes. After all, you were unlikely to require the use of both at the same time.

During 2017 and 2018, the round the UK idea rarely got discussed. It had been consigned to the dustbin of a million other half-hearted, half-started ideas, never to see the light of day again.

Chapter 4

Mad May

2019 started very strangely. For the first time in more than 20 years, I had no children at home. My eldest boy, William, was living and working in Hong Kong and my other two boys, George and Freddie, were at university in Newcastle and Southampton respectively.

Suddenly, after 25 years of raising kids, my wife, Emma, and I found a new freedom to travel. We searched for the cheapest deals and near the end of February 2019 set off to visit our son Will in Hong Kong for a few days (strange that you wait a quarter of a century to get rid of them and then at the first opportunity you go and find them!). Our plan was to carry on for a week of relaxation and unwinding together in northern Thailand. We travelled for what felt like days from Bangkok along the Cambodian border in an assortment of crafts including a van, a speedy bath boat and a Toyota Hilux. At sea, you're only given a safety briefing and life jacket as you come to the end of the trip! I could only surmise this was a formality they couldn't be bothered to waste any energy on at the outset and at least this way, the transport company could guarantee everyone disembarking could confirm they'd been given a safety briefing.

My favourite transport on this trip was the 30-foot long bath boat with two enormous 200hp outboards, home fashioned to transport tourists. The trick with this boat, in case you ever get in one, is to sit at the front. Oh, and duck as you climb in so as not to knock yourself out on the sun canopy cage like Emma did as she jumped in and almost swallowed her teeth. The bath boat had bench seats down both sides. Luggage was arranged along the full length of the boat in the centre. Tourists were squeezed in on both sides of the luggage along and between the single benches, facing inwards, almost kneeling on their luggage in the centre aisle. The captain, wearing the appropriate captain's hat, in case we didn't realise he was in charge, gently taxied away from the rickety wooden pontoon. As soon as the boat was clear, he absolutely gunned it. Full throttle in a speed boat as anyone who owns one knows – especially one with high powered rear engines – lifts up out of the water at the front. The effect of such instant power coming in made everyone onboard and everything, including the luggage, slide somewhat rapidly backwards (hence my tip about sitting at the front). Those unwise enough to sit right at the back of the boat spent most of their three hour journey squashed by 20 other foreign tourists being forced backwards by gravity. There was nothing to be done except grin and bear it.

The other exceptionally exciting part of our Thailand trip came on the island of Koh Kut. Here, the mode of transport was moped and Toyota Hilux. Hilux was our first choice for transfer from the bath boat to the jungle lodge we were staying in.

This was an incredible experience. Somehow, each Hilux managed to squeeze five into the front cab where they nearly boiled alive on the journey or each guest could elect for the cooler open-air rear pick-up where 10 more could be squashed in, clinging onto the canopy frame on the rear. The roof was covered in suitcases and other luggage; bench seats on both sides, no seat belts or even a roll cage. We would catapult along partially made-up roads, bouncing around at speeds you couldn't possibly think a Hilux with 15 people and a tonne of luggage could move at without falling over round corners. The added difficulty for me was that, due to my height and with the canopy being so low, I had to double over in half just to fit in the back. I ended up staring at the groin of the person opposite me for most of the journey. So that was February into March 2019 done.

As soon as I arrived back from Thailand, I had a mountain of doors to renovate and then deliver to Belgium in May. I checked the sailing calendar and worked out I could compete in a Europa Cup race week in Ostend and combine the trip with work. I also got into planning mode and arranged for Alan Davis, one of the British sailors also racing and living in his van throughout the summer, to transport my race boat by road trailer to Roses in Spain for the European Championships taking place in June. I could then drive back to the UK in my van and start preparing my other Laser MOD27 to sail around the UK then fly back out to Roses and compete in the Laser Masters European races. It all fitted perfectly.

However, between returning from Thailand and going to Belgium and Roses I still had to squeeze in another trip. Several months earlier I'd cleverly realised Emma may need a bit of buttering up before my big voyage. A treat for her, I thought. So, in a flash of impetuousness, I'd booked weekend flights to Iceland. I'd bought the tickets for £25 each on a special EasyJet flash sale six months earlier. This was way before I'd seriously contemplated sailing around the UK and before Emma had decided we needed to visit Will in Hong Kong including a second phase in Thailand with him.

Three years earlier, Emma had bought me a fabulous surprise 50th birthday present, a trip to Iceland. We'd travelled all over the southern island and had a fantastic time. We saw the Northern Lights, hot geezers, electric blue ice boulders emerging from a massive glacier onto the beach, amazing waterfalls and had consumed numerous and delicious steaming hot broths. Of course, Emma had planned this trip superbly. She's good at planning trips. Except on this occasion, she'd kept it a secret from me so I'd extract the maximum enjoyment from her surprise present but we were doing the trip on the cheap (we're well-trained). It wasn't until we were actually in the airport, just before checking in for Reykjavik (unbeknown to me at the time) when she asked me where my jacket was. I said I'd left it in the car as I didn't think I'd need it in Tenerife. She still wouldn't reveal our destination but she looked horrified and soon sent me off to buy a new jacket from an airport shop while she checked in our luggage. So, I bought a FatFace lightweight bomber jacket for £50 thinking it would do since "we must be going ski-ing" and I didn't really fancy spending £200 on a proper ski jacket for the slopes of France. I had a perfectly good ski jacket as it happened that I'd left in the car. Anyway, my logic was that I was usually too warm in France wearing a ski jacket at this time of year (December.) Emma continued to look worried when I turned up sporting my casual and wholly unsuitable new FatFace jacket.

When we landed in Iceland it was minus 7 degrees and blowing a force 9 gale. Needless to say, I spent most of the trip wearing all the clothes I'd brought with me and was still freezing. But it was a truly great trip!

So, when I booked Iceland again, I'd planned for us to cycle across the island and do some rough camping. I convinced Emma it would be great fun. When we actually arrived in Iceland, we found out all of the cycle routes were closed especially the one that crossed the 'highlands'. The roads in the middle are only open for a relatively short period of time in their summer which commences in late May/June. I'd chosen early May, the wrong time of year. I suppose the clue for future research and planning by me is to – well, 'do some' as Emma would say.

We also found out very quickly that we couldn't afford anything. The pound had sunk 20% against most currencies due to the Brexit uncertainty and this was coupled with the fact Iceland was officially the fastest growth currency in the world. The value of the Krona against Sterling had doubled in value in the three years since we'd been there in 2016. We spent three days in Reykjavik. It rained relentlessly in sheets and the buildings seemed to match the sky's concrete grey. To make things worse, the UK was having an early spring heatwave. Two mediocre pizzas and two small beers cost £75. We resorted to watching the Eurovision song contest in a bar on the Saturday evening. Beer was on a two-for-one offer so it was the only place in town we could afford at £10 a half pint. This bar also happened to be the only transvestite club in town with live dancing acts throughout the evening. It turned out to be a very funny night even when reluctantly sober!

Sunday, we spent most of the day in the local swimming baths. Top tip, this is the cheapest place to hang out in Iceland. Freezing cold plunge pools followed by hot baths, saunas and steam rooms – all for a few Icelandic Krona. This was a bargain compared to our first day when we paid close on £200 for a ridiculously short boat trip to see a few puffins. In truth, we were both relieved to land back at Gatwick. And starving, like nearly all the other tourists who'd returned.

Now, I'm not quite sure if, when I left for Belgium at the end of May, I'd definitely decided to go round Britain that year, 2019, or defer it until 2020. I'd talked a lot about doing it. I'd thought a lot about doing it but I hadn't actually done anything about doing it at that moment in time as far as I recall which doesn't mean I hadn't prepared anything – I just can't recall having done anything, yet!

I'd employed a neighbour on a contractor basis to help me in the workshop and with on-site fitting. I'd also taken on a friend of Emma's to manage the online and phone sales enquiries and trained her up between my trips to encourage her to become 'me' at work. It all seemed to be going quite well. Sales were up 50% and we had loads of jobs on. The local joiner I used, Neil, was banging out his usual top-quality frames and door accessories and also helped out with some of my more technical door jobs. I was starting to feel really confident about leaving the business in their hands for a few months in the summer.

And then it just unravelled. It started to go wrong when I kept finding my workshop mate skulking around our car park whenever I returned from the suppliers or from visiting customers. He was always furiously typing or talking into his phone. More noticeably, he never seemed to be working so eventually I had it out with him.

It turns out he'd spent all the hard-earned money I'd paid him to buy a pick-up truck – yes, the very one I'd advised him not to go near as it was on eBay and very likely to be a scam – too late! The scammers had got all his money and he'd got nothing! And it got worse. He confessed to me that he was, in fact, in the midst of setting up a door renovation business. "Where?" I asked. "Eastbourne," he replied. Seriously! He was going to be in direct competition with my business in the town we both lived in? Well, that didn't end too well for him that day. I was back on the tools.

It was now mid-May. I had so much work on and no-one to do it except me. Everyone I knew locally who was any good was just flat out. The sun was shining so all my 'usuals' were busy, super busy. Neil, the local joiner, came and helped out when he could and I bribed him with too much money and beer. I also pulled in 'Terry the Wand', a local fine furniture restorer. I got him polishing and painting doors and doing everything and anything I could. I had jobs coming out of my ears. Terry was great but my type of work was a bit rough for him compared to his usual fine polishing of priceless antiques. Nevertheless, Terry and his wife, Nerys, stepped up to the plate and did a great job for me.

After my Belgium delivery and sailing event, I returned to England at the end of May. Neil and I fitted an amazingly beautiful double period front door and triple Edwardian set of back doors in a stunning Eastbourne house. It was a lovely job but needed a bit of on-site snagging and finishing. No time, I was off to the European Laser Masters in Roses. It was now 14th June. I still hadn't done anything about sorting out my round Britain boat, the kit or the route. I was just too busy.

Chapter 5

Countdown From Roses, A Place of Rest

I'd just landed in Roses, northern Spain. Aussie Jeff (different to Jeff who'd moved to Inverness) picked me up at the mainline station in Figueres, home of the amazing Salvador Dali exhibition. Aussie Jeff is a legend! He was old when I first started sailing Lasers in the 1980s but somehow he hadn't really aged much in all the 35 years I'd known him and he still looked just as old. The endearing thing about Jeff is he always seems so relaxed, always laughing at whatever came his way. I've rarely seen Aussie Jeff upset about anything and, even when he was, it would have been difficult to tell.

As a lifestyle, Jeff spends half the year sailing Lasers competitively in Australia during the summer months and in the winter heads off to the northern hemisphere, sailing and racing against anyone he could find.

At that time there was (and still is), a big Laser race circuit in Europe. It mainly attracted youngsters hoping to qualify to represent their country in the Laser sailing class at the Olympics. Jeff was well into his sixties. He always described himself as just an 'athlete.' In Europe, he kept a van parked up undercover somewhere in Manchester during the English winter (Aussie summer) and retrieved it in our summer (their winter). The van was his kind of motel on wheels and it was legendary. This Vauxhall Vivaro was customised for living in. Well, if you were small and didn't need to move much. It had everything in it you could ever need including three fridges, two still boxed just in case the main one broke, two gas cookers, also boxed, a host of solar panels, electric plugs and chargers for every conceivable device, 12v, 24v, 110v, 240v step up and step down converters, inverters and a host of adapter cables, half of which I'd never seen before. Sails, masts, booms, ropes, boxes and boxes of unknown stuff, clothes, wetsuits, tools and more unknown stuff. Even a BMX bicycle which I once saw him trying to ride blind drunk. Jeff didn't really drink until he did then just watch out for Coco the Laughing Clown!

I once witnessed Jeff whizzing off after a reasonable drinking evening at the end of a regatta in France or Spain, I can't recall which. He set off wobbling along the road in the most comical way. Not surprisingly, it didn't end well, upending and face-planting himself Laurel and Hardy style after riding straight into the kerb of a pavement he was trying to cross. He got up and explained sincerely, "The reason I crashed was I wasn't going fast enough." He then set off flat out on the tiny blue BMX bike, weaving across both sides of the wide promenade along the seafront, soon disappearing into the darkness of the night.

Aussie Jeff was a seasoned traveller, a proper nomad, moving around with the Laser sailing circuit wherever it went. The inside of the rear of his van overflowed into the front seat. If you needed a lift with Jeff, your head was cranked over to one side to avoid part of a mast or more commonly seven masts poking through into the front seat. In the rear of the van, every millimetre of panelling was lined with tin foil. The roof insulation was a metalised, plastic bubble wrap stuck on with duct tape. The outside of the roof was covered in roof racks, spars and solar panels. The solar panels were the budget sort you could buy in Maplins in the UK a few years ago when it still existed. If you drove at more than 45 mph, the panels started to lift off and blow away so they had to be gathered in when embarking on a long journey. His navigation was via a 1990s style TomTom. It was so obsolete the maps were virtually hand drawn and it never seemed to work when you needed it. Aussie Jeff swore by its accuracy. He had a surprisingly useless sense of direction but if you needed an explanation on the Coriolis effect or the differences in wind patterns in the Southern Hemisphere versus the Northern Hemisphere, he was the go-to resource.

Roses didn't actually have a train station. I'd caught the very last train from Barcelona to arrive at Figueres around 12.00 pm. Aussie Jeff arrived half an hour late to pick me up as he'd gone to the other station in Figueres – Vilafant where the high-speed train arrives. I'd already had a manic moment earlier in the journey in Barcelona charging back and forth, running across an enormous marble concourse, trying to figure out which platform was the fast train and which platform, the slow train. I'd nearly made it to the fast train, just missing it by a whisker! This was mainly because I'd bought the wrong ticket so I couldn't get through the barriers. Hence, I ended up on the slow train and hence Jeff had spent an hour in the wrong McDonald's car park waiting for me to arrive.

The Roses regatta – the Laser Masters European Championship – was great fun. I barely recall anything about it except for the fact that I slept in my own hotel room – a first for me as I'm usually racked up in my van. I had an enormous balcony you could play football on. I used this only once, walking out stark naked first thing in the morning, stretching up full height and then practising a few press-ups. When I'd finished, I was greeted by looks from a group of elderly ladies breakfasting and staring disapprovingly at me from an overlooking balcony. I finished my stretches and work-out and casually walked back into my room.

I returned to England, hitching a lift back to the airport with Aussie Jeff. The day I landed I went to work for a debrief on the latest catastrophes to beset my little business, Historic Doors. There were plenty. The next day I ignored them all and got the MOD27 into the workshop. It was 22nd June 2019. I should have already left by now. The longest day was gone. From now on, every day I delayed meant less light during sailing days.

That first day of preparation I fixed on the keel band. Well, keel band is a loose description. It was actually a set of doorstep water bars I'd bought from Screwfix. Made of aluminium in 1.5 metre lengths, four pieces were glued into position along the centre line of the boat set into a built-up moulding that I'd cast in resin using, of course, duct tape. I applied Voodoo glue to secure the bands. The bow had to be curved using masking tape to keep the shape until the glue went off. The idea was to try to protect the underside of the boat from damage if it had to be dragged up a hard surface (which would be almost a daily occurrence).

On the same day, my new gelcoat spray kit was delivered. It needed a minimum of 50 litres of air in a compressor to work. My two compressors were only 25 litres so although I tried pairing them, I soon worked out there wouldn't be enough pressure. What to do? Call Terry the Wand, of course.

Terry the Wand had a proper compressor and loads of spraying experience although in 35 years of spraying, he admitted to having no experience in spraying gelcoat but what did that matter? He had loads of experience spraying French polish and lacquer. I packed up the MOD27 and agreed to drive down the following week on Saturday 29th June.

It was a boiling hot day. The sun was scorching – just perfect for a bit of outdoor spraying. I packed the MOD27 up and towed her the mile down the dual carriageway from my own workshop to Terry's. When I got there, the boat wouldn't fit in his workshop so we ran an extra-long hose to the spray gun and set up the boat on pallets outside. We turned on the compressor, let the pressure build up and then watched most of the gelcoat dribble out the end of the gun into a giant blob onto the floor. After a bit of fiddling around, we tipped the reservoir on the gun up the other way and bingo it came out in a thick spray. Terry did a grand job and we left the MOD27 to bake in the sun.

I returned to assess the handy work on Monday and was shocked to find the hull still really sticky. Perhaps we hadn't added enough catalyser or made the mix wrong. I left her another day and by Tuesday, after having googled the issue, I'd handpainted the bottom of the boat with PVA! I smothered it on neat out of a 2 litre bottle making the bottom of the boat look as if she'd been smeared with yoghurt. Then I went home. On Wednesday 3rd July I went back. I was beginning to get a bit desperate. The original plan was to take the MOD27 down to Torbay on the 5th July, sailing away for my grand tour after competing in the Laser Masters Nationals. Thank God I didn't do that!

On Thursday 4th July I checked the MOD27 hull again and it had worked. The gelcoat had set. I packed the MOD27 up on the trailer and towed her back to my workshop to start checking and replacing all the fittings, to cut in the hatches and generally make her ready for a sea trial. I was getting lots of issues at work for jobs unfinished and, just to add to the things to do list, I'd agreed to run an America's Cup racing match fundraising night for Prostate Cancer UK at the Laser Masters Nationals. It needed working out how we would play a game to entertain a group of wizened old cynical Laser master sailors. Fortunately, I'm quite good at improvising and doing this, certainly better than almost everything else.

So, I delayed my departure to set off round the UK again and set my mind to arranging an event for the Laser Masters America's Cup fun evening. I planned a game that involved teams having to build a replica America's Cup yacht out of a £2 Baker Ross children's 3D wooden boat kit. The kit included a mast and sail, the type of model boat you put in your bath if you're aged five years plus according to the instructions. I'd bought 20 kits to dish out, £5 each to enter. Well, everyone in the room was definitely over five years old. I tested the idea in the bar 15 minutes before hosting my first prostate cancer fundraiser. Mark Lyttle, reigning World Master Laser Champion, and Stuart Hudson, a legend in the Laser for most of his life, set a build time of 2 minutes 20 seconds. I then set up a team challenge for all the competitors to build their boats in sub 3 minutes. I made up some sort of arbitrary time penalty. The slower each team built their yacht, the later they started in the match races I subsequently organised.

On the night, I found a set of fishing rods and came up with a brainwave. I organised the racing as follows: one member of the team had a fishing rod and stood at one end of the room and the other team member held the boat at the other end of the room. The boat was attached to the line and spooled out. The winning team was the fastest one to reel in the boats across the sailing club's parquet floor until it touched the end of their rod. Of course, I made it up as we went along but that night we had World Champion sailors crawling around the floors on their hands and knees repairing their America's Cup yachts as if it was a gold rush. We raised hundreds of pounds for Prostate Cancer UK and had a good laugh. Would my impending sail round UK be this easy and this much fun?

With my duty to entertain the masses now fully discharged, all I had to do was go racing the next day. I can't recall what happened, probably no wind as I ended up spending half the day in Tony's Torquay Chandlers. I went in with PY and Aussie Jeff but they soon tired of my relentless questions on kit, radios, this and that. They left me to it. Pressure off, I had a pocket full of money and I was going to spend it in this shop. My round Britain kit list was made up on the spot, there and then, in the Torquay Chandlers, that very day.

Not surprisingly I bought most of the wrong kit: two unknown bargain brands of ex-display waterproof bags and a 60 litre and a 20 litre dry bag, both of which leaked almost immediately (no such thing as a bargain), an Entel VHF radio with the words 'waterproof' in red letters printed on the front (lasted eight weeks before it died in the middle of the Irish Sea from water ingress when I was 20 miles from nowhere and going through a handover between the Holyhead and Belfast coastguard), my Spot X tracker and satellite messaging unit which took me the best part of my trip and two more units to figure out how to use and configure.

The first Spot X stopped working due to water ingress in the charger socket within the first few days. Apparently, the waterproof flap covering the slot didn't like the type of water. The second unit was washed off me in a storm en route to the Mull of Kintyre and the third unit was a demo one, very kindly supplied free of charge by the distributor which worked really well after I'd figured out how to mount it on my lifejacket unobscured so it got a satellite signal. The tracking function was only mastered properly on the final day home.

Tony Chandler gave me a free discarded old plastic flares tube with a red threaded handle cap. It looked perfect but leaked. Flares and safety kit were stored in it mounted on the mast until I discarded it near Beadnell Bay in Northumberland as it was worse than having no bag at all and kept the contents of the tube permanently wet.

I have little recall of the race on the Sunday at Torbay as my mind was now firmly set on setting off from Eastbourne as soon as possible. I still hadn't announced exactly when I was going. Jon Emmett, a renowned sailor, coach and podcaster, interviewed me on the Saturday evening before the America's Cup racing I was hosting which had the effect of ramping up the pressure I'd now put myself under. (Emma says I do this a lot – apparently I talk about something I want to do, talk about it some more and then talk about nothing else. Yet I'm surprised when anyone believes me and then immediately feel a sense of panic about having to do it). It was a funny moment talking about my plans which were still far from fixed or prepared. I made up a lot of it on the fly. Jon was delicate in his assessment of my chances but I understood enough from his reaction that he clearly believed this was going to be the last time he ever saw me. I was still blissfully ignorant of the task ahead.

Monday came and work was going bonkers. Jack, the new work experience lad, had bailed out due to a lack of money and excessive responsibility. I just couldn't understand why he wasn't going to take over while I was away. My lady who'd been trained up to hold the admin fort and in whom I'd invested heavily in time and money over the past five months grew increasingly anxious and was starting to have sleep problems. I ignored it. The MOD27 was now top priority. Daylight was getting less and less every day I delayed. Every hour was now being spent working on the boat. She still hadn't been through a sea trial with all of the kit with me – rig, oars, any of it!

On Thursday 11th July, finally I managed to get the MOD27 back down to Pevensey Bay Sailing Club with most of the kit fitted to the boat. There had been no time to finalise my kit list for clothing, sleeping, cooking and everything else. The new dry bags got stuffed with whatever I could find at the time. The large dry bag was strapped with a Velcro strap under the toe strap, the other dry bag stowed inside the newly fitted RWO branded eight inch rear hatch. I removed the inflatable masthead float that I occasionally used on one of my other boats, a Boss. It was a bit embarrassing sailing with a masthead float but if you know how mental a Boss is, you'd probably forgive me for doing so. I stuffed this bag at the back of the cockpit to provide additional buoyancy using another Velcro strap.

For those too young or uninitiated, a Boss is a twin trapezing wing-shaped boat. I'd bought mine for £250 from another boatyard jumble clearance and driven 250 miles to Derbyshire to buy it. I was told the trailer was sound except it had no wheels so I took a pair with me. When I tried to add the wheels, they didn't fit of course. I then spent two days in Derbyshire searching for the right size wheel nuts to fit the new trailer wheels on with. I still have a lot of different sized wheel bolts and nuts if anyone ever needs some. The trailer was a relic of the extreme sailing fad that dinghy sailing went through in the 90s. In its day, the Boss was the fastest dinghy you could buy with way too much sail area and way too little control. I'd used the Boss on 10 occasions since buying and rebuilding it. Every outing was a new experience of terror. Not surprisingly, I burned through nine different crew members. My 20 year old first cousin once removed, Hannah, proved to be the most resilient. The Boss requires a very athletic and agile crew to keep it upright, hence the need for a blow-up airbag hoisted on the top of the mast. As I rarely did keep it upright, when I removed the airbag, I found it had a very slow puncture.

"Ah well it should be fine," I kept thinking.

I Velcroed that airbag into the back of the MOD27's cockpit, figuring this would compensate for the extra weight I'd added and the loss of buoyancy caused by storing a lot of my gear inside the hull. My 60 litre dry bag was stowed under the central toe strap in the front of the cockpit. This left just enough room for my two feet.

My new sail, a Rooster replica, Laser standard size, radial cut sail was ready. I'd bought this from Gary Smith, a Rooster dealer and member of Eastbourne Sailing Club. He'd done me a special price which included sewing on a second pair of vertical battens so I could reef the sail by rolling it round the mast at sea in the event of high winds. Well, that was the idea but it proved to be mindless optimism on the water as it was just impossible! Gary had also previously helped me adapt the larger Rooster 8.1 rig by adding the zip which failed on its first outing. Although I was definitely thinking along the right lines, I was guessing at this stage but later was proven right that a lack of wind would be more of an issue than high winds, hence the larger 8.1 rig idea.

By 7 pm I was ready to launch the MOD27 for her maiden sea trial. It would be dark by 8 pm. I sailed the boat out from the Pevensey Bay Sailing Club beach in no wind then proceeded to deliberately capsize several times. I tried out my wooden oars. The first set were massive, so long that I couldn't row with them as they banged into my knees as they came together at each stroke. I'd fixed the new rollocks too far forward in the boat and they were way too low down. It took me 20 minutes to make it back rowing the 200 feet to shore in a flat calm sea. I went ashore and borrowed a shorter set of oars from a Mirror dinghy owned by James Allerton from our club. If you're not sure, a Mirror is a small, wooden lightweight dinghy designed for children to learn how to sail. I tried these shorter oars and, although they were better, I found I still had a similar issue. I thought it was just a technique problem so I said thanks to James and agreed to borrow them. Test complete. I even managed to pull the boat up the beach on my own despite numerous offers of help from other club members. I used a tiny plastic oval fender my friend Ellie had bought for me in a boat jumble at Newhaven. I only just managed to pull the boat back up the beach though and spent an age recovering afterwards, huffing and puffing like I'd just run a marathon. Worryingly, the boat was unloaded and I was pretty fresh as I hadn't been sailing all day.

Friday 12th July was manic. I had door issues everywhere. My Miss Moneypenny who was going to be me at work was getting super jumpy and was now threatening to pull out. I tried to reassure her that everything would be fine. I resolved that her worries were just pre-hand over nerves and Emma was doing an amazing job trying to help to reassure her.

All weekend I worked on the kit and boat. The bags inside the rear hatch had punctured. Screws attaching the toe strap and the rudder were poking into the hull about three inches. I hacked them off (easier said than done). Once I'd managed to cut them shorter, I capped off the screw ends with plastic rawlplugs but now the fittings felt too wobbly so I replaced all of these screws with fatter, shorter ones and capped them off with the proper Laser rear traveller, plastic screw caps, normally supplied with new boats. Fortunately, I had a load of these in my spares box. I then gelcoated the inside of the boat with a paintbrush and stuck down a sheet of the micro plastic parcel bubble wrap to act as a blanket inside my storage area. I stuck this on while the gelcoat was still tacky. This bubble wrap survived the whole trip and I'm sure stopped the dry bags inside the boat from chaffing through on the journey. Nevertheless, again unbeknown to me at the time, I set off with two bags already compromised from being punctured in the first sea trial by the screws!

Ron Pattenden turned up on the Sunday at my workshop to bring me a bit of kit he thought I might be able to use – his tent, a solar battery charger for my mobile, his Sealskinz socks, a blue spray suit and the famous fender which was much larger than the tiny oval one I'd struggled up the beach with. He'd already used this fender instead of a trolley when he did his own circumnavigation – over about nine months – the other way round back in 2004. He gave me a lot of confidence until right at the very end when he exclaimed after my less than detailed route preparation and mapping evidence,

"Blimey you're pushing it!"

My Spot X tracker and VHF Entel radio finally turned up on Monday 15th July. It was sent directly from Torquay Chandlers and both the product and the contact had been missing in transit for a week. Now I decided to focus on safety and made a trip to Simpson Marine in Newhaven where I'd originally bought the MOD27 for £50. Here I bought some out of date flares that they gave me as part of a deal for buying a useless hatch I never used, string, sail repair tape and two bright orange spray cans plus a few other odds and sods. I thought at the time, 'I can't believe they've given me out of date flares". I said nothing, I was grateful for any help. Money was super tight. I really couldn't afford to go at all – both my small businesses were in trouble. Determinedly, I pushed this iron fact to the back of my mind.

'There's never a right time to go on a trip like this one. It's bound to be tense just before the off,' I kept telling myself.

That evening I painted the MOD27 deck 'safety orange' and grey. I sprayed my lovely best centreboard and rudder half orange so I could be seen if I capsized and turned turtle. This was PY's idea. In fact, I hated doing this as these were my race boat foils (accessories) and were worth considerably more than the whole boat. I had an older set of foils but decided to use my good ones as I regarded these as being critical equipment. Same with my mast and boom. Again, I used a brand new carbon fibre top section mast and relatively new boom and bottom section mast. The kicking strap and control lines – essential to be of good quality for what I was about to put them through – were also virtually brand new. My tiller for steering was a new Laser factory issue made from carbon fibre. Superb. However, the deck cleats weren't good and nor was the mainsheet ratchet block, used to pull the sail in and out. In fact, the ratchet was broken before I left and I knew it but pretended it wasn't because I just couldn't afford to spend £70 on a new one.

"It'll be fine," I blagged.

I went to work on Monday 15th July and my temporary replacement employee who was going to be me, wasn't in. We were supposed to be doing the final handover. I'd revealed all the bank accounts and passwords to her on the previous Friday so she'd seen the true gravity of the cash position of my door renovation and sales business for the first time – bloody awful! Still, early on Monday morning I received a message from Emma to say there was an issue.

This was the woman who I'd trained up for the past five months, spent umpteen hours and hours making sure she knew everything there possibly was to know about my door business from stock, suppliers, customers, projects, pricing, storage, treatments, subcontractors, marketing, the website and everything I could ever think of. She was a friend of Emma's through her Pilates teaching.

"We need to go to her house and collect the work phone and all the files" read Emma's text. I took a deep breath then another, slower, and a few more.

"I'm supposed to be fucking leaving tomorrow!" I shouted out loud to myself. "SHIT!"

I looked at the mass of ongoing jobs that needed managing. Most of the work I'd subcontracted out but they still needed careful managing and checking and there were two important jobs still outstanding which needed finishing. I couldn't do it. I just couldn't – I was about to set sail in my Laser, the MOD27.

Emma arranged a meeting with my employee 'lady' on the morning of Tuesday 16th. We both arrived to collect the work mobile phone and all the files she'd kept at home so that she could conveniently work whenever she wanted around whatever she was doing – this was a good eight months before anyone had even sniffed the merest whiff of Covid! We met on her doorstep; she was ashen-faced. She hadn't slept properly for the past week and was shaking. She'd been having nightmares about taking on the responsibility of the business for an indeterminate length of time. It was clear she was completely the wrong person. Emma immediately said,

"Don't worry, I'll deal with it."

I knew Emma could manage it. We'd run businesses together for most of our lives. The irony was we agreed from the start that Emma wouldn't be involved with the door business as the previous publishing business we'd run together for seven years had nearly destroyed our marriage and, besides that, she was a very happy Pilates instructor and part-time English teacher who enjoyed what she already did. But now she was coming in totally unbriefed and with no idea how anything worked at a day's notice.

The rest of the day, I spent time with Emma showing her passwords, administration systems, banking systems, stock control, locations of doors, customer histories, supplier details, subcontractor contacts, invoicing procedures and where I kept the coffee. You name it – we went through it. I then packed a bag load of gear. Then another and another and let a few close friends know I was leaving in two days' time on Thursday 17th July. This wasn't quite the stress-free departure countdown I'd originally planned.

That evening I posted my first proper Facebook post on my 'stickdaringrounduk' page. This page had been put together three years earlier, unbeknown to me, by Rupert Bedell. Rupert was running the Laser Masters Race Circuit and website at the time and subsequently became part of a small team of five that evolved working remotely to monitor my movements as I went round the coast. That was the theory anyway. The Facebook page had come about after Rupert and I had been discussing the idea at one of the sailing events only for my plan to materialise shortly afterwards. This proved to be one of the catalysts for me taking the idea of a circumnavigation in my Laser more seriously, rather bizarrely. The page had been lying dormant for the past three years with one single 'like'. Not that I really understood what a like on Facebook was at the time. Clearly the page had already been seen by a few people who didn't particularly like it so they didn't give me an all-important thumbs-up. If I'm honest, from as far back as 2016, I started bumping into people at sailing events who were surprised to see me. Other sailors didn't expect me to be at a circuit race meeting as they thought I was off on my trip sailing round the UK. The pressure to go for it had been accruing as far back as then.

I planned to leave level with the pier at Eastbourne at 12 noon on Thursday 17th July and sail anti-clockwise round mainland UK. The day before I left, I had so many must-do tasks still unresolved, I'd barely properly had a chance to worry too much about the danger or endurance of the way ahead. I was too busy trying to find something or work out how to pack something or where best to stow the oars or where my wetsuit was. That's a good point. Where was my wetsuit? I couldn't locate it. I made a call to Alan Davis who'd brought my boat and most of my gear back on his trailer from the Roses European Championships in Spain. At the event, I'd stored all my gear in his trailer which was parked next to where the 300 boats competing in the event were lined up. I'd been living out of his trailer and changing each day on the quayside where it was parked up. Had I left it with him mistakenly? I had several other wetsuits but they were all completely worn-out with holes in the bum panel. I really did want my preferred one – a Sandiline long john with built-in hikers. Alan called back and confirmed he didn't have it. I spent a whole evening chasing round to see if I could scrounge one from any of my other sailing contacts.

Finally, I made a few desperate calls in the hope of securing a freebie from any one of the companies in the business. One call was to Joel, who used to work for Laser Performance, the manufacturers of the Laser in the UK and Europe. He'd recently changed jobs and was now working for the marine corporate wear division of Gill Marine who also had a full range of dinghy sailing gear. He offered to sell me an old wetsuit of his; not really the answer I was looking for! I'd already texted Rooster Sailing looking for some free gear several weeks earlier but hadn't received a reply. My problem was I really had zero money to spare as I had to leave Emma with some chance of keeping the door business alive and although I was only a few thousand within the overdraft limit, I knew it would need every penny while I was away.

I'd planned to fund my own day-to-day expenses out of my Barclays bank overdraft and a few hundred pounds of cash I'd put aside. That night, I hunted high and low for that wetsuit and eventually located it in a plastic bag that had fallen down behind a racking panel in my van. Phew!

Wednesday 16th is now a blur – it was on the actual day too! So many work issues still to wade through! George, my middle son, was brought in to help Emma with the physical aspect of lifting and moving customer doors. George was in his second year of a four-year degree course in Business Finance & Accountancy at Newcastle University, sponsored by PWC. He'd just come back from a trip of his own around Europe and agreed to sort out the purchase and sales ledger and help Emma in any way he could, including wrapping and packing online orders. We agreed we would sub-contract out any fitting of doors while I was away but try to avoid taking on any new fitting work until I was back. I found a member of Pevensey Sailing Club, Jono, who agreed to do some of the manual and technical restoration work, finishing off jobs still ongoing and unresolved. Jono (John Ostler, his real name) proved to be invaluable to Emma during my absence. George was given access to the accounts and just laughed when he saw the balance sheet and bank account. Somehow, we'd scrimped and saved to give him a top-notch private education but you'd never know how looking at my figures.

Thursday 17th July arrived. I was going. I loaded the boat onto the trailer still in my workshop. The orange paint was just about set and the bright sunlight glinted off it as I opened the workshop doors. I checked everything. Behind, the workshop cum warehouse was a total mess but there was no time to clear up before I set off. Usually, I cleared up every single time I left but not today – no time!

I arrived at Eastbourne Sailing Club at 10.30 am. I was instantly met by one of my oldest friends, Nick, from 'the FAFF gang', my very early group of mates who all sailed Lasers back in the 80s. Nick had cycled down from London for my launch! I was really touched and quite surprised to see him. I'd had numerous calls and texts from David Giles, another one of the current Laser sailing gang, who'd also come to see me off. My cousin Gemma was there along with Anne and Richard and a few other local Eastbourne friends. Ron had also come down to wave goodbye and wish me luck which I thought was nice of him. Graeme, whose Vintage Bike Cave was next door to my Historic Doors emporium, also came down and again I was surprised to see him.

With all this attention, it then seemed to take me an age to rig up, load gear into the boat, get changed and generally be ready to go. At last, I'd got it all together. I posed for a few pictures, kissed Emma goodbye in the shallows, waved to everyone and then launched at 11.30 am. I'm sure some of the onlookers thought this might be the last time they'd ever see me!

There was then a bit of an anti-climax as I actually had to sail west, the wrong way, in order to reach Eastbourne Pier. There was a light south westerly breeze which required me to sail very slowly into the wind to reach the pier. I got to the buoy just beyond the end of the pier and decided that was close enough as the tide was against me now. Once again, I turned to wave to anyone who was still bothering to watch and at 12 noon I turned swiftly around and headed east with a warm breeze behind me and brilliant sunshine above. This was it!

Chapter 6

The First Day

The first week remains a bit of a blur. I went through probably the steepest learning curve of my entire life: tides, waves, ships, fishing fleets, windfarms and, not least, an active military firing range. The latter, extraordinary as it might seem, had never come up or even occurred to me. It was quite a shock! I'd no idea what to expect from this new challenge from the British military whose active ranges are apparently dotted all around the UK coastline and regularly impact seafarers such as myself.

My first experience of this nature occurred at the end of my very first day. I'd made good progress in a moderate breeze, sailing for 11 hours with no breaks, when I started looking for a stopping point. It was approaching dusk. The light was just beginning to drop, making the horizon blur into the sky. I'd left it a bit late to start planning my overnight camping place but as I started assessing the options, all I could see was one continuous barrage of man-made sea defences, on and on, stretching for miles. In the dimming distance, I could just make out a dot of what could be sand on a beach which looked good for a landing. The tide allowed me to drift towards it. There was no turning around now as the wind was far too light to take me back home.

Very soon I passed a set of red traffic lights planted somewhat out of place on the concrete wall. I could see the end of the wall and a set of sandy dunes in the far-off distance. The lights concerned me. I made a call to PY, my very professional Safety Channel co-ordinator who'd also served as an officer in the British Army and unbeknown to me at the time was once in charge of a live firing range. He was the best person I could think of for any kind of safety check – meticulous, accurate and very direct. I phoned him:

"Pete, it's me. I'm just trying to find somewhere to stop, I think I'm near Hythe. Do you have any idea what the red lights mean on the shore?"

There was no reply. Just silence on an open line. I waited. He was scanning Google Maps. It seemed an age before he responded with a question.

"Can you hear anything?"

"No." The air was very still and not even the sound of any cars could be heard in the distance.

"Ah! I think you're in the Hythe Firing Range. If you can't hear anything you're probably OK to keep going." He sounded confident.

I thanked him and quickly hung up as I needed to save the battery on my mobile which was very low. Almost as soon as I passed the lights, a large inflatable looking rib-like vessel came racing flat out towards me. It had a rail full of flood lights all pointing in my direction and came hurtling right alongside swashing a large bow wave that knocked what little wind I had in my sail totally out of it. An officious and rather annoyed-looking uniformed man started mouthing things at me.

I couldn't really hear him so I just carried on trying to sail. Eventually, he made it clear I was to stop but, after trying a few verbal exchanges, I still couldn't really hear, so he tried to pass me a rope. The diameter and weight of it may have been suitable to fasten on the Queen Mary but not my 13-foot Laser. He indicated I should take hold of it so they could tow me but if I'd taken the rope, it would probably have sunk my bow completely so I declined his kind offer and indicated I'd carry on. From his facial expression and gestures, he wasn't pleased. Very begrudgingly, he eventually began escorting me without a tow an agonisingly slow mile along the shoreline until we both came to a large tower and another set of red lights. Just before the lights I could now clearly see a set of 10 round discs standing tall on poles numbered 1 to 10.

As soon as I passed the number 10 disc, which happened to be the last one, a crescendo of deafening gunfire volleyed out of the sky from nowhere. It was so loud I very nearly fell out of the boat. My heart was pounding and my ears were almost burning from the pain of the noise!

"Go and report to the watch tower," the grumpy escort ordered me, pointing aggressively towards the shore.

He muttered something about messing up their firing exercises earlier in the day at Lydd. I pretended not to hear but I did recall wondering why all the boats I'd seen that day near Lydd in Kent had gone so far offshore despite the most direct route being straight across the bay as I'd sailed. It turns out the firing range there extends four miles out to sea.

I beached the boat onto a near vertical shingle bank 100 metres along from the watch tower. The rib (or launch as I sometimes call them) had by now disappeared. My friend hadn't waved goodbye. The light was failing now and I had to unload all my kit to make any progress heaving the boat ashore. It seemed to take an age. Darkness loomed and it took me almost an hour to get the boat high enough up the beach to avoid the high tide line. Pushing it like a wheelbarrow on top of the cylindrical plastic fender, I finally parked the MOD27 at about the same height as a few tatty-looking fishing boats lying around me.

No-one with guns was coming to arrest me. I doubted that a visit to the watch tower would be in my favour, especially if they were as unfriendly as my rib escort had been. I decided it was probably best to give the visit a miss so, very quickly, I scrambled my gear together and pitched the rather tired old tent that I'd borrowed from Ron.

Ron had used this tent when he was sailing his Laser the other way round Britain some 15 years ago. It was the first time I'd inspected it closely and was surprised just how worn out it was. With a positive hat on you might describe it as 'tried and tested' or more realistically 'well used'. Still, it went up quite easily. Once safely inside, I stretched out and got changed out of the wet sailing gear. Ron had told me he used to stow his gear in one corner of the tent and sleep on the other side. There was an issue – either I must be twice the size of Ron or his tent had shrunk! There was no way I could fit anything except myself in there. I threw the wet, salty gear outside, struggled into my Trek trousers, t-shirt, jumper and shoes and set about figuring out what I could eat.

When I eventually located the single gas burner at the bottom of a bag, I discovered it needed to be assembled. It resembled a stove for a children's dolls' house! The saucepan and cup I'd bought were also minute. I had just enough water left to make one tiny pot of noodles and also had half a tin of chickpeas. I boiled it all together and scoffed it down only to suddenly feel absolutely starving hungry. A coffee and powdered milk helped slightly so then I turned my attention to my next day.

I needed water and, almost as urgently, electricity to charge my phone, VHF radio and my Spot X tracker/satellite text machine without which I'd have no means of navigating or communicating tomorrow.

I now felt weary but forced myself out of the tent. It was almost pitch black. Incredibly, I found my head torch amongst so much other stuff I'd brought with me – way too much stuff to manage every night. Trudging off in the darkness towards a block of smart looking flats, I spent half an hour trying to find some life – a pub, restaurant or cafe, any sign of life at all. Nope, nothing. I'd landed miles from anything even remotely resembling civilisation.

There were virtually no lights on in the block of flats either. They must all be holiday flats, I thought. I was now becoming concerned about my lack of water too. The darkness began to feel heavier. I spotted an up-and-over garage door slightly ajar at the bottom. Quietly, I crept forwards towards it, trying to ignore the salty taste in my mouth and my need to drink something. The door pushed open further and I just made out the silhouette of a tap. Warily, scouting round to see if anyone was watching I flicked up the garage door and filled one large and one small bottle with water. The tap was really noisy and, at any moment, someone might easily come out and accost me! Both bottles were full. I hurriedly closed the door and sloped off back towards my tent. Everything electrical had to be turned off and my phone put on the solar-powered charger that Ron had also lent me. It was all done and I was exhausted. I fell into the tent and into a deep sleep almost immediately.

Chapter 7

The White Cliffs of Dover

The following day was bright and warm but the wind was blowing so hard it could have pulled 'dogs off chains' as Aussie Jeff would often exclaim. I'd had a bit of sleep but the tent was way too short for my six foot two inch frame and I couldn't stretch out properly without touching the sides. If I did, my feet would get soaking as the rain just poured in through the worn-out walls. I assembled the tiny gas cooker and wedged it into the shingle outside the door. I carefully lit the stove to heat up some water in the tiny saucepan. It seemed to take an age but eventually, after searching through nearly all my bags, I located a coffee sachet and added it to the now boiling water. I added powdered milk and produced a cup of coffee – at least enough to give me two mouthfuls. I refilled the cup and stuck my head outside the tent. The wind was whipping across the sea making white horses dance as far out as I could see.

Scanning the beach, I noticed a lone fisherman trying to secure his boat which looked like it would be washed away any minute by the breaking surf. The stones and shingle rolled backwards and forwards in time to the sea, creating an incredible rhythmic noise like music. I made my way across to the fisherman with my water bottle. He looked warily towards me. I think I must have looked like a vagrant and he probably thought I was going to ask him for money.

"I don't suppose you could tell me where I can get some water?" I asked in my most humble voice.

The fisherman, whose name turned out to be Richard, proved to be a very fortuitous find. We struck up a conversation. He and his mate were clearly involved in securing the boat which, to my untrained eye, looked in worse condition and even older than mine. He downed the tools he was using to fix something unrecognisable and told me to follow him. Climbing up the steep shingle beach, we approached a derelict shiplap shed. Inside, glistened a clean, wet, concrete floor, a large industrial walk-in cold store and a few empty plastic boxes (probably used for fish storage). He pointed to a tap in the corner above which was a double plug socket, about eight feet up the wall. I must have spent too long gazing at it because, before I could ask, Richard said in a thick Hythe accent I'd never heard before,

"Do you need to charge your phone?"

I looked sheepish. "Yes please."

He made his way back to the fishing boat and I went back to the tent to retrieve my charger packs. There was a mobile phone charger, VHF base charger, Spot X tracker charger and a spare recharging battery pack for the mobile. I had a triple plug so I was able to assemble all the units into one socket and the spare battery charger into the second wall socket. The leads were mostly too short so I improvised using string to support all the devices and save them from hanging off their electrical cords. By the time I'd managed to get this to work, Richard had returned. I did wonder if he was just checking to see I hadn't stolen anything of his but he actually said,

"Do you need to get any food?"

I was surprised he'd even considered this. I hadn't really told him much about myself at this stage. The truth was, I had loads of gear but no idea. Most of the kit I was dragging around seemed totally superfluous. I really wanted a coffee and a croissant. I also needed a sandwich or some food for the day's trip.

"Yes, I could use some food for today. Is there a shop nearby?"

"Waitrose is the nearest, about two miles away," Richard replied in a flat rather factual delivery.

He looked at me and then pulled out his phone. Before I could interrupt, he'd asked his wife to come down and take me, a total stranger, to the supermarket. Jacqui arrived in minutes. I felt a little awkward and slightly embarrassed. Just as I climbed into her car, Richard grunted to her questioning eyes,

"He's awright."

So off we went with me making polite conversation all the way. I bought various items of food for the day as well as coffee and croissants. As an afterthought, I picked up a bunch of cheap flowers by the checkout and presented them to Jacqui who was waiting for me in the car.

"This is just a small thank you," I said, smiling and handing them to her.

She accepted them slightly awkwardly but then handed them back for me to look after while she drove me back to my tent on the beach!

Richard greeted us and we talked about the weather. He shook his head when I prodded him about fishing that day.

"It's gonna be rough, very rough round by Dover," he explained. "With this north easterly, the waves'll be bouncing back off the harbour wall – standing waves with up to a four metre swell. Add that to gusts of 30 knots and it'll be pretty bumpy!"

I felt frightened. The main problem with this trip was that I didn't have a clue...not a Scooby Doo about what to expect anywhere from hereon in. I decided to go back to my tent and change into my wet gear, convincing myself this would make me feel more confident. It took a while to struggle into my wetsuit and top because they were both still wet from the day before. It was an unwelcome feeling – wet and salty and my skin was already itching. By the time I'd changed, Richard was ready to go home. He told me to lock the door once I'd collected my electronics and showed me a place to hide the key. As he departed, he uttered some words to the effect that he knew I knew what I was doing but if it was him, he'd wait until tomorrow. He then wished me good luck and left, turning to call back,

"If I see your tent still on the beach in the morning, I'll bring you some food. We're off at 5.30 am tomorrow. It's going to be a lot calmer". Then he was gone.

I felt very alone. Back in my tent, I sat staring out of the doorway looking at the now howling sea smashing into the shingle beach. The visibility was poor with spray everywhere and a fine drizzle coming down. An hour or so later, at around 11 am, I saw some more fishermen fiddling with their boats further down the beach so hurriedly changed back into my normal clothes and wandered along towards them. I was wearing my Henri-Lloyd sailing jacket, a jacket I'd owned since the late 1990s. One of the fishermen, although shorter than me, had a giant physique. His arms looked like Popeye's and his stomach was a bit like Big Daddy's from TV wrestling fame in the 70s.

"Are you going out fishing today?" I piped up.

They all stopped and looked me up and down. The largest fisherman eventually replied,

"Whaaat in thaat weather? Thaaat'll be skull 'n' crossbones round Dover."

It was amazing how pirate-like they really did sound! They started laughing at me, at the idea of me going out!

What exactly skull and crossbones meant I wasn't sure but I got the gist. I didn't hang around chatting long but listened carefully to their few pointers for navigating the next part of the journey. I felt a little bit intimidated to be honest and slightly stupid that I'd even asked if they were sailing today. It was obvious they had no intention. Like Richard, they would go tomorrow when the swell had died down. I trudged back across the steep shingle bank to my tent, climbed into my sleeping bag and fell sound asleep.

Somewhere around midday, I was woken by someone knocking on the tent wall calling out my name. I opened the zip and saw Richard again. He'd returned to the beach to find me.

"You'll be OK now," he chirped up.

I could hear the sea and wind had moderated a bit but it didn't actually look much better when I stuck my head outside. The tide was nearly at full height and the waves were still smashing into the beach. I hardly knew this man, Richard, but he clearly knew what he was doing when it came to the sea. I instantly took his word at face value, surprised that he'd bothered to return to the beach to find me. I felt a great deal of respect for him then and thanked him. Hurriedly, I packed my kit away and changed into my wet wetsuit for the second time in one day.

When I say I 'packed hurriedly' it actually took at least 45 minutes and at the end of my efforts I was left with a 20-litre dry bag full of gear. I couldn't recall where or how I had previously stowed it. There just didn't seem to be enough room to put everything back in the boat. After repacking several times, I just gave up. Richard kindly agreed to hold on to this excess kit for me and told me he'd see me when I got back. When he said this, I thought to myself, "if I ever make it."

I trudged back up the beach to Richard's store, deposited my bag and retrieved all the electrical kit I'd put on charge. On the way back down to my boat I seriously thought about making a call to Emma. I didn't like this sailing round Britain idea any longer. Perhaps she'd drive out and pick me up? I could just pretend it had never happened. Somehow, I resisted making that call.

Launching off the beach at Hythe was pretty hectic. It's an incredibly steep shingle beach. It took four or five attempts to make it through the surf which meant being capsized in the shore dump, smashing me off my feet on each occasion. On the last attempt I made it through the surf, once clear of the breakers, it was very windy but not a disaster – in range of my sailing abilities. Visibility was poor though and I headed about two miles offshore to clear the harbour walls and avoid any of the skull and crossbones.

I'd already learnt a valuable lesson that fishermen and locals such as Richard are not only the font of all sea knowledge but kind people and, luckily in my case, good judges of character. Richard and his wife were the first of many I'd meet on my adventure to whom I will always hold a debt of gratitude.

When approaching the harbour at the Port of Dover, the second group of fishermen had told me I must radio the Harbour Control on Channel 74 when two miles off. They suggested if it was very bumpy, I should request entering the western entrance. If Dover Harbour Control let me through, I could pop out through the eastern entrance. By doing this, the fishermen suggested I'd avoid the worst of the enormous swell. The short cut would take me inside the eastern corner of England and miss out the giant waves bouncing back off the massive harbour walls and the 300-foot high Dover cliffs. Apparently, they do this a lot in their fishing boats when the swell is really bad. However, I recall the fishermen all laughed mischievously at the recounting of this idea, giving me the distinct impression at the time it might not be entirely permitted.

When I radioed in to Dover Harbour Control, they were having none of it. I'm not sure if it was my hesitation on the radio or my lack of conviction when requesting this from them. This was, in effect, my first time ever speaking to a Port Controller let alone the busiest Port Controller in Europe, managing 13 million passenger movements annually. The breeze was blowing the tops off the waves as I rode up and down an increasingly confusing sea. I could see huge ships everywhere I looked. I tried to explain I was circumnavigating the UK in an open 13-foot long sailing dinghy with no engine. I can only assume they'd no idea what a Laser was as they advised,

"If you're having difficulties where you are now you need to sail four miles offshore."

I swallowed. "But I'm in a Laser."

They were very polite but simply repeated the instruction. I looked further out to sea. It looked rough everywhere and there seemed to be ships in every direction. Then I felt annoyed. I wasn't having difficulties. I just didn't fancy going any further offshore into the path of one of these massive ferries. Nevertheless I carried on.

It was with great relief that, after an hour of sailing, I could see the lee of the Dover cliffs. A further hour later, I was cruising along close to the famous White Cliffs of Dover, now protecting me from the most exposed direction of wind, responsible for kicking up such a large and confused sea. It was a tighter reaching angle to the wind now I'd turned the corner of England, a more stable angle than before when I was running before the wind. I carried on sailing all afternoon until thoughts of my next stopping point came to mind. Whitstable Sailing Club was possibly within reach, just.

The issue now was that I'd lost the advantageous tidal flow behind me although the light would be good until 9 pm as it was almost the height of summer. The tides here were really strong. I carried on, heading directly north thinking if I could just get round past Margate, I might make it to Whitstable on the north coast of Kent by sunset.

I'd raced my Laser at Whitstable several times and knew they had club bunk rooms. These seemed considerably more attractive than I'd previously ever remembered them being and I was sure I could scrounge a bed if I could just get there. I soon passed the Port of Ramsgate which was a lot less eventful than Dover and thankfully with fewer big ships. The tide was pushing me strongly and it was a fight to press on to be honest. The idea of getting stuck short of Whitstable at Margate was the only thought keeping me going.

If you're not familiar with it, Margate is an up-and-coming town again, famous for 'Dreamland', a 1950s style retro rollercoaster fun park that was being lovingly restored even as I approached. I felt sure that a night on Margate beach would result in trouble though, for both me and my kit. My door business had taken me there on a delivery earlier in the year and although I enjoyed my trip, and even stopped to have a haircut (which afterwards Emma had said was 'amazing'), I preferred to avoid large towns on this journey. For the first time in my life, I felt vulnerable.

My only real memory of that previous experience of Margate is about the man who cut my hair. He's worthy of a mention. He was a young, first-generation Turkish immigrant. He used all sorts of unusual cutting techniques I'd never experienced before, the most notable was a ruler length thin candle wand. When he produced the wand, I'd no idea what it was for. Lighting one end, it flared up as soon as it ignited. He took aim and flicked it at my ears, setting fire to all of the hairs inside them! It was an extraordinary experience. He flicked the wand at my ears several times, hitting the hole perfectly every time. A sizzling, scorching sound was quickly followed each time by an acrid smell of burning every time impact was made. The result was the rapid and thorough removal of all of my ear hair. He even clipped my nostrils too! To this day, Emma asks when I'm going back for another 'flaming wand'?

The problem of where to stop soon got resolved. In the distance, shortly after passing Ramsgate, I thought I could see what looked like a small fleet of boats the same as mine. They seemed to be coming out of the cliff but, as I got closer, I realised there was a tiny harbour. Of course, Broadstairs had a sailing club. In fact, I'd even visited their Laser Open Meeting once in the past. Evening club racing must take place on a Thursday. How funny. I closed in on the area they were sailing in. Scanning the horizon, I noticed a motor boat whizzing around dropping buoys.

"They must be setting up a race course," I told myself.

As I arrived at the harbour entrance the boat had now completed dropping the final mark which looked to me like the start/finish line. I sailed directly down the line and hailed them.

"Are you racing?" I shouted out.

The two men on the boat looked at me as if it was perfectly normal for an orange boat such as mine, looking something like a lunar module from Mars, to ask them this every day of the week. Casually they smiled and nodded which I took to mean yes.

"Do you think I could join in with your club race? I'm sailing round the UK."

"Of course!" they chorused back.

I pulled alongside the tiny inflatable rib and offloaded my large 20-litre dry bag, strapped down under the toe strap in my cockpit. Encouraged by their willingness, I then untied the two long wooden oars strapped to the foredeck and also handed them the fender I used for a trolley, tied to the side deck. By the time they'd stowed all my gear in their tiny inflatable rib there was no room for anyone else. I didn't bother emptying all of the gear out of the rear hatch where I had a load more kit. I felt I was beginning to take advantage of their offer. I passed them the heaviest bag containing food tins etc. but left the tent and sleeping bag still inside the boat.

Unburdened by my kit, I turned my attention to the race and whizzed up and down the start line, sizing up the layout of the course whilst waiting for the remaining boats to come out of the harbour to join me.

It was great to be amongst fellow Laser enthusiasts and I managed to finish in third place. There were some strange looks when I went ashore; no-one had seen a bright orange-decked Laser before, let alone one slightly low in the water with hidden weight. The fender I used for a trolley was going to take ages to get up the now dried-out muddy harbour so I borrowed a club trolley. An hour later, I was recounting stories at the bar and utilising all the spare power sockets in the quaint but aged clubhouse building of Broadstairs Sailing Club. Much of the evening I perched on the staircase sending messages from my phone while it was plugged in with all my other electrical appliances, utilising the only spare socket I could find.

After food and a few pints, I lost interest in the messaging and batteries and got chatting to various members about the day I'd had. My ears pricked up at one important question,

"Where are you staying?"

I paused. A second later I admitted, "I have a tent."

And so Simon Field became the first victim of my round Britain adventure. He very kindly offered me a bed at his house – probably out of politeness but,

"That would be great. Thank you," I replied without allowing him to draw breath.

This technique I learnt very quickly was going to be an essential skill in the art of sailing a Laser around the UK. Never miss an opportunity!

It turned out Simon was the only member of the club who didn't drive and he lived five miles away. He had his bike with him that evening. Five miles after a full day's sailing and evening race? Hmm. Luckily, another very kind member offered us both a lift back to the house. By 10 pm I'd had a few beers but I needed to figure out my next route which was going to be a big one – crossing the Thames Estuary. Crikey, I'd no idea how wide it was until I looked properly at the map. I needed to find someone in this club to talk to who knew something about it as it looked quite scary.

Eventually, I was directed to two of the more senior club members, supping halves of bitter in the corner. I can't recall their names now but they certainly proved to be very informative. One of the men was a seasoned yachtsman and the other had an in-depth understanding of the commercial traffic moving along the estuary into the Port of London.

London was once the largest port in the world but has since been relegated to now only being the third largest port in the UK after Felixstowe and Southampton Docks. Nevertheless, it still handles some 12,500 shipping movements a year with the greatest number of activities located close to the mouth of the estuary where the waters are deepest. The Port of London Authority, the PLA, which manages all shipping in and out, is a trust first established in 1908. It's responsible for managing the area from Teddington Lock sailing eastwards towards the North Sea, stretching up to Foulness in Essex, via Gunfleet Old

Lighthouse across to Warden Point Battery, located just west (inland) of Whitstable on the Isle of Sheppey in Kent.

After a lengthy discussion with the two wise men of Broadstairs, they advised me to sail around the headland at Margate and along the coastline towards the Isle of Sheppey along the Kent shore. They told me that once I made the commitment to cross the Thames I had only four hours to get to the other side. If I didn't cross in four hours, I'd be washed out to the North Sea. The tone in which they explained this left me in no doubt that there were very strong tides indeed and, if I missed the tidal gate, I'd be swished out to the North Sea, never to be seen again.

The beer continued to flow and I kept dragging out more and more information from these two highly knowledgeable gentlemen. The more questions I asked, the worse tomorrow seemed to become. Time was dragging on. Simon was looking anxiously over to me indicating it was time to leave. I felt guilty for holding him up but also slightly terrified about the imminent crossing I was planning and wanted to extract the maximum information from my counsel.

The advice of locals, I was beginning to discover, was a double-edged sword. On the one hand, the information being relayed is absolutely invaluable. On the other hand, prior to any fact-finding, I was blissfully ignorant about the forthcoming level of danger. Before speaking to these two experienced sailors, the scale of the task hadn't fully dawned on me. By the time I left that evening, I'd identified the optimum time to start my crossing to maximise the tide, the best locations to start crossing from and the places to aim at, an estimated time to get across the estuary (based on the forecast for the next day), a safe location to rest up in the middle where I wouldn't be run down by BFS (code for Big F***ing Ships which Ron had told me about before setting off).

The wind farm was suggested as a 'safe zone' (thank God) as ships weren't allowed near it. I later discovered the London Array Wind Farm, as it's known, is located 20 kilometres (12 miles) off the Kent coast in the outer Thames Estuary and was, until September 2018, the largest offshore wind farm in the world.

By now, Simon had started making moves towards the clubhouse door. Our table was the last to empty. I thanked both men and made my way to the changing rooms. This was up a rickety narrow staircase. I unplugged and gathered up my now fully charged electrical devices and packed my wetsuit and kit bags. Struggling down the stairs, barely able to carry everything, Simon relieved me of the most awkward bag and we made our way to our volunteer taxi waiting outside.

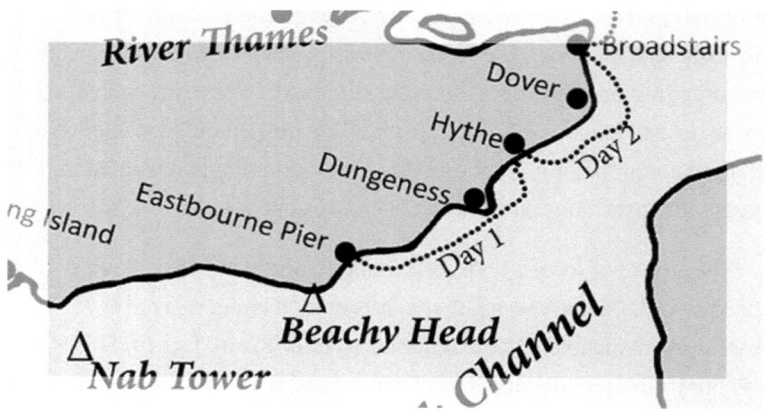

These experiences are strange. I can nearly always recall the details of the buildings, rooms and faces of the people, what they were wearing and their clothes. What I really struggle to remember is the flood of different names of the people I met along my journey. I'm not sure if it's the sheer volume of names or something in my head that just can't retain names – in all honesty I've always been poor this way. Hopefully, those who helped me will forgive my amnesia. As I progressed along my journey, I took it upon myself to keep better notes but at this stage of the trip I was woefully ill-prepared for the recording of information, other than via my Navionics app. Fortunately, my mother-in-law, Jo, kept a record of every location I stopped at and a quick summary of the places and many of the people I met.

By the time I arrived at Simon's house, I had just enough energy to inspect his partner's homemade jewellery collection before making my way to the bed he'd kindly organised and falling asleep the instant my head hit the pillow!

Chapter 8

First Crossing: Thames Estuary

I was fortunate that the breeze for my big first crossing was a decent south westerly, blowing around 18 mph when I set off. The wind strength was forecast to build to around up to 25 mph as the day progressed which meant I could sail on a broad reach. For the uninitiated, this is the best point (fastest) of sailing for a Laser, closing in on speeds of between 8 to 14 knots. Once I started my crossing there would be no options to bail out – I'd be fully signed up. I kept recalling the words of my bar room advisors from the night before,

"Once you go, you have to commit. You have four hours to get across before the tide sucks you out into the North Sea. You can't fight it; you'll be pulled out like you're in a Dyson vacuum cleaner!"

Very reassuring. My plan was to sail past Margate and head inland hugging the coastline past Whitstable. This meant heading west towards London, the wrong way for a while in order to shorten the crossing distance. The idea behind this was to minimise the distance I was offshore by crossing somewhere close to the Isle of Sheppey. That way, if I got into trouble, I was closer to land. Well, that was the theory discussed in the bar the night before.

Setting off at 10.50 am with the last of the ebb, I pushed off feeling slightly anxious but weirdly confident after my late night briefing at Broadstairs Sailing Club. Today's journey would be the longest and farthest offshore I'd ever sailed alone, let alone in a Laser. I started slowly as I had to fight my way against a foul tide. I went parallel to the rock-strewn coastline of North Foreland for an hour as soon as I rounded past Margate, then turned west. Very quickly I realised the original plan to sail inland towards London was futile. It meant beating into the wind. This is not only tiring, but also very slow.

"Four hours to cross. Four hours to cross. When you decide to go you have got to just go for it." These words rang in my ears repeatedly. "You'll be flushed out to the North Sea if you misjudge it."

I could see a large chimney on the shore which I believe was something to do with Margate's wastewater treatment plant at Foreness Point. Unbeknown to me at the time, I was in an area that is famous for shipwrecks. With such a shallow draught I feel fortunate I didn't encounter any such wrecks, rocks or sandbanks and carried on oblivious to any dangers below the surface. My mind was racing. It made no sense to continue hugging the coast and sailing inshore. I needed to go for it and cross. If I aimed for Southend-on-Sea, 29 miles on the other side, the wind would be across me.

"29 miles! Blimey, that sounds a long way!" I said out loud.

It's further than crossing the English Channel from Dover to Calais in France. I stopped to consider my position. After a few attempts at swiping my Samsung phone with wet hands through a waterproof case, I managed to open the Navionics app. I double-checked my track and my position and then plotted the distance and compass setting to make Southend. This was easier said than done as I was being tossed around in the sea and wind, making drawing the plots on my tiny screen very tricky. Finally, I got a plot to roughly where I thought I needed to aim. My guess was right. It was 28.9 miles in a straight line from my current position. The tide would be pushing me into London for a little over four hours. This meant I could afford to aim a little out to sea and increase my speed to assume a broad reach thus gaining the maximum speed from the MOD27. A broad reach, as this is known in sailing vernacular, with 17 mph of wind, is quick. I could make an average of 7.5 knots an hour. Travelling for four hours should get me pretty close to Southend. This was certainly within my comfort zone as it would be in sight of land. Pulling out the VHF radio I was carrying from inside my life jacket, I made contact with the coastguard for a radio check.

"Thames Coastguard, Thames Coastguard this is Pevensey Laser, repeat Pevensey Laser, radio check over."

Pause.

I tried again, "Thames Coastguard, Thames Coastguard this is Pevensey Laser, repeat Pevensey Laser radio check over."

Pause.

Suddenly I heard a crackly response.

"Thames Coastguard, call sign Laser receiving you over."

"Thames Coastguard, Thames Coastguard this is Pevensey Laser, I'd like to file a passage plan over."

"Pevensey Laser, Thames Coastguard go to Channel 69 and stand by."

I was sent to a working channel to clear me off the emergency Channel 16. This is standard procedure. I stood by for what seemed an age then a very pleasant and helpful sounding voice came back over the radio. They'd got my name wrong as there was no record of a Pevensey Laser on their maritime database so I went through a series of fairly lengthy questions whilst bobbing around on the edge of the estuary. Conscious of my four hour window now being eaten up by what I perceived to be pointless bureaucracy, I began to grow impatient. I soon changed my tune about that however as their help provided me with great reassurance. I periodically checked in with the coast guard and Port of London Authority on Channel 69 throughout the day. It was a comforting thought to know that they were aware of my tiny 13-foot boat crossing in front of 25,000 tonne cargo ships ploughing into London at speeds ranging between 18 and 24 knots. I secretly hoped that they'd be alerting every vessel in the area about my presence. Perhaps this might have been me having delusions of grandeur but at the time this thought was a definite reality as I'm certain I witnessed ship after ship slowing down or altering course to swerve around me.

I took one last look at the mainland, one deep breath and then I decided now was the moment. Adjusting my sail to increase the power, I hiked out from the toe strap and went flat out towards the other side. I steered a compass heading of 290 degrees. There was no going back now. I checked the Navionics app quite frequently when I first got going. That is, when the screen saver hadn't kicked in!

When it got cold and wet, I struggled to open my phone apps. When I swiped the screen to open it, often the wrong app would appear, most often Samsung Pay or some other obscure app! My cold, wet hands just didn't have the dexterity or contact with the screen to operate it as normal. I found that the screen lock wouldn't undo and my fingers couldn't open the screen. I experimented trying to swipe the phone on my jacket, then on my wetsuit both of which failed miserably. As a last resort, I tried swiping it across my woolly hat. Bingo, it worked!

Throughout the process of swiping, I successfully managed to make numerous inadvertent phone calls to various people in my phone book and was unable to hang up as the screen was locked open. This left them listening to heavy breathing and sploshing noises! On one occasion I even got the playlist to the Kinks on Spotify stuck for a good few minutes and played it to someone before managing to close the app.

At that moment, my Navionics app was open and my location was showing on the screen. Squinting through the waterproof cover that was peppered with seawater droplets, I made my first position check. I was being pushed west towards London. I corrected my heading by five degrees using my manual compass located on the deck. It was positioned just in front of the mast. I'm short sighted and wear prescription sunglasses. These were now encrusted in salt and wiping them made the lenses smeary. To read the compass I had to lean forwards and lift my glasses to see the numbers. When I did this, I often found my weight was too far forward making the bow of the boat dig into a wave which then broke over me and stopped the boat dead in its tracks. When this happened, the cockpit filled with water and soaked my head, sending freezing water down my neck.

I kept sailing as fast as I could. The visibility was starting to worsen and the breeze was building as I moved further offshore. I could make out the enormous metal masts of the wind farm on the dim distant horizon and headed directly at them. The giant windmills seemed to remain the same size for ages but gradually I was closing in. Stupidly, I hadn't checked how far offshore these were before leaving and now it was just proving too time-consuming to keep checking the app. Also, I noticed the more I used the Navionics app, the more alarmingly quickly my battery on the Samsung phone was draining. At this rate it would be flat before I reached the other side. I was going to need all the juice I could get.

"Four hours to cross. Four hours. You'll be flushed out to the North Sea if you misjudge it."

I just couldn't shake off those words in my head. Did they really mean it or were they just exaggerating? Two hours in. I was now clock watching and behind schedule. I made it under the cover of the first wind turbines sited on the Kentish Flats at 13.04 according to the time stamp on the picture I took. I needed a break so sailed in between the third row of steel trees and got my sandwiches out, ate a tin of mackerel fillets and drank half of my first bottle of water. I devoured most of the food in no time, saving the fruit and oat bars for later.

Looking around, I could see very little other than the astonishing sight of these enormous bladed turbines. I could just make out the shape of a few tankers and roll-on roll-off car ferries that glided past in the distance. The turbines stood ominously all around, as if standing guard. There were several boats attached to the steel trees by some sort of bow line. I couldn't see any people inside the boats as the windows had smoked glass. The huge windmill upright posts seemed to defy gravity, standing so tall and the huge blades created a loud whooshing sound as they spun around at a rate of knots. One of the service boats made its way towards me and stood off watching. I've no idea what they must have thought. I tried to radio them on my VHF but couldn't make contact. Instead, I packed everything away and sailed directly across the farm aiming for the furthest western diagonal corner.

I think the tide must have changed because in this section it was growing stronger. The wind was definitely increasing but my recorded tracks show I headed much further west than I needed to. I radioed the Port of London on Channel 69 and confirmed I'd reached the wind farm and would be continuing across to Southend. They acknowledged but offered no more than the minimum confirmation and dropped out. I was hoping for a cheer! But they probably had no idea what a Laser was let alone why someone would want to sail one across their estuary. Probably that was a good thing as I'm sure if they'd realised, they'd have prohibited it.

After an hour sailing, again the breeze was now full on, gusting over 20 knots and the sea state was now much steeper with higher waves and rougher than before. Visibility was poor and I couldn't see land in front or the wind farm I'd left behind. The increased wind strength was great for my boat speed, though the lack of visibility and large, breaking waves were beginning to scare me a bit. Some way off I saw a massive ship come out of nowhere but it just went past, approaching from the North Sea side which was obscured by my sail. I swivelled my head and picked out ships everywhere. It was really difficult to assess which direction they were moving in. What seems most likely now is that they were anchored.

Looking back at the charts I plotted at this stage of my crossing, I can see I was in the middle of a large ship anchorage area. It was impossible to tell what the other vessels were doing at the time. I doubled down and just hiked out as hard as I could. The boat was smacking against the steep waves. It felt like I was crossing a shallow section of water as the waves were really kicking up, standing then breaking on me from unpredictable directions. Every time I hit one badly, it sent a jarring thud through the boat. It was an unnerving experience.

Eventually, I could just about make out the faint outline of the northern side of the Thames coastline through my salt-encrusted sunglasses. I'd no idea what I was aiming at any longer except the land. I'd been sailing for four hours and the tide was definitely starting to turn, exerting a huge pull to sweep me out to the cruel North Sea. Forcing any negative thoughts to the back of my head and locking my eyes on the land, I estimated I was an hour away from anything solid. As I closed in, my confidence grew.

My thoughts turned to how far I could sail today from this point. Should I stop at Southend or somewhere nearby or should I continue northwards along the coast? I was now entering Phase 2 so I must have subconsciously assumed Phase 1 had been completed. I don't recall cheering. I still felt reasonably fresh and believed it possible to go further than Southend. It seemed clear to me that I was going to make it across. Now the only problem was, what was Phase 2?

The tide was definitely drawing me out to sea. Altering course, tentatively at first, still conscious of the advice to avoid being lost, I started heading more easterly; flowing with the tide out towards the North Sea. My speed had improved by my altering the course and so now I was screaming along with spray everywhere and the land was whizzing by but I was unsure of the course to steer since I was unable to open my phone again. It was time to improvise – to use line of sight and dead reckoning. I was now very close to land so looked for large objects, aiming at large buildings on the shore on the far-off horizon. The beach looked like a fortified Normandy landing area. As it transpired, this area was actually modelled on the German fortifications of France. A replica beach defence had been constructed in World War 2 for British forces to practise invasions and knock out the sea defences of the German army. There were loads of large but derelict-looking buildings behind the sea walls. I found out later that these buildings had been constructed to manufacture the casings and assembly of Britain's first atomic bomb in 1947.

This lump of land I was sailing parallel to, heading out towards the North Sea, was Foulness Island. Foulness was thought to have derived its name from the 12th century name 'Fugla-naess' meaning 'Wild Bird's Headland'. It had a desolate, eerie feeling; an ominous place housing many dark secrets. I didn't like it so kept going until a headland appeared, Foulness Point (not that I knew its name at the time). Checking my watch, I still had at least four hours of daylight remaining and the tide behind me for most of this so I elected to carry on.

Crossing the river at Burnham-on-Crouch, I knew there was a famous sailing club along this stretch that I felt sure would give me a bed for the night. So, resisting the temptation to turn left, I continued northwards out towards the North Sea. I remembered I'd visited Brightlingsea Sailing Club on a few previous occasions and felt confident that someone at the club would help me out for the night. I stopped with my sail flogging noisily while I checked the app. It took an age but finally I worked out where I had got to and a Phase 2 plan, albeit a draft plan at this stage.

Heading out across open water for the second time that day, I started an 11 mile crossing, aiming for the far north eastern shore of the Mersey Island estuary. When I saw land, I'd need to beach and in fact I did so at a place called Colne Point. There was nothing in sight, just dunes and marram grass. Having beached the boat because I was finding it impossible to read my Navionics app bouncing up and down on the water, I tried to locate Brightlingsea Sailing Club. At sea, I just couldn't seem to find it on the app. Once on shore it became a lot easier and I identified its location quite quickly.

The club lay due north west up the estuary. It looked pretty confusing with bars and sandbanks everywhere. Assuming my Laser would be able to go across most things, I ignored the navigational warnings, only to pretty quickly realise this was a bad mistake. I was heading into a sandbank; there was no way through. The bank was kicking up some pretty nasty waves and then, suddenly, my centreboard grounded. I did an immediate about turn, retracing my steps back to the point I'd landed. I scanned the horizon and studied a host of yachts in the distance on the other side of the water to me, all of which were sailing towards Brightlingsea.

I made a decision to follow the herd and sail towards them in search of the main channel. Again, very quickly I found myself directly in the middle of a shallow bar. The waves were horrendous, short and suddenly breaking. What a nightmare! Surely I wasn't going to get smashed up here. I pulled my centreboard up halfway which was far from ideal as I was beating into the wind now. I could feel the boat sliding sideways further into the bar and turbulent waters, smashing me up and down and breaking with frightening ferocity. I was so close to Brightlingsea! I quickly made a number of U-turns and eventually found a way through to the main channel. My nerves were shot. I followed the channel markers into the Brightlingsea estuary and when I reached the sailing club slipway, I was totally done in. The relief that I was safe and in a place I knew flooded through me physically. The time was 18.17. I'd been on the move for eight hours and eight minutes and covered a distance of 49.7 nautical miles (57 miles). It was the furthest I'd ever sailed in a Laser in my life.

As I dismounted from my boat straight into what looked like shallow water, I immediately sank waist deep in black, silty mud. A concrete walkway jutted out into the calm estuary mud flats a few metres away so, forcing my legs forward against the heavy resistance, I slowly reached it. The next challenge was how to get the boat up the 200 metre concrete ramp when the tide was all the way out like this.

The clubhouse, which seemed miles away, looked deserted. I was forced to leave the boat stuck fast in the mud and make my way along the slipway, trudging up to the dinghy park where I located an old discarded launching trolley. It was pretty small but I felt it would be better than trying to roll my boat up the concrete walkway covered in gluey mud on a fender. The clubhouse looked closed so there was no-one around to request permission or help from. I spent the next half hour hauling the MOD27 across the thick, black mud onto the walkway getting even more covered in the filthy stuff. Eventually in the grassy boat park, I collapsed, lying spread-eagled on the soft grass and fell asleep.

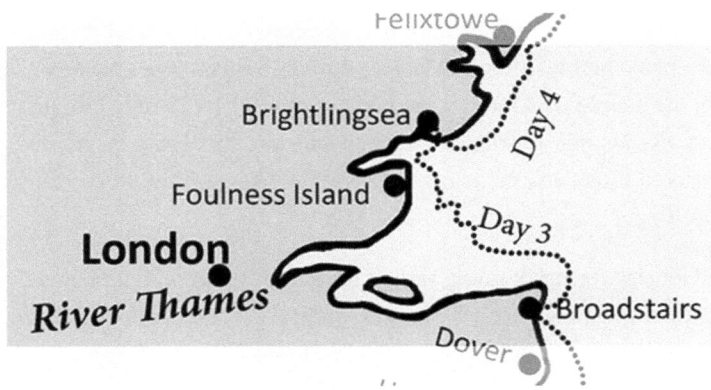

I was rudely awoken by spots of cold water falling on my face. I opened my eyes and above me the sky was full of densely packed, towering black clouds. Then, almost without warning, a deafening clap of thunder jolted me into action. As soon as I'd gathered up my bags, the sky released a torrent of water directly onto my head. I shot for cover in the clubhouse where thankfully there now appeared to be some form of life.

The door was still shut to the main area so I shivered inside the entranceway out of the worst of the rain. Fairly soon, a smartly dressed young woman came out to collect some bags from her car which was parked directly opposite the entrance.

"Would it be ok if I left my boat and camped here tonight?" I blurted out, making her jump.

She smiled but said she didn't know and explained she was only visiting, running a charity fundraising evening at the club tonight but offered to call Fiona, the Club President, on her mobile to see if that would be OK. By this time the battery on my mobile phone had totally died. Thank God that Fiona was excited by my trip and proved very helpful. She immediately offered me the use of the club's facilities but warned me I'd have to pitch my tent in the council campsite behind their dinghy park as they weren't permitted any camping in their grounds. My spirits sank when she said this.

The council campsite is a long walk from the club and I'd stayed there twice before at Laser Masters sailing events. I knew there was no way the people who ran it would let me stay for free. Added to this fact, a thunderous rainstorm had blown up and was still going on outside. I thanked Fiona and made my way into the club's showers to clean myself up.

Hot showers after going sailing normally feel good but this one was the best shower I'd ever had in my life! I wrestled my boots off before carefully stepping into the cubicle still in my spraytop and wetsuit. The warm water slowly permeated my skin and felt fantastic. I stripped off slowly, peeling away layer after layer. The salt from my matted hair ran into my eyes making them sting. My skin felt tender and sore. Foolishly, I hadn't put any cream on my face as it had seemed unnecessary when I set off in the gloomy, grey light of that morning. My face was raw now.

I carried out a detailed assessment of other injuries. The little finger of my left hand had got bent back on my first day's sailing and was now sticking out at a funny angle. It felt like I'd dislocated it and maybe damaged the tendon. My backside was seriously sore and my legs ached; the pre-existing tennis elbow in both my arms that I'd got from lifting too many doors was aggravated but there were no other issues to report. Dressing after my shower was fast. I'd dispensed with the underpants idea after Day One. I needed to lighten the load so anything I could dump I had. I pulled on my black trousers, Prostate Cancer UK t-shirt, shoes, no socks and tied the belt (which was a spare sailing control line) and I felt brand new again.

I decided to defer the tent issue until later and headed back to the bar. I was the only person sitting at it although the main room was packed with guests for the fundraising evening. To my surprise, this involved making things in origami in order to raise money for a school in Africa. The club was heaving with women laughing and drinking wine, and lots of it from what I could see. We were in Essex of course – home of the white wine spritzer.

Most of the evening was spent sitting at the bar on my own drinking beer and talking to Tom, the young bar steward. My phone had a charging issue which Tom managed to fix. Turns out the charging contact point was already beginning to get corroded from sea water. Tom immersed the contact charging plug and phone input jack in vodka, leaving it soaking while I drank beer and talked to him about the drama of my day. After an hour of soaking, he plugged it back in and bingo – the phone was back up and running. Several hours later I made sure the vodka didn't go to waste now its primary function had been completed.

Samsung 8 Galaxy phone sorted, phew! My one and only navigation tool was back up and running. In between fixing my phone I made a call to Emma and messaged in on the Safety Channel using Tom's phone. This was to reassure everyone and ensure that the coastguard wasn't out scanning the Thames estuary for a bright orange and grey knackered old Laser. There was great relief from Emma. It was my first big offshore crossing of the trip but what's more, my GPS tracker had stopped working just after I left the shore. The supposedly waterproof satellite unit I'd invested my hard earned £200 in had lasted not even two days. The Spot X tracker's power input socket had got wet and so it stopped working. Unlike my mobile, Tom's recovery method failed to resuscitate the Spot X. I'd hardly started my journey and the list of stuff breaking was growing rapidly. Losing both my phone and tracker had been a great cause for concern to those following me as they couldn't see my position any more. Whilst pondering on what to do about the Spot X over another pint of beer, Tom presented me with my now fully charged mobile phone.

"You're back up and running again," he exclaimed excitedly.

Finally I could start planning tomorrow's journey. It was gone 10 o'clock again. I felt exhausted and very hungry. I was scribbling down notes for the next day's trip when the origami fundraisers interrupted me,

"Help yourself to whatever's left – pizza and salad leftovers," they said.

I managed to hoover up everything left on the table. Then I felt super tired but remembered I still had nowhere to sleep. After my brief planning session, I'd figured out that I needed to leave with the tide at first light in the morning at 5.30 am!

"Oh my God," I thought, "it's 11 o'clock now and I've no idea what to do about camping."

I didn't want to flout the club rules but the campsite owners were probably tucked up in bed now and it was still teeming down with rain outside. Tom then mentioned,

"In case you need them in the morning the changing rooms are left open at night. They have a separate entrance to the main clubhouse."

"Really?"

I waved him goodnight, slipping into the changing rooms unnoticed. Pulling my sleeping bag out of the waterproof bag, it felt soggy. Apparently the waterproof bag was not so waterproof after all. Another kit failure. I dried the bag as best I could under the hand dryers in the toilets and made a makeshift bed on the floor. My mat was only very thin and I could feel every bone in my body being pushed back by the solid changing room floor. I propped up my head using various bags and clothes as a pillow which improved things slightly. I've slept in more comfortable places but outside the rain was lashing it down and I wouldn't have traded this location for a tent for any money in England. Plugging in my VHF radio and phone to ensure maximum charge, I set the alarm in time to make the first tide and allowed a full hour to get ready and rigged – it would go off at 4.15 am. Five hours sleep. Lovely!

Chapter 9

It's a Blast – East Coast

There was a sudden, loud, rude shock to my system. My alarm. I lunged at it, barely connecting with the phone. Pulling on my wetsuit and rash vest, I appeared in full sailing gear in the canteen bar area that a young French cleaner was hoovering vigorously. She almost leapt into the air when she stopped her noisy work and heard my mumbled, "Morning." I carried on as if it was perfectly normal to be going sailing at half past four in the morning. After a few polite please and thank yous or should I say, "s'il vous plait and mercies, she kindly filled my water bottles and I was out of there.

Rigging in record time meant I had to wait for sunrise. It was cold and damp outside. The sun climbed slowly, providing no warmth as it first appeared. I made my way down the dark slipway that still seemed to disappear into the night. I can't recall ever launching to go sailing at 5 am in the morning before. Somehow it just seemed the natural thing to do that day. Pushing the boat along the concrete slipway on the borrowed tiny trolley, I felt some resistance in it which I ignored, assuming the axle must just be corroded and carried on. It was only when I pushed the boat off the trolley and it partially blew over that I realised the boat's bottom had been rubbing against the trolley wheel. A significant groove had worn through the new gelcoat layer, exposing the fibreglass mat underneath. I was seriously annoyed with myself for not taking more care. I left the boat floating on the edge of the muddy beach and returned the trolley to its original abandoned position in the boat park.

Today was going to be another big day. My plan was to make it to Lowestoft. This was some 60 nautical miles; an ambitious task. As luck would have it, the forecast was perfect for another long run. The wind was still blowing from the south west, except today the forecast looked really ominous further south with strong winds moving across the country. Electrical storms were expected.

Today I'd be passing the ports of both Harwich and Felixstowe. Somewhere near one of these was Shotley Sailing Club, home to Terry Scutcher, who was better known in the fleet as 'F'ing Terry'. Terry was one of the diehard Laser Master regulars who attended all the racing circuit events I usually went to. I was really looking forward to tucking into a full English breakfast with him and had set my sights on getting to Shotley and surprising him with an early morning visit, around 8 am. Terry was known for his thick East coast accent and use of 'colourful' language. He was the Laser fleet's answer to Gordon Ramsay. I hadn't actually forewarned Terry of my ambitions but just assumed he'd be free. Just in case, I pinged him a messenger note advising him of my target ETA just before I set off. I also asked the Safety Channel members to try to make contact with him. A deafening silence was the response there. Perhaps he was away?

Making good progress out of Brightlingsea, avoiding the shallows and bar that had caught me out the previous day, I noticed how the coastline architecture was so contrasting. It ranged from the unspoilt and isolated sandy dunes of St Osyth Naturist Beach, which I passed as I turned left into the North Sea after leaving the river estuary, into what I think of as a typical English style seaside town. Clacton-on-Sea was heavily lined with groynes; sea defence breakwaters, made of the toughest greenheart timber that are piled metres into the shifting golden sand below. They're reinforced by large man-made bays formed of black boulders designed to break up the erosive effects of longshore drift. It was all to hold back the relentless force of the North Sea; a sea with twice daily spring tidal ranges exceeding seven metres. In front of the town stands a continuous man-made wall – a thin line protecting row upon row of houses. It was a picture book of time. Houses from all eras were dotted along the front here from grand Victorian buildings with elegant and ornate facades to simplistic 1960s sprawling bungalows with plain glass viewing windows. Every now and then a collection of more modern four storey blocks of apartments stuck out of the ground, arranged in large four and five storey towers evenly spaced just behind the wall line. These were advertised by estate agents as retirement apartments with sea views and priced to maximise 'your luxury retirement and enjoyment.' The frontage of these blocks had overly manicured communal gardens, fenced off by red brick walls with white iron arrow tipped railings positioned along the top.

I observed how the beach huts lined the actual promenade next to the beach with the occasional large green tree interrupting the open walkways. Close to the town centre, a Victorian pier stood out proudly amongst the waves. This was a truly British eccentricity. A flat, 30-foot high platform jutting out, somewhat bizarrely, into the North Sea, defying the forces of nature with its obstinacy. It looked like a Meccano set from where I was. On the end of it, a rickety roller coaster offered the thrills of a ride designed to shake up your jellied eels and ice cream.

As I closed in on Clacton Pier, a range of ugly square buildings became visible. I could just make out the contours of one, a large pleasure building with 'AMUSEMENTS' in gaudy, glaring letters printed above it. This building probably contained every manner of slot machine designed with the sole purpose of making the customer lose money. High pitched electronic music drifted into earshot which got louder and louder until I was well past then thankfully ebbed away.

I was hungry now. I'd been sailing for two hours and it was still only 7.30 on a Saturday morning. I decided to beach the boat close to the pier and go in search of a cafe or shop. Landing was easy and I pulled the boat up the sandy beach dragging her on her side in the capsized position. Whilst sorting out my bags, looking for my debit card and some money, a dog bounded over to say hello. He was a small brown wiry-haired type. I didn't recognise the breed but he was incredibly cute and friendly. The lady owner approached and apologised. (it's funny how people think a dog being friendly needs an apology). We got chatting and I asked if she knew of a cafe nearby. She said nowhere would be open until at least 9 o'clock. We talked a bit more and then she went on with her early morning walk.

What's wrong with this place? Didn't everyone know they were getting a visit from Stick Daring, intrepid explorer and circumnavigator – hopefully. Apparently not, and of course why should they? Only a handful of people knew I was on this voyage. The town was hardly going to break a sweat for some aged wannabe idiot. So, I resorted to emptying my food store bag located in the rear hatch. This sounds easy but it took me quite some time to find and extract a crumpled muesli bar and handful of pepperami sticks. I unloaded nearly all my gear through the hatch cover, the aperture of which was clearly designed to only allow a Mars Bar to pass through, not a tent and three months' worth of overnight bags!

I relaunched and continued on up the coast, having consoled myself that Terry would soon come up trumps. He was probably asleep like most normal people. Passing Walton-on-the-Naze further up was quite a sight from the sea. It looked like it had had a beach hut steroid injection! If it was compared to childbirth, you would say there had been an explosion of triplets. Tiers upon tiers of beach huts were arranged vertically in terraces – making them look stacked six high. They were squeezed together on concrete bases, some so tightly arranged you couldn't fit a cigarette paper between them, each painted in contrasting Farrow and Ball colours –- Middleton Pink, Nancy's Blushes, Citron, Green Ground, Blue Ground and Wimborne White. I recognised them from my doors. It was a full metal jacket beach hut frenzy!

By 8 am I'd made it to Harwich, taking a short break at the mouth of the rivers Stour and Orwell. Checking my phone there was still no word from Terry. I was pretty hungry but there wasn't much point stopping this early, I mused. I tucked into another pepperami stick which had been stuffed into my life jacket pocket. There was a strong tide against me now as I approached Harwich and it became slow going. I sent a WhatsApp message to the Safety Channel to double check if Terry had messaged them.

"Negative," came the WhatsApp reply.

Oh well, I'd carry on and see if I could beach and find a cafe somewhere nearby. I'd kill for a bacon buttie and cup of coffee. To my left I could see a wide estuary mouth that was divided into two separate rivers, the Stour and the Orwell. Scenes from the Stour Valley are famous for their depictions in paintings by the famous early nineteenth century English landscape artist, John Constable.

The estuary mouth is where Essex meets Suffolk with Felixstowe sitting further seaward, looking a little as though it's guarding the mouth of these rivers. The fortress' high walls and pontoons are festooned with every type of industrial-looking ship imaginable. Cranes as tall as Nelson's Column stand proudly on the quayside. A mishmash of industrial shipyard buildings is strewn around the docking areas. It was quite imposing and felt slightly intimidating.

The Port of Felixstowe is the UK's busiest container port. There were a lot of seriously large ships that looked like they were either loading or unloading their cargo. Some had a continuous flow of water pouring out from their sides. Fortunately for me, not many of them were on the move as I passed by. Perhaps I was too early but then again, I doubt that industrial marine traffic only works 9 to 5 Monday to Friday!

Behind the industrial docks I could see elegant sailing boats making their way down the River Orwell in the distance, flowing gracefully and effortlessly past the rolling green land and bright blue sea. They were grey; silhouetted by the morning sun poking its face through a rounded nest of cumulus clouds. As the sailing boats came closer, it became clear they were an assortment of racing yachts making their way out towards the North Sea. It seemed like an early start. Perhaps they were off for a long weekend race? I double-checked what day it was; I'd lost track of the days already. Ah yes, Saturday I reminded myself. That might explain it.

I felt a bit deflated that I hadn't managed to link up with Terry and the next hour seemed to drag. The largest yacht I'd seen earlier was slowly beginning to catch me up. I could see nine crew members sitting with their legs dangling through the wire guard rails all dressed in matching blue and red oilskins. I assumed there must be another two, maybe even three people in the cockpit, one trimming the mainsail and spinnaker and the other steering but I couldn't see them from my position. I doubted they would have any spare bacon butties on board to toss to me either!

The spinnaker on this first yacht looked massive and was straining to its maximum. As it got closer, I could see the spinnaker trimmer on board was having a very busy time trying to keep it under control. It looked too large a kite for this wind strength. Watching the yacht struggle with this power, it occurred to me that the wind had been steadily building. I looked behind me and saw a thick mass of black clouds in chase. The forecast for today was thunderstorms and very strong winds approaching from the south.

I was now sailing just off dead before the wind. This is fast and relatively stable if you're an experienced Laser sailor but for the yachts it seemed to be pretty rocky. They appeared to be in constant danger of broaching every time a strong gust came through. A broach occurs when the wind overpowers the yacht causing it to heel over. The rudder stalls making the boat unsteerable. It's a bit like when an aeroplane stalls if it flies too slowly and loses lift off the wings. The boat's rudder loses lift, rendering it useless.

The sequence of events for a broach starts with a strong gust and culminates in the boat screwing up violently into the wind and heeling over sideways, often until the sail is laid flat on the water with the tip of the mask submerged. It becomes very messy and is an unpleasant experience for the people sitting on the yacht's side with their legs trapped underneath the guard rail. Usually one of two things then happen, either these helpless victims get dunked in the sea or they're flung across the roof of the yacht.

I was surfing very close to my maximum speed now, sliding down increasingly large waves. The trick in these seas is to avoid running into the wave in front and burying the boat's nose. I was really having to concentrate at 100%. The largest yacht was catching me and annoyingly started to bear down on me from behind. I was weaving back and forth to keep my balance and take advantage of the waves picking me up and forcing, racing me downhill in front of the rolling crest. When the spinnaker of the first yacht came close to my stern, I headed up a bit to keep out of the way of its wind shadow.

Right now, I could do without the additional randomness of my sail being blanketed then exposed to a strong gust from behind. After an hour or so of this, the large yacht finally drew level and moved slowly past me. I must have been going pretty fast as this yacht looked at least 50-foot long and had just about every hi-tech device imaginable bolted to it. I chuckled to myself. Here I was in a £50 Laser in the middle of the North Sea, sailing alone, travelling only slightly more slowly than this million pound plus super yacht, packed with 10 times the people to control it. It seemed very amusing to me to know my investment per mile per hour represented such a big differential. People who say sailing is a rich man's sport are frankly misinformed. Several more yachts started catching up and overtaking me. They were slightly smaller than the first one.

"They must all be racing – everyone looks very intent and focused," I decided.

I carried on heading towards Orford Ness Lighthouse which sits on a promontory and can be seen for miles and miles, standing out like the gateway to the North Sea. While concentrating hard on keeping clear of the overtaking yachts, I missed the entrance to the River Alde on the shore side. I couldn't consult my navigation app on account of the fact that I was desperately trying to stay upright and only just avoiding a capsize with every new wave. Had I taken the river turn-off, I could have sailed parallel to my current position cutting off the Orford Ness Lighthouse. Inland would have offered more protection and smaller waves but, as it was, I was in a 'lane of no escape' until I reached and rounded the lighthouse. The large headland was now kicking up huge rolling waves.

I just kept going as fast as I could, weaving in and out of the waves. I saw more yachts approaching from behind, more like the 30-foot type I'd sailed regularly at Cowes Week. After being overtaken by several of them, one suddenly broached. I witnessed another yacht's spinnaker simultaneously explode as they passed, surfing within just a few metres of me. A massive gust came out of nowhere, bigger than anything so far and forced me to bear off down a particularly large wave to avoid being capsized. I was now hurtling past another yacht on my inside track that was also struggling to stay in control; we only just avoided a collision. At the same instance I noticed the first yacht that had passed me was now a long way ahead, broached and screwed up into the wind which looked frightening.

Most of the crews of the overtaking yachts had given me a quizzical look, scratching their heads and questioning why such a tiny boat would be so far out to sea in such weather. I couldn't give them or indeed myself a logical answer to that question. Most waved at me sympathetically enough. As we closed in on Orford Ness Lighthouse, it felt like the sea was squeezed between the land and the lighthouse like a tube of toothpaste. The waves became much bigger and far less predictable. I was surfing on the ragged edge amongst some of the smaller yachts, matching many of them for speed. Most would go on then suddenly broach violently out of control, some careering towards me. We were all hugging the shoreline; a continuous solid wall.

There was no bail out option along this section. I was stuck and just had to keep going. At times, the yachts and I were surfing within 10 metres of the sea wall. I'd become trapped on the seaward side amongst several yachts. We kept watching each other. I was getting tired and started to feel irritated that they were so close to me but in all honesty, they seemed to be struggling more than I was. The difference as I saw it for me was that if I capsized (quite probable), I'd be in real trouble in the current sea state – unlike the yachts who were more stable.

Soon it became clear we were going to have to cross paths. The leading yachts were heading out to sea after the lighthouse whereas I was heading inshore after rounding the headland. Following a particularly large wave, I managed to surf across and just in front of one of the yachts that had been pinning me out to sea. As I crossed, it broached suddenly and was out of control twisting into the wind, narrowly missing the back of my boat. I may well have caused them to do this but I feel no remorse as they should have kept clear since they were overtaking me on the wrong side. The skipper had a perfect picture postcard face of horror as their boat flattened onto its side, spinnaker whipping in the maddening wind.

I'd now been surfing by the lee for seven hours. My legs were shaking, my elbows screaming, arms and fingers barely able to continue the constant sheeting in and out of the sail. I started to recognise a few landmarks and finally saw a beach that I knew.

Aldeburgh is home to one of the UK's oldest sailing clubs. The only problem was, I'd missed the river entrance to sail into it. The club is inaccessible from the shingle beach lying directly in front of it. Instead, the approach is a mile's sail up the river I'd missed earlier. Nonetheless, I could see the sailing club from the sea and decided I'd had enough. I pointed my boat at the beach and sailed at it flat out, capsizing on the shore and falling out the back as I landed!

I just lay there totally exhausted. Thank God it had ended! I turned and squinted to see directly in front of my landing spot were two wooden fishing boats, behind which sat a small wooden hut. I couldn't move yet. I was lying flat on my back, arms spread wide apart, prostrate on the beach – absolutely knackered! Time slowed at last. Then I became aware it was hot lying on the pebbles as I was sheltered from the wind. Out to sea it was really, really windy now. The black cloud that had been following me all day was still growing ominously in the distance. I had just sailed downwind by the lee of the wind for 40 continuous miles in over 20 knots, gusting loads more at times.

"You can't park your boat there, mate!"

I turned around to see a large fisherman standing and pointing his finger at a sign.

"No Landing"

I didn't quite believe what I was hearing. Did this bloke really think I cared? I barely had the energy to answer.

"Well, you gonna mooove it?" he persisted in a slightly threatening way.

"I've just come from Brightlingsea," I managed to faintly reply.

His mouth opened disbelievingly, "What in thaaa thing?"

I nodded but made no noise as I lay back on the beach absorbing as much of the sun as possible, trying to muster up the energy to reset and move on.

After some silence and to my complete surprise, he added, "Do you want fish and chips and a cup of tea?"

I smiled and came back with the standard answer I was now learning to perfect, "Yes, please."

I couldn't quite believe how delicious fish and chips and a cup of tea could taste. By now I was chatting with both fishermen, scoffing and slurping outside their hut on Aldeburgh beach. I could quite easily have stayed there all night.

The problem was that I'd already made a plan. I'd alerted Gemma, my cousin, the day before that I might just make it to Southwold. She'd asked her parents, my Uncle Mick and Aunty Jenny, if they might be able to put me up. They had a big house in Southwold and had prepared a bed and Gemma, who also lives in Eastbourne, was driving up to meet me – about four hours. They would be so disappointed if I didn't make it. I really fancied a comfortable bed and hot meal. Jenny is my mother's younger middle sister. I knew she'd look after me.

I used to stay in my aunt and uncle's house off Corton Road in Lowestoft most summers when we were kids. My older brother, sister and me, being the youngest, would be packed off for the school holidays. I have four cousins, the eldest two are Sarah and Martyn then Gemma, who is nearly the same age as me, and Phillip, the baby, a few years younger. We spent most school holidays charging around the sand dunes of Corton Road, Lowestoft playing soldiers, hiding in the disused pill boxes left over from World War 2 which are still standing and set into the dunes. We used to always swim in the freezing thunderous surf of the North Sea and sail on nearby Oulton Broad. Martyn was the first person I ever sailed with in fact. His dad, Uncle Mick, and Martyn raced Enterprise sailing dinghies on the Broads.

I remember I was eight years old the first time I set foot in a boat. Martyn had a Mirror dinghy – the 'boat of choice' for kids to learn to sail and race in those days. They came as a kit which your dad would spend hours in his garage stitching and glueing together, making good the joints with fibreglass tape and painting the wooden hull any colour of paint left lying around in the garage. The sails were bright red so they could be seen for miles which I can only imagine was a deliberate decision by the designers. The Mirror dinghy had the feel of a mini pirate ship to me because, as you hoisted the sail, the top half of the mast slid up doubling the mast height, forming what is called a gaff rig. There's a small triangular sail at the bow and a third sail, launched for sailing before the wind – the spinnaker. The crew had to pull this sail up and down and attach a single pole onto the mast and then onto the guy which is always difficult to understand for non-sailors but, in simple terms, it stops the sail from collapsing. The crew's job (this was me in this instance) was to let the spinnaker sheet, the rope that is attached to one corner of the sail, in and out as the wind gusts. If you were too slow, the boat capsized which we sometimes did. I couldn't believe we were allowed out on our own. It was just fantastic! Screaming around the Broads weaving in and out of the pleasure boats, spinnaker up, waving at every boat that went past usually with spray all around us. I didn't know it at the time but those were magical days. Really, my sailing story started here. How could I possibly not stop at Southwold?

I texted Gemma to tell her I'd be coming and started packing up again to get going. I really didn't fancy it at all and kept warily looking up at the ever-darkening sky. She replied to my text saying her dad had made arrangements for me to come into the harbour at Southwold. I'd never before even noticed the harbour at Southwold and had to check my Navionics app before setting off. It looked to me more like a river estuary and seemed like an incredibly long and thin entrance. I thought little more of it as I pushed off waving goodbye to my now best friends, the fishermen.

Chapter 10

Southwold Ahoy!

It was very windy and as soon as I was properly set, I was surfing along. The wind was nearly dead behind but I was making good speed. At this rate, I'd cover the 10 miles and be in Southwold in little over an hour. I settled down in the boat and found myself a comfortable position. I found lying in the boat with my feet dangling out one side and my head the other reduced further chafing of my backside.

Although very flat, this section of coastline is breathtakingly picturesque, if you ignore the monstrous Sizewell Nuclear Power Station just north along the coast from Aldeburgh. The unspoilt marshes and dunes of the RSPB Minsmere area, which supports a mix of habitats, has a triple SSSi rating for scientific importance. However, as with much of the UK coastline, this area is under threat from global warming and rising sea levels as it is dependent on a single sluice to drain fresh water off the land at Minsmere. With increased tidal surges, the sluice is often overwhelmed and clogged by shingle so blocks land drainage. As with much of the UK's coastline, the Environment Agency is presently looking at ways of reducing the impact of rising sea levels to protect this area.

All was going very smoothly. The weather system that had been chasing me all day was still just behind. I felt so relaxed now I even afforded myself the luxury of calling Jeff in Inverness to have a chat. He'd been tracking the weather system I was just managing to stay ahead of all day, monitoring my position on his computer screen, using some weather radar app to compare how far away it was from my present location. Jeff was really into weather. He just loved it. He eulogised about how I'd managed to stay a step in front of the storm coming up behind, telling me tales of fallen trees and general mayhem being wreaked by the storm further south. I laughed and just carried on.

At Jeff's old house in Eastbourne, his garden was littered with weird weather contraptions. When he worked with me as a Surface Enhancement Technician (painter) at my door business, his morning opener would go something like this:

"Yeah at 11 o'clock it's going to rain – only a slight drizzle coming in over the Downs. It's only going to go on for 20 minutes and then the wind is coming round to the north east, alright."

And he'd go on enthusiastically, continuing to divulge every minute detail of the day's weather patterns. What to expect, why and the time to expect it. To most people, this might seem reasonable but given Jeff's background it was interesting that he found it so important. Jeff had had a

turbulent childhood, mostly spent living with friend's parents or on his own in social housing. I never met Jeff's parents and I'm not sure he did very often. He told me he couldn't read and write very well which I was surprised at given how articulate he is.

Jeff told me that many times he'd turn up for school to get a free meal and then go home or round to a mate's house. He lost 12 years of his life to drugs yet somehow saved himself and turned his attention to healthier pursuits. When you know what he went through from the age of about 12 (after his mum and dad split up and he was basically on his own), he's a total miracle. His unassuming, laidback, good nature is impossible not to warm to.

I first met him cycling over the South Downs near Eastbourne and was introduced through a group of mutual friends. Whenever we set off on a cycle with him, we only really saw Jeff when we'd got to the pub we'd agreed to rendezvous at. This is on account of the fact that he always rode totally flat out, leading from the front of the group. He was unbelievably fast the entire way. His infectious laugh is what endeared him to me from the start and his humorous, if slightly tragic, outlook on life. When all seemed lost, somehow we'd laugh it off. He'd regale various tales of worries and strife yet always see the funny side and point out the ridiculous. Underneath I'm not sure his earlier insecurities have ever gone away though and often he's struggled with his demons but found a positive way of carrying on. Everybody likes Jeff. I think he saw me as a sort of dad figure which I felt far too young for as he's only about 12 years younger than me!

After completing my call with Jeff, I began to admire the approaching shoreline coming up to Southwold. The Georgian town of Walberswick is one of the prettiest places on this stretch. It's known for its understated beach huts which are mostly painted black. There's a picturesque harbour wall you can crab from and where the enticing Crab World Championship is staged annually in August.

Just as I was musing about the sunny days I'd spent crabbing with my cousins and later my own three boys, a huge gust of wind walloped me squarely from behind. My legs were still dangling out of the side of the boat at the time and I was in total relaxation mode. So much so, I was unable to react fast enough and found myself unexpectedly in the water with the boat lying on her side. Luckily, I was tied on by the end of my mainsheet – the rope used to pull the sail in and out – but because everything had happened so quickly, I found myself on the wrong side which was annoying.

The mainsheet was taut and pulled me under the hull of the boat. I was being blown along with the boat on her side and the sail was still filling. It felt very similar to my experience during the trial run when I sailed to Bexhill while Jeff raced me on his bike. Trapped in this awkward position, I couldn't figure out a way of freeing myself except to either cut the rope or try to untie the knot. My knife was inside my life jacket pocket and it was always difficult to unfold the blade at the best of times so therefore I chose option two, untie the knot.

This was my first proper capsize of the trip! Suddenly my mind was deluged with concerns about the amount of kit I was carrying dragging the hull under; my thoughts started racing. My additional bag was in the cockpit coupled with the punctured (now deflated) mast head float that I hadn't bothered re-inflating for the last 10 mile stretch. It was now useless as a buoyancy aid. My fingers worked away at the knot whilst my feet were kicking away, keeping my head just about out of the water. After a few minutes, I released the knot and swam clear, just clutching onto the centreboard to pull the boat upright. I was surprised how easily she righted herself once I'd managed to get into the correct position. The waterproof bag strapped under my toe strap in the cockpit acted as a really good buoyancy bag and the open hull area instantly drained dry. "Bingo," I thought at the time. Then I made a mental note to myself not to tie onto the boat ever again. Well, the MOD27 had finally had her first proper sea trial and had come out with flying colours.

After sailing for another 10 minutes, Southwold pier came into view. The harbour entrance was somewhere before the beach which was before the pier. The strong breeze had begun to whip the sea up and the storm was nearly on me. Despite blue skies and the heat of the sun still being palpable, the wind had gathered strength. I needed to get in as soon as possible. Ahead, I could see a promenade supported by big criss-cross timbers underneath. Then, when I got closer, I could clearly make out a solid wall on the far side. The water between the two was about as wide as a main A road and I didn't particularly like the look of the width of this gap or the swell between the wall and the wooden prom. At the mouth, waves were swashing through the lattice work, hitting the far wall hard, then bouncing back forming this horrendous standing wave swell. I hadn't really taken any time to consider how I'd approach this until I was 50 feet into this cauldron of boiling water. The sea state was bumpy but when I had wind at the mouth it was manageable. Now I was halfway along the entry walls and I ran out of wind because the height of the walls on either side was almost as tall as my sail. They blanketed the wind almost entirely. At this point, I was helplessly being washed towards the very concrete looking far wall.

"Stuff this" I thought, "I'm outta here!" and made an abrupt U-turn and headed straight back out to the harbour entrance and the safety of the open sea.

Once out of the harbour, I sailed parallel to the beautiful, golden, sandy beach that is Southwold. There was quite a shore dump but the tide was a way out so I surfed in aiming for the centre of the beach. I'm proud to say I executed one of my tried and tested beach landings perfectly.

A few moments later I looked out to sea and felt relieved I was finally ashore. It was 15.23. That meant I'd been running for 11 hours and had covered 49.9 nautical miles (92.4 km) – my biggest day so far. I knew at the time I was running too fast. I'd never be able to keep up this pace all the way round, though little did I know there would be some more very big days to come.

Uncle Mick had been expecting me at the harbour. It turned out where I'd landed was exactly halfway between both major car parks. I felt a pang of guilt for a moment when I realised this as Mick was being treated for cancer at the time and my landing spot meant a long walk for him to find me.

By the time he arrived, I'd unrigged and unloaded my bags. With his help, I pulled the boat all the way up the long, inclined, sandy beach; this was the most energy-sapping type of surface for humping a boat around on. Mick was concerned it was a weekend and there was a nearby open-air festival that night. The dunes on this beach often received late night revellers pairing off apparently and the worry was that for a few big laughs maybe they would cast the boat off. Armed with this knowledge, I dragged the boat as far into a dune as I could manage in order to dissuade anyone from attempting to move her all the way back down to the sea. It took an age to hide her upside down and bury the mast and bits underneath out of sight.

Carrying as much kit as possible, including my large dry bag with clothes and overnight stuff, rudder, centreboard and tiller, we trudged off to Mick's car and back to his house. Aunty Jenny ensured I was well-fed and even washed all my sailing gear for the first time in the trip for me! That evening was a lovely experience; talking about old times, eating and then sleeping in a luxurious bed.

Gemma arrived late in the evening but just in time for a short visit to the pub next door. She ordered a few pints of Adnams and I pulled out Uncle Mick's road map to plan the next day. I made a call to Gemma's older brother, Martyn, from the pub to ask his advice on crossing The Wash – the stretch of water in the north west of East Anglia that separates Norfolk from Lincolnshire. In particular, I wanted to know any places I could bail out to and generally get the lie of the land along that northern coast. Martyn ran the family bakery in Lowestoft with his younger brother, Phillip. He too was nearby and free the next morning (a Sunday) so we arranged to meet for a cousins' family breakfast on the beach to go over some details in person before I set off.

Breakfast on Southwold beach was a large affair with my immediate cousins, their wives, friends and my aunt and uncle all gathering round one tiny outdoor table at a cafe! I had very little chance to recap my conversation with Martyn from the night before about places to stop but I did find out about a few optimum landing locations called Sheringham, Cromer and Mundesley, any of which I decided could be my next end point. Martyn's chuckle after I told him where I thought I could get to was slightly troubling. There was the issue of a lack of water close to land, vast tidal dunes in the middle of the sea and the prospect of total nothingness for miles if the wind dropped and I didn't make any of my target destinations. He also made the point, which lodged some serious doubt in my mind, that this bit was the easy section.

"What about the top of Scotland?" He ventured.

"What about the top of Scotland? I replied.

There was no reply, just a nervous laugh and a frown. I parked that thought deep in the recesses of my imagination, shut the door and threw away the key.

To my relief, the boat was untouched by the previous night's revellers. It was a lovely sunny morning when I hauled the MOD27 out of the sand dunes, dusted and washed out all the fittings and tried to revive my lovely ball-bearing blocks which had seized solid from the worst combination of sand and salt. I took a picture or two, packed my gear back into the hull, squeezing it all through what seemed like an ever-shrinking hatch and already it was nearly 1 pm. I was just in time to catch the ebb tide to carry me north towards Sheringham where I hoped to set up for my second long crossing across The Wash the following day.

The day proved to be surprisingly challenging given the benign launching conditions at Southwold. Changeable winds soon switched on then off, on then off leaving me drifting around miles offshore, often running across turbulent waters that appeared from nowhere. I was scooped up and swished around like socks in a washing machine, unable to do much about it as there was too little breeze to get me out of trouble. Miles away from land, I hit the bottom in shallows then was whacked with buckets of breeze coming in from a completely new direction.

I barely noticed Lowestoft and Corton Road beach where I'd spent so many summer holidays as a child messing about. I was well past there now – the most easterly point of the UK so from here on in, I was at least heading north west if nothing else.

After six hours of flowing with the tide, I'd had enough. I was wrung out mentally and physically from the cumulative efforts of the previous days. From the very first hour of the day when I was totally becalmed trying to pass the entrance to Great Yarmouth, my senses had been on red alert. The wind had just vanished right in front of the harbour mouth and I found myself frantically trying to waft the sail in and out to get out of the way of a very large and unwelcoming-looking ship that was oblivious to my presence.

I realised around half past five in the afternoon that I wasn't going to make Sheringham. I thought it unlikely I'd even reach Cromer so my next bail out location from the discussion the night before was a place called Mundesley. I'd no real idea what I might find there as I hadn't researched it before leaving. The tide would turn in less than an hour and the wind was dropping. I was still miles off shore as every time I approached land it seemed as though I'd hit quicksand or something worse might happen. I had visions of Captain Nemo and the Nautilus rearing up out of the sea with some giant sea monster in pursuit about to swallow him up with me – both never to be seen again! It was definitely time to land. Quickly checking the Navionics app, I aimed straight for Mundesley.

I actually made shore at 18.12 and contacted the Safety Channel confirming as much. Mundesley had a small sandy picturesque beach with a lifeboat station squeezed high up into the cliff face. This was connected by a long ramp, down which the lifeboat was launched. Adjacent to this ramp was an elevated wooden platform where a number of small power boats and tractors were stored and a slatted set of wooden steps reached down amongst the rocks, also giving access to the beach.

It didn't take long to arouse some interest from some locals walking dogs nearby. I started chatting to them and recounted the story of my journey and the day's events to them. A few very soon became a lot more and before I knew it, I had a big crowd of people helping to carry my boat up to the cliff face near the steps, far enough to avoid the imminent high tide. I was hoping one of them would have a key to the lifeboat station. Sadly no-one did.

There was no fresh water on the beach and at this stage of my journey I hadn't mastered the useful technique of hinting for somewhere to stay without actually asking directly. Mario, one of the onlookers, came forward and suggested that the fountain up on top of the cliff on the town's green would be the nearest source of freshwater. He helped me to assemble my bags and I struggled up the cliff with him, still dressed in my now seriously itchy wetsuit. I needed to find somewhere to rinse off fast – my backside was on fire!

The rest of the beach group arranged their own social plans for the evening and told Mario to meet them at some pub, whose name I didn't catch. When he initially mentioned the town square, I imagined there would be a toilet block or small building I could change in. There was in fact, but it was now eight o'clock and the toilets were locked for the night. The only running water was the fountain right out on show in the open on the green next to the road. It was very public to put it mildly.

A steady stream of people was passing by, making their way to one of Mundesley's many pubs and restaurants. I felt slightly awkward with Mario loitering waiting for me and started to wish he'd go away. We hovered there a bit longer. I was already stripped half naked in the middle of the high street so, after another five minutes I thought, "Sod it" and sluiced myself down in the fountain in full view of everyone. I told Mario I'd catch him up once I'd had a good wash and changed. Finally, he took the hint, waved a hand vaguely in the direction of the pub and disappeared. That was a relief. At least I could just get on with it pretending no-one had noticed. I stood stark naked in the middle of the town, washing myself all over in the wonderfully refreshing cold fountain water. It was absolute bliss. People were walking within a few yards of me but I think they were more embarrassed than I was now that Mario had gone. I'd felt oddly self-conscious when Mario was waiting. Maybe it was the thought that he was about to witness my tiny shrivelled up manhood! Total strangers? Well, I couldn't give a 'Castlemaine XXXX' about them. I'd just sailed 49.4 nautical miles (91.5 km) today. No-one even looked – they all ignored me except for two teenage girls who cracked up with laughter when they were further down the street!

That felt much better now. I rinsed all my gear thoroughly and applied a load of nappy cream to my affected parts, pulled on my clothes and trudged off in search of the pub that Mario and his posse had headed to. It was now pitch dark. Embarrassingly, I actually passed those two teenage girls sitting outside one of the pubs in the high street. I finally arrived at what I thought to be the correct pub but Mario and co were nowhere to be seen. I'd just missed the last call for food and couldn't believe it. The time was nine o'clock. No food! I made do with beer, crisps and peanuts, followed by crisps, beer and peanuts....and the same again once or twice more.

The pub was the olde worlde type with low beams and dark wood, beige cream nicotine-stained ceilings and chintzy, frilled, twin wall lamp shades covering fake candle-shaped bulbs. The bar was short with two high stools but it was one of several in the building. It was actually a hotel. I sat at the bar and asked if I could plug in all of my electrical devices. The bar lady looked slightly bemused as I pulled out device after device but obliged and laughed when I even supplied a four way single plug to connect everything into one socket. In the process of asking, I'd sat down on one of the bar stools vacated by what I assumed to be one of the locals. I'd clocked his Liverpudlian accent which seemed strangely out of place in this cosy hotel bar so much further south. I'd noticed him when I first arrived, being the loudest voice in the bar. When he returned to his seat with a new friend, I smiled and apologised for taking his seat, offering it back. I tried to explain I thought he'd left. He instantly pretended to take offence and in a very loud voice invited me to step outside. I instantly felt threatened and alert to the danger and momentarily considered his proposition seriously. I even instinctively thought of responding with the well-known army double hand raise to simulate surrender, throwing him off guard only to follow up with a full metal jacket attack! Fortunately, it just wasn't in my nature to respond like this and my frontal lobes soon rehydrated by this point. My fatigue was total. I smiled and took up a seat on a low stool next to the table, where my kit and gear was dumped, a safe distance away from the bar. I felt irritated by him but ignored it, returning only once more to the bar for a refill whilst waiting for my electrical kit to fully charge.

Where was I going to stay? I really didn't fancy splashing out on one of the hotels but would have loved to have curled up in Egyptian cotton sheets that second. I simply didn't have the funds for that level of luxury so, instead, I trudged back down to the beach where the boat was parked up. Mario had mentioned that people often slept underneath the steps in the summer months. I thought about this for a bit and decided that, given the circumstances, it was a good plan. The night was properly black with little or no moon showing at all. I groped my way back down the long hill yet again passing the two teenage girls on the way back. This time we all laughed out loudly but said nothing more.

At the bottom of the steep hill, I could hear the sea gently lapping on the soft sandy seabed. A slight shimmer was reflecting on the water. It was difficult to see much and I'd forgotten my head torch. After a lot of groping around in the dark, I found my tent and sleeping bag and pulled them out from underneath the upturned MOD27, exactly where I'd hidden them earlier.

There was a short flight of steps coming down off the prom so I crawled underneath the bottom step, my stomach scraping on the sand to squeeze under it. I was about to pull my tent out of its bag and pitch it in a void next to a large crop of rocks when I heard a sort of groaning...then a mumbled 'sssshhh'.... Then quiet which shortly afterwards was interrupted by the sound of zips and rhythmic breathing starting up which was definitely growing in speed.

"Oh FFS! What next?"

I was camping directly underneath two local youngsters bonking. I was properly irritated now but for some unknown reason felt I should keep quiet and let them ride it out. It went on for ages. It was beyond midnight by the time they'd done their business and disappeared back to their respective homes, probably pretending they'd just been to the pub with friends for the night. I fell asleep on the sand without the tent. In the middle of the night, it was cold and sand flies crawled on my face, ears and neck. Dusting them off as best I could, I struggled to pitch the tent in the cramped space beneath the steps with no light to see by. Dispensing with the guy ropes and finally succeeding, I zipped up the door and crashed back into my sleeping bag. My face was smarting from the rash of stinging bites. This was still only Day 5 and I'd covered only a few hundred miles. Worse was that, according to my cousin Martyn, this was still the easy bit.

I was now getting irritated by my lack of distance. People online kept telling me it wasn't a race. To me, it felt like slow progress. I wanted to just get this thing done. I'd never been very good at planning but I did begin to understand this journey was no sprint; it was going to be a long laborious and probably dangerous slog. What on earth had possessed me to take it on? At first light the following morning I'd almost had enough. The sun was working itself into another hot day and my face already felt crispy before I stuck it out of the tent. My backside was raw, my hands, elbows, neck and especially shoulders really ached and my lower back felt as stiff as a board. In fact, my whole body was aching and sore. I just wasn't in the mood for another long slog today. I checked the tides on my phone. The ebb started at 10.30 am. This was good news as it gave me a bit of time so I set off in search of a cafe and a full cooked breakfast.

Mundesley is well supplied with pubs and restaurants but could I find one cafe open? On the upside, I did bump into Paul who was out walking his dog. We got chatting and when I mentioned I was raising money for Prostate Cancer UK by sailing my Laser around the UK, he seemed captivated by my story. I was quite taken aback when he then invited me to have breakfast with him and his family at their holiday home. I could think of nothing I'd rather do. On the good 10 minute walk we chatted. It turned out Paul was ex-military police I think he said. He looked incredibly fit. I guessed he was slightly older than I was but he looked like he could push up a good 50 times if asked to. His hair was close cut, dark and he had a strong-boned face with deep penetrating eyes. He seemed to love everything about my adventure.

When we finally arrived at the holiday cottage, I'd pretty much told him about my entire journey. His two young daughters and wife or partner had obviously just woken up and were in their pyjamas watching telly. It felt slightly awkward to start with, like a bit of a rude intrusion, probably because accepting help was such an alien thing to me. At this stage of my journey, I was a relative newbie to the art of gracious acceptance. His wife/partner coped well with my arrival as if it was something she was virtually expecting and used to. She knocked up a superb cooked breakfast and supplied me with repeated coffee and toast. I ate everything in front of me; I was starving hungry. I wonder now if she thought I was a vagrant? I must have looked like one with the number of pink sand fly bites all over my face plus weird clothes, stinking hair and a knackered look. It transpired that since retiring, Paul had always hankered after the idea of undertaking an adventure like mine. Like many ex-servicemen, I think he missed the army life and hungered for the excitement, discipline and routine you get from being in the forces, difficult if impossible to replicate on civvy street.

By 9.52 am I was back by the boat, now fully fed and setting up for another day on the sea. I perched on top of the MOD27 still buried where I had left her upside down in the sand. Sending the Safety Channel my plan for the day, I simultaneously arranged my day's food rations into small plastic bags and dusted off the sand as best I could. Once rigged, I took one final look at Mundesley and said goodbye to the deserted beach, pushing off into smooth waters exactly at 10.30 am.

Emma was planning on driving up in my new Transit work van to meet me today. I wasn't sure where but I thought my best hope would be to make it to Wells-next-the-Sea (and besides, what a name). I decided to try to set up there to make my crossing of The Wash from the north Norfolk coast over to Skegness the following day. In the pub I'd found out there are a complex network of channels and sandbanks littered all the way along this coastline. My cousin, Martyn, had mentioned in conversation something about the bells at Wells-next-the-Sea ringing to warn the town every time the tide comes in. He also mentioned quicksand and sandbanks strewn everywhere. All these folklore stories weren't really helping my nerves too much.

It was another boiling hot, beautiful day from the start. When I pushed off, I was sure it was going to be stress-free. It didn't take long though before I revised my opinion. Almost as soon as I got a few miles offshore, the wind switched off! I just bobbed around and around, drifting with the tide for several hours. The forecast had suggested a decent breeze and yet I was barely making two knots. My mind kept wandering back to 'the bells at Wells-next-the-Sea'. My imagination started to unwind and before long it was running wild – I saw visions of screaming hordes fleeing the incoming tide, all trying to escape the near death experience this daily phenomenon brought. Clearly, I needed to get a grip so gave myself a talking to and then, just as I was dismissing the idea as ridiculous, I ground to a gentle halt.

In the middle of the sea, I felt my centreboard dragging on something soft – sandbanks no doubt. Pulling up the board, I looked around just feeling mildly worried. In the distance, I could see two clearly defined sets of channel marker buoys. They were enormous red and green buoys and, further into the distance, I saw a large ship which looked to me to be snaking along what seemed like a tiny corridor, miles off shore. Spooked by Martyn's words about the quicksand, I headed directly offshore towards the large marker buoys. I couldn't quite believe how far out I was – I could barely make out anything on the land now. There was little wind but just enough to make some kind of headway. Fortunately, it was a tight reach so what wind there was did at least move me at my maximum potential speed.

By now, I was cooking in the boiling hot sun. The first of my two water bottles was already drained as I sat squinting into the horizon for the next channel marker. They were miles apart, designed for large ship navigation systems, not line of sight. After several hours working my way along this narrow lane of buoys, I came across a different looking marker buoy. This one was rusty, metal-coloured and much much taller. On top was mounted a frame with a large bell cast underneath it. The bell clanged eerily in time with the tidal flow and waves. Getting more ominous the nearer and nearer I came, there was a section of water that looked different to the rest of the sea around me. Up to this point I'd started to relax and was even beginning to enjoy the sunshine and easy sailing conditions.

I checked my Navionics app which was impossible to read due to the dazzling sunshine; I just couldn't make out anything obvious. Dismissing it as nothing of importance, I just carried on. The one thing I've now learnt from my trip sailing around the UK is that there is never a buoy marked with a bell in the middle of the sea for no reason at all. Shortly I found out why it was there.

As I passed the bell, the sea started to form into steep waves and became confused, tossing me around in all directions. In spite of the little breeze, it was unnerving and spooked me. I scanned the horizon for another channel marker but the next green marker was at least a mile further out to sea and at 90 degrees to my current position. I aimed in that direction and couldn't get away quick enough from this unexpectedly turbulent patch of water. Maybe it was a wreck or a bar, bank or obstruction. To this day I've no idea but, whatever it was, I didn't like it one bit.

Back in the main channel I felt safer. Just the odd big ship to contend with but even they'd all evaporated like magic. I was alone in this vast expanse of water; nothing to see except a tiny dot on the horizon where I was following the coastline and ahead, even smaller red and green dots denoting the channel markers. It was still quite early in the afternoon but the wind had become so light I was hardly making any headway. It felt like I was fighting the tide now. Checking the Navionics, I could see there was a place that looked good for a landing at a beach called West Runton. I googled it on my phone, trying to get a satellite view of the area. It looked sandy. I just hoped I'd be able to make it inshore with the breeze dying and the lack of water. It must be low water by now as it felt like the tide had turned on me.

The sail in was still unnerving. I just couldn't shake off the thought of getting stuck in quicksand. It looked like sand bars all around me and here I was, all alone, poised on the brink, soon to be a tasty morsel for the next quicksand bar to suck me down and consume me without trace. It was East Anglia's answer to the Bermuda Triangle for Laser circumnavigators. All this time spent alone by myself was spiking my imagination into creating jittery delusions and fantasies that were starting to feel more and more real.

Reaching the shore at what I thought to be West Runton, I encountered an idyllic sandy beach that was jam-packed full of holiday makers enjoying the blazing sun and golden sands that stretched for miles in both directions. Sitting on the side of the MOD27 in the calm shallows, I reflected on how anyone could possibly believe for one second how stressful this day had been for me. It was 14.42 when I checked into the Safety Channel with my location. Looking at the chart, it looked like I'd hardly gone anywhere. In fact, I'd hardly moved along the map at all, only managing four and a half hours of sailing today and making less than 10 nautical miles (16.8 km). Tellingly, my mobile phone battery was virtually flat which shows how much I'd been checking the Navionics app for directions, positions and obstacles.

I couldn't see Emma anywhere so I climbed up the lifeguards' wooden tower which was a perfect lookout to see everything going on. The three lifeguards were all really friendly, plugged my phone in and made me a cup of tea. I tried to connect with Emma again and told her I was with the lifeguards.

It came as a surprise when she said, "So am I!"

A number of VHF calls later between the two lifeguard towers and finally we identified that one of us was definitely on the wrong beach – she was indeed at West Runton and it turned out I was on East Runton next door. At least she now knew where I was. A text message came through on my finally recharged phone, telling me an hour earlier she'd abandoned the van and looking for me and had made for the sea to cool off. She'd driven constantly from Eastbourne for about seven hours in 30 plus degrees and was sweltering. A while later, up she popped round the corner of the tower where I was waiting and all was well.

That evening, Emma and I made our way to a large and welcoming pub nearby and I tucked into fish and chips, apple crumble, cheese and biscuits all washed down with my staple diet of beer, the 'food of athletes' as PY would say.

This was the first night I'd slept in our new van. I'd bought it less than a month before leaving. Sadly, my old one, also a Transit, was dying too regularly to be trusted as a support vehicle. It was a shame as the old van had everything perfectly kitted out inside for a trip like this. I'd honed it to perfection for living in and had travelled all over Europe in it for many years on the Laser Masters' circuit. Although it looked like a normal van on the outside, the inside was like a Tardis.

Behind the smoked glass windows was a fold down three-quarter double bed, shower, toilet, fridge, microwave, gas cooker, heater and sunroof. It even had surround-sound tv. I'd often boasted that you could shave, shower, cook and wash up all whilst sitting down on the onboard convenience. In contrast, the new van had virtually nothing in it: a recycled gas cooker I'd acquired from the local dump for £15, a large gas cylinder to power it, a row of metal racking down one side that I'd hurriedly installed in order to carry a load of doors shortly before leaving and the fold up chair bed I'd removed from the old van. This was only installed as an afterthought the day before I left. Sleeping arrangements were awful. We just couldn't fit on the fold down bed as it needed the side extension piece I'd built into the old van for us both to fit. After a lot of re-organising, we both slept on the van's boarded floor on a tiny mattress, head to toe in separate sleeping bags. How romantic! I vowed to sort the van out along the way.

I was very tired, always short on preparation time and having a number of ongoing issues with the boat that urgently needed some attention to the corners, all of which were leaking. My communications kit was also struggling. Unable to track my position since Brightlingsea, due to the Spot X tracker failing, Emma had brought a replacement unit with her. This was an important priority for the Safety Channel but seemed less pressing to me at this very moment in time. The new Spot X needed to be synced with the old data on a laptop. This involved quiet time sitting and reading instructions. My brain was overloaded trying to figure out what had happened with the weather today. There should have been a sea breeze, surely it had been warm enough to generate one.

The principle of a sea breeze from my A level Geography limited understanding is as follows: hot air rises over warming land like being passed over a hot plate. The hot air cools as it travels out over the colder sea, a cold plate which draws it back towards the land where the hot air has left a void, forming a circular motion creating the sea breeze. It works on a temperature differential between the land and the sea. After today's forecast failed to generate any sea breeze, I felt puzzled and needed some expert weather advice. Inevitably it felt like there were just too many parameters to consider and store for my tiny brain. I needed to somehow reduce the number of thinking moments along this journey.

I suddenly thought of Roger Williams, a Laser Master whom I'd first met in the Hayling Island Sailing Club bar during an event we'd both attended. We'd chatted about the weather in detail then because he'd been in charge of the Bermuda weather station for many years. He was the ideal advisor to have to hand since there wasn't much he didn't understand. Well, I certainly needed some expertise now.

I found Roger's card which had been in my phone case for months for just this moment and called him from the pub. Digesting my food, I listened intently to his analysis of today's gradient wind which, he explained, was down to the wind direction. The next few days he believed would be more southerly which was a more favourable direction for a sea breeze. What a relief! I felt much happier then.

Even if he was wrong, it was reassuring for someone else to provide an opinion from a basis of some credibility rather than depending on my poor knowledge and weather apps like Windfinder, Windguru or Predict Wind, all of which seemed to offer conflicting and multiple forecasts depending on which weather model of theirs you decided to choose. They offered a forecast for all directions these days. When they first came on the market, it was much simpler and either just right or wrong but now they seemed to be hedging their bets which didn't help me much.

I was still a good distance away from crossing The Wash. Hunstanton was really my target location from where to leave from and, even from this point, it was a minimum of 12 nautical miles to the nearest point on the other side let alone reaching Skegness, the nearest main town.

It was after my chat with Roger that I communicated to PY my desire to try to include Roger onto our daily WhatsApp Safety Channel messaging system. This way it would be possible for him to communicate any weather risks likely to come my way and share this with everyone else simultaneously. So far, only PY was on the channel with Emma as a back-up for when PY couldn't be there (though as anyone who has ever witnessed Emma in a Pico at Pevensey Bay, Emma's skills are somewhat less useful except for what she can see on Google Maps!). I was quite surprised at the resistance PY put up against my idea of having Roger. He sent a message in a slightly stronger than usual acerbic tone. I sucked in through my teeth on reading it and breathed out slowly to try to contain my automatic negative response.

I'd been sailing hard for six days and the relentlessness of this journey was clearly starting to tell on everyone. I was oblivious of the strain I must have been putting on PY. I think he too was unaware of the scale of difficulties I was trying to cope with. It's always hard to see the other opinion when there's a deliberately limited communications flow. We kept it factual, minimal and clear as PY had insisted we would at the beginning following, no doubt, his knowledge of comms in the British Army where he'd served for many years. Small misunderstandings can quickly escalate into something entirely different from what is meant. PY was clearly busy with his normal work life and the WhatsApp bleeps he received during the day were probably like a small twinge of stress every time they went off. If you have no control over the beeps, it's often more stressful receiving one than being the one sending them. I felt a surge of frustration but decided to back off and agree I'd liaise with Roger directly separately. In spite of my best efforts, this gnawed away at me for some time afterwards.

The following day, shortly after waking I received a message from PY at 7.41 am asking if he should assume I'd left the beach. The tone clearly suggested he was still irritated about last night's WhatsApp message exchange too. I responded with my seven point plan at 08.32 am. I'd overslept after another really uncomfortable night with Emma in the van! I really needed a day to sort our sleeping arrangements out. Even before the day's sailing started, I felt shattered.

Pushing off the beach at 10.30 am, I intended to head for Hunstanton Sailing Club if the wind allowed. Emma set off in advance to recce the club and find out if I might be able to use their shower. The sailing started slowly but soon the wind freshened and, following the navigation buoys again, I made good progress – so good in fact that I considered having a go at crossing The Wash that day. The weather was good, wind from behind and visibility as far as you could see. The only downside was the continuous thumping of the boat into the short chop which was typical of the conditions I'd been experiencing for the past few days.

In the shallow water, the mast was smashing up and down in the hull's fibreglass tube with every single wave. I tried everything I knew to mitigate the slamming but nothing really seemed to work. It felt like a real slog bashing against the short chop all day long but the wind direction remained kind and was pushing me northwards. I just hoped the boat would keep holding together – the corners were showing serious signs of fatigue and the boat was taking on water although not enough to be a serious concern. Enough, however, to make the contents of my dry bags stored inside the hull get totally damp.

By three o'clock I'd pretty much decided I needed to get out of this relentless chop. There would never be a better forecast to cross to Skegness so I messaged the Safety Channel via WhatsApp and said I was thinking of going for a crossing. Emma was the first to respond. She'd made contact with one of the members of Hunstanton Sailing Club and he thought it should be fine to cross, given my approximate location and time. That was enough to convince me. I altered course and set out into open water, leaving the perceived safety of the coastline.

Changing the angle significantly increased my boat speed and reduced the slamming as it altered the angle I sailed over the waves. As the water got deeper, the waves increased in size and I was properly surfing across this open expanse of sea. It felt fantastic – what I call champagne sailing. Sun, surf and miles and miles of sea. What more can anyone ask for in life?

I easily made it across The Wash and passed Skegness just before 6 pm. There was good light but I was feeling seriously tired. The week of continuous sailing and lack of sleep was beginning to catch up with me. My new target was Mablethorpe, a quaint, ancient town with a long history dating back to medieval days. It had apparently been named after the abundant number of maple trees that it once had, the stumps of which can still be seen at low water. I checked the Navionics app and calculated an approximate ETA of 19.30. I was now up into the county of Lincolnshire – another one to tick off the long list. The coastline was absolutely stunning with long expanses of beautiful, wide, sandy beaches.

By now, I was scanning the coastline for a place to stop, somewhere picturesque but close to civilisation for food and water. As I studied the strange assortment of beach huts widely spaced along the top of the sand dunes, one caught my eye. It was more of a house than a hut. From the sea all I could see was a glass dome turret sitting above a silver rectangular box about three times the size of a standard beach hut. I thought that would do and felt I needed to investigate so headed to shore. Approaching from the sea, it looked just like a Martian spaceship had landed on top of a landing pad. I found out later it had only recently been built. Funny how something unusual like that was enough to bring me in.

The place I landed was actually 29 miles short of Mablethorpe on a secret beach called Sandilands. It was just dazzling with soft golden sand, little shore dump and artistically designed beach side huts dotted along the marram grass ridge. I lapped my way into the gently sloping beach with the tide now a long way out. The water was bright blue in the distance, mimicking the sky and transparent close up in the surf.

Suddenly I noticed a lone man appearing from between two huts set deep in the sandy dunes. He was making his way towards me. I'm not really a great believer in destiny, fate or religion. My upbringing as a Roman Catholic has actually put me off such things but what would be the odds of me sailing onto a remote sandy beach and the first person to see me and come up to greet me being the best Laser Master sailor in Lincolnshire? At times like this, I reconsidered divine intervention. Jim Hawkins, who I didn't know but had heard of, was famous on the Laser scene from a period in time just before I came back on the racing circuit following my 15-year Laser sailing sabbatical while I was raising my three boys.

Jim sauntered over to me and smiling said. "Is that a Laser?"

"Yes," I replied without offering any other details.
He started chatting about his days racing the Laser, mentioning a whole string of names I recognised. Of course, he asked me where I'd come from and what I was doing and while we were chatting I was also trying to contact Emma and guide her to the beach. She was racing towards Mablethorpe in the van. I was next to hopeless by now so Jim eventually took over with the directions and got her to turn around while I started unpacking the boat. Then I set about the daily ritual of

hauling the MOD27 up the beach on her single plastic rolling fender safely above the high tide mark.

When Emma arrived, Jim introduced his family and friends from his beach hut and instantly invited us to use their shower and kitchen and go and join them for a BBQ at his house nearby. We willingly parked the van for the night on his driveway and ate fantastically well that evening.

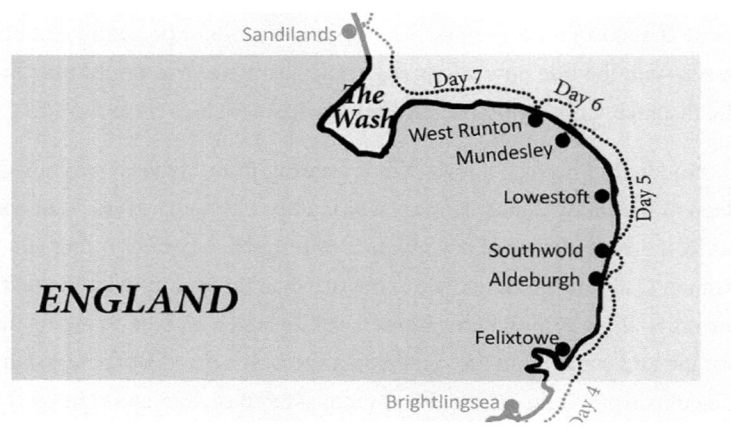

I was aware, however, of the need to plan for the next day. Usually, I'd begin almost as soon as I landed. Jim warned me about the firing range at Donna Nook which I checked out the contact details for before departing. I'd learned my lesson. He also mused about the seals that enjoyed the sanctuary of Donna Nook where no people were allowed. It was a protected area of beach just before the Humber. He didn't mention very much about the tides, except that I should watch out for the bar on the far shore and mentioned this can be navigated by an inside channel which takes you very close to shore. I may have been told more but my concentration was closing down now through fatigue and I retained little more. Jim seemed very reassuring.

"Crossing the Humber should be straight forward," he said.

Sandilands turned out to be quite an oasis – a perfect place to stop and recuperate with people it felt like we already knew. All from a fluke stop on a stretch of beach little known to anyone.

"Don't tell anyone else," Jim whispered to me before I departed the next day.

Sorry, Jim.

Chapter 11

Humber Crossing

Setting off from the glorious beach at Sandilands the following morning, all seemed good. The day started with a full, cooked English breakfast at the house before Emma, Jim, his wife and family plus now a few friends accompanied me and the boat down onto the sand. The sun was out, the winds were light blowing 11 knots from the south. I planned to catch the ebb tide heading north at 10.30 am but had to wait half an hour until the breeze filled. There was no rush. Even when I pushed off, there was plenty of time The plan for the day was a quick spin across the Humber and onwards north to Flamborough Head. I'd stop overnight at Filey Brigg which has a famous dinghy sailing club. I hadn't actually made any contact with anyone at Filey SC in advance but felt sure they'd respond if I called them up en route.

The Humber is a crossing I knew very little about so, being unaware of any dangers before now, I hadn't really bothered doing any planning for this stretch of water if I'm honest. However, the previous day's experience had shocked me into action so this morning I'd been looking up everything there was to know about the River Humber since first light. When I typed into Google, 'River Humber dangers', you can imagine my horror when the first line to appear from a contribution by the Yorkshire Post read: *"The Humber is said to be one of the most dangerous rivers in the world and with currents anything up to seven knots and sandbanks that can change almost daily – it is no place for the unwary"*.

Sailing away, looking back at Emma beaming on the beach in glorious sunshine with Jim, his family and friends waving me goodbye, nothing could have felt less dangerous. The sea was smooth, the winds were quite light and above me were beautiful blue skies with a warming sun.

"What could possibly be dangerous about this place?" I thought to myself confidently.

The firing range at Donna Nook was only a few miles along the coast. I thought I'd be organised for once and call them up long before I reached the range. The officer in charge was very friendly and had no issue with me crossing their range because no firing was scheduled for that day. I felt really chuffed with myself for my expert planning.

I cast my eyes towards the shore where I could see military-style Land Rovers moving up and down the beach. The noise of them towing heavy machinery echoed in the distance and travelled across the water in a low continuous droning sound. Squinting towards the vehicles churning back and forth, I noticed a mass of black dots spread out across miles of the beach. Initially I thought they were some sort of sea defences but soon the sea defences started moving. Shortly after this, I nearly jumped out of my skin when a seal shot out of the water just beside my boat and made a giant splashing noise with its tail before shooting off under the boat. Several more seal heads then appeared around me. First two, three, four, five. I soon lost count. There were masses of them. They looked very interested in me. Some smaller seals swam under the boat. They raced around rapidly before disappearing into the depths of the sea. Then one jumped out of the water in front of me, then another to the side and one from behind. They were playing with me. The wind had totally disappeared so I settled down, perched in the middle of the boat and watched their antics – becalmed.

Soon the smaller seals disappeared and I thought they'd got bored with me. It was lunchtime so, breaking out a tin of sardines from my life jacket pocket, I was just about to take a mouthful when a male bull seal pulled itself up nearly as tall as I was, three feet off the transom of my Laser. It let out a blood curdling snort, looked me square in the eyes for several seconds then ducked back underwater. Seconds later, I felt activity right beneath the boat. Something kept bumping into my centreboard. I was totally surrounded by seals of all sizes, many of which started leaping at me, landing a few feet away and smashing their flippers down in what I began to realise was an aggressive splashing manner. This went on for ages. I was a sitting duck, slowly drifting towards their breeding grounds. There was no wind at all to get away. I was beginning to get quite concerned that one of the seals would try to make a lunge for my food which I am sure they could smell. Stuffing the rest of the sardines down as quickly as I could, I reached forwards and untied the oars strapped to the bow. I needed some weapons. These creatures looked like they meant business. And I think it was my sardines.

The seals' antics continued for at least an hour. I felt relieved when the wind eventually filled in. They didn't get onboard the boat but, if one had, it would have filled the entire cockpit. At one point, the large bull definitely looked like he was sizing this move up, making the most unpleasant nose-blowing noises as he peered directly at me from less than a few feet away. Fortunately, there was just enough wind to allow me to sail further out to sea, escaping the seal colony. As I made it more seaward, the seals melted away into the distance. The largest seal and a posse of 10 or 15 of his mates were still pursuing but had dropped back into the distance.

I was just starting to relax a little when the sky overhead started to look very strange. It gradually turned very overcast and the humidity levels seemed to go through the roof. I was perspiring uncontrollably onboard and felt the air had been sucked away into a large black cloud that was quickly descending from the sky. For the second time today, the wind evaporated and shortly afterwards the black cloud came directly at me from over the horizon. It appeared to be touching the water and was moving at an incredible pace.

"What next?!" I cried out loud.

Shortly after my yell of despair, I was engulfed by a swarm of flying ants. They completely overwhelmed me, the boat and my sail. My face started stinging as the ants bit chunks out of my skin. Millions of them. They were big and every bite produced a tiny red sting. My face was literally covered in them. Meanwhile, the seals had returned as I drifted back to their breeding grounds with the tide sending me helplessly back across the firing range.

"You couldn't make this up!" I thought to myself.

I should have radioed the firing range marshals to request permission to reverse back across their range but other events seemed more pressing. This was a nightmare. I had so few options.

"What to do?"

No wind and the current racing against me. There was only one option, turn around and try to head back towards Sandilands using the tide to drive me. I spun around and was actually being driven closer than before into the seal colony. Covered in flies, I was attracting the seals' attention again. The sea was literally full of them. I couldn't land on the beach here, especially with the attractive stench of my sardine breath. The seal sanctuary went on for miles, 6.25 miles to be precise, although I didn't know that at the time. Pulling on the oars I managed to make some headway trying to row away from the colony out to sea. The tide was so strong though it was hopeless. I did succeed in losing the majority of the seals however and the boat bumping and splashing had stopped. More importantly, the large bull seemed to have got bored and disappeared. I hoped!

Making virtually no progress rowing like a light switch, the wind was back on again and it felt like the tide had changed direction. What was going on? I was now beating the wrong way round the UK. So, turning around again, I set off in a freshening breeze back towards the Humber and across the firing range. The ants had mostly departed in the freshening breeze and I felt confident I'd make it across the Humber now. Moving a long way off shore to avoid a repeat of the seal 'two step', I was still being monitored by them but not harassed.

The River Humber looked so benign. Not so much as a ripple yet something wasn't right. I had some breeze but looking at the banks of the river, I wasn't making any headway. I was sure the tide should have been carrying me across. Perhaps it was some kind of channel eddy. I elected to head west along the river in the direction of Grimsby.

"Perhaps the tidal flow will change if I can get further on shore and then make my crossing,"

I thought out loud to myself.

Bad idea! After half an hour of battling towards the southern bank of the Humber, the wind evaporated again. The tide was now really strong and started pushing me back towards the Donna Nook nature reserve and that less than friendly seal colony would not be very pleased to see me again.

This drifting back and forth between the edge of the Humber and the Donna Nook firing range went on most of the day. As soon as the wind came in and I got going, it changed direction and switched off. Every time I thought I was clear and could start the Humber crossing, it stopped. Fortunately, the swarm of flying insects had disappeared. Apparently, these swarms were so dense the Met Office had picked them up from satellites in the southern part of Britain a few days earlier looking like rain on their interactive maps.

Finally, at around 4 pm, the wind changed and started blowing more consistently from the south, enough to get me into the very centre of the River Humber, only to change its mind and switch off again. Now I was drifting into the middle of the main shipping channel. The visibility was hazy from the heat of the day and my concerns had changed. Ships were the new danger. Loads of large ships were steaming in and out of the main channel. I was so small there was no way I thought they'd notice me. Jumping on the radio, I made contact with the Humber coastguard to make them aware of my predicament.

They asked, "Do you require assistance?"

Hesitating, I replied "No."

But I actually wanted them to make a great big red cross on the map so no one would run me down. Obviously I didn't ask this. The coastguard suggested I call up the Humber Port Authority on Channel 14 to alert them of my position. Unlike sailing a yacht, undertaking extensive amounts of admin like this when afloat is a considerable distraction. It was only as I connected with the Port Authority on the VHF that I noticed an enormous ship steaming directly past me, silently gliding towards Grimsby or Immingham Docks. It was so close I could read all the lettering on the containers stacked on top of the enormous deck. This wasn't funny anymore.

"AAAAAAAAhhhhhhhh come on wind!" I shouted as loudly as I could.

Fortunately the transmit button wasn't depressed on my VHF otherwise I'd have blown the poor man's eardrums off at the other end. After a calming chat with the Port Authority, almost as soon as I disconnected from the VHF I picked up some fresh breeze. Someone in a much higher powered office must have been listening to my plea for wind.

I was off again and I cheered out loud.

With the fresh breeze, I was moving at good speed, hiking as hard as I could, straining to keep the boat flat on a fast reach towards Spurn Head. This headland on the other side of the Humber is hook shaped, a bit like a coat hook on the back of a period door. On the map, Spurn Head looks quite innocuous but the charts suggest this is an area of turbulent water. Unfortunately, reading the Navionics charts on my mobile app didn't show this level of detail so I sailed directly into a set of horrendous vertical standing waves and found myself ripping along in a current of unknown speed. I made a fast about turn, back the way I'd come. Once clear of the immediate danger and now breathing heavily, feeling my heart leaping out of the insides of my wetsuit, I tried taking some slow deep breaths and to remember what Jim had told me before departing from Sandilands. This felt like a lifetime ago.

"There's an inner channel at Spurn Head you can take," Jim had said.

I scanned the shoreline and yet again today had to sail the wrong way to escape. I was now travelling west, inland towards Kingston-upon-Hull, instead of east to Skegness. I transited around the sandbanks kicking up the dangerous waves I'd narrowly survived and followed along the Humber's banks until the water looked safe enough to head in shore. Skirting around the obvious overfalls, I safely made it to the north side of the Humber.

"Thank you, God!!" I exclaimed out loud.

Now all that was required was to hug the shore and start working east back out to sea. Jim's advice was good and I safely made it round Spurn Head using the narrow channel he'd told me about, away from the treacherous banks where the sea looked like it would eat anything floating on top. It was nearly six o'clock in the evening by the time I finally passed Spurn Head. I'd been messing about all day to make what I believed this morning was just a tiny crossing. Looking back on it, this was one of the most dangerous days of my journey. Before setting out, I hadn't been aware of any of the risks. I had no idea the Humber has the second largest tidal range in the UK at 7.2 metres. I also wasn't aware that the Humber is the dividing line between the Midlands and the north of England. More crucially, the tidal flows from the Atlantic start to reverse direction after the Humber so the ebb tide flows north and the flood tide south. Or is it the other way around? Answers on a postcard please.

You'd have thought making landfall after the day's drama would be plain sailing from here. I sent a text message to Emma confirming I'd made it across. She'd been hedging her bets, staying on the south side of the River Humber in case I didn't make it. Now she had a pretty long drive to cross the Humber herself and try to catch me up. I carried on up the coastline for another hour until I finally found what looked like a soft beach under a low cliff. I'd landed at Tunstall, directly below a campsite called Sand-Le-Mere. I wasn't sure what state the tide was at now but it looked like it was coming in. After crossing the Humber, it seemed to have changed dramatically on this side. I suddenly remembered I hadn't communicated anything to the Safety Channel and had missed a rendezvous at 16.00 hours. In all the chaos I'd forgotten. I was over three hours late. Leaving the boat abandoned floating in a small lagoon on the stony beach, I climbed the near vertical 12-foot cliff to get a better signal and sent a Safety Channel confirming my position.

"Landed at Tunstall 19.00. What a day! Again!"

I'd managed to sail 18.3 nautical miles today at an average speed of 3 knots. I could have walked it quicker and saved myself a whole artic lorry load of stress.

The near vertical red sandstone cliffs were very tricky to climb and even harder to descend. Roughly carved out footsteps made by other climbers were the only aid. They didn't seem to be made very well, certainly not National Trust quality. At the bottom of the cliff there was rubbish left strewn around the beach. I even noticed a used nappy at the base of the steps. What sort of people do that?

Randomly scattered across the beach was an assortment of rocks, some tall as a house and some small. They formed a barricade in front of the cliffs, I assumed to slow down coastal erosion which is a very big problem on this coastline. I looked for the high tide mark but there wasn't anything obvious. After a frantic drive, Emma had now found me and was chatting away to two local fishermen to ascertain my whereabouts while I'd been off climbing the cliff. I mentioned to Emma I wasn't sure about this beach as it looked like it might totally flood at high water. I dragged the boat as high as I could, finding a route to the cliff base navigating across a group of the smaller rocks. I used the rock pools to float the MOD27 higher up the beach. These small pools were rapidly beginning to fill up with water as the tide came in. After I'd spent half an hour heaving the MOD27 into a circle of very large rocks where I thought she'd be safely above the high tide line, two fishermen approached. One by the name of Brad came and told me he thought the beach would probably flood tonight as it was spring tides.

"You can't leave that boat here overnight," Brad said in a thick north east accent. "The tide will come up to the first step on that cliff tonight," he carried on, pointing in the direction I'd just climbed up.

By now the wind had dropped to nothing. Even if I could be bothered to relaunch and paddle further along the coastline there was nowhere for miles to safely store the boat overnight. After a few minutes of head scratching and scanning around the beach, I made a decision. We were going to need to find some help. I'd have to carry her up that cliff.

It took an hour to round up enough helpers, un-rig and empty out all my gear from inside. By this time, it was nearly dark. Brad and his fishing friend joined us and Emma found a few more locals including Mark, the Sand-Le-Mere campsite maintenance man. With a number of his friends, we carried the MOD27 15 feet above sea level, up a near vertical crumbling cliff face. Parked on the grass at the top, it made for a great photo.

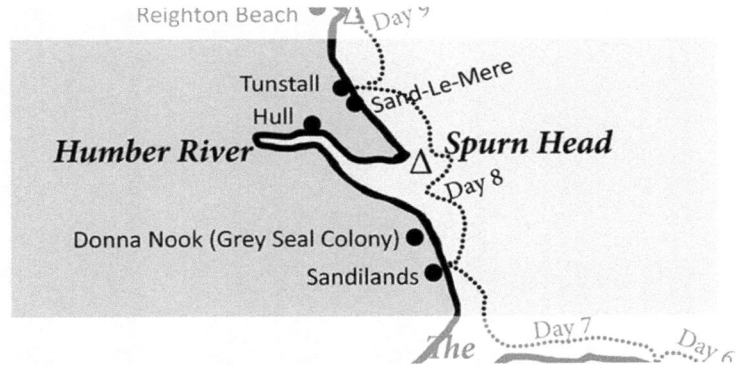

That night, Mark sorted us out a free space for the van on their site and the use of all Sand-Le-Mere's facilities. Mark was terrific, a larger-than-life character in all senses of the word, who came to my rescue. A totally 'up' person who had an endearing, soft, local accent and a similarly melancholic attitude to the world. His boss was slightly suspicious about us and asked Mark to get us to provide evidence of my story. Mark said that even if his boss didn't believe I was sailing around the UK for Prostate Cancer, he did, and would pay for our camping spot out of his own money. Mark's boss came on board once she'd seen the Facebook page. Sand-Le-Mere was a great ending to a truly traumatic day.

Chapter 12

The Slow Route North

Tunstall turned out to be a friendly place to stop. I seemed to be making a habit of finding nice people. If you read the national newspapers, or worse spend your life consuming tweets or other social media, you could be forgiven for believing most people in Britain were either mass murderers, paedophiles, villains or some other sort of miscreant. My experience so far was quite the contrary. Nearly everywhere I was stopping the people were helpful, interested and friendly. In many cases, like Mark at Tunstall, they made incredibly kind gestures of support which left me feeling uncharacteristically emotional. I was finding the real Britain on this journey into the unknown.

The daily chore of packing my gear into the minute hatch on the MOD27 every morning, then launching into a new adventure of unknown daily hazards, negotiating whatever weather was laid down in front of me, coupled with the basic needs was like a cleansing process. I was transitioning away from normal life into this nomadic reality where the only things that mattered now were food, drink, shelter and warmth. As with any process of purging, it was having some side effects whilst the toxins were being stripped away from my body. Twenty first century contaminants like money, desire, greed and ambition were just less relevant when battling along through the North Sea in my Laser. The focus of my mind became so much smaller than normal. All I had to do was survive. Chip away at each mile, look for every minute to count and consume the miles until I reached home again. Whenever that would be. This was the most common question people asked me.

"How long is it going to take to circumnavigate the UK?"

At this rate, probably until Christmas. The reality of the situation was that I really didn't have a clue.

The departure from Tunstall was the same mission as last night in reverse. This time, the MOD27 had to be lowered down the crumbling red stone cliff. It was too big a drop to attempt on my own so a new posse of helpers was required. As if by magic, four unsuspecting men sauntered towards me along the grassy cliff top. They looked like they were on their way to chop down a tree or something similarly agricultural. They were all covered in dirt and had matching green rugby style shirts on. It took very little persuasion to recruit their help and I assembled them into a row holding the mainsheet attached to the bow cleat at the front of the hull. They looked a bit like a tug of war team getting ready to heave. I hurriedly clambered down the same carved out footholds I'd climbed last night and directed the men to lower away, positioning myself directly below the boat so I could catch her when she came into reach. Standing on the beach, I could hear the four men chuckling and chatting to each other cracking jokes and puffing on cigarettes as they lowered the MOD27 vertically down the cliff. She came down to my outstretched arms, slowly arriving rear end first. I guided her transom onto the beach whilst the four men played out the bow line steadying her gently into position. When she was firmly wedged on the stones standing upright as if on parade, I took over and lowered her until she lay flat on her bottom. Once she was successfully down, I checked the plastic bow cleat that had the rope tied to it and found it was hanging on by the end thread of one screw. When I pulled, it came away in my hand. That was lucky! Had it failed coming down the cliff, the boat would have dropped directly on top of my head.

The strain on the MOD27 was beginning to show. She had taken a lot of punishment. Aside from the dislodged bowline cleat and cracks in all three corners of the hull, the new 8 inch RWO plastic hatch cover was the most worrying. This was showing a hairline crack where I'd accidentally sat on it falling off a wave a few days ago. I used this hatch twice daily and knew when I installed it this was a potential point of serious weakness. If the hatch failed and I capsized, the hull would fill with water really quickly and most probably sink. Although I'd installed additional airbags inside for extra buoyancy, I'd never tested the hull's buoyancy full of water. I parked this idea in the lock up box of ideas not to worry about and set about today's mission.

The plan today was to get to Whitby. I'd looked at the tides and was confused. It all seemed to be in very different directions to those I'd expected. Everything was back to front. I've subsequently discovered I'd moved into the Atlantic tidal influence on the east coast. This divides somewhere near Middlesbrough. It looked like to gain the maximum assistance from the tide, I'd be following the ebb tidal flow from now until Scotland. According to my app, this meant departing Tunstall at 10.30 am. A leisurely start time. Pushing off, the plan I'd set to make it to Whitby was an ambitious distance of 91 km especially given the wind forecast was only 11 mph. The sun was out though and the sky looked beautiful with a few wispy clouds dotted around. I'd spotted a very tall headland when putting together my Safety Channel briefing just before launching. It was called Flamborough Head. I thought it worthy of a cautious mention in the notes as a potential hazard but gave it little consideration really and set off on my way.

Chapter 13

Climbing Out of a Big Hole

The Yorkshire coastline was providing me with plenty of testing moments but nothing life threatening. My mind was the biggest battle. An excessive imagination left unchecked was starting to run away with me. I was dreaming at night about a swarm of man-eating flies and packs of seals about to drag me off my boat for a tin of sardines. As if! However, my mental health had already become quite shaky at times even before the events of today.

Approaching Flamborough Head was different to anything I'd previously experienced so far. I approached this giant headland on a sunny day in a pleasant 10 knots of breeze. Halfway round the headland, a mile or two offshore, the wind disappeared. The sea state was quite smooth but there were very large and long, rolling waves pressing me in towards the headland. I was quite relaxed at first as I was a reasonably safe distance offshore. However, half an hour of surfing along in no wind left me being rolled worryingly close to the headland. Looking up from the sea, the cliff was enormous, hanging over the top of me as if suspended from the clouds. I could feel the anxiety levels rising deep down in the pit of my stomach. There was so little wind. I flapped the sail back and forth for an hour trying to gain speed and propel myself away from the murderous breaking waves smashing into the rocky cliff face. I found myself a few hundred feet off and could see every rock, nook and cranny. I was mesmerised by its brutalness. It was a miracle it was still standing so defiantly against the relentless crashing of waves. There was no getting away from it. The wind had completely evaporated. I was surfing helplessly into the cliffs. Everything was happening in slow motion, there was no rush, the sea was going to consume me in its own time.

The oars. Quick use the oars. Why hadn't I thought of that before?

I scrambled across the foredeck trying to untie the oars. These had been lashed down all the way from Eastbourne, fixed to the bow with Velcro straps and rope threaded through tiny holes I'd drilled into the side gunnels. They'd been a constant irritation, often nearly falling overboard when it got rough. They were so well secured I nearly fell overboard trying to undo them. The sea was throwing me some really big rollers, like a slalom course of waves. After several near capsizes, the Velcro strap at the bow came free. I threaded the oars through the metal rollocks I had clanking around in the bottom of the boat which I'd inserted into the special slots I'd built into the MOD27's deck. Pulling on the oars I found, as I had on my test run at Pevensey Bay Sailing Club, that they were useless. Every time I pulled them through the water, their ends banged into my knees. I couldn't get any leverage or force. Fairly quickly abandoning one of the oars I tried paddling with a single oar. The problem with this was, I couldn't steer and paddle at the same time so all I succeeded in doing was going round in circles. Looking up at the cliff, I started to panic.

I'm going to be surfed into this cliff face. The reality of my predicament had now sunk in.

Taking several deep breaths, I then swore my head off at the top of my voice, shouting as loudly as I could at the cliffs and wind. This didn't work either. Getting a grip of myself, I tried to consider my options. One of these was climbing the cliff. I was thinking that maybe I could get a handhold to jump onto the cliff face. Was I seriously thinking I was going to abandon the boat and try to climb up this massive wall? Clearly this was totally unrealistic, not to mention insane. Firstly, the only climbing I'd ever done was a bit of bouldering at an indoor climbing centre. Secondly, I had no climbing gear and, even if I had, I wouldn't know how to use it. Thirdly, how on earth was I going to leap from the boat without falling into the smashing waves, washing 20 feet up the cliff face? It's amazing what your brain does when you're stuck in a situation like this. I dismissed climbing and re-focused on paddling and wafting the sail back and forth. I did this for an hour, maybe more. My technique improved over time and I was managing to just about maintain my position far enough off the cliff to avoid the breaking waves. However, I was so close to disaster all the time and getting tired. I was boiling hot as well so, if something didn't change soon, I might sweat to death inside my wetsuit. I was hot before I started all this frantic activity.

Anyway, I'm very glad to report there is a God because, just when I thought I was beginning to lose the battle, from out of nowhere the wind came in. At first it was quite light and teased me into thinking it was coming before disappearing again but then it became stronger and kept on building and building. I sailed around the rest of the headland not much more than 30 feet from the breaking waves in an increasing wind as if nothing could be simpler. Very shortly after rounding, I found myself surfing along almost out of control on a screaming reach being covered with wash and spray, now unable to see anything due to the water cascading into my face. I was looking for a soft beach to land as soon as I was clear. The wind was now gusting 30 knots or more. When the gusts hit, the whole boat lifted out of the water onto a screaming plane, throwing spray and surf everywhere.

I battled on for another hour but it was getting too much. Heading inland, I eventually made landfall on a wide open expanse of sand stretching miles. I was at a place called Reighton Sands only a few miles short of Filey Sailing Club. I skidded to a halt on the soft golden sands and promptly capsized the boat, lying the sail flat to stop it flogging itself to death in the near gale force wind.

I was safe. Wow! What a day! No wind. Then too much wind. Wind from in front then from behind. Massive rolling swells, headlands, tidal rips and now a mile of soft golden flat sand to drag my boat over to reach the safety of the high-water mark. I sat on the sand lapping up the blazing sunshine. Lying flat on the beach reduced the wind chill and warmed me inside. Now all the drama had subsided, I noticed how extremely itchy and uncomfortable my wetsuit felt. I had an attack of the wetsuit itches and anyone who has experienced this will know it's a bit like falling into a hedge full of stinging nettles.

Whilst I was writhing around in the shallows trying to relieve my itching, a few holidaymakers appeared, attracted by my dramatic landing. I just wanted to strip off all my clothes but there were children around. Squirting the remains of my fresh water down the front of my suit helped and when a young lad with his dad came over to investigate what I was up to, my itches had nearly gone away. The boy was fascinated with the boat. He wanted his dad to get one. I chatted to another father with his teenage daughter. She said she'd never been outside of Scarborough. When I told her I was sailing around Britain she didn't realise the United Kingdom was an island surrounded by sea.

I waited for over an hour sitting out the breeze. There was little sign of the wind abating in spite of my weather forecast predicting it would. Over an hour passed before Emma arrived. I sent her a text message with my approximate position. She was carrying a cold cup of coffee for me. I was several miles from the nearest car park, somewhere away in the distance at the top of the sandy cliffs. She pointed to it but I couldn't see it.

After surveying the beach, it was obvious to me the boat needed to be dragged up for miles to reach the high tide line. The soft golden sand stretched out before me was only a shallow incline. It was a hopeless surface for the fender trolley system. It would take me at least another hour to roll the boat up to the high tide line. Added to this the sea was still dropping so there was still an hour or more to wait before low water. This would mean waiting seven hours for high water until I could use the tide to float the boat up the beach on its own.

After a bit of deliberation, I decided the best option was to reef the sail and make my way across the bay to Filey Sailing Club two miles away. I planned to stay close to the shore so if the wind went berserk again, I could get in quickly. The worst that would happen was I'd be blown onto the beach so I reefed the rig by rolling the sail around the mast and switching the top batten from its horizontal position to the customised vertical pocket using the facility that Gary Smith, the sailmaker in Eastbourne, had added.

I fixed all the sail control lines back on the reefed sail but discovered the outhaul (the rope used to pull the sail out to the end of the boom) was now too short to be adjustable. This is because by rolling the sail around the mast it required the outhaul rope to be one metre longer. I bodged it together (an invaluable sailing skill) and simply tied the outhaul so it was fixed in one position. The downside of this was it could not now be adjusted. I wasn't too bothered though as I'd only need to adjust the outhaul if the wind dropped and it wasn't showing any signs of abating soon, I convinced myself. It was tied tightly to make the sail the least powerful that I could. Finally I was ready to relaunch.

Agreeing with Emma to rendezvous at Filey Sailing Club, I set off. All was fine at first, the boat felt very controllable but a bit slow. Almost as soon as I launched, the wind strength moderated and shortly after started dropping quite quickly. By the time I was halfway across the bay, the wind switched off again. Stuck a mile offshore, I had just enough momentum to head inshore but was irritated that the outhaul and reef couldn't be shaken out at sea. I now needed all the sail power I could get. It was a slow process getting in close to Filey beach but finally I could see a lifeguards' rib on the beach in front of a long concrete ramp. This ran downhill adjacent to the sea wall defences that marked the start of the town's beach. A large number of people were still in the water even though it was now evening. As I approached, I could see they had surfboards and were messing about quite close to the shore. The wind had completely died and I was being washed in on the waves and tide, unable to control the MOD27 much with my tiny sail surfing down the breakers. The closer to shore I came, the more concerned I became.

"This is a surf beach. Oh shit!" I shouted out loud.

Two things a Laser sailor on a circumnavigation doesn't want to see are surfboards and surfers. By now, the breakers were obvious. Incredibly powerful but very short steep waves, the worst sort for a boat like mine. Too short to catch properly and the type that just picks you up and tips you head first into the next wave, usually resulting in barrel rolling the Laser. Not good as the pointy bit sticking up above the deck with the sail on it usually snaps off during the roll. I'd learned this through personal experience during my sailing years.

For the second time in a day, I wrestled one of the oars free from the tie down and, dipping the paddle in the water and pulling like mad, I tried to improvise my steering. I found that by dragging one leg overboard I could slow the boat down a bit. It must have looked ridiculous from the shore. This idiot half swimming and surfing, schizophrenically wobbling through a dramatic shore dump in an overgrown surfboard with a mast! I didn't much care what it looked like, right now I urgently had to generate some speed. Speed was my friend, this would be the only way I could surf in with any control. I felt a sudden lurch forwards and paddled like mad. The bow of the boat was burying itself into the wave in front. I moved my weight back along the boat trying to keep the front end of the MOD27 from digging in. I was now in the middle of the most horrendous shore break with steep short waves pitching me up and down, surfing me onto Muston Sands.

Some 400 yards off this point is a collection of stones known as Mile Haven Stones. I can only assume it was these stones that were creating the breaking waves and ferocious surf. I paddled furiously and managed to keep the boat pointing forwards towards the shore, riding on the front of a particularly long wave. I'd made it through the worst and kept paddling right into the beach, crashing into the sand. The abrupt stop tipped me out onto my back as the boat continued on another 15 feet up the beach. It was quite a scramble to catch up and prevent her from being sucked back out to sea and smashed to bits in the following set of waves.

Meanwhile, Emma who had been watching this present drama unfold, had the foresight to ignore all the local signs and drove directly down the lifeguards' ramp used to launch and recover their ribs on the beach. She'd seen me floundering around for the past half hour. I was shattered. The beach was still busy with people even though it was nearly seven o'clock in the evening. There were so many surfers it was difficult to drive the van along the sand as it honked and revved to encourage the astonished onlookers to get out of the way.

Having recovered the MOD27 from any further damage, I waded along the shallows dragging her behind me using the mainsheet which I'd lashed around the mast towards. I sloshed my way towards Filey Brigg where the sailing club was. It was the only place I could see that wouldn't be covered by the high tide once it came in. After 20 minutes of wading I got fed up and waved to Emma. She reversed the van towards me. I fixed the mainsheet to the van's tow bar and climbed into the front seat.

"Let's go."

Emma fired up the van and dragged the poor old MOD27 across the sand. The aluminium plate stuck onto the bottom took a lot of the punishment but nevertheless I could feel the gelcoat scraping off as we bumped across the sand and stones. It was almost half a mile to the safety of the sailing club's ramp. Once close enough, a few helpful locals ambling along came to help me lift the boat up the sailing club's concrete ramp where she was abandoned in a small hollow, just high enough to avoid the next high tide.

Somehow I'd made it through another day but it still wasn't over. I still had to de-rig and hide my sailing gear and unload everything. Scanning around the club's dinghy park there was no sign of life. It was a Thursday so no club sailing. I didn't bother phoning anyone. I just wanted to wash, eat and sleep. After unrigging, we eventually hid all of the gear under the cover of one of the sailing club's training boats, parked directly under a floodlight outside the clubhouse. It involved removing and refitting the top cover and making good again in the morning but at least it was well hidden from curious eyes and hands.

I changed in the van and my shower that evening was squirting myself with a 2 litre fresh water bottle. By the time we made it into town, we were the last customers into the restaurant, an Italian pizza and pasta place. We ate well that night. I've no recollection of what it was but it all went down. Emma parked the van on top of the promenade on a relatively flat spot where we camped for the night. Opposite was a smart Victorian three storey semi-detached house that overlooked the sea. Next to our parking space was a beautifully manicured, lush green lawn leading down to the promenade wall. The grass was slightly lusher by morning.

Chapter 14

Beat the North East

It felt like I was mostly beating up through the top of England, working my way slowly up the north east coast into northerly winds. This journey felt like it was never going to end. It seemed the winds knew I was coming, switching on enough to get me launched only to suddenly turn off, often leaving me marooned several miles offshore; far enough away from the shoreline so I could see it but uncomfortably distanced so as to make it deeply unnerving every time it died.

I found warm and cold patches of weather as I followed a weather front along most of this section of the route. The weather front was running parallel to the north east coast. When it went cold, the wind moved north in front and lighter. If there was a warm spot, it went southerly, behind me and stronger. The problem was, the coastline wasn't straight. Had it been, I could probably have stayed in the warm sector. But life isn't like that. Straight lines would be so simple.

Headlands were particularly tricky. Throughout my entire north easterly journey I could never predict what was coming next. Often

I'd approach a headland that had a large cloud mass hanging over the top of the cliff, extending out onto the sea. I always dreaded these situations. I found out from two sailors further up the coastline from Beadnell Bay Sailing Club that this cloud mass was locally referred to as a 'haar'. In meteorology, a haar or sea fret is a cold sea fog and it occurs most often on the east coast of England or Scotland between April and September. The haar forms when warm air passes over the cold North Sea and is also known as a har, hare, harl, harr and hoar. Whatever you wanted to call it, I found it super stressful. What to do? Sail offshore further and risk getting marooned for the entire day, bobbing about in zero visibility and the chance of shipping mowing me down? Or stay tight to the cliff line where land effects, tidal currents and rocks became another trigger for a full load of anxiety?

Along this rugged coastline I often went days without seeing any shipping. I expected to see other yachts or sailing boats but don't recall seeing any. The odd fishing boat passed by, usually picking up or laying pots, a highlight of my day until I started running into the long trailing mooring lines of the pots.

Apparently, if you're trying to catch lobsters the best places to lay pots are rocky areas on contour lines. Sand and mud flats are ideal for catching prawns and in between both of these geologies is best if you're looking for crabs. These three bases were being well covered by Britain's fishermen, rendering the whole coastline of the north east and much of the rest of the UK a total hazard for small keel boats and Lasers. After hitting a few of the mooring lines (which tied a mass of pots together), I started to become very wary of the poorly made black or faded yellow and pink flags sitting on top of tiny buoys marking the position of pots below. Often 30 pots were roped together spreading out under the sea and stretching for miles. To be honest, it wasn't too bad getting caught up in these obstacles in a Laser. The remedy was to simply pull up the rudder and centreboard which I found quickly untangled me. However, it was the shock every time I hit one of these obstacles that did the damage. I was never quite sure if something else had gone wrong; another thing to add to the list of things unsettling me, along this slow, treacherous and stressful part of the journey. The continuous changes in wind speed and direction were wearing me down. Unable to relax and enjoy the scenery, I found myself in a state of high tension most of the day navigating this stretch of water. It wasn't until I reached Whitby that my mood improved.

I was in a phase where the ebb tide was getting later every day. As there was such an advantage moving with the tide, I found myself with a few spare hours each morning to explore where I'd landed the previous night. The downside to late ebb tides though is it meant I wasn't arriving at my destination until dusk. Late stops usually resulted in poor accommodation options and nowhere open to find food. Approaching Whitby at nearly 6 pm, I'd had enough for one day. I'd hit every obstacle I could imagine that day. Added to this, the haar had kept me becalmed for hours out to sea and, to cap it all, I was now sitting in a torrential hailstorm with thunder and lightning, trying to find a phone number for Whitby Yacht Club on my mobile phone.

Locating a number on Google, I called it.

"Hello Whitby Yacht Club," said a beautifully smooth and measured voice.

"Hello! Hello! Is that the Yacht Club?" I shouted down the phone raising my voice above the clap of thunder erupting a few hundred metres above my head.

"I'm sorry darling, I can't hear you. It sounds ever so noisy where you are," replied my sweet angel on the end of the phone.

"Hello. If you can hear me, can you just reply yes or no please," I said in the clearest and most restrained voice I could muster.

"I'm at the harbour entrance," I carried on not waiting for a reply, "Can I land a Laser sailing dinghy in the harbour?"

"Sorry darling I've no idea, I'm just the stewardess here. What's a Laser sailing dinghy?" she politely asked.

I asked a few more questions but received a similar set of answers. This lovely, sweet lady was trying to help but clearly didn't have any nautical skills. She sounded slightly exasperated with me for pressing her for answers she didn't have but laughed at the hopelessness of our conversation. She wished me good luck and said I was welcome to use the Yacht Club's showers if I could find somewhere to land. The heavens erupted at this point and all I could hear was the clattering of marble sized hailstones banging down onto my decks. I hung up.

The waves were breaking into and over the towering harbour piers which guarded the very narrow looking entrance. I was a safe distance away from them, sitting on the sea trying to decide whether to go in or carry on. The concern I had was getting caught in the swell at the harbour mouth and losing all wind from the huge walls surrounding the entrance, leaving me at the mercy of the sea.

According to local history records, people used to say that 'the only road to Whitby is the sea' because crossing the North Yorkshire moors was very difficult until the first turnpike road was built in 1764. Thus, while many towns centre on a market square, Whitby's heart is its harbour. The bottle-shaped estuary of the River Esk is the only natural harbour along the 100 miles (160 km) of treacherous coastline between the rivers Tees and Humber.

At this precise moment in history, I was less interested in Whitby's rise to prominence as a trading port in the 1300s and more about how the 13-foot boat I was being deluged in could get ashore somewhere safely. Just my luck, I'd found the only non-sailor at Whitby Yacht Club to talk to. I'm not entirely sure my angel had really grasped how small and delicate my vessel was nor how massively exposed I was feeling with thunder and lightning bolts shooting all around me.

I decided to give up on the idea of going into the harbour. On the plus side, I'd at least managed to get agreement from this very patient and rather lovely lady on reception to use the club's showers. If I could get there. Looking beyond the harbour walls, there was a lifeguard's flag flying limply in the downpour, sitting on what looked like a sandy yellow beach. There looked like a big shore dump on this beach and I hesitated about landing here. However, the storm was getting so scary I decided to surf in and beach it. To hell with the consequences of getting off the beach in the morning, the fear of being electrocuted at sea convinced me this was a better alternative.

Usually, lifeguards are stationed on a beach for a reason. It turned out this beach was no exception. Whitby is one of the more popular surf beaches of the north east. Lining up for the shore, all I could see was rain cascading down on the white surf. This usually has the effect of flattening the waves but they still looked pretty rough to me. Setting up for maximum speed, I aimed directly for the softest looking area on the beach and was picked up by a powerful roller 50 yards off shore. The nose of the MOD27 was precariously pointing downwards in danger of running into the wave in front. I shifted my weight so I was hanging out the back of the boat to counter the nose dive and drove in on this single wave, crashing down on the foreshore to be unceremoniously ejected as I landed. I was quickly surrounded by three youngsters wearing lifeguard's shorts and waterproof jackets, smiling and laughing at me as they each grabbed a corner of the MOD27 and carried her up the beach. I was abandoned to scrape myself out of the surf and stagger gratefully after them. They carried the boat all the way up to the 10-foot high yorkstone sea defence wall which ran around the whole promenade. The rain was pelting down but the young lifeguards were still laughing and joking. We chatted as they helped me roll up the sail and remove all the gear. The tide line was high, up close to the wall but they assured me it would be safe here tonight. They invited me to shelter from the storm in their building, producing a cup of tea as soon as I went through the door. Shortly after, Emma made it down onto the promenade with the van and within an hour we were packed up and traipsing through Whitby Yacht Club to locate the showers.

Whitby Yacht Club sat in a narrow side street close to the harbour. It was a wonderfully welcoming place. It was clearly a very social club, comfortably set out for dining and drinking. The showers, when we located them, were cluttered with items being stored or perhaps abandoned. The showers didn't look regularly used and it took a while before anyone even knew how to turn them on! That evening there was a quiz night planned, most of the members attending looked like they were retired yachties. Emma and I ate sitting at the bar and smiling at people but swerved the quiz. I'd had enough challenges for one day and preferred to attempt to not fall asleep in my dinner at the bar.

I was stuffed and ready for bed. Just as we were thinking of leaving to make camp in the van, Angela Walton, one of the senior club members, started chatting and invited us over to join them on their table. Eric, Angela's husband, had sailed extensively along this north eastern stretch of coastline in his yacht. Eric turned out to be an invaluable font of knowledge and I picked away at his brain until at 11 pm, Angela asked,

"Where are you staying tonight?"

Emma's forlorn facial expression clearly gave a clue that suggested wherever it was, it wasn't very desirable. Angela's female intuition rapidly recognised this look and kindly offered us a bed for the night at their house which we both jumped at instantly.

Angela and Eric lived in one part of a large Georgian manor house. Several brandies later and a headful of the north east coastline, protrusions, currents and dangers to watch out for, too many to digest at half past midnight, we slumped into our beds.

The next morning, I didn't need to leave until the afternoon to catch the ebb tide at 1.30 pm. To my delight, our hosts provided us with a superb full English breakfast. This was cooked and served up by Eric, suitably attired in his MasterChef apron, accompanied by Angela recounting riveting stories of their own sailing escapades. We cemented a new friendship over egg and bacon that continued all the way around the UK with Angela and Eric being two of my most loyal supporters.

Angela said to me in the morning, "I get it!"

After explaining I was raising money for Prostate Cancer UK, she helped me to raise thousands of pounds through her online enthusiasm and Facebook sharing.

The tricky winds continued along this north east coastline. When I arrived at the beach the wind was gusting over 20 knots. Rigging up on the beach I could barely take my eyes off the surf piling in. How was I going to get through that? The waves were steep but short. The challenge would be finding a break in the wave sets and somehow get enough speed to break through the crests of the breakers before they washed me back onshore. One bad wave could easily roll me and most likely snap my mast or worse. The young lifeguards were assembled around the MOD27 and keen to help escort me off the beach. They'd already launched their jet ski which was patrolling up and down leaping through the surf as if to say, see it's easy, just do it like this. I looked on with growing trepidation. Three of the lifeguards helped steady the boat and we waited patiently searching for a flat spot between waves. There was nothing even close to a lull for minutes. The lifeguards were only dressed in shorts and raincoats. I could sense they were getting cold and keen to get rid of me. Standing up to my chest in water I spotted an opportunity and shouted "go". Everyone pushed me off as I rolled into the cockpit and knelt on the rear of the boat, keeping the bow high so as to ride over the top of the incoming waves. The sail filled instantly and the rudder was working, thanks to one of the lads pushing it down as I took off. I made it through the first two waves quite comfortably then, 100 metres further out, I saw the jet ski take off, leaping over a particularly large set of waves which were still building and heading directly for me. I needed speed and very urgently. There was no time to adjust my position in the boat so kneeling with my feet hanging over the back of the transom, I rode up the face of the first wave and just made it over the top although my speed had dropped significantly. There was no riding over this next wave and it broke over the top of me, swamping the cockpit and almost washed me off the back. I clung onto the mainsheet and just kept sailing, lying on my stomach steering with my knee wrapped over the tiller. I made it through a third smaller wave and carried on another 50 metres, still spreadeagled face down on top of the MOD27. I'd done it! I was through the surf. Looking back to shore all I could see was a mass of foaming white water but where I was sitting, the waves were rolling gently beneath me. The jet ski came racing over and we waved at each other, both laughing.

Once on my way, the wind soon started playing tricks again, dying off badly just as I sailed past Staithes where Captain Cook grew up before he set off on HMS Endeavour to discover New Zealand and Australia in 1761. Cook made landfall near Point Hicks and then proceeded to Botany Bay. The weather where I was felt a far cry from the weather in Australia.

My wetsuit and clothing were inadequate. They were too thin and I was shivering for much of the day. The further north I headed, the colder it was getting. I was regretting leaving my oilskin trousers with Richard the fisherman at Hythe on my first day to save weight. Heading towards Middlesbrough and the magnificent River Tees, my legs were shaking permanently as I dragged my way, shivering along this steely landscape. The wind was turning on and off like a light switch, marooning me miles offshore, stuck in the haar for hours at a time. When I came in close to shore looking for more breeze, I found myself looking up at dark rocky cliffs with jagged rocks and no friendly stopping points. This was truly a rugged, treacherous coastline. Baron and brutal; tempting me in to try landing whenever the wind evaporated, always knowing I'd be consumed if I gave into this temptation.

I struggled on for six hours following the ebb tide. I'd only covered a mere 20 km and by the time I eventually landed, my nerves were frayed. I'd been marooned for three hours just outside a small inlet called Skinningrove, sandwiched between the high-rise cliffs. The rocks projected a long way out to sea and were drying underneath me. I could see how razor sharp they were as I sank towards them, sitting helplessly above as the tide slipped away. A faint puff of breeze rescued me, blowing just enough for me to limp my way towards the safety of land. I narrowly missed the partially submerged concrete breakwater dividing the beach in two at Skinningrove on the way in.

Looking up at the overhanging cliffs I knew immediately this was a far from ideal landing spot. I had no choice. It was either here or get swept back from where I'd come with the new flood tide. With no wind, my options were nil.

The beach was deserted. A few hundred yards inland I could see a short row of tired, small terraced houses. In front of the houses was an area of rough ground. Strewn all around lay a mishmash of rotting old fishing boats, rusting tractors and abandoned cars. It was deadly quiet then two locals sauntered out of their house and sat themselves down on a boulder just beneath the cliff. There was a man dressed in scruffy jeans three sizes too big for him and a black t-shirt and a large woman with similarly ill-fitting clothes, only hers seemed three sizes too small. They kept their distance and watched me with expressionless faces whilst smoking a cigarette which they shared.

A local fisherman covered in tattoos also appeared, drawing deeply on a Woodbine. I hadn't noticed him before but he seemed to have come from behind a shabby looking fishing boat. He looked at me with suspicion and a slight air of malice. He made no motion towards me until I engaged with him. I can't recall his name but he had a slow, deep, Geordie accent, a muscular wiry physique and slicked black hair. His cheeks were hollow and under the tattoos he was tanned. I guessed he was about my age but his weather-beaten face made him seem older.

I tried to make conversation with him but I really just wanted a lift with the boat across the rocks. He enjoyed the way I had to tease the question out of him. He knew that was why I was investing so much time in pointless conversation. His self-confidence was not unfriendly but he volunteered no verbal commitment and I wasn't really in the mood for idle chatter myself.

"Don't suppose you would mind helping me up over these rocks, would you?" I enquired.

"Aye" was his curt but helpful reply.

We both struggled to carry the fully loaded MOD27 over the rocks, they were uneven and slippery, smoothed off by years of rolling in the sea and with an assortment of sizes and shapes making it difficult to get a sure footing. My fisherman friend was strong. He managed to make it all the way up the beach without stopping. By the time we parked the boat, my fingers were cramping and screaming with pain. He nodded at me then just strolled off.

What a relief. I could never have got across this boulder strewn beach without his help.

By now, Emma had made it to Skinningrove in the van. She could see I was close to the end of my patience for the day. Around the same time, I realised I'd missed my 17.00 hrs rendezvous with the Safety Channel so I checked in as soon as I could find a place where my phone would work. PY was kicking off with messages to me about chaos on the Safety Channel. Missing deadlines, discipline and the like. I'm not sure he fully appreciated how stressful today had been. I wanted to tell him to "eff off". It had been bad enough launching through a tsunami this morning, dealing with the wind changing continuously, being becalmed then drenched in a mass of rain, stuck adrift in the fog and now negotiating with locals to get the boat to safety across a boulder bank. I couldn't fully appreciate at the time the stress my lack of comms was causing.

I then received a message from Brad, via Facebook messenger. Brad was the fisherman who had helped me up the cliff at Tunstall a few days earlier. It read,

"Stick. You need to pack up your gear and get out of Skinningrove or you'll be catching the bus home. This is the worst town in Britain."

Brad had seen a Facebook video I'd posted after making contact with the Safety Channel describing my arrival at Skinningrove. I was a bit shocked by this. It looked a bit run down here but the fisherman I'd met seemed nice enough. The rain had started coming down heavily again. After some deliberation, I took Brad seriously. He was from these parts and had been very helpful when he and his mate had carried the boat up the cliffs at Tunstall with me. He had no reason to warn me unless he genuinely thought there was some risk. I took the unusual decision to load the boat onto the roof of the van for the night, just to be safe. That was the first time I'd ever attempted to do this with my new van.

As I've mentioned, my normal sailing van, the half-arse camper, had a special Laser loading mechanism that I'd invented called the Easy Loader. Sadly, the half-arse had died just before this trip and I hadn't found time to modify and transfer this Easy Loader system over to the new van before leaving. The new van had a different roof rack system which I'd never had an opportunity to test out. There were four aero bars on the roof with a roller on the rear bar. My idea was to stand the boat upright against the van's rear doors resting against the roller with the bow just above the roof height then, to load her onto the roof, I planned to pick up the back of the boat and effectively clean and jerk her upright then push her forwards onto the roof over the roller. I'd thought out the theory but had no idea if it would work. It's a medium high-top transit which is a long way up, 3.2 metres to be precise.

The same fisherman who'd helped earlier reappeared. To my surprise, he volunteered to help Emma and I heave the MOD27 over the rocks to the closest point we could drive the van onto the beach. Unrigging everything, we executed my plan, only for the right-hand rear roller fixing to snap half way through the initial clean and jerk manoeuvre. The MOD27 was dangling precariously half over the side of the roof. If she fell now, she would not only damage the panels on the new van but most likely smash the hull on the uneven rocks below. The rain was teeming down. I managed to convince the fisherman to hold her in the air with his arms fully extended to prevent her slipping off any further. Meanwhile, I attempted to climb up onto the roof to pull her onto the bars. With my first attempt to climb up, I opened the front passenger door and, jamming my foot in the gap, made a lunge for the front aero bar end to try to pull myself up. This was a disaster and I went sprawling in through the open side sliding doorway, hitting the van's floor on the way down before ending up on my backside on the rocky beach.

Meanwhile my fisherman friend was going for a record on how long he could hold a 65 kg Laser above his head. I tried again, only this time I clambered up the windscreen pushing off from the windscreen wipers and made it onto the dripping wet roof slipping around once on top, narrowly missing falling off before catching hold of the boat's bow. The fisherman looked quite pleased to be relieved of his strong man endurance challenge. I hauled her onto the roof. She was safe but there were still a few dodgy moments as the main cleats on the deck kept catching on the roof bars as I dragged her on. On one occasion, I nearly toppled straight off the side of the roof backwards as the boat shot forwards after releasing her from a particularly difficult snagging. All three of us were drenched to the skin. Once it was clear his assistance was no longer required, the fisherman tipped his cap and sloped off into the night saying very little. If this place is the worst town in Britain, we have nothing to worry about in this country.

It was dark by the time we left the beach. We hit a pub called The Ship Inn at Saltburn, caught the last food order and ate fish and chips, sank several beers and then followed that up with a few brandies. We stumbled our way back to the van in the pitch-black night and crashed out in the public car park next to the toilet block where earlier that evening we'd both strip-washed. Incredibly for a public convenience, it had hot running water. In a public loo!

It rained most of the night and the following day. We had another pretty terrible night's sleep in the van. We'd already had several hurried changes to the sleeping arrangements. I'd finally given up with the fold down bed which I'd stripped out of the half-arse. It wasn't wide enough for two to sleep on and too bulky for one person. To try to improve things, we'd dumped it at Sand-Le-Mere. Whilst this had improved the internal space, we were now sleeping on a one-inch mat on the van floor. There was still a way to go. The upside of the van was that it was dry, unlike the tent.

Next morning, I started late and it became a bit of a rush to get fed and sorted. It was taking even longer than usual to get going. The prospect of unloading the boat off the roof on my own weighed on my mind. Then there was the rocky beach to get across. I needn't have worried because unbelievably when we arrived, the same fisherman was coming into shore in his fishing boat. He was on his way back in from an early morning pot laying. Without even a word, the fisherman from Skinningrove came over and offered to help again. This time it went more smoothly and we were carrying the MOD27 across the assault course of rocks in no time. Any sane person would have turned around and driven back out to sea.

My plan was to push off against the flood tide for several hours in the hope of using what little wind there was, making extra time on the water, taking maximum advantage of the ebb tide all afternoon when the winds were forecast to be very light – sub 6 knots. The haar was already clinging to the overhanging cliffs around Skinningrove. Out to sea, it looked like there was still surf breaking, probably caused by the submerged rocks that had nearly dried out beneath me yesterday. The wind shadow of the giant headlands stretched out as far as the breaking water. I didn't like it and had a scan around for a better place to launch.

The other side of the natural harbour was a sandy beach with lower cliffs behind.

"Why hadn't I landed there?" I thought.

Perhaps I could launch from this beach; it was only about 500 metres further north. Did that matter?

I dismissed this idea on the grounds of practicality rather than any conscious decision for purity. I couldn't face loading the boat back onto the van roof. There was no wind when I waded into the water. The tide gradually sucked me out into the surf. I really didn't like the look of the breakers; they weren't big but looked very powerful. I climbed into the boat and sat waiting for some wind. There was none. When the first wave hit me, it was tiny but I was surprised how easily it washed me back into shore. Jumping out of the boat, standing up to my waist in water I tried again, this time pushing the boat deeper, hoping I could wade through the worst of the surf to get to more breeze further offshore. This didn't work either. I was just washed back in again with the first wave I encountered. There were several more attempts, each time failing to clear even the first wave. I tried paddling through the surf next but pretty quickly was washed back to where I started. Wading out again, I lost my grip on the boat when a slightly bigger wave caught me off guard and flicked the aluminium boom up into the air before whipping me across the corner of my eye. I was sent reeling away, unsure what had happened. Instinctively, I grabbed hold of the boat before it hit the rocks as it washed back inshore. My head was throbbing with blood pouring onto the deck. Emma had seen the whole sorry episode unfold in front of her and brought down a cloth to stem the blood pouring from my eyebrow. Game over today. This time I decided Skinningrove could have my boat if they wanted to steal her and I hid her behind a pile of rocks near the cliffs, stripping anything moveable off her and leaving a trail of blood back to the van where the gear was stowed safely for the night.

This is how we met Stephen Drury. For something to do, we visited Saltburn to see the town's famous tourist attraction, the New Cliff lift. The lift was built in 1883 to transport Victorian tourists from the top to the bottom of the cliff and back up again. It was 120 feet tall and ran on rails up a 71 percent (1:1.4) incline. According to the tourist literature, the two 12-person cars are the oldest remaining funicular rail system in the world. The way it works is that each car is fitted with a 240-gallon water tank and runs on parallel funicular railway tracks. Double steel wire ropes are attached to both cars, controlled by a brakeman based in the upper station. The car at the top has its water tank filled until the weight of the upper car just exceeds that of the car at the bottom. It then travels down the incline, almost exactly counterbalanced by the other car which travels back up to the top. The brakeman controls the speed of travel. When the car reaches the bottom, its water is run out and pumped back up to the top of the cliff. Of course we tried it out.

Afterwards, we sauntered into town in search of a local bar. The food festival, which had been running all day, was just packing up. Hearing some live music, we were drawn to a place called Signals Bar. A few rows of hay bales were dotted outside surrounding an old-fashioned dray cart on top of which were a few lads strumming guitars and murdering one of the Killers' best songs. Grabbing two beers, we joined a small group of like-minded music lovers and settled down for the entertainment.

While these youngsters were 'pogoing' up and down, there seemed a very real danger their stage might disappear into a pile of matchsticks beneath them. Stephen Drury introduced himself to me. He was sitting on the adjacent bale of straw dressed in a pair of blue shorts, a t-shirt and a 1970s style tracksuit top which was doing a poor job of disguising a slight paunch. His polished pate curtained by wispy grey hair made him look slightly papal and his monotone Yorkshire accent had a hypnotic rhythm. We started chatting and after I'd told him my reason for being in Saltburn he rolled smoothly into a story about being Britain's first ever speed walker. This was back in the 1970s when no one thought walking was a real sport. Stephen tells a great yarn and both Emma and I were mesmerised by his tale of how he'd walked across America being followed by a campervan full of spare trainers and special food with a harem of sponsors supporting him. He also told us how he'd walked close on 2,700 marathons in his lifetime and other significant trips including walking the Pennine Way and Land's End to John O'Groats.

Stephen was highly engaging and full of amusing stories. He discussed my journey and we laughed at similar experiences of chaos and mishaps. The only difference between our tours seemed to me was that I didn't have a posse of sponsors. I did have a Transit panel van though and a one woman support team, not to mention the Safety Channel chomping away at my heels every day. Somehow in our conversation, I touched upon the notion of launching from the sandy beach next door to Skinningrove where I was presently stuck. I mentioned I thought it would be easier to launch there and was quite taken aback when Stephen said quite forcefully to me,

"You can't do that! If you relocate your boat further up the coast and you do eventually make it all the way round the UK, one day someone will say you didn't sail it all. You missed out the 400 metres between Skinningrove and that beach."

I sat silently feeling a lot less jolly than a few seconds earlier. I thought I'd found a strategy to escape the permanent shore break and wind shadow surrounding Skinningrove. I knew Stephen was right. As we carried on chatting, it became clear he spoke from experience. There were some dark clouds sitting over Stephen's past. He told us how his daughter had died of a drug overdose in her late thirties and how he went to the High Court to convict the drug dealer who'd injected her, known ironically as 'The Doctor'. He talked compassionately about the man who had administered the lethal dose and mentioned he forgave him and felt sorry for him as a hopeless drug addict himself.

He talked a lot about how he'd missed a section of his walk across America through illness which clearly haunts him to this day. He also told of how, at the end of each day's walk of 80 miles or more, they would mark the road where they stopped with chalk and return to the same spot the following day. On a few occasions it rained, washing off the chalk marks, and this resulted in him deliberately walking back several miles further the wrong way. This was to make absolutely sure he'd not missed out any metres.

There was a lifetime of experience relayed through every word of his conversation which I admired and often found charming and amusing but at the same time my instincts made me slightly wary. I liked Stephen a lot and found his company entertaining and his advice helpful. And, because of him, I made sure I completed every inch of my circumnavigation around the UK.

The following morning, I set off at first light to catch the ebb tide and yet again met the same fisherman I still didn't know the name of. Again, he helped me down the same rocky beach and somehow this time I made it through the surf, paddling like mad in a desperate bid to escape Skinningrove, the "worst town in Britain". Looking back at it as I sailed on, I said to myself.

"That place ain't so bad... in fact. I rather like it!"

Chapter 15

Geordie Shore

The breeze was back on as I made my way towards Tynemouth, crossing the Tees estuary mouth, moving past the remnants of the former industrial iron and steel might that once dominated the Middlesbrough waterside then on past Hartlepool, once famous for being the poorest town in Britain and Sunderland crossing the River Wear, the second of the three north east's great rivers emptying out into the North Sea. Finally I arrived at the River Tyne which is the gateway to Newcastle, the best party town in Britain. It was here I was starting to fade. The mileage was back up with one of the best days I'd had since before crossing the Humber, close to 60 km covered today. All I had to do was make it to land safely. Easier said than done in the increasing breeze and sea state. I looked at the landscape to see if I could recognise anything.

All day I'd been having issues reading my Navionics. For some reason, the screen had gone completely black on my phone. I must have accidentally changed the brightness setting. I couldn't see anything on the screen. I was sailing by instinct unable to work out where I was. I had no other map and hadn't studied any place names or landmarks the previous day. I was guessing from my limited knowledge acquired when I worked in Newcastle back in the 1980s. My knowledge was pretty sketchy as was my memory.

"Just keep the land on my left and head north," I told myself to try to be self-reassuring.

It was only at the end of the day when I caught sight of yet another massive walled harbour with waves crashing into the narrow entrance ahead of me that I was sure that was the Tyne I'd just crossed. It must be!

The swell at the harbour entrance looked way too dangerous to navigate so instead I elected to land on the beach just past it. Aiming again for the lifeguards' flags flogging madly in the middle of a wide bay covered in sand. The surf seemed quite big, but I thought,

"Stuff it."

I'd had enough of sitting in this uncomfortable plastic boat any longer. I released the rudder downhaul rope and eased off the kicking strap. A large wave picked me up and I surfed down the face of this fantastically powerful rollercoaster. The wave pushed me straight up the beach, at the last minute I flicked the centreboard most of the way up which unbalanced the boat and tipped me out the back of it, before capsizing on the sand. Tynemouth beach had now witnessed a Stick Daring landing. A great ending to a great day. Only it wasn't quite over yet. The boat still needed to be hauled up the beach and all the gear safely stowed, but first I made sure I filed a Safety Channel report and contacted Emma.

Washing facilities here were a cold shower located just outside the promenade beach cafe. It was still sunny and quite warm so the showers felt very refreshing. More importantly, my body was salt free. I hoped my rinsed kit would dry quickly and be safe where I'd left it drying camouflaged behind the wooden fence hiding the cafe's industrial size bin. Day-trippers passed by as I stripped down to my naked flesh, as if it was perfectly normal to strip-wash in these very public showers. I didn't care anymore. My backside was on fire and it needed putting out.

Whilst hanging my sailing clothes to dry on the fencing I disturbed a swarm of wasps feasting on the cafe's throwaways and beat a hasty retreat back to the van being pursued by a number of them keen to tuck into my naked bottom. As I fled, I ran straight into the path of a poor unsuspecting Indian lady who was leaving the beach with her family and five children. I smiled as I raced past her hoping to avert her gaze from my rapidly bouncing manhood.

The town of Tynemouth is picturesque and there is a mass of amazing Victorian buildings housing restaurants and shops, so many that it took Emma an hour to decide which Indian restaurant we should eat at. This decision was made only after we'd trudged up and down the high street looking at every menu. The first one looked good to me. My fatigued temperament acceded to her choice. Once inside the restaurant, I was gratified to find that the lady from the earlier manhood beach incident was neither a customer nor the proprietor! We slept in the van overlooking the cliffs opposite a row of magnificent white, four storey, Victorian terraced houses. Finally, the van accommodation was starting to get more comfortable after further modifications had been made.

The following day was another bad light wind and big surf day. There was no way I'd get off this beach. It was mega surf and there was no or little wind. I was beginning to regret my decision to land here again. The harbour would have been a much better option. John Pythkelly, one of my Facebook followers from Tynemouth Sailing Club, made contact. As I was stuck here, I responded to his message and hoped I might get a hot shower at the club if nothing else. After talking with John via messenger he told me they raced around inside the harbour on a Wednesday evening. I didn't hesitate when he invited me to join in. It meant moving the boat back to the harbour off the beach. As I couldn't launch, I borrowed John's trailer from the club and tied the MOD27 to it, hitched up to the van and set about making my way back to Tynemouth harbour.

Tynemouth harbour is as big as a reservoir, and a large one at that. Once I'd made myself known at the club and rigged, I launched on the shingle bank just outside the clubhouse, protected by the huge harbour walls. Getting to the start line required me to try to sail out under the cover of a 20-foot high wall that completely blanketed the wind. As the cover of the wall was out of range, a great gust of wind hit me. I narrowly avoided capsizing and after a series of very dodgy wobbles continued my way towards the start line.

On the way to the starting boat, I passed a series of racing buoys that had been laid around the harbour, creating an entirely unintelligible course to sail. The buoys forming the course were unmarked. What names, letters or numbers they did have on them were either invisible or bore no resemblance to the course displayed on the starting boat as far as I could tell. A few legends of the sailing world I recognised by name, if not by face, were present including Alan Johnson of Enterprise class fame. I remember following his results when I was sailing an Enterprise myself as a young teenager.

The breeze was full hiking conditions and the MOD27 and I had good boat speed so elected to get a safe start and follow the lead Laser around the course for the first lap, mainly to figure out where to go. This plan didn't go very well, I actually found myself over 100 metres ahead of the next boat at the first mark, so much so I had to slow down and let it pass as I had no idea where the second buoy of the course was. The problem then was the boat I let through was actually very quick so I spent the rest of the next two laps huffing and puffing like mad to overhaul and eventually just overtook him on the finish line.

I felt pleased with the win and particularly enjoyed the Miami Beach size waves coming in through the bottleneck harbour entrance, running down the course like a tidal wave. We had a great evening's entertainment. Many thanks to all at Tynemouth Sailing Club for their hospitality, especially John Pythkelly for setting it up.

The breeze was up in the morning and setting off from the harbour was a relief, although it meant navigating the enormous seas around the harbour mouth and sailing back over an area I'd already previously sailed. I decided to go a long way offshore and investigate the massive car container ships anchored up. Approaching them at 7 am in the morning made me wonder if they were all sitting down munching their way through a full English breakfast. The thought of it made me hungry as I'd stuffed nothing of any note down me this morning, hurriedly leaving very early with the ebb tide.

Chapter 16

Impossible Task!

It was Day 16 of my trip and I'd covered close on 450 miles since leaving Eastbourne. This was only a guesstimate calculated by using Google Maps. My Navionics tracker wasn't always turned on to conserve battery life so this meant it was unable to give me accurate distance readings. My very crude navigational calculations estimated I must be just over halfway to Jeff's in Inverness. Sixteen days, 450 miles, an average of only 28 miles per day. Obviously this included some days off but looking at the distance, this journey felt like an impossible task. And that was just to get myself to Jeff's!

My body was falling to bits. Suffering with tennis elbow, both arms were painful to bend. My neck was cramping on one side as I was sailing on one side of the boat for hours on end. My right knee was starting to cause me some pain so I spent as much time hiking off my left leg as possible. My fingers were forming into stiff balls every night from constant gripping. On a plus note, my backside was starting to heal after a very painful first 10 days. Thank God for Sudocrem!

The MOD27 was fairing a little better than my body but was slowly leaking through cracks in the corners and the cockpit was partially full with water all day because the plastic bailer was broken. The brand new Rooster sail looked badly worn around the batten pockets and had a few holes where it had caught on barbed wire fences, rocks and other sharp obstructions. My mainsheet ratchet block was broken but to be fair it had been dodgy from the first day. Both side deck cleats used to secure the mainsail were unreliable, especially in strong winds, releasing with no warning. The additional masthead air buoyancy bag, impolitely referred to by Jim in Sandilands as my whoopee cushion, was punctured and would only remain inflated for its first hour after full inflation. The windex was regularly stuck with sand and most of the ball-bearing blocks on the boat were encrusted with salt and sand making them virtually useless.

All my communication devices had problems, as did my power packs. The rechargeable battery units had all failed. The phone charger packs had failed; the leads had become rusty. My Spot X satellite tracker and emergency transmitter, which failed after the first day with sea water ingress and had now been replaced with a new unit, was intermittent at best and sometimes didn't work at all. I think there was some user error in this but it certainly was becoming an irritation to the Safety Channel. My personal FM radio had died early on and been discarded. My head torch was still working but the batteries were low. The flare packs looked sound in spite of soaking in water all day but it was difficult to tell though until one was lit. All my waterproof phone bags had now failed and were leaking, as were most of my waterproof dry bags stowed inside the hull of the boat. I was triple bagging everything. A lot of the kit was being carried in the van during this stage so I hadn't bothered to think too much about this problem. Once I reached Scotland, this would be a different matter. I realised that my challenge might not be described as plain sailing. The weather had been pretty good so far, mostly sunny and dry. It was the first day of August after all, holiday season.

"How long do you think it's going to take you to get to Jeff's?" was a question the radio presenter on Tees radio had asked me the previous day.

"I have no idea" was my genuine response. "A lifetime," I quipped.

Jeff had been excitedly tracking me both on the Spot X device and my mobile phone using an app on Google Maps. He'd periodically contact me to advise on weather concerns and progress updates on the media interest he was getting in Scotland. He had visions of celebrity status – appearing on breakfast TV which was probably as realistic as appearing on the Christmas edition of the Morecambe and Wise show.

Jeff was a great inspiration and encouragement but nevertheless I felt myself sinking. I wasn't really convinced I'd even get to Jeff's, let alone around the UK. Twenty-eight measly miles a day. I'm sure I could have walked that distance more quickly. What was troubling me was I was getting more and more fatigued as the journey went on. I'd spent an enormous amount of energy already. Coupled with poor sleep for two weeks, I was now being disturbed each night with bad dreams, finding myself hot and sweaty waking just before some virtual moment of doom occurred.

During the day, my anxiety levels were on permanent alert. As soon as I saw anything move in the water, a strange ripple, a weird breaking wave, a headland, dark sky above, animals in the water, seaweed, fishing buoys, rocks, anything that I considered unusual, my senses moved to red alert. I think this may be a penalty of sailing alone. If I compare how I was on the day of leaving Eastbourne to now, in just a few short weeks I'd become aware of much more danger and, in many respects, this was proving to be a problem. I'd now regularly wake in the mornings and think, I'm not going today. The wind is too light, the shore dump too big or the wind direction is wrong. I found myself looking for the slightest excuse not to get back into the boat. Emma was virtually booting me out of the van and off the shore each day.

I was trying to find a reason why I was doing this daft journey. What was it for? Notoriety, fame and fortune? A mad dare that had gone a step too far? I chatted to PY about my reasons for doing it. The relentlessness of each day; the expectation of the unknown of what was to come. The mental pressure of the Facebook pages that were beginning to attract more and more followers was starting to place additional burdens on my already overloaded shoulders. I'd started off this passage very low key with little PR probably because deep down inside I didn't really have any confidence I was going to make it. I wanted to be able to melt away into the sunset if it all went pear shaped and pretend it was just a laugh. That was gone now. People were talking about me and, more crucially, throwing money at me through the Prostate Cancer UK appeal. I'd only set up the Just Giving page the day before leaving. Somehow this charity element was becoming more important as I went further into the experience. I was getting real joy and motivation from the money I was raising, far more than I'd ever have imagined at the beginning.

My personal finances were shot to bits. The bank overdraft was bumping along at its maximum. I couldn't really think about this now. Emma and Jon Jono, who'd stepped in the day before I left to take over the reins of my business, were doing a grand job; a job neither Emma or Jon Jono had been trained for. They were managing really well given the circumstances. Emma was quizzing me about the management of my doors business every time I landed. Relentless questions to be answered about how to do this? Where was the password for that? How much does this cost? Who does this for you? Where can we get this? Most of the time I was pretty dismissive. I just didn't want to know. I was Stick Daring now, intrepid adventurer, Stick of Historic Doors, Britain's finest reclaimed door was morphing into someone else. Stick Daring, as he was now known, couldn't sail round the UK and keep a failing reclaimed door business afloat. Something had to give and at this moment it was the doors. They would stay afloat or sink and frankly that was in the lap of the gods, or just God. I didn't really care which it was. Emma, on the other hand, did care and was rising to the challenge with an enthusiasm no one had put into the business for years.

Throughout the journey and leading up to my departure I was getting increasingly irritated by one particularly difficult customer whose front door I'd installed two days before leaving Eastbourne. I'd personally gone to the site and completed the job. The painting and preparation of the job had been done by one of my subcontractors, without my supervision, as I was distracted preparing the MOD27. The day before I installed Brian's door (not his real name but for the purposes of this account I'll call him Brian) I realised it was below a standard I'd usually have let out of the workshop. There was just no time to do anything about it so I tried to make good on any issues on the day of installation. In fairness, I thought I'd done a pretty decent job by the end. The problem was that this particular customer happened to have an exceptional case of OCD or just didn't fully appreciate the difficulties of planning a circumnavigation while refurbishing and fitting a period front door. More than any customer I'd previously had dealings with in the past 12 years, I had to pick this one two days before leaving.

Committing the fatal error of trusting Brian to pay the last instalment on the day of completion, as agreed, I left his premises in a hurry and said it was fine if he paid online before rushing off at top speed so I could continue my preparations which were woefully behind schedule. Looking back, as I reversed my van out of Brian's driveway I knew when he smiled and waved me off in the friendliest manner that we'd never see any more money from this job.

Two weeks later we were still waiting for over half the money from Brian's job. Emma was now actively engaged in responding to page long emails on a daily basis as to why he wouldn't pay and even having to fend off reasons why he should get a full refund. I found my daily exchanges with Emma as I came ashore usually ended with a discussion about Brian. The problem just wouldn't go away. I needed to kill this issue. It was getting out of hand. Although the business was nearly out of cash, I called him and agreed to everything Brian asked and unbelievably the problem still carried on. How much more can you give someone?

"Go away! Please."

"Take whatever you want off the bill. I'm trying to sail around Britain. Please just let me get on with it."

These were words I was speaking down the phone to Brian. Phone calls I made, snatched often after sailing long days along some of the most treacherous coastline in the UK in a Laser sailing dinghy. They weren't good calls for either party. I must have made three or four calls to try to resolve the dispute. It seemed the more we agreed to everything Brian wanted, the more he came back asking for even more. In the end, I told Emma to block his emails and phone number and write off 100% of the outstanding monies - a painful day given this was desperately needed to fund the next week's payroll. By sheer good fortune, the very day after my last Brian call, a top level new online order came in for some very large period room dividers. Thank God, the payroll and bills were safe for another month.

Chapter 17

The God Effect

I can't recall who it was but I was once told by someone and the words stuck with me when they said,

"You will never find an atheist sitting in a life raft."

I didn't dwell on this comment at the time or even register the significance of such a statement. My own religious upbringing was what I'd describe as 'reluctant Catholicism'. That is to say, my mother was Catholic. My father was raised by his mum as Church of England but I only ever saw my father worshipping around Christmas time and this usually with the enthusiasm of a tail-ender facing the opposition fast bowler in the final over of a cricket match.

I was educated in the ways of the Catholic faith. I attended St. Joseph's Catholic Primary in Epsom, Surrey where I took my first confession and holy communion with Monsignor Westlake. Aged eight, I then moved to St. Peter's Middle School in Ashtead, Surrey where I grew up. My parents bought a derelict house in Cray Avenue, Lower

Ashtead that they then renovated. I managed to fall in the pond on the first day we moved in, fortunately being rescued by my older brother. My father made the pond into a rockery the following day using rubble from a chimney stack he'd dismantled. It was an adventurous first year in this house for me, managing to fall out of the apple tree, restyling my nose into the shape it is today; best described as 'Roman' by my friends, Roman all over my face.

My secondary school religious education brought me into contact with the Church of England for the first time. A former grammar school, Glyn School, based in Ewell Village, was an all-boys secondary modern. It changed its name the year I arrived from Glyn Grammar School on account of the then government abolishing grammar education. Glyn was miles from my home village in Ashtead, way outside of the catchment area but because my older brother Guy was very bright, I qualified to attend. He'd passed the 11 plus four years earlier and my parents had managed to bend a rule that allowed siblings to attend the same school even if it was outside the local catchment area.

Glyn was quite a shock at first. To start with, there were no girls. Weird! Then we had to stand up every time a teacher entered or left the classroom, address the teachers as Sir or Ma'am and attend a daily assembly to sing hymns. I barely recognised the prayers; the words were similar but different to those I'd been accustomed to in my Catholic upbringing. I found myself resisting the C of E influence. I think this is called Catholic indoctrination.

However, please don't get the wrong impression of me. My religious fervour would at best be described as limp if not indeed non-existent from a very young age. I became a serial yawner on contact with the doors of St Michael's Church in Ashtead where my mother had dragged, coerced, manipulated and bribed me with sweets to attend Mass every Sunday for years. The introduction of a Saturday evening service instead of Sunday morning had helped to extend my religious appearances on account that it didn't interfere with the weekend's football fixtures or local car washing round I ran called Posh Wash. I was always active as a kid, playing football for Glyn School on Saturdays and Pelham Ashtead on Sundays where I was even the captain for a few years.

I was happy to go along with the religious thing, mainly because I was in the system and partially to please my mother. In fact, I had moments in my early teenage years where my religious fervour upgraded from limp to enthusiastic. I even attended two pilgrimages, one to Canterbury Cathedral and the other to Buckfast Abbey. Both were organised through the local diocese church group based in Arundel and Brighton. My brother had trodden the same pilgrim path and had stories of walking 20 miles each day, sleeping in sleeping bags in church halls and barns with 200 other pilgrims. Here's the crucial bit though, it was with girls, coupled with daily God Stops (churches) to pray followed by Pub Stops (pubs) to drink and sing your heart out until you either fell over or threw up. The Pub Stops were the clincher for me. At 15 years old I was already investing most of my car washing money into liquid assets. The idea of going on a 15-day, 240-mile pub crawl with a group of young like-minded, mixed sex teenagers was enough to convince anyone my age to join in. What a brilliant recruitment idea the church had come up with.

It was at a similar time in my life that I was also reading Chaucer's Canterbury Tales for my English O-level. My young English teacher, Miss Bond, would sit me at the front of the class whilst reciting the lewdest stories of Chaucer. They were probably described as pornography when they first were told in the Middle Ages and a worthwhile read if you've never read them – motivating and amusing, once you work out how to decipher Ye Olde English. The Wyf of Bathe tale is my favourite. I felt I was living out a real-life role in the Tales of Chaucer on the pilgrimage holidays.

The God Effect

Why am I telling you all of this? I think it's important. My journey through the north east of England was seriously testing me. I was regularly scared witless. My belief in a God watching out for me was growing. I was having so many close escapes from danger. Every day I was having at least one life threatening incident when, out of nowhere, I'd be rescued from what seemed like an inescapable situation. Call it destiny, religion or whatever you want – when you're about to be smashed onto rocks in a plastic sailing boat with no wind and from out of nowhere the wind blows to save you or you are adrift in the North Sea becalmed in the main shipping channel where it's only a matter of time before a 20,000 tonne super tanker will mow you down and the wind blows again or you happen to land on a beach where, by pure luck or some other higher influence, you miss every jagged rock lying inches below the surface to land safely, unwittingly taking the narrowest of routes to avoid the forces of nature – if it was happening to you, you'd start believing in something too. The God effect was becoming a growing reality.

This is why most ports in the Middle Ages had chapels built right next to the sea. Sailors would drag their scurvy ravaged bodies ashore and before plunging themselves into the local hostelry to consume copious amounts of mead and pounce on the nearest flaunting wench, they'd pray and thank God they were still alive.

I was getting it!

Evidence of some other force in play kept on making appearances and there was a clear sign of this when I made a long sail up to Amble from Tynemouth. A Facebook follower whom I'd never met offered me his yacht to sleep on for the night.

My trip into Amble was hairy to say the least. I'd stopped halfway through the day at Newbiggin to rest up for four hours while I waited for the tide to turn then, approaching the Amble harbour sandbank late in the day after continuously beating into the wind for four hours, I had to make a decision – take the short cut and risk crossing the bar or figure out a way around it. The wind was blowing around 20 knots and waves were overfalling everywhere. This was not my idea of fun. I ended up taking the long way round, beating parallel to the bar for a further hour into the distressingly large waves that are typical of this coastline. Having navigated around this cascading mass of confused seas, I carried on a mile further offshore to sea to seek shelter behind the lee of a tiny island before finally entering the tall harbour walls protecting the Amble yacht haven. It was dusk when I arrived, barely able to see Emma standing on the end of the pontoon with our host for the night, Steve Vogel.

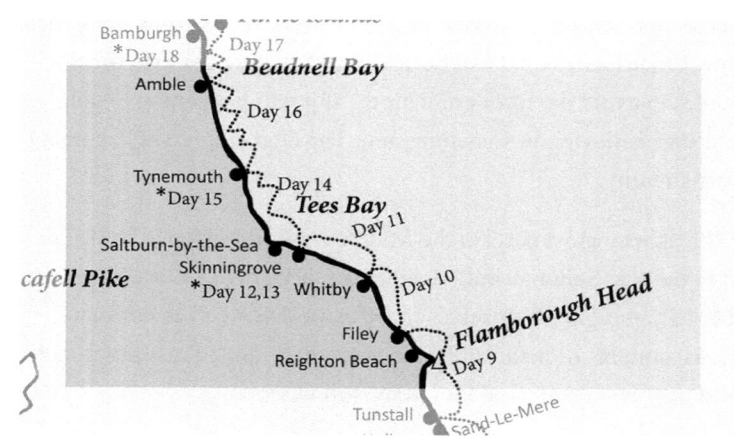

Steve and Emma helped me to de-rig and then we abandoned the MOD27 on the end of a long wooden pontoon for the night, half-heartedly lashing her down with the mainsheet. I was ushered off to have a quick wash before heading to a local fish shack which was closing at 9 pm. Steve talked about his yacht and his dream of sailing around the Mediterranean next year when he was planning to retire. Little did he know at the time that, shortly after I completed my circumnavigation, he'd be diagnosed with prostate cancer. Very kindly, he paid for our suppers that night. Emma and I ended up sleeping back in the van that evening as it just seemed easier than fiddling around on an unfamiliar yacht in the darkness and then figuring out how to hand the keys back at the crack of dawn the next morning. It was because of our chance meeting that Steve first heard of prostate cancer and at the time of writing this chapter, he was undergoing treatment.

A similarly odd coincidence happened further along the coast at my next stop in Beadnell Bay, one of the most picturesque harbour and beach locations I'd encounter across the whole of the UK. Close to Bamburgh Castle and the Farne Islands, I was fortunate to have a beautiful sunny day on my arrival at Beadnell Bay. I'd sailed 36 km beating all day again, this time up from Amble. I recall pulling into this incredible, golden sand, horseshoe shaped bay. In the far corner was a solitary house with a tiny drying harbour next to it. Dotted along the sand dunes were a few other buildings. The Beadnell Bay Sailing Club sat somewhere just behind the harbour wall, accessible through a short made-up track with a single bar gate dropped across it. I arrived at Beadnell with the tide all the way out. It was miles to pull the MOD27 up to the safety of the club's grounds.

A local tractor was towing ski boats up and down the beach but didn't show any interest in helping me. Apparently he charged £20 a tow. I'd made no advance contact with anyone here and just hoped the local sailing club would be open. As I was rolling up my sail down on the beach, a familiar voice said:

"Hello are you here for the Laser open meeting tomorrow?"

I was stunned. Not only was the voice incredibly familiar but the fact that there was a person on the beach who knew something about a Laser and secondly was the first person I met in Beadnell Bay seemed a surprising coincidence.

I didn't really register what this person was saying to me as they continued talking, then he said,

"Neil! Hello Neil," and he laughed.

I was struggling to place his face and where I knew this stranger from. He was looking elated and smiling at my arrival in Beadnell Bay. Then the penny dropped. Benson... master Laser sailor... and yes that was it, he ran the only RYA coaching course I've ever attended; the race coach course at Pevensey Bay three years ago.

"Richard Benson!" I exclaimed. Unbelievable!

"What are you doing here?" we both asked simultaneously and laughed at our synchronised timing.

I explained my bit and he explained his. The next day, Sunday, Richard was the race officer for the first Laser open meeting to be held at Beadnell Bay Sailing Club for 20 years. Explain that one, non-believers!

That afternoon I ended up at Richard's house, just round the corner from the sailing club. We drank tea together with his wife, Aida, and reminisced about Laser events. Emma and I even took their lovely little dog for a walk along the beach up to Bamburgh Castle, almost losing her along the way. When we returned, Richard ran through the weather forecast for the next day which in summary was less than 5 knots of wind and boiling hot sunshine. He convinced me to take a day off and sail in their event. I agreed and worked on the MOD27 to set her up for racing early the following morning.

The Beadnell Laser Open took place in 3 knots of breeze. Most of the day, we drifted back and forth. Six boats attended and, after a narrowly fought duel, I finished in fourth place. Second place was the highlight for me in race two. We had a great day. That evening my attention turned to the next day's challenge: getting to Scotland. I studied some of the local maps on the club's walls and two members offered to help me to plan a route. I exchanged a glass of wine as payment. We chatted late into the evening before they departed leaving me the use of the clubhouse and entrusting me with the keys to lock up.

Chapter 18

Last English Stronghold then Scotland

    The Northumberland coastline is the most northern province of England. I had no idea until sailing through this wild but beautiful area of England how stunning Northumberland's beaches are. This 30 mile stretch of coastline has one of the bloodiest histories of England with an abundance of ancient fortifications strewn almost everywhere you look, built first by Romans and many more by Norman lords guarding a contested walled border with Scotland to suppress rebellion and defend against the attacks from Celts. Northumberland is the most heavily castellated county of the UK, boasting 70 castle sites.

    I sailed past one of the finest in England, Bamburgh Castle, standing on its colossal rocky plateau guarding the sea. I could imagine myself hundreds of years ago stealthily making my way ashore. I visualised creeping along, using the tide that races past the Farne Islands, before pulling my boat ashore under the cover of the local haar, armed to the back teeth with steel, ready to set upon the locals to plunder their crops, women and livestock.

The currents ripped me past Bamburgh Castle like riding a magic carpet, moving silently with the tide in a near still wind. I was steering the MOD27 but not really sailing, looking at small seals diving in and around the rocks racing by with dolphin fins momentarily breaking the surface of the water in the distance. It was a silent mesmeric place with strange crumbling monuments from the past dotted around sitting on top of large granite rocks.

I reached the birthplace of the Lindisfarne Gospels. This is where St. Aidan built a monastery in 635 after King Oswald gave the Holy Island of Lindisfarne to him. It's been a place of pilgrimage ever since. It was 11 o'clock and Emma called me to say she'd driven across the three mile causeway that linked the island to the mainland. The tide covers the adjoining road twice a day. I guessed I couldn't sail across the causeway if she'd just driven it so headed seaward around the eastern side of the imposing island. I considered stopping for a coffee at the Pilgrims Coffee House but there was nowhere obvious to land.

The wind was a light 7 knot southerly and I relaxed, lying across the boat, steering with my elbow with the mainsheet in the one deck cleat that still worked. I sailed past a tall ship. Everyone on board lined up on one side of the ship looking at me and took a million pictures. We were close together for quite some time but we soon got bored of each other as I slowly inched ahead. The day's forecast was light all day. My target was to round St. Abb's Head but by early afternoon it was clear this was going to be unrealistic. I passed Marshall Meadows, the most northern settlement in England, and crossed the Scottish border at 1.30 pm. No one noticed and waved any flags but I felt a giant milestone had been reached. Scotland at last!

Chapter 19

Écosse de bas

I spent my first night in Scotland perched on a 20 degree slope, camping in the van at the car park just above Coldingham Bay. Approaching the bay, I was drawn into the centre, aiming at the lifeguards' flags mounted high up on a building up the cliffs. All around the entrance were signs of submerged rocks with breaking, foaming seas threateningly festooned across both sides of the mouth. I sailed past with caution, peering hard down at the dark green water looking for any errant rocks poking up that might pierce the hull. Once through into the main bay it looked very sandy and calm, perfect for an easy landing. John and Jenny, two young lifeguards, helped me drag the MOD27 up the beach above high tide to the sand dunes. John did mention that boats were banned from landing on this beach but he said he didn't think I qualified! I laughed. Jenny who helped too asked about my journey. It turned out Jenny, whose surname is Lattam in case you want to look her up, had her own adventure planned for the autumn. She was training to swim the channel in October, fundraising for the

RNLI. I shivered when she told me she swam daily in these freezing waters in only a swimming costume; part of the rules for her channel crossing. No wetsuit allowed.

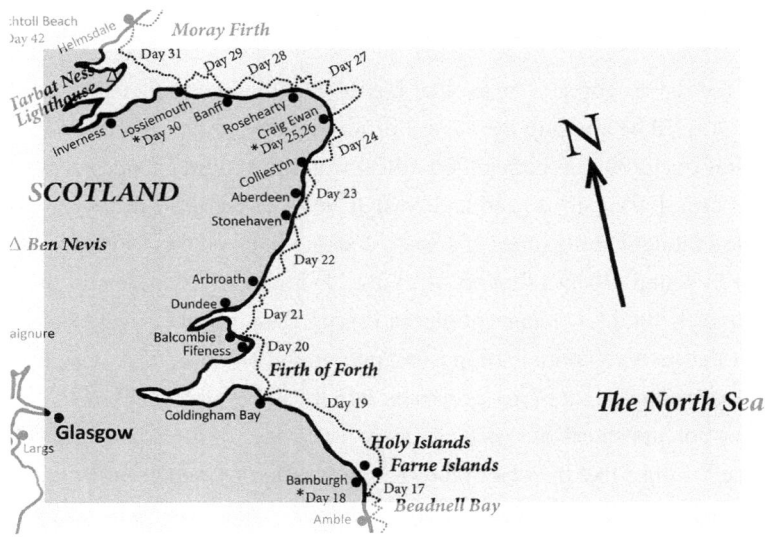

Once ashore, I inspected the MOD27. I was growing increasingly concerned about the amount she was leaking. The cracked hatch cover was seriously close to breaking in half. There was a surf shop near the car park so I went in hoping they'd have a kayak hatch I might be able to swap for the cracked RWO one. They had nothing suitable so I doubled down on the duct tape and hoped I'd be able to keep her airtight with my temporary repair. This was a concern though as I feared that in any capsize, the hatch would fail, swamping the hull.

The following morning John, who was a young fitness fanatic in his late teens, showed off his skipping rope training talent out on the wooden deck of the pretty lifeguard hut. He appeared to want to put on a show demonstrating the incredible speed of the rope whirring through the air as he jumped rapidly through it for about five full minutes. It was astonishing, and I felt quite touched that he'd clearly decided he'd want to show me! I resisted any attempt to compete as I knew full well that I'd lose. Skipping over, he and two other lifeguards, all decked out in yellow and orange kit, enthusiastically helped me down the long sandy beach with the boat to launch. I was careful to sail straight out through the centre of the bay, continuing some distance past the headland to avoid any submerged rocks before heading north again.

Today was going to be another big day. As if any of the others weren't. I'd be crossing the River Forth, the gateway to Edinburgh. This is over 800 kilometres (500 miles) from Eastbourne. Once across the Forth, I was only a headland away from reaching Jeff's in Inverness or so I thought at the time. It's funny looking back on this trip how naive I sound. When I first set off, I used to look at the contours of the map, pick out a few names of places I recognised, vaguely figure out the tides on my Navionics app using my mobile phone, spend an age trying to squeeze all of my gear back into the impossibly small hatch in the boat, push off and go for it. How hard can it be? I used to ask myself. Looks like the rest of the UK. Now, after my numerous brutal close encounters with death, I was researching every nook and cranny along the route, talking to the locals, agonising over headlands and hoovering up every last drop of local knowledge I could find.

What I wasn't quite sure of was why I increasingly found myself suddenly breaking down emotionally in the middle of the sea. Always on my own, I found I was quite frequently and unexpectedly uncontrollably crying my eyes out, sometimes with no reason for doing so. It was strange, often taking me several minutes before I got myself under control. When I landed, I didn't have this feeling. I was getting tired and could be pretty grumpy, especially in the mornings. Emma witnessed my low mood, particularly if I'd had a long one the previous day or something had gone wrong. But no tears. I didn't mention this to her or anyone else.

I had continuous pain in my hands and elbows and my right knee was becoming excruciatingly painful but I never felt like crying about it. I wasn't the crying type. In fact, before this trip I nearly never cried.

But I was finding sometimes on my own, I just couldn't control this behaviour. Sometimes it was sparked by remembering a kind deed someone had shown me, other times there seemed to be no reason at all. I'd never experienced anything like this before. It touched a rawness inside I didn't believe I possessed. A human compassion I'd not experienced before. I started wondering if a homeless person gets these feelings of overwhelming emotion when they're helped by a total stranger. In modern society we've lost touch with this side of ourselves it seems, not everyone, but I count myself in this category. Modern life desensitises human beings. I'd become quite cynical about the hungry and homeless beggars on the local streets where I come from. I was now increasingly reappraising my position on this.

The Firth of Forth was looming. This crossing is technically a fjord, formed by glaciers during the Ice Age. The River Forth acts as an estuary for several rivers joining the North Sea at Fifeness in the north and Lothian in the south. The shortest distance across the mouth of the river is sailing from North Berwick to Earlsferry, a distance of 16 km. I was planning on making my crossing here. However, as I approached Dunbar, still a long way south east of North Berwick, the wind direction was more favourable to crack off and sail directly across the North Sea from Torness Power Station to Anstruther on the other side. The distance when I checked on my Navionics app was almost 30 km. I went for it.

I was on a tight reach and surfing along at a good 7 to 8 knots until I reached the middle of the estuary. Here, the wind started going weird and then very soon completely switched off. I was becalmed in the middle of the sea for 25 minutes. The first signs of the new breeze came in from the north, making it a beat into the wind. This was slow, really slow! I had an anxious half an hour before the wind came back in fully. This time it moved more southerly and came in lumps, gusting around 20 knots. As I approached the coastline of Anstruther, the breeze built further. I was flat out surfing along on very large waves. In spite of the power and direction of the wind I still seemed to be moving very slowly relative to the buildings on the land. I fought for several hours to make progress along the coastline up to Craighead, Fifeness. This was the eastern most point of Fife, after this I had to turn north west to make my way to Jeff's across the Moray Firth. Here at the headland, several tidal influences are in play from the rivers Tay, Eden and Forth. These three rivers join and flow out into the North Sea at Craighead. The waves had become really steep now and I was hardly making any headway against the tidal race.

According to local folklore, old boatmen used to shiver at the names Kneestone, Mary's Skerry, Englishman's Skerry, Long Man's Grave and Tullybothy Crags, all wreckers which kept the old coastguard station busy along this stretch of water. At the time, I was unaware of those notorious buried obstacles I was sailing above. I'd accumulated enough experience to recognise that when hiking flat out in 20 knots and barely moving it meant it was time to land. I headed towards land and cut close inshore, traversing across the strongest part of the tide which was ripping underneath me. After 50 minutes of battling away, I found calmer water and could see a small bay in the distance. Squinting hard through the spray on my glasses, it looked like this might be a possible landing place. There was a horseshoe shaped small beach surrounded by low grassy banks.

Balcomie Bay is the name of this spot. Surfing in with my rudder and centreboard half raised, I skirted across Englishman's Skelly, oblivious of this rocky outcrop just beneath the sea, missing it by a matter of inches. If I'd hit this at speed who knows what damage would have been done. This danger only fully revealed itself to me when the tide went out. Later that evening I was able to see the many rocks I'd dodged when landing. What a fluke! Safe!

Balcomie was a deserted stony bay strewn with seaweed. Long grassy banks surrounded it, rising two feet above sea level. Where the grass banks finished, they were replaced by craggy, razor-sharp rocks at both ends of the bay that disappeared into the sea, popping up every

Écosse de bas

so often further offshore in rocky outcrop formations. Lush, perfectly manicured grass was visible in the distance. It looked a lot like a golf course with a few pretty small huts dotted around. The sun was out, it was a lovely spot. I thought I'd landed in the middle of St Andrews Golf Course at first. That would be amusing. I messaged the Safety Channel and told them I thought this was where I'd landed.

Wherever it was, this looked like a good place to stop for the day. I set about hauling the boat across the seaweed bay and after a lengthy struggle managed to get the MOD27 up onto the top of the long grassy bank. As I was unrigging, a very small lady walking two Scottie dogs attached to extraordinary long leads appeared on the beach. If you wanted a perfect picture postcard, this was it. I approached her and we chatted. Her name was Isla. She was half my height with bright electric blue eyes piercing out from behind small rimmed spectacles. Her face was friendly and welcoming and she spoke with a melodic soft east coast accent. Isla lived in alone in a small cottage on the headland with one of the finest views of Scotland overlooking the sea. She introduced me to her Scottish Terrier dogs, Finlay aged two and Seamus aged four; two of the most iconic Scottish Terriers you could find.

As it turned out, I wasn't at St. Andrews Golf Course but Crail Golf Society. When PY checked the maps, he accused me of navigating with a potato. That would probably have been more useful today given the conditions, making it nearly impossible to swipe the phone open whilst sailing through these seas. I'd chosen my location well. Isla invited me back for tea and cake and later Emma joined us, finally catching me up after driving the van 100 miles wiggling along some of Scotland's tiniest lanes. She'd seen me start the crossing from the power station at Torness and then made a dash for the Forth Bridge, arriving almost an hour after I'd landed, an indication of the speed I'd been running at today.

PY made a call to the golf club on my behalf and deployed some of the Irish flattery he'd clearly been holding back from me. He charmed Amy David, the lovely American receptionist, to help me along my way. The result of his Irish blarney was that Emma and I enjoyed the most luxurious shower facilities of the entire journey and a complimentary VIP guest pass for two which gave us access to the restaurant, bar and breakfast in the morning. Absolute jackpot! Plus, we were allowed to park the van in their club car park and sleep with one of the best views in Britain outside the window.

Yesterday had been a big day, covering 60 km and bumping up the average a bit. Today was likely to be another big one, crossing the River Tay, continuing my route northwards. So, a Crail Golf Society breakfast was the order of the day; a late rise at 9 am with the luxury of a sumptuous shower to beat all showers. What an incredible facility and as many full size super soft white towels as you could use.

After seeing the plethora of rocks littering the bay at low tide the previous night, I was being extra careful to stay very central as I gingerly picked my way out from Balcomie Bay. Isla had shown me an ancient mariners' map hanging on her dining room wall featuring Englishman's Skelly which she seemed to find quite amusing. I maintained a course for at least a mile offshore to triple check that I wasn't going to hit anything before turning westwards, keeping closer to shore for the more favourable tides. If I sailed straight out to sea, the wind direction made for a less physical ride so, after an hour of beating into the wind, I eased off my sails and aimed directly at Arbroath. This meant going far offshore, crossing the Tay shoal. God knows what that would be like. Isla had said to me very bluntly that she wouldn't cross this stretch of water in a small boat like mine. Her brother or uncles were fishermen so she spoke with some authority. I moved back into deaf mode and filed another demon in the ever-growing box at the back of my head.

The crossing was going well; fast reaching, sailing in 20 knots with lots of spray and rolling waves. All was under control until I reached an area approximately 8 km west of Bell Rock Lighthouse. Here, the sea state became very confused with standing waves which seemed to break on all sides. Had this happened the day I'd left Eastbourne, I'd have been pretty unnerved by the conditions but, at this stage of the journey, I'd become more used to navigating difficult and scary seas. It felt like I was passing directly across a shoal or rocky outcrop but after a serious buffeting I made it through to smoother waters without capsizing, conscious at all times of my badly damaged hatch cover.

Reaching the mainland somewhere close to Carnoustie, another famous golf club on the other side, was a great relief and I travelled north staying close to the shoreline. I sailed past Arbroath Harbour at 2.30 pm and decided it was too early to stop. Today, I'd sailed 37 km and felt I could carry on but just as I sailed past Arbroath harbour, the wind faded. Two fishing boats sat a few hundred metres apart north of the harbour. At first, I thought they might have a net strung out between them so I went towards the shoreside boat. There were half a dozen people onboard all standing on one side holding fishing rods. It became clear there were no nets out. I drifted around for a further half an hour fighting against the tide in no wind. It was futile trying to go on so, turning round, I headed back into Arbroath harbour.

Before entering I called up the harbour master on the VHF. Roddy the harbour master answered in a welcoming manner, enough to convince me it was worth risking sailing through the tight harbour entrance. Once inside, the harbour was full of commercial boats. Roddy was an extremely friendly man with a broad perma-smile. He directed me to a pontoon in the inner harbour via his VHF radio. His thick accent was difficult to understand but I found my way into the pontoon I thought he was directing me to. This was a working harbour, there were no yachts in here.

Parking the MOD27 was an interesting exercise. It required me to haul her up on top of one of the narrow wooden pontoons. The first task was to remove the rig. The easiest way to do this seemed to be to pull out the mast, still attached to the boom and sail. I attempted this in one movement. As soon as I lifted the rig out, a puff of breeze caught the sail and unceremoniously spun me round. I narrowly avoided falling off the pontoon three feet into the harbour below. Once out of the boat, I had the sail standing upright on the pontoon. Laying it flat was quite a challenge as it was so narrow. As I lowered it down, the rig overhung the pontoon on both sides. The next task was unloading all the kit and then draining out the leaking MOD27 before hauling her onto the top of the pontoon. I lay on my stomach, dangling head first over the water lying across the pontoon and reached down to untape the hatch cover. The cover was gently prised off making sure not to damage it anymore and crucially not to drop it in the water. Pulling the gear out of the hatch as the boat bobbed around in the water was another tricky affair. As usual, the large tent bag was obstructing the hatch opening and it took ages to prise this through the hole. I had to open the dry bags inside the hull. This involved unclipping the securing fastener then unrolling the tops to let any air out before I could squeeze them through the aperture of the tiny hatch.

By the time I was finished I was surrounded by an assortment of part opened bags that I piled together on top of the sail to stop it blowing away. The next task was to get the hull up on top of the pontoon, turn her over and lash her down for the night. Heaving her up the three feet was surprisingly easy compared to the previous exercises. Once on the deck, I needed to make her secure. Lashing the boat to the tie up loops on the side of the pontoon was harder than it sounds. The pontoon was so narrow I had to crawl across the upturned boat to reach the far side, and again very nearly lost my grip lying prostrate on my belly across the hull to reach the end loops. This whole process went on for almost an hour before I finally made it up to the harbour office. It would have made an epic comic film except I hadn't delivered the perfect finale of falling in. Once safely ashore, I went through the usual ritual of contacting the Safety Channel to update them and then phoned Emma to liaise with her and find out where she was.

Roddy was a jovial, laid-back harbour master. He offered me the use of their office shower as the harbour didn't have any other facilities for visitors. I gratefully accepted. It looked like this shower was rarely used but the water was warm and I was freezing cold. Before showering, Roddy and I posed for a quick picture which was later nicknamed the Arbroath smile off, on account of our grinning faces. I think Roddy won this contest with a slightly wider grin than me. A famous picture from the trip.

Chapter 20

Oil Country

A little-known fact about Aberdeen is that it's the home to some of the wealthiest people in Britain. A study in 2019 found that four in every 10 households in the village of Milltimber near Aberdeen earn more than £100,000 a year – higher than any other area in Scotland. This is according to an article in the Aberdeen Evening Express based on statistics compiled by the estate agents, Savills.

"Victorian villas line the generous streets of this suburb, six miles outside Aberdeen, whose prosperity and high average house prices are founded on oil wealth."

Although this was 'oil country', and in spite of the apparent wealth of this area, it certainly wasn't making it any easier to sail in. In fact, it was now impossible to find any safe havens where I might bail out if the weather turned bad. It was a brutal craggy coastline. Once I'd cast off from Arbroath, the only realistic place to land was Stonehaven. I'd no idea at all what to do if the wind switched off today. I must have been concerned about this as I cast off at the start of the ebb tide, flowing north from Arbroath harbour. On this occasion, to make the tide I was up at 4.45 am and I slipped silently out the harbour mouth at 5.20 am where I was rudely interrupted by the wash from two rapidly moving fishing boats. Men were hurriedly scrambling on deck pulling in ropes and struggling into their wet weather gear whilst steering their boats within inches of me racing to catch the same tide.

The breeze was pretty incredible. One minute it was steady at 10 knots, then gusting 20 knots followed by torrential rain, then sun, then freezing cold then hot, switching on then off. It was like someone had a light switch they kept playing with just for fun. Jeff's felt a very long way away from me this morning. The skies were grey and drizzly and I was flipping chilly. I had chattering teeth pretty much all the way along the coastline leading up to Stonehaven. As I arrived, just before 1 pm, the sun poked its head through the clouds.

My right knee was agony. It felt worse now than at any point on the trip. Every time I tacked the boat, I yelled as a shooting pain went straight up from my knee to my hip. I was beating into the wind all day hiking solely off my left leg. It had taken eight hours to crawl my way another 56 km closer to Jeff's.

By the time I made it into Stonehaven harbour, I was glad to see the welcoming face of Emma. She was accompanied by Ditta, Stonehaven Sailing Club's training officer. The concrete ramp I pulled into was slippery but fortunately it was a shallow incline to ascend. Ditta waded in with her yellow boots and with a club trolley helped pull me up the ramp. I was extremely grateful that passage was over.

Our stay in Stonehaven was particularly comfortable. Ditta had offered to put us up and we had anything we wanted including a sumptuous bed and ensuite bathroom. She lived with her daughter and husband in a Victorian three storey town house very close to the harbour. That evening she invited me to join in with their club's evening dinghy race. I politely declined on account of being totally exhausted and in extreme discomfort with my right leg which I now had tightly strapped. Emma and I watched the racing on a public bench on the harbour wall whilst eating fish and chips. We'd bought these from the internationally renowned Carron Fish Bar which claims to be home of the deep-fried Mars Bar. We swerved sampling one of these specialities at £1.50 each.

The evening turned out to be surprisingly warm with the added bonus of the rain having stopped. We just sat quietly, absorbing the picturesque harbour scene, watching a dozen or so keen club sailors racing each other around the cans. I felt slightly disappointed I couldn't join in but I really enjoyed this short moment of calm. Drinks at the sailing club after the racing were pleasant and we chatted with a few of the locals before we returned to our luxurious bed at Ditta's.

Overnight, I'd left my sail still connected to the boom and mast and stored it inside the cavernous Stonehaven sailing club boat shed. This was large enough for me to lay it down on the floor which would save me time rigging up in the morning. Stupidly though, as I dragged the rig out the next day, the sail snagged on a barbed wire fence, tearing a batten pocket and making several other small rips along the luff tube. I couldn't quite believe how careless I'd been. I made a hurried temporary repair using the sail tape I had stowed at the bottom of one of my bags and after a lot of cutting and sticking, I pushed off with my patched-up sail, aiming for my next unknown destination. Ditta had given me a small plastic 'praddle' her cadet sailors used after I told her how I was struggling with the oars when the wind dropped. The oars were unloaded into the van, never to return.

The Safety Channel notes suggested my plan that day was to make it to Aberdeen. I don't really remember much about this. The wind was yet again northerly so it meant another whole day beating. My leg was so heavily strapped I couldn't bend it so, every time I tacked, I ended up doing this weird back roll across the boat to avoid putting any pressure on my knee.

The forecast was 18 knots which actually I didn't mind. I was more concerned at the size of the swell which seemed to vary depending on which report I read. One forecast eight foot swells around Aberdeen. I spent all day smashing into really steep but very short choppy waves. Every time I hit one, it felt like the boat was going to break in two. The relentlessness of this sea state was playing on my mind all day. I was having a lot of trouble avoiding some really negative thinking. I was fed up with this journey and wanted it done. Jeff's would be far enough. I could bow out gracefully once I reached Inverness. I'd done what I'd set out to do. Make it just to Jeff's.

By midday, I was freezing, tired and hurting all over. The "bloody sea" was smashing me every few seconds. I was trying to sail using a technique my other mate Jeff, the Aussie from Sydney, had taught me – rapidly wiggling the tiller to force the boat through the short chop, steering through the banging waves to keep the boat moving. You can sail like this for a few hours but when you have to do this all day, you find your elbow gives up, cramping, burning and aching, screaming out to stop. When you stop applying this technique, the ride becomes even more uncomfortable as wave after wave crashes over the bow and fills up the cockpit with sea water, making it even harder to steer.

Approaching Aberdeen harbour, I'd seen a ton of ships. Big ships, very big ships. Fortunately, I'd had the foresight to read up the previous night about Aberdeen harbour and the requirements for crossing. It's a long wide open harbour mouth with a lot of very large shipping movements daily, mostly servicing the oil industry. Before crossing, small ships have to radio up the harbour master control. The wind was dropping as I approached so I radioed ahead to check if it was OK to cross. The harbour control was surprisingly helpful and after a few moments of translation from thick Aberdeen to southern English, I was given the all clear to cross.

The only problem was that I was beating directly into the tide and the wind had dropped to little more than 5 knots. It took almost an hour to reach the start of the crossing. I radioed again, this time giving the harbour master an update on my position. He confirmed it was still OK to go so I carried on my slow beat across the harbour mouth. It looked like there were ships coming and going everywhere around me. They were so big they hardly seemed to be moving until you got close to one, which I was seriously hoping I didn't. I left the VHF radio open on the harbour channel, listening to the chatter between various boats and the control room. One Norwegian tanker seemed to be getting quite heated as they wanted to slip their lines and then I heard them referring to a small yacht.

"Is anyone aware there is a small sailing boat blocking the harbour?"

The harbour control report back to the Norwegian captain made me chuckle as the controller replied, "Aye we're aware of the solo yacht crossing, standby until given permission to move."

It took me over an hour to get across the harbour mouth. I've no idea how much it costs to keep a super tanker on standby for an hour in harbour with its engines turning but, judging by the chatter I was hearing, obviously quite a lot. Perhaps I should have told them how much I had paid for the MOD27! The day improved after this, the sun came out and by the time the wind was dying completely, I'd made it into a wonderful place called Collieston Bay, arriving in brilliant sunshine. There was a sandy beach surrounded by a high circular stone harbour wall. Inside the harbour were a series of white detached houses, two of which stood right on the walkway around the harbour. Several larger houses were set further up the cliffs on both sides. The harbour wall had a narrow concrete car park on the northern side and the opposite flank was steep cliffs. Winches were set half way up the cliff face. Attached to these were a small fleet of open fishing boats and pleasure craft. They'd been hoisted well clear of the slabs of granite laid out below on the exposed beach. Looking at the high tide marks, it seemed the harbour and beach completely flooded. Slabs of craggy rocks filled much of the harbour with two distinct narrow channels. Green weed attached to the rocks disguised their danger.

The only option for parking tonight was to copy the fishing boats and haul the MOD27 halfway up the cliff with the rest of the boats sheltering on the southern face of the cliffs. I sailed over to this side of the bay. After scrambling around for a trolley to borrow, I found a rusty set of wheels attached to an axle with a piece of angle iron poking out the front. It took a bit of engineering improvisation but I managed to make myself a rope trolley tied onto the axle. Attaching the mainsheet to a winch set high up the cliffs, I hauled the boat up until she was nearly vertical, bow down against the jagged rocks. Making her fast, I left turning back occasionally to see if the continuous flow of water pouring out of the transom bung hole had stopped.

The MOD27 was looking tired and slowly starting to sink. Her corners looked terrible and the RWO hatch was hanging on by a thread and plastered with duct tape. I had no idea what would happen if I capsized but I needed to get this hatch fixed and quickly. I'd been hunting online for a replacement hatch for sale. Everyone seemed to be out of stock of this unusually large 8 inch size hatch. I even called RWO who confirmed they were out of stock in the UK and didn't expect any more for weeks. This was a disaster. My whole trip now hung in the balance because of a tiny plastic 8 inch cover. PY had pointed out before the start of my trip that any hatch I put in the boat was a potential point of weakness. His words resonating inside my head were beginning to irritate me.

I put out a Facebook appeal but although I had plenty of offers, no one could find a hatch cover this large. I found plenty of smaller hatches but could think of no other solution other than to keep looking. Meanwhile, I'd just have to continue taping the hatch up the best I could and try to avoid putting any stress on it. Difficult when you're loading gear in and out each day.

That evening, Emma and I parked on the quayside in the tiny car park protected by the thick outer walls. We chatted with two couples grappling with their St. Ayles skiff, a type of Scottish clinker-built fishing boat powered by four oarsmen. Setting out into the still night, to me this looked like a harder way to travel than sailing around in a Laser. I watched with amusement as they tried to synchronise their stroke as they weaved out through the harbour entrance.

We found the local pub, The Kilmarnock Arms, which was more a restaurant than a pub and grander than we wanted but it was our only option so we took a seat. Only one other table was occupied. I pulled out my box of chargers and plugged my array of electrical devices around the power points in the pub. I'm surprised we didn't get turfed out as we looked pretty suspicious with all this gear.

Chapter 21

Peterhead "Blood Draining!"

Safety Channel forecast:

"09/08/2019,

09:11 - Stick: Pre-departure format:

Collieston Bay 2. ETD 9.20 am.

3. Peterhead ETA 12.00. via Cruden Bay

Primary safety Comms method: VHF

5. Secondary safety Comms method: mobile

6. Expected Comms frequency: update at 12.00.00 via WhatsApp channel or relayed via phone or coastguard to advise on route progress.

Weather concern: easterly winds at first 18 - 23 knots gusting upwards of 30. Concerns: big storm coming in later circa 14.00 - 16.00 up to 40 knots

Swell later, 4ft -6ft, 8ft on the beach. Rocks, very limited landing places. Peterhead or Fraserburgh"

This is the exact message I sent to the Safety Channel before pushing off from Collieston Beach. I really didn't want to go back out in the MOD27 today. My knee was heavily strapped, I liked it here. The wind direction was mostly going to be a beat again and it was going to go bonkers sometime in the afternoon, depending on which forecast you believed. The wind forecast didn't really bother me as much as the size of the swell. There were no safe places to stop on the way to Peterhead. It was craggy dark cliffs and the easterly breeze was blowing the sea directly into them. As I typed the wind speed into the WhatsApp message to the Safety Channel, I wrote it so objectively now that I didn't even give the 4 in front of the nought for the wind speed a second thought.

It wasn't nice. As soon as I left the shelter of the harbour, I was back out into the wild North Sea again. I felt alone. Really alone today. Battling along the coastline there was a serious swell running. The strong winds hadn't even kicked in yet. An hour into the trip I could make out an ominous looking building perched high above the cliffs. This was Slains Castle, now lying in ruins, crumbling, overlooking the coast of Cruden Bay.

The original castle has been rebuilt many times since its construction in 1597 by the Earl of Erroll. The ruin today is the inevitable result of the castle's location and the misfortunes that befell the various owners over time. The most recent owner, Sir John Ellerman, finally gave up the castle in 1925 and removed the roof to avoid paying taxes. The castle is now most famous for being known as Bram Stoker's inspiration for the setting of the tale of Count Dracula (1897). How appropriate to pass by in such inclement weather.

I really didn't want to hang around here but the wind was pushing me back into the cliff line all along the coast. I'd tack out to sea and

Peterhead "Blood Draining!"

then back into the cliff, watching the waves smashing into the face until I knew it was becoming dangerous for me. Tacking back out to sea again, there was no escape. It was a boiling cauldron. I just kept plugging away, getting drenched with every wave crashing over the bow. My eyes were stinging and my hands cramped from pulling the mainsheet relentlessly in and out. Every gust and wave were an effort, steering through the surf, trying not to slam into the next confused set of waves. Visibility was terrible, I could hardly see anything. The tops of the waves were being blown off the crests and all I could see was white spray everywhere. I tried to remain focused on steering through the maelstrom and not worry too much about the violent scene around me.

"Try to relax," I kept telling myself as I climbed out of one giant hollow reaching the top of the next humongous, tumbling wave as I approached what looked like Peterhead, although I couldn't be sure. There was no way I could check any navigation kit in this sea. I saw a giant tower. The sight of this was awesome. By now, the breeze was going as bonkers as the forecasters had predicted. The waves were impossible to distinguish, bubbling into a fiery spray. The terrifying sight of foam smashing over the tops of the harbour walls and ricocheting up to the top of the 17 metre tall chimney was enough to put me off venturing too near them. I was approaching from the seaward side, at least a mile out. I couldn't see anything and I didn't know how to sail in through the southern side of the harbour wall where the lighthouse stood (not a chimney). Once through this, I'd have found the relative safety of the outer harbour. If I'd carried on further in, there were two giant walls protecting the Aberdeen Sailing Trust building on the inner, inner harbour which I later discovered.

I didn't like it, bizarrely feeling much safer out at sea. I aimed for the headland that was Peterhead. I was sure once round this point the sea would flatten off a bit and I could try to find a beach to land on. I vaguely remembered seeing sand on the other side of the headland from looking at my maps that morning. The headland rounding was even worse than I imagined. The waves seemed to be as tall as my mast and so confused they were coming from every direction. I followed the harbour wall contours, watching in terror at the size of the sea smashing into it. Somehow, I made it round Peterhead without capsizing. Bearing off, I surfed down the most enormous wave in towards a sandy bay that I could barely make out in the distance. I was now sailing on a broad reach moving in the gusts at uncontrollable speeds, broaching numerous times, but crucially avoiding any capsizes in the screaming gale, letting my sail flap violently when I became overwhelmed by the wind's strength. The noise from the roaring surf was deafening as I approached the beach. The middle of the bay looked safest. I was hoping there would be no hidden rocks here so I aimed for the centre of the miles of golden sand which looked like safety.

After a hairy 20 minutes, I blasted up the sands of Craig Ewan beach, arriving on a tidal wave which deposited me unceremoniously out onto golden sand halfway up the beach before the surf retreated. Before it had time to rebuild and drive back in, I staggered to the bow and started dragging the MOD27 up the beach. It was as much as I could do to stand up before the next wave hit me. I was plumb in the middle of a golden horseshoe of sand. The wave surged in and smashed me off my feet. The MOD27 was upright as I was hit and my feeble attempt at dragging her up had at least left her stern facing the full force of the incoming wave. The wave drove over her and forced her deep into the sand filling the cockpit with water. The power of the wave was ferocious, depositing shingle and sand all over the hull. However, this extra weight may have saved her as it helped to prevent her being drawn out with the sucking wave as it retreated once again. Back on my feet, I grabbed the mast and pulled her over onto her side. Most of the sand had emptied by the time the next wave hit. This time holding on tightly to the mast I used the wave to drive the MOD27 higher up the beach to reach safety. It worked. A further wave hit but it was too far away to be of any concern. I'd made it. Untying the fender, I managed to drag the MOD27 to the safety of the soft sands underneath the cliffs. I was alive!

I cannot recall feeling so exposed at sea and yet so exhilarated at the same time. So scared and yet excited. I let out a mahoosive shout of joy, scaring the life out of a lone dog walker hurriedly trying to avoid this mad banshee on her remote beach. My teeth chattering and every bit of me shaking violently from cold and adrenalin, how I had survived that madness was beyond me. I was so lucky to be safely on firm ground. I could hardly hold my phone to make contact with Emma, I was shaking so badly. In the end, I persuaded the lady dog walker to dial the number for me as I was unable to. She quickly disappeared as soon as I started talking. As I spoke, my voice sounded weird. My lips wouldn't move and my tongue felt like an elastic band was stopping it moving correctly.

I discovered later that I'd rounded Peterhead in close on 40 knots of breeze and landed on Craig Ewan Sands, a famous surf beach that was smack bang in the middle of nowhere two miles away from the nearest car park which was at the Peterhead Golf Clubhouse. The links course extended along the bay directly above the 20-foot high sandy cliff behind me. There was no way I could sail to the car park; I'd never get through the surf and I didn't want to go anywhere near water ever again at that precise moment. There was nothing else I could do. I'd have to park the MOD27 in the sand dunes. Easier said than done. They were near vertical dunes with thick tufts of spiky marram grass sown to protect the cliff line. After a lot of effort, I manhandled the boat halfway up the dune and rolled her over so the upturned hull was almost invisible. Rolling up the sail, I slid it under the hull, burying the rudder, tiller and centreboard deep in the sand next to it. I pulled out what valuables and clothes I could carry and left the rest of my gear inside the upturned hull. It was a long cold walk to meet Emma who was waiting for me in the golf club car park. However, the effort of parking the MOD27 and walking through soft sand for two miles with all my kit had warmed me up a lot and my teeth had stopped bouncing up and down uncontrollably by the time we made contact.

Before leaving, Ditta had passed on a number for a lady called Angie. She ran the Aberdeen Sailing Trust (AST) which was located in the harbour, the safety of which I had so skilfully avoided. Angie had already made contact with Emma and we drove round to see her as she'd offered me the use of the club's showers. When we arrived, I couldn't believe what I was seeing. It seemed there were hundreds of kids charging around in shorts and t-shirts, some in small dinghies, some in the AST clubhouse making things from plasticine or painting pictures. It was freezing cold and very wet. Didn't these children know what cold was? Within the safety of the multiple harbour walls, it felt surprisingly sheltered from the gale blowing outside. Nevertheless, as soon as your head poked out from the cover it nearly got blown off. It was a truly inspirational sight to see this youthful enthusiasm on such a grand scale.

Angie absorbed me into her fold of kids and coaches as if it was pretty common practice to help out a circumnavigator. By the accounts of other UK circumnavigators, I discovered it probably was quite a regular event for Angie. Peterhead was one of the few places you can stop for miles along this coastline so Angie had seen most of the other mad folk who'd dropped in on their circumnavigation journeys. Once I'd showered and warmed up, she told me about one woman in particular she'd helped.

Fran Gifford had sailed around the UK in a two-man Wayfarer called Viper in the summer of 2010. She'd bought the boat quite cheaply from Hartley Boats in Derby. By most accounts it was cheap for a reason. Similar to my own experience, her boat had been leaking after pounding around the Scottish Coast, travelling clockwise in the opposite direction to myself. She'd sought refuge in Peterhead harbour in a 30 knot gale, similar to the one I was in. Angie recalled how six adults were unable to lift her Wayfarer out of the harbour on account of the hull being completely full of water. Fran was storm-bound in Peterhead for several days and Angie and her team patched the boat up during this time to ensure Fran completed her circumnavigation.

I wasn't planning to be storm-bound but it seemed fate had dealt me the same cards as Fran. The following day's forecast was just as terrible as today so, after spending the night sleeping in the van in the pouring rain outside the AST's clubhouse, I decided to sit it out today. We drove back to Peterhead Golf Course car park then walked the two miles along the beach dressed in full wet weather gear to check on the MOD27. When I finally located her again, she was still where I'd left her near to a half-buried World War 2 pillbox which amazingly I hadn't noticed the day before. The boat was only just above the high tide mark in spite of being half way up an impossibly steep, collapsing sand dune.

After returning to the van, I slept in the car park the rest of that morning. When I woke, I started looking online for a local chandlery. There was one at MacDuff. They were closed but I managed to find a phone number for an emergency call-out by their marine engineer. When I connected, he was very friendly and although he didn't have a new hatch cover in stock which would fit mine, he seemed to think one of the boats in their yard did have. He told me to take it if it fitted. We drove an hour to the yard only to find it was the wrong size.

Driving back to Peterhead, Emma wanted to let her hair down and go dancing. It was, after all, a Saturday night. Reluctantly I agreed and we ended up in a pretty rough local boozer with live music. I was really tired and grumpy and had an aching knee and stiff neck so I didn't want to dance. Emma made up for my absence, spending most of the evening strutting her stuff on the dance floor. By 1 am, I'd had enough and we left but only after Emma polished off her last whisky.

Whilst Emma had been swinging herself around the pub dance floor, I'd been outside having a crisis of confidence, exchanging WhatsApp messages with the G7 group, suggesting to them I was thinking of moving the following morning. Roger O'Gorman, one of the members of our group, was insisting that I promised him I didn't go. I was desperate to get to Jeff's but the forecast was terrible, howling gales worse than today. PY and Rupert Bedell were more level headed in their comments. PY stated most matter of factly that if it was a red zone forecast it was a non-moving day. Dave Freeman and Rupert agreed. Discussion ended!

The following day was Sunday. It was Emma's turn to be grumpy. Nothing to do with her sore head from too many whiskies but the porridge I made was too watery and the coffee had no sugar and tasted disgusting. We dithered about most of the morning. The weather was terrible, pouring with rain. We arranged to meet up with Angie and Kieran at the AST clubhouse and chatted for a while about her project helping underprivileged kids get sailing. It was a really moving story. She talked of how the club provided food and a safe place for a lot of local kids whose parents were in poverty. Sailing formed a small part of her one-woman community effort to address some of the imbalances of society in Peterhead and show the kids opportunities they wouldn't otherwise have a chance to experience. An amazing woman!

After this chat, Emma and I went swimming at the local leisure centre. My neck, shoulders, back and knee felt terrible so a swim seemed a good idea to try to loosen them up. We went shopping and ate a terrible meal in a Morrisons cafe then decided to drive up the coast to look at the Bay of St Fergus. On the way, we battled through roads that resembled lakes they were so flooded. The rain was torrential. At Rattray Head, the sea was boiling. I looked out and was thankful I wasn't out there again. I slept in the van most of the afternoon, parked in a grassy layby. That evening, I made contact with Peter Crawford. He lived in Rosehearty just near Macduff, further north along the coast. Annie had passed me his number as a potential source of information and assistance.

Peter was involved in running the Rosehearty Community Sailing Club, another inspiring local community initiative to get youngsters sailing. We drove out to visit him and spent a cosy evening in front of their fire, sipping whisky, chatting with Anna, his wife, and stroking Huntly, their gigantic Golden Retriever. Peter invited me to stop off when I sailed past the next day.

It was now Monday 12th August. The middle of August and the air temperature when I rose at 5 am the following day was four degrees. My plan was to set off with the ebb tide at 6.30 am. I had a long walk back to the boat and hoped it would still be there on Craig Ewan sands. I said bye to Emma who carried on sleeping in the freezing van. I ran to warm up in my soggy wetsuit. Arriving at the boat, it looked like someone had moved her. Most of the bits I'd buried had also been moved. I was slightly worried the police had received reports and perhaps they thought the boat had washed up onto the beach and were looking for a body. I dismissed this and got my ship together, washing sand off the boat with salty sea water. It took an hour before I was ready to launch. The biggest problem now was that there wasn't much wind and the surf piling into the shoreline was enormous.

I spent three hours trying to get off Craig Ewan beach. Every time I waded up to my neck trying to walk beyond the largest surf, just when I thought I'd gone far enough to clamber onboard, a giant wave came in and washed me back into the shore, bowling me over and smashing the MOD27 into the beach. On one occasion I got quite a long way out, making it through what I thought was the worst of the surf, then from nowhere a curling wave broke on my foredeck when I was hardly moving. It tipped me out and the boat capsized, careering into the shore. When I finally made it back on shore and recovered, I discovered the tiller had snapped clean off at the rudder stock. All the battens had snapped, the sail was ripped and the MOD27 looked a pretty sorry sight. I called Emma and asked her to bring a spare set of battens and my spare tiller with her as quickly as possible. I was pretty shaken by the aborted launch but determined to try again so I set about fixing the damage.

Unpacking the sail tape from inside the hull, I was surprised to see the hatch cover was still intact. By the time Emma arrived, the sail was covered with tape which wasn't really sticking as the sail was still wet. I swapped over the tiller and replaced one of the broken battens which was all Emma could find. Setting off again into the surf, I had several more aborted attempts. Following a call to Neil Pamment, my surfing friend from Eastbourne, he suggested I try to find the rip current. This is the area on the beach where the water sucks back out to sea. After a lengthy study of the shore, I felt I'd identified a rip. Dragging the boat along the shoreline in the shallows, I set up to try to use this rip current to suck me out through the surf. It worked and I finally managed to make it out, narrowly avoiding a catastrophe with another super steep wave which I climbed over, swamping the boat. Fortunately, I was far enough offshore to catch some breeze which was just enough to propel me away from the dangerous surf of Craig Ewan Beach. Missing Peterhead harbour had added three days to my journey.

Chapter 22

Take Rosehearty

I did stop to see Peter Crawford and several members of the Rosehearty Community Sailing Trust. It was another long beat all day to reach them, recording 35 km sailing in my log. Approaching Rosehearty harbour was a nightmare. When I'd looked the previous day with Peter at how I might get in, it seemed like an impossible rock-strewn entrance. He told me even the locals struggled to navigate their way in. All I could see were breaking waves over semi-submerged rocks. It wasn't very windy but the swell was large from the previous few days' gales. I called Peter on his mobile as I approached for a few clues on getting into the harbour. He passed the phone over to Ian, one of the most experienced sailors in the trust. The only problem with Ian was I couldn't understand much of what he said on account of his thick local accent.

"Tak a wee dip 'n' sheet thru the oooter lochon aye then ...aye… and well …aye then.. tooook the shoooot an cannee beee hard to misss the …."

Ian was giving me probably the best advice I could have ever hoped for. Sadly, I really didn't have a clue what he was telling me. The sea noise, a poor mobile signal, wind and Ian's accent made his entire pilotage unintelligible. In the end I just went for it by instinct, narrowly missing several hard looking semi-submerged obstacles.

I was sucked in on a large wave which looked like it would drive me straight into the harbour wall. Once safely in the shelter of the outer wall, all wind evaporated, leaving me at the mercy of the swell piling in through the narrow entrance. It wasn't pretty but I made it to a soft landing spot on the small shingle beach set back deep inside the harbour.

Peter had rallied the Rosehearty Community troops and a small welcoming committee turned out to meet me. He was keen to show off their brand new boathouse, built with the assistance of Sport Scotland and lottery funding. It was a great advert for regional sailing.

Once ashore, I started looking at the damage the morning's capsize had caused. The battens were all snapped and two of the pockets they sat in were ripped. The hatch cover was as good as dead, nearly cracked in two and the tiller was snapped in two at the stock of the rudder with a small jagged bit sticking out the top. Ian looked over the damage and made noises that I really couldn't fully comprehend but fortunately Peter translated. Together we wheeled the MOD27 up the lane on a borrowed children's Optimist sailing trolley to the Rosehearty Community boatshed.

Once inside the boatshed there was an Aladdin's cave of boats and a fully spec-ed workshop. Ian set to work on making me a set of new battens with just a saw and his hand plane. Graham was introduced to me and he made an assessment of the hatch cover and tiller. Quite quickly he told me he had a plan and set about removing the cover. I hung around for an hour or so fetching fibreglass mat, glue and an assortment of bits from the supplies I was carrying in the van. I watched the two men until I excused myself saying I really had to change and eat and thanked them for their help. They were far too busy to be bothered with such niceties and just carried on.

When I returned later that night, the newly fashioned battens were sitting on the bench. They were a bit softer than my normal ones but would get me out of trouble. The sail had been dried and glued up then repaired with the tape I'd supplied but the tiller was back in one piece, jointed and glued and wrapped in carbon fibre mat. The best bit was the hatch cover sporting a new top made out of double skinned plywood with two finger holes which made unscrewing the hatch a million times easier than before. Graham had managed to re-glue the plastic thread and fixed the wooden plate to it with glue and screws. It worked a treat.

Meanwhile at the local pub, the Durrant Hotel, where Emma and I just made it in time to catch last orders for some grub, we had another unexpected treat. The waitress who served us was a young, chatty and inquisitive girl, fascinated by our story. After we'd finished our meal, we asked to pay but she said that her boss had requested we donate the £50 cost of the meal to my Prostate Cancer UK fund. I was really touched. We had a group picture of all the staff outside the pub and posted it on my Facebook page as a small thank you.

Peter, Huntley the dog and most of the Rosehearty team turned out again in force the following day to assist with rigging and just about everything they could. It was a truly heart-warming experience, one that at the time really mattered to the continuation of my journey.

Chapter 23

Keep on Trouping

My mental state was see-sawing every day. Each morning when I woke, I found myself increasingly tired and often quite depressed at the prospect of another day sitting in the boat. It usually made me grumpy with Emma. I found I didn't want to talk much in the mornings. She did a great job of managing me around and then getting rid of me again. Today was different. Rosehearty had really lifted my energy levels, especially the new hatch cover. I felt secure in the knowledge that whatever went wrong, the MOD27 was watertight again. Well, not exactly, but at least for now she wasn't likely to sink if I tipped her in. Sailing away from the harbour mouth, looking back through the cascading surf around the partially submerged rocks at the entrance, I felt good! I just had to knuckle down and keep on trooping. Chipping away at this ridiculous task.

I used the term trooping as my day was about to be dominated by a headland known as Troup Head. The high cliffs of Troup Head provide a spectacular setting for Scotland's largest mainland gannet colony. Thousands of kittiwakes, guillemots and razorbills live here as well alongside several other species including puffins. Troup Head is the highest point on this stretch of the Buchan coast and, as I'd found out on previous occasions, was likely to cause me problems rounding unless I was very lucky which, unfortunately for me, I wasn't.

There were light winds, blowing around 9 knots when I sailed past the picturesque village of Pennan, famed for the film Local Hero when it featured as the fictional village of Ferness. Film enthusiasts have come from all over the world to make a phone call in the red telephone box that featured in the film here but apparently this was a prop that was installed for the film and removed when they finished. There was such disappointment from tourists looking for the box that it was eventually reinstated. Just beyond the village, set under the cliff line, lies Troup Head. You can barely see an inch of the 376 foot high cliff face because it's covered in birds. Passing by, I was surrounded by dive bombing gannets. The stench emanating from their bird poop was nauseating. I headed inshore with some trepidation, staying close to the cliffs.

Before leaving Rosehearty, Ian had advised me that the inshore route was the best route round Troup Head. I wasn't convinced as I was continuously bombarded by every type of bird diving into the water. After I'd struggled halfway round, avoiding the relentless bombing of birds, the wind died and I started drifting backwards in the current towards Pennan. Three hours I sat under the cliffs, watching and dodging the diving birds, often skewering the water only a few feet away, moving forwards slowly in the soft breeze, counting every painfully slow inch only for all my gains to be rubbed out as the wind switched off halfway round the headland. Again and again I tried, each time drifting back from where I had come.

Eventually I gave up and drifted back with the tide towards Pennan. I was planning on landing and giving up but couldn't see where I could get in safely. I called Emma who'd driven down the cliff road into the village but the mobile signal vanished as soon as she arrived on the small road overlooking the sea. She couldn't tell me there was a harbour. From where I was sitting out to sea, I could only see a sea wall but no harbour entrance. This was obscured on the cliff side and, like most exposed harbours is a dog leg entrance, deliberately designed this way to prevent waves smashing into the moored boats inside the safety of the walls. I sat for ages scanning a continuous wall but couldn't see any entrance. The waves were crashing into the shore and I didn't fancy getting caught up in that lot with no breeze.

After another wasted hour, I waved to Emma standing on the shoreline, a tiny spec in the distance, indicating I was carrying on. I sent a message but knew she wouldn't receive it until she was back up the top of the cliff. I'd wasted precious time. I turned round and headed out to sea in search of a fresher breeze. I passed several fishing boats that were transiting up and down repeatedly along the headland, a bit like they were mowing the grass. They came close to me on several occasions as if to say get out of the way. On the back of the boats were giant hoovers that apparently suck up razorfish from the sand on the seabed, hardly a sporting chance for the sea life when these things are deployed. I didn't know what the fishermen thought I could do to get out of their way as they headed directly at me. The wind was nearly non-existent. I'd just about had enough of this weather. I vented my frustration letting out a thunderous shout at the top of my voice, cursing this bloody headland and the shitty weather. Not long after I did this, a thunderous black cloud deposited its entire contents directly on top of me and my tiny boat. As if to say, you ain't seen nothing yet. The only good news about this reply to my outpouring was that with the rain clouds came an almighty squall. I surfed around Troup Head after five hours of drifting and made a course towards Banff where Emma had arranged to meet me again.

The sea looked like steel, a charcoal greyness shimmered across the surface with fountains of white breaking out now and then. Choppy waves crashed randomly; bursting into each other with white caps in a chaotic yet regular pattern for as far as I could see. I was finally starting to relax today and enjoy watching the sun dipping down towards the horizon. At this rate I should make Banff just before dark. After all today's events, the prospect of a dry warm night in the yacht club was what had kept me going the last few hours. Landfall was close – hopefully within an hour's reach assuming I could make it before the tide turned more powerfully against me. It already felt like I was fighting some current that was only going to get stronger.

Then, in the far distance, something caught my attention. I noticed a change in the water pattern. It was different but a long way off so I couldn't be sure. I squinted into the dimming light, straining my eyes; not the best at distance even in good light. It had my full focus.

"'Surely not!", I thought. I was still a long south but there it was again. The hairs on my neck suddenly stood up like soldiers on parade.

"Was I in danger?" was my first thought.

It felt dangerous. I was alone five miles off shore in open water which was beginning to feel like hostile territory. It wasn't my domain. This was a place where nature had created a different top dog. I counted the sleek shadows aloud – 1, 2, 3, even 4. There was no doubting it was a pod of orcas. Their fins gave them away, followed by plumes of white foam erupting powerfully through the surface, jetting metres into the air. Their silhouettes were becoming clearer, cutting through the water like torpedoes pulling oil slicks, barely breaking the surface as they moved in silent convoy like a fleet of black limousines heading for a mafioso rendezvous. These guys were hunting and I had no intention of being dinner! Pulling hard in on the sail, I tacked away aiming inshore with the objective of being as far away from where they were as quickly as possible.

Don't be mistaken. I love watching orcas or killer whales as they are often referred to. I thought of David Attenborough eulogising in his mesmeric tones, lulling me into the illusion these creatures are harmless or even friendly. I'm sure they are if they have sadly been intensively trained by a Sealife centre coach bribing them into submission through the strict control of food. But these fellas looked to me like they meant business. My nerves had reached their limit for one day. I just kept hiking as hard as my weary legs would allow, not looking back. It took another hour of battling against the racing tide before I laid sight on the small harbour. Finally my racing heart returned to something resembling normal.

Rain, sun, squalls, becalmed, 60 degree wind shifts and a lot of grumbling later, I made it across the River Devron fighting the ebbing tide and sailed into Banff harbour in the dying light at 8.30 pm. I was freezing, the temperature was little more than six degrees. This was August in Scotland.

"Don't they do summer up here?" I wondered to myself.

Standing on the end of a pontoon was a man called Mark Donnelly. It was virtually dark when I pulled into the harbour. Mark had been recruited very last minute via the Banff Yacht Club Facebook page. He'd turned out mid-dinner to assist, helping me hurriedly pull up the boat onto the tiny wooden pontoon and tie her down before we totally lost all the light. Somehow, we managed this without falling in. This was almost as big a feat as the day's sail.

"What time do you call this?" Mark asked.

I chuckled. A smile from my grimacing face at last. Thank God for humour.

The Banff Yacht Club was opened up for me. Mark introduced me to Alistair Mackie and Jim Henderson, local sailors who turned up for a chat and a beer. They lit the fire and allowed us to use the kitchen to cook dinner. Emma set about her task of cheffing while I tried to defrost in the club's shower. £1 bought me seven minutes, I indulgently spent £2, finally able to feel my toes by the time I'd finished. After cleaning up, I had a beer in the upstairs lounge and picked the brains of the three sailors. I wanted to know everything about crossing the Moray Firth and then going round the top of Scotland. While they talked, I was simultaneously stuffing in the box load of biscuits Mark had set out on the small table in front of me. I was at the final crossing before reaching Jeff's, the Moray Firth and that was it. Why was I talking about the top of Scotland? I was just going to Jeff's. The sailors left us to enjoy Emma's steak pie. I fell asleep on the club's sofa to Emma's questions about the latest door orders only to wake at 9 am the next day.

Chapter 24

Just to Jeff's

This was it. I was on the last day of my mad adventure. One good day's sailing and I was home and dry. I only had 80 km to go to reach Lossiemouth, 110 km to Jeff's back door but that would mean sailing up the Moray Firth the wrong way for rounding Britain. I was planning on reaching Lossiemouth but thinking Inverness. I was done. I'd made it to Jeff's. That was the original objective we'd agreed in the pub back God knows when this madcap idea started. Just to Jeff's! It didn't feel right though. Was I mad? Had the sea affected my brain?

Before I'd left Pevensey Bay, PY had compared my trip to that of Donald Crowhurst's. At the time I felt slightly offended but quickly dismissed it as his acerbic wit. For those of you unaware, Donald Crowhurst was one of the first solo sailor circumnavigators. He entered the Sunday Times Golden Globe Race in 1968, a competition to be the first person to sail non-stop single-handedly around the world. There was a £5,000 prize and Crowhurst saw this as a way of saving his failing electronic navigation business. His yacht, Teignmouth Electron, rather like my MOD27, started taking on water almost the moment he left harbour.

The boat was still only half built when he set off. Crucially, a key component of the bilge pump was left behind on the shore in England along with a mass of other equipment in his haste to make the race deadline. There was no official start time but you had to commence the circumnavigation before a set cut-off date. Donald just made the date but spent most of the time circling in the Atlantic Ocean knowing his boat could not withstand a rounding of the Cape of Good Hope. Unwilling to face financial ruin and the humiliation of pulling out, he started faking his positions, recording some record winning distances which attracted suspicion from several yachting experts. Crowhurst must have been feeling the strain and went into radio silence for 111 days. In the spring, when he was scheduled to re-enter the Atlantic Ocean, he announced that he had completed his circumnavigation and was heading home. He was told that Robin Knox-Johnston, who had started the race earlier than Crowhurst, had completed the race and Nigel Tetley would soon follow with a faster time.

Crowhurst began sailing home, hoping that Knox-Johnston and Tetley would claim the prizes. However, when Tetley sank, pushing too hard and capsizing, thinking Crowhurst was going to beat his time and be in a position to win the fastest-time prize, Crowhurst must have realised his logs and account of the race couldn't withstand the scrutiny if he won. He is believed to have become depressed and mentally ill. His boat was found abandoned drifting mid Atlantic. His logs indicated he'd never left the Atlantic. His final log entry on July 1 read,

"It is finished. It is finished. It is the mercy." He ended, "There is no reason for harmful …"

There are no clues as to what became of Donald Crowhurst but many think he committed suicide. His body was never found.

Knox-Johnson, the only finisher of the race, gave the £5,000 prize to Crowhurst's widow.

On his return to dry land, Tetley also struggled mentally to adapt to normal life and a few years later was found hanging from a tree in a wood near Dover in 1972. He was dressed in lingerie with bound hands and the coroner recorded an open verdict attributing his death to masochistic sexual tendencies.

Another competitor in the race also displayed unusual behaviour – Bernard Moitessier, a Frenchman who could have won the race but had either gone insane or didn't care for the fame and glory associated with winning. After passing Cape Horn, he decided to turn round and sail back the way he had come across the Southern Ocean twice rather than return to England.

So, I was in good company. My mind was clearly displaying similar behaviour. Here I was within touching distance of ending this insanity, allowing my broken body to rest. The perfect ending; get to Jeff's and have a few beers. A good laugh. A few nights out, a curry perhaps. Maybe even a bit of sightseeing at Loch Ness.

I didn't want it to end here!

WHAT? What was I thinking!

"Fool! Don't be so stupid," said my right brain.

"It won't take long to get around the rest of the UK. How bad can it be?" said my left brain.

It was time to go. I trudged down in the morning darkness and crawled across the top of the MOD27 sitting upside down on the pontoon. There was no room to put my feet down either side because the platform it was resting on was narrower than the hull so I was balancing on the upturned hull. The rig was lying further along the jetty. I hadn't even bothered untying any of it when I landed late last night. I simply took the whole sail connected to the boom out of the mast step and tied it flat on the concrete wharf. I'd done this a lot in the past 29 days but not often on such a rickety, wobbly pontoon. Rigging my boat in Banff harbour was a proper high wire act, one that required my full concentration. I clearly wasn't giving it today. I was thinking over and over about the end of my journey. Struggling with my inner thoughts, I lowered the boat off the pontoon into the water and by a miracle, stepped the rig in the hole, without falling in. Only to realise the MOD27 was pointing the wrong way round, facing downwind.

"Oh for God's sake," I swore at myself.

"What an idiot!" I said out loud.

The harbour mouth was too narrow to sail round in a circle. I didn't want to go through the effort of untying the rig, spinning the boat round and re-tying everything again. All I needed to do was tack or gybe round. Very cautiously, I tried pushing the MOD27 around but the wind was too strong. I pushed a bit further, keeping one leg on the pontoon and one on the boat then…

"Aaaaah" Splash!

I was in the freezing water, head fully submerged, thrashing around trying to keep hold of the boat which now wanted to sail off down wind. One hand on the pontoon, I let go of the boat. It capsized after the mainsheet very fortuitously snagged on the mooring eye attached to the pontoon.

"What a calamity. Thank goodness no one is up and watching," I thought.

It took me a good 20 minutes to sort myself out and by now I was shivering, cold and wet before I even got started. That was a wake up call. Scrambling back up onto the pontoon, I lost all thoughts of tomorrow and focused 100% on the now. I was shivering badly when I headed out of the harbour in the direction of Lossiemouth. Hello today, here I am again.

In the world on this day, the 14th August 2019, the day I was hoping to complete my trip to Jeff's, across the other side of the world in Hong Kong, protests were erupting. New Chinese laws resulted in the international airport terminals being barricaded by hordes of masked objectors. William, my eldest son, was flying back from Hong Kong airport that day to visit his parents for a few weeks in the summer, only neither of his parents would be at home when he arrived. Apparently, he'd risked life and limb to come back to see us in England, making a dash for it through the airport protest lines when they were distracted by a baton charge by the police. A day later, the Hong Kong government closed the airport so Will made it back to England to see Mum and Dad in Eastbourne. Another reason to stop at Jeff's.

I was lucky with the breeze. It was a brisk southerly to start. I raced around another load of dangerous headlands. Same style, different names. Whitehills, Strathmarcin, past Portsoy harbour and around Redhythe Point, on past the ruins of Findlater Castle which looks like it's been carved into the cliff face, sailing as close to the rock face as I dare to shorten the distance of travel, knowing somewhere not very far underneath the breaking surf, lapping under the cliff would be jagged rocks just lying in wait especially to stop stupid sailors of tiny Lasers from making it to Jeff's. I was wise to it by now. When I came in very tight to the rocks, I got so close sometimes I could nearly reach out and touch the cliff faces, I'd slightly heel the boat over. Instead of looking forwards where I was heading, I'd crane my neck over the side of the boat and look underneath at the front of the centreboard protruding a few feet into the sea. I could see the outline of the rocks I was skimming above. Every now and again I'd lose my nerve in shallow water and dive inboard, rapidly pulling up the board, hoping my rudder would still clear the underwater obstruction. I sailed like this for hours and often got my head stuck in this position with a neck spasm and cramp down one side of my body.

The MOD27 and I felt happy together. I knew she was leaking quite badly through the bow but I still trusted her. She'd looked after me when it mattered. Nothing had broken of any significance. The sail looked pretty tired as did my sailing clothes. My hands were tough as leather now, my fingers curled in a semi-permanent grip shape. Although my knee still hurt, it wasn't as bad now I wasn't hiking into the wind every day. I was cracking off these final miles averaging 7 knots through the water and the tide was with me. It was looking good for Lossiemouth. I'd decided to defer any big decisions about the journey until after I saw Jeff. I planned to leave the boat at Lossiemouth. This meant if I carried on, I wouldn't have to sail all the way inland to Inverness then back again. I could sail directly across the Moray Firth to Dornoch, Golspie or Brora, depending how brave I was feeling. If I stopped here, it would be easy enough to lift the boat onto the van roof and drive away south.

The winds had lightened as I approached Lossiemouth harbour. The entrance to the harbour is quite imposing, it has a high wall acting as an arm extending well out into the sea. Sitting at 90 degrees to me as I approached, there was a big swell running around the arm. I didn't like the look of the northern end of the wall, all I could see were white surf and rocks so I steered for where I imagined the opening to the entrance was. It was only when I was within 50 metres from the opening when it became obvious. Initially I thought I was travelling to the wrong side of the harbour. I slid past the wall riding a big wave and spun in behind the protection of the harbour arm, being careful to keep my distance so as not to lose all of my wind from the high wall. Once inside the harbour there is a labyrinth of smaller harbours and pontoons. I found my way through one wall, then another, then through a narrow entrance way. Inside the inner harbour were rows of neatly lined up yachts and a narrow concrete slipway sitting at the end. I tied up to the pontoon just before the slipway. Emma had met a local yachtsman by the name of Billy who'd helped me navigate the harbour, directing me over the phone.

On shore, Billy helped roll up the sail and then watched in shock at how much water was draining out of the hull as I tipped the MOD27 up. I removed everything that could be stolen and loaded it into the van, lashed the boat down on top of the rolled-up mast and sail and thanked Billy for his help. The harbour was deserted but I found a shower block and with the help of a man working on his boat, managed to get into the block using his passcode to rinse the salt off.

I'd done it! Eastbourne to Inverness. Well almost.

Jeff cracked up into a fit of giggles when he saw Emma pull up with me in the van outside his house in Ardersier on the shore of Loch Ness. I hadn't sailed up to the shingle bank outside his back garden as we originally discussed. I could tell he was slightly disappointed.

I wasn't!

Dedication

For Chris Fyans

Special Thanks

Part 1 – Just to Jeff's

To everyone who assisted and donated to make this incredible journey a success including to name a few...

The Safety Channel - Emma, Peter, Rupert, Dave, Roger G, Roger O G,

Others who assisted before and during the journey Jeffski, Terry the Wand, Ron, Jeremy, Aussie Jeff, John Jono, James A (for the oars), Roger W (Weatherman), Gary S (Eastbourne's special genius), Ellie, the Jevington Eight Bells gang, Aaron at Simpson Marine, George my son.

People who assisted along the way-

Richard & Jaqui (Hythe). Simon his partner and all at Broadstairs SC. Fiona - President of Brightlingsea SC and Tom the barman (solid changing room floors have never felt so comfortable). The fisherman at Aldeburgh (for parking and fish n chips). Aunty Jenny, Uncle Mick, Gemma and Martyn (Southwold). Mario (top tip to sleep under the steps) and Paul and his family (Mundesley) for the massive breakfast. The young Lifeguards at West Runton. Jim Hawkins and his family (Sandilands), Brad his fishing mate and Mark from Sand-Le-Mere. The lovely receptionist and Angela and Eric from Whitby Yacht Club. The fisherman at Skinningrove and Stephen at Saltburn (for the advice and entertainment). John and everyone at Tynemouth SC. Steve from Amble Yacht Club (thanks for the diner). Richard, Aida and all Beadnell Bay SC (I'll be back in 20 years for the next Laser regatta). John and the life guards at Coldingham Bay (amazing skipping talent). Isla, her two Scottish Terriers - Seamus and Finlay and Amy the receptionist at Crail Golf Society (Lovely towels). Roddy the Arbroath harbour master (thanks for the shower). Ditta, her family and everyone at Stonehaven SC. (Sorry I lost your praddle at sea). The Aberdeen harbour master for keeping me safe from impatient "FBS". Angie and the Aberdeen Sailing Trust (hugely inspiring work). Neil from Eastbourne (for the phone rip tide advice getting off the beach). Buccaneer Marine Supplies, MacDuff (for the offer to take a hatch cover off one of their storage boats). Peter, Anna and Huntley the dog and the Rosehearty Community Boat Club especially Ian and Graham for the repairs. Durrant Hotel for the free meal. Mark and Banff Yacht Club (for the biscuits and allowing us to use the kitchen and warm up by the fire). Billy at Lossiemouth Harbour (assisting with navigation and hauling the slowly sinking MOD27 out of the water).

Big thanks to everyone who followed on Facebook and all of the messages of support and donations to Prostate Cancer UK, and anyone I might have overlooked or forgotten.

Finally, thanks to my Mum and Dad for encouraging me to get into sailing.

EMMA & STICK

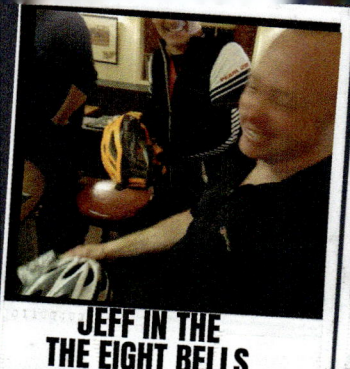
JEFF IN THE THE EIGHT BELLS

RON

G5 (L-R) PETE, RUPERT, DAVE, STICK ROGER

£50 BOAT PURCHASE

KEELBAND P31

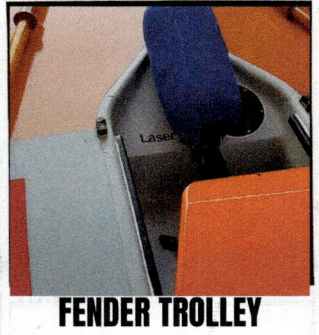
FENDER TROLLEY

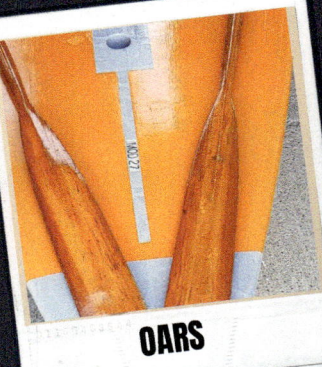
OARS

ELECTRICAL PACK

SPOTX, VHF, MOBILE P34

MINI FLARE PACK

EASTBOURNE PIER
LEAVING DAY 1

17TH JULY
EASTBOURNE DAY 1

HYTHE FIRING RANGE
ESCORT P46

RONS LEAKY TENT
1ST NIGHT HYTHE

JAQUI & RICHARD
HYTHE P53

SIMON FIELD & PT
BROADSTAIRS DAY

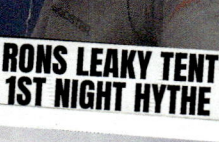
ARRAY WIND FARM
THAMES ESTUARY P62

DAY 3 COLNE POINT
P72

DAY 4 UNCLE MICK
& FAMILY P88

GEMMA WITH A PINT
OF ADNAMS BEER P96

DAY 5 MUNDESLEY
LIFEBOAT STATION P99

DAY 6 WEST RUNTON
P107

DAY 7 JIM HAWKINS SANDILANDS P115

DAY 7 UFO SANDILANDS P115

DAY 8 BRAD (2L) & MARK (2R) SAND-LE-MERE

DAY 9 FILEY 1ST CONTACT ON LANDING

DAY 10 WHITBY ERIC & ANGELA P143

RECEPTIONIST WHITBY YACHT CLUB

PACKING UP AT WHITBY

SAFE STORAGE SKINNINGROVE

SHORE DUMP STUCK SKINNINGROVE

SKINNINGROVE DAY 12-14

SIGNALS BAR SALTBURN

DAY 12 STEVEN DRURY SALTBURN P 152

A NORTH SEA "BFS"

MOD

TYNEMOUTH LIFEGUARDS

DAY 15 TYNEMOUTH SAILING CLU

DAY 16 STATUES NEWBIGGIN P169

DAY 16 AMBLE STEVE VOGEL P170

DAY 17 BEADNELL BAY RICHARD & AISLA P171

DAY 19 COLDINGHAM BAY

DAY 20 ISLA CRAIL FIFENESS

FINLAY & SEAMUS P181

UNRIGGING - CRAIL

RODDY HARBOURMASTER SMILE OFF P62

DAY 21 ARBROATH HARBOUR

DAY 22 DITTA STONEHAVEN P187

DAY 23 CROSSING ABERDEEN HARBOUR

COLLIESTON BAY

DAY 24 PETERHEAD

DAY 25 CRAIG EWAN BEACH P196

KIERAN & ANGIE ABERDEEN SAILING TRUST

DAY 27 ROSEHEARTY

IAN & GRAEME ROSEHEARTY P204

DAVRON HOTEL

PETER CRAWFORD & HUNTLEY DOG

DAY 28 BANFF SAILING CLUB P210

FIRE ON IN BANFF 13TH AUGUST

BILLY HELPS ME AT LOSSIEMOUTH HARBOUR

DAY 29 - AUGUST 14TH ARRIVED AT JEFFS

EMMA ARRIVES WITH LEO LOOKING FOR NES

The Amazing Adventures of Stick Daring

Part 2
Laugh? I Nearly Died

Chapter 25

Monsters and Madness

When I mentioned to Jeff I was coming to see him back in June, a month before departing, he fell about laughing. After a few days he then started to take it a bit more seriously and bombarded me with facts about Loch Ness and the Cairngorms. He told me how he wakes up each morning and looks out on great hanging clouds over looming mountain ranges. There was so much information to digest I didn't bother and just pretended to listen.

Until Jeff moved to Ardersier, I'd only ever learnt about Loch Ness from a primary school project I did on the monster there, known affectionately by the locals as Nessie. Even back then I don't think I placed where it was on the UK map except that it was in Scotland. For those of you unfamiliar with the fable of the Loch Ness monster, it dates back to the 6th century. The Irish saint, St Columba, was ordered by one of his monks to swim across the loch and fetch a boat. Halfway across, the monster appeared and went for the swimmer.

Shouting loudly at the monster as it approached, Columba cried out, "Go no further, nor touch the man! Go back!"

The monster is said to have fled!

Since then, Nessie has been seen many times and no one has been harmed. Sightings have been sporadic over the centuries but in the 20th century Nessie has apparently been more active which has attracted significant numbers of tourists.

The first photograph taken of the monster was in 1933 showing an eel-like creature with a long neck arched over a thick body. This photograph, taken by a London surgeon, caused a sensation when it was first published in the Daily Mail.

The circus owner, Bertram Mills, offered a £20,000 reward (the equivalent of £2 million today) to anyone who could capture the monster for his circus but so far no one has claimed the reward.

In 1951, Lachlan Stuart, a forestry worker, also managed to photograph the monster. He saw three humps in the water appear in a line and ran back to his house to get his camera. After taking one photograph, his camera shutter jammed but his photograph got wide publicity.

Over the years, several scientific investigations have taken place, attracting two submarines and a number of sonar experts! When the submarine Pisces was diving off Castle Urquhart, a vast underwater cavern 950 feet deep was found and some suggested it was Nessie's home.

In 1975, four firemen from Hemel Hempstead decided that the monster must be a male and built a 309-foot long papier-mâché 'lady monster' to attract 'Mr Nessie'. Her false eyelashes, full make-up and a pre-recorded mating call, which turned out to be that of a male walrus, still weren't enough to tempt Nessie out of hiding!

Here I was parked outside Jeff's having completed our dare. I felt numb; not really sure what had just happened to me for the past 29 days. Sailing around 700 miles in every weather condition, experiencing more emotions I'd ever known bar one – death – which I felt I'd never come that close to except perhaps on one occasion.

It was over. I'd made it!

Jeff greeted Emma and I and spent an age directing us where to park the van. We ended up directly outside one of his neighbour's windows, blocking out most of their light. I could sense the net curtains twitching as we tried to reduce the impact of our somewhat out of place white Transit van in this picturesque little hamlet.

As soon as we got out the van, Jeff immediately took us across the road to see his new house. We were given a guided tour of his property, surrounded by acres of mud following the relentless monsoon Scotland had been experiencing that summer. Jeff was positively exploding with enthusiasm and excitement though, oblivious of the ankle-deep mud we were tip-toeing over. He eulogised about the new front door I'd sent him before I departed. He was bouncing off the ceiling telling us every detail about the village, the shore view and his new- found life in Scotland.

We were joined by their two dogs including Leo, the English Bull Terrier that Jeff had brought up from a puppy over the past 11 years, and a ridiculously large bouncy wire-haired thing belonging to his new partner Louise. Leo was well known to us from Eastbourne, a terrifying looking dog like Bill Sykes' in Oliver Twist. He looked like he would eat you if you made a false move. Fortunately, Jeff had raised him from a baby and Leo had assumed a similar personality to his owner, preferring to lick you to death than any sort of confrontation. He was an absolute baby. Be it a rather smelly and extraordinarily powerful one.

The following day we did the tourist thing, visiting the shores of Loch Ness. Nessie clearly hadn't heard I was coming or was busy but dispatched an advance party of mosquitoes to greet us anyway. We ate at the local pub, The Dores Inn, appropriately named. Emma and I then spent another chilly night sleeping in the van. I think I'd already made up my mind before arriving at Jeff's. I'd got some momentum via Facebook and my fledgling following was growing, sending messages of support. Their fascination and desire for me to succeed really buoyed me on. I'd promised to circumnavigate the UK to raise money for Prostate Cancer UK and people had already been so generous in coughing up their cash on our Just Giving page. Yet a bit of me had been holding back in my mind and I hadn't quite committed. Emma tried deliberately not to influence me. She loved the challenge and liked to see my 'grit' but she knew it would be much more dangerous so assured me it was entirely a personal decision for me. This was a big moment. I felt drained but strangely like this was just what I needed to do. I was carrying on.

We hurriedly hatched a plan that night to leave the van at Jeff's. Emma wanted to return to Eastbourne to meet Will. She booked a flight from Inverness airport, which was literally a mile away, for two days' time and set off with me the following morning. We headed back to Lossiemouth where the MOD27 was stored. Emma planned to travel one more day with me before returning to Jeff's and leave me until I'd made it around the top of Scotland. The geography along the top of Scotland would make it very difficult to follow me in a vehicle.

When I sailed out of Lossiemouth harbour I was on Day 31 of the trip. Jeff and everyone I met kept asking me how long it would take me to complete the rest of the way around the UK. They asked me in a way that assumed I might have some idea. I'd usually reply,

"I don't actually have a scoobies."

This didn't have any impact upon the questioners who would press me for a more accurate answer, thinking I was just hedging.

When I followed up with, "Honestly I have no idea," they seemed rather deflated, as if I could magic up a number for them instantly.

"It's not like I've done this before," I privately muttered. "I'm just making it up as I go along!"

Chapter 26

Fun and Games at Helmsdale

How nice of Helmsdale to lay on the Highland Games for me especially after making such a lengthy crossing today. Setting off on part two of this voyage this morning hadn't been easy. In fact, as I'd sailed out through Lossiemouth harbour I nearly turned back as the boat careered off on a screaming reach out into the next chapter of a very alien place to me.

It was windy. Again! I was running before the wind, sitting right back in the boat and the surf was still soaking me. I'd set a course to Durnock initially but this was proving just too square to the wind to be comfortable so I eased the MOD27 onto a broader reach aiming more northerly. No chance of hugging the coastline with this breeze. I was just going to have to aim for the middle of the sea, heading miles off shore and grit my teeth.

Tarbat Ness Lighthouse sits on the end of a long promontory opposite Durnock on the other side of the Moray Firth. Heading further north east set me on a course to the open sea but the tighter angle was quicker and more stable. As I passed by the lighthouse, I gave her a wide berth. The shoals around were kicking up some seriously steep, short waves. The weather closed in and rain obscured most of my view of the lighthouse for an hour or more. As it cleared, I realised I'd made it past and was now heading directly towards the north east tip of Scotland. How brave was I feeling? Well, I must have been reasonably confident because I made it across to Brora, sailing a straight line across a stretch of open water which I recorded as close to 50 km.

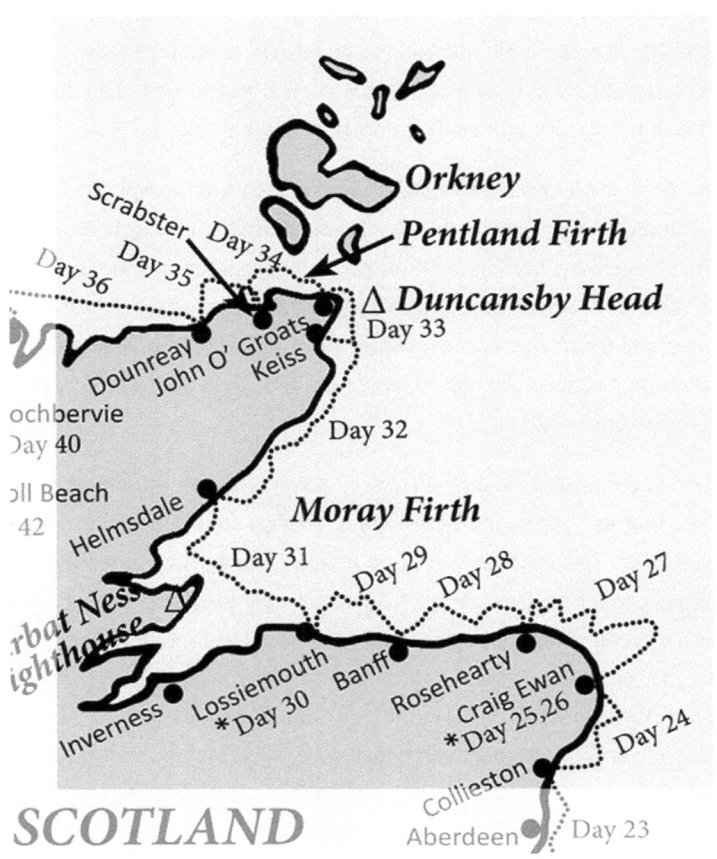

Once I reached Brora, I made my way along the coastline again, staying reasonably tight to the shore. The thing that struck me here was the sheer scale of the mountain ranges with billowing clouds all around them. Vari-coloured grey, white and black, it looked as if someone had taken a ball of cotton wool and rolled it in charcoal unevenly then spread this out over the sky. It looked strikingly powerful; way too powerful for me to want to hang around here much longer. I paused and checked the Navionics app. Helmsdale harbour looked a good option. I had no idea at all what it would be like but communicated this plan to Emma.

She was on her last day with me in the van. Emma would have to return to Inverness to catch her plane, taking off at 7 am tomorrow. She couldn't believe how far I'd managed to travel. The drive for her by road was 107 miles. She was only part of the way so it was going to take her an age to catch me up through winding narrow mountain roads.

Coming in to Helmsdale harbour, I very nearly went through the wrong entrance. Many years ago, after a particularly poor season, the local fishermen blamed the harbour wall for preventing salmon making their way up river to their spawning grounds. As they paid for leases to catch salmon around the foreshore, this was an urgent situation that required similarly urgent action. The agreed solution was to dynamite a hole in the side of the harbour wall.

When I approached the harbour, I very nearly sailed in through the giant hole that still had debris all around it left over from the day it was dynamited. The swell and sea were foaming. Fortunately it looked treacherous enough to dissuade me from attempting to enter here and after turning around and sailing back along the wall, I discovered the real entrance. This too wasn't easy as there was a tidal wave rolling in between the high walls flanking the harbour mouth. Taking a particularly large roller, I made it through safely and bundled my way onto the end of one of the floating pontoons nestled amongst the commercial fishing boats.

The place was deserted. So, following the same process I'd perfected at Banff, I hauled the MOD27 out of the water onto the pontoon two feet above, turning the hull upside down and lashing her to the mooring eyes. She sat proudly on the tip of the pontoon. I'd unstepped the rig in the water first and it was lying flat rather precariously further along the jetty. Not surprisingly, it took off in the wind while still attached to the boat by the mainsheet. Fortunately nothing was lost. Nevertheless, another small rip in the sail was added to the previous ones. I felt especially unhappy about this.

I was in no hurry as I knew Emma would be ages. Looking around, there was no one in the harbour at all, it was like a ghost town. So, making my way up the pontoons, climbing along the steep ramp to the village road I could see a congregation of camper vans parked up close by. There were a few people just sitting around in folding chairs outside, drinking and chatting.

I sat on the wooden bench in my wetsuit observing and realised everyone was doing the same to me. I felt quite self-conscious. I must have looked pretty odd to this lot. They looked a lot like tourists but oddly all had a similar dishevelled long-haired look. Almost a uniform, but not quite.

The sun had broken through the cloud and it felt good to be warm. I really wished I had some food with me. This was still inside the boat and would be a real pain to retrieve now. All my spare clothes were in the van. I decided to dry out the sail over the slipway railings so that the repair tape would stick better when I applied it.

Making my way to the harbour master's office, there was a note pinned to the door advising that the toilet facilities would be closed during the Highland Games. Visiting boats could call a mobile number that was scribbled in handwriting on an A4 sheet of paper. I rang the number and reached a voicemail leaving a short message but also texted the number.

Returning to the bench, I could see the sail was taking off so, running flat out, I just caught it before it blew into the harbour sea 20 feet below. Having narrowly averted disaster, I bundled the sail up and stuffed it under the bench to stop it flying away again. Drying could wait. Time dragged and nothing happened.

Several hours later, Emma arrived in a fizz. She'd been driving flat out to catch up along some tiny roads. Shortly after she arrived, the harbour master, Donald Sutherland, texted me. I called him back and he offered me the use of the toilets and shower facilities. There was a combination code. He said they weren't usually closed but because today was the Highland Games, they shut them to prevent campers abusing them.

I have to say they were good toilets. The entrance was a tiny green brace and ledge door but once inside it was like an atrium with vaulted high ceilings and beams. It was spotless and laid out like a public swimming baths changing room. There were two shower cubicles and two toilets. The showers not only had hot water, they also had heated rails along the inside of each cubicle and, get this, a large infra-red heat lamp suspended from the ceiling. I pressed on all the switches and revived my aged body basking in the glowing red heat and boiling hot water.

Donald made an appearance as I exited the block. He was a softly spoken man with thick set eyes and a strong Viking jaw. Grey hair disguised his weather-beaten face but I figured he was probably about my age. He was very friendly and we talked a little about John O'Groats. Emma was disappointed she'd come all this way with me but wasn't going to make it to the top of Scotland because she had to return home. We were only 50 miles away. Still, there was no appetite on my part to drive with her to John O'Groats just to say we had, especially as it was a 100 mile round trip. I don't think Emma wanted to drive any more really either. We were both tired. Looking around for a place to pitch the tent, Donald suggested inside the toilets might be preferable as the forecast was torrential rain overnight. I quickly agreed, thanking him and watching him disappear almost as soon as he'd arrived.

The nearest pub in town was packed and had very low ceilings so I sat in a small side room because standing up was so uncomfortable. I needed to recharge everything so I brought the bag full of chargers. These took up every plug socket in the pub, even the locals public bar. I was nervous as I couldn't see all of the appliances from the tiny room I was sitting in. Anyone could walk off with my phone or VHF or Spot X or, worse still, the whole lot and I probably wouldn't have noticed. It made me edgy and even after a few pints whilst talking with the landlord and his son, I never really felt at ease.

The town was hopping. The Highland Games were a big deal here with the population swelling by some 700 people for this event. There was lots of drinking and laughter, a bit of punchy behaviour with a couple of youngsters and plenty of arm wrestling and beer spilling. I was tempted to stay a day to watch the opening ceremony tomorrow. Emma really wanted to stay too and the thought of her leaving was stressful for us both.

I'd be back on my own again. Carrying all my gear, getting wet in Ron's leaky tent. She'd be back in Eastbourne within 24 hours, 600 miles away.

I left the pub feeling tired and irritable. The pressure of Emma getting up tomorrow at 5 am to catch a plane from Inverness was nagging in the back of my mind. Where to park the van in Inverness for four weeks? Would Jeff get his girlfriend out of bed in time to drive Emma to the airport? How long would it take her to get back from here in the morning? What about the forecast of floods? I think these stresses were beginning to tell and, not entirely surprisingly, Emma and I had an argument by the time we'd reached the van. Neither of us could sleep, pressed together uncomfortably closely in the van. By 4 am she decided enough was enough. I was turfed out of the van and decamped to the toilet block while Emma set off in the driving rain to weave her way back to Inverness and fly back home to Eastbourne. She was gone in an instant. I felt sad and pretty low after she left. It was a terrible way to say goodbye.

In spite of the circumstances, my memories of Helmsdale are warm. I believe they have the best harbour toilets in the whole of Scotland, certainly the warmest. Breakfast was minimal in the morning, cooking up porridge on my tiny single ring gas burner inside the toilets.

My thoughts now turned to Duncansby Head. This is the notorious north east tip of Scotland, with up to 10 knot tidal races and standing waves. I needed to look up and plan this bit thoroughly. No one I'd spoken to about this headland thought it was a good idea to go around it in such a small boat. In fact, nearly everyone had said I was mad. I dismissed this as negative thinking. That is until I chatted with Donald on the quayside as I was rigging up the following morning.

Donald owned a small yacht he kept in the harbour. Casually he asked me if I wanted to look at the charts on his yacht whilst I was rigging on the pontoon. I was very keen to learn more so, finishing off tying everything together, I hurriedly made my way to his boat that was moored on the same pontoon. Very soon we were pouring over his charts and Donald was explaining where I should aim to set up camp the night before rounding Duncansby Head. He explained that going round the headland, it was crucial to get there during or just before slack water. His advice was to stay tight to the cliffs, he was convinced this was the best way to round.

I said, "Donald, everyone I've met so far tells me Duncansby Head is terrible but can you tell me honestly? How bad is it?"

"Honestly?" he replied questioningly.

"Yes honestly," I said, looking him squarely in the eyes.

He paused before answering, looking downcast and deadly serious,

"Bloody awful!"

Chapter 27

Moine Schists at Duncansby Head

After a very informative conversation with Donald Sutherland, I was apprehensive about the next two days and determined to get as close to Duncansby Head and its 60 metre high twin sea stacks as I could. This was my best chance to navigate the complex tidal flows around the north east tip of Scotland.

Setting off from Helmsdale, I was sailing along the coast of Caithness and Sutherland. This area of Scotland is notable for its sheer rocky cliffs and sheltered coves – a landscape fashioned by geology formed from an ancient continent that included Canada and Greenland. More than five hundred million years of geological history are recorded in the rocks. Thick piles of sea-floor sediments have accumulated over millions of years. Twentieth century geologists have termed the rock formed by the pressure of time as the Moine Schists laid on top of Gneiss bedrock, believed to be even more ancient, possibly as much as 3,000 million years old.

To me, it looked just like granite. I don't recall being particularly interested in its geological foundation at the time. However, the term "Oh Schist" did come to mind when approaching Keiss harbour. Of the 40 mile journey, my only recollection was passing a terrifyingly beautiful natural harbour. I subsequently found out this was Whaligoe Steps. If you approach from the land side, there are steps down the cliff that allow you to see into the harbour, protected by vast slabs of semi-submerged quartzite rock, where breakers crash, foam and gouge holes in the cliffs. Not a place I was naturally attracted to in my Laser.

Keiss was the nearest soft landing point before the Duncansby headland. Surfing in towards the harbour, all I could see was another ancient wreck of a castle standing precariously on the cliff edge overlooking the harbour walls like a protective old warrior. I assumed when it was originally built there was more rock beneath the walls but for now it looked vulnerable, as if it was about to topple into the sea any second. It's extraordinary that the sea had managed to pulverise this incredibly hard rock to such an extent in just a few hundred years.

The harbour had a tiny entrance. A flat, concrete wall protected the front with a gap just wide enough to squeeze two boats through if side by side. All around, the sea was whipping into the beach, driving in long, foaming rollers as far as I could see. Dark shadows were visible just beneath the shoreline and great slabs of rock framed the entrance ominously. From previous beach landing experiences, the harbour definitely looked like the safest option. I reached in, it was blowing close on 25 knots and the sky was dark with drizzly rain. There was nothing comforting about this place. It looked uninviting. Visibility was poor so it was impossible to tell how to get in safely. As I closed in, I couldn't figure out how a sailing boat like mine could get in without hitting the wall. I'd have to sail on a reach through the entrance then immediately gybe to get to the inner harbour. It was super narrow and very windy and the restricted manoeuvrability in an unknown place suddenly put me off. I bailed out, turned around and headed straight back out to sea well away from the rocky shoreline. It was late, very late and getting dark. Bloody scary to be honest!

I surfed up and down the coastline, sailing back and forth along the vast bay before I could see what I was looking for. Sand dunes. I'd formulated a plan. I was now a mile or two south of the harbour. It looked like all the submerged rocks were congregated along the northern end of the bay. The surf felt stronger here in the south but I could see the beach and dunes behind with green bits on top. There were no obvious rocks and I was tired and needed to stop so decided to go for it. Approaching at maximum speed, a decent size wave washed me up onto the wet sand, far enough up the beach to allow me to escape from the next wave cascading onto the shore.

Here I was, standing on Sinclair Bay, Keiss. Not a thing close by, just a set of dunes 30 feet tall and miles of crescent beach laid out before me. In the distance, the outline of the castle ruin was silhouetted against the granite sky. There was nothing else for it; I'd have to unpack my tent and find a spot in the dunes and set up for a solitary night with my rice and mackerel rations.

Just after I'd hauled the boat up the beach and resigned myself to a night of solitude, in the distance I thought I could make out a man walking in my direction. It was windy and raining, the time was around 7.30 pm. Anywhere else, this wouldn't have seemed out of the ordinary but here, in the middle of nowhere, in this weather at this time, it did! The man approached and started talking to me a long way off:

"Hello is that a Laser? Are you staying here? I saw you coming out of the harbour and wondered if you needed any help."

My new friend was called Richard. He was a German tourist, visiting Scotland in his camper van with his wife, Regula. They were parked about a mile along the beach towards the lights of some civilisation. Richard had been looking out to sea when he saw me surf up the beach. He thought I was staying in the harbour and that I may have broken something. He had a flask of hot coffee with him and offered me a drink. I couldn't quite believe it and accepted gratefully. He then offered me some soup and bread. Before I could even pretend to resist, he was off at lightning speed, making his way back to his camper van to fetch more supplies.

When he returned, I'd successfully located a hollow high up in the dunes out of the direct wind blowing hats off anything that moved onshore. My tent was pitched and all my gear unpacked and stowed. Richard had brought Regula with him. I ravenously stuffed as much hot noodle soup and crusty bread in as he could give me as if I hadn't eaten for a week. We decided to visit a pub together in the village later that evening once I'd struggled out of my wetsuit which was feeling very itchy. We agreed to meet at their van, a mile back along the beach.

By the time I'd sorted my gear out, changed and walked the mile back to Richard's van which he then drove into town it was past 9 pm. We stopped at the first pub we found, The Sinclair Arms. I was still starving and after buying Regula and Richard both a drink enquired of the bar staff if they had any food. The young bar girl, Emmaline, looked like she might have already eaten most of the food but very politely explained the kitchen was closed. She did have some Monster Munch crisps though! So, dinner was several packets of Monster Munch in assorted flavours and beer. Quite a few of each in the end. We had a cracking evening talking to the locals including James, Gordon and Kettie. Richard joined in the conversation, becoming increasingly more animated with his near perfect English and then German as the beer flowed. Regula smiled in the corner talking to two other German visitors touring Scotland. I was engrossed in conversation with the three Scottish lads, all of whom were seafarers of some description or other. I was digging for any tips on rounding Duncansby Head and its infamously dangerous tidal flows and cliffs. Had I understood the thick Glaswegian accent of the most knowledgeable conversant, who's name I forget, it would have been very useful indeed. Sadly, our mutual excessive consumption of beer and a very slurred dialect made most of the gold coming from his lips completely unintelligible to me!

Dropping me off in the car park on the beach where their van still stood, Richard and Regula said goodbye. As I stepped cautiously along the sand dune path, I realised I hadn't any idea where my tent was. There was no moon and it was very dark. I trudged back along the beach trying to follow my footsteps. I had a tiny head torch but the battery was low so it was of little use. After 20 minutes of walking I guessed I must have missed the hollow dune in which I had pitched my tent. This was high above me in a hollow invisible from where I was standing. It took an hour to locate the tent. Crawling inside, I collapsed into my sleeping bag and was snoring within seconds.

Next morning at 6 am it was still raining. All my gear was wet inside and outside the tent. The only good bit was the makeshift washing line made from my boom where I'd strung my wetsuit and buoyancy aid both of which had been rinsed out by the rain. Looking out to sea, the view was of relentless white surf. I pulled out my notebook and scribbled down the tide times I'd worked out in the pub late last night then set about making breakfast. This consisted of cheesy pasta made from a dried packet and coffee, both cooked on my single pocket size gas stove. Studying my notes from the night before, I tried to calculate the best time to leave Keiss for Duncansby Head. In one of my dry bags I had a few torn out pages from the Cruising Almanac published by Imray. I'd only brought the pages I thought covered the most notorious bits of the journey. Duncansby Head was one of them. Reading aloud to myself it read,

> *"Duncansby Head to Cape Wrath*
>
> *Passage through or across the Pentland Firth, which is one of the most dangerous stretches of water in the British Isles, where tidal streams may reach 16kn, requires accurate timing...It should not be*

attempted at Spring tides, wind over Force 4, wind against tide or swell, or in poor visibility."

When I checked my weather app after reading this it was showing 20 knots gusting 30, at 7 am, moderating to 16 knots gusting 29 by midday.

"Oh shit!" I said out loud.

I kept looking at the soggy pages of the Almanac and re-reading the last paragraph.

"Hmm!" I thought to myself as the jitters welled up in my stomach.

I recalled Donald Sutherland's parting words about Duncansby Head as we'd both poured over the tidal charts in his yacht at Helmsdale.

"It's bloody awful."

Those were his exact words. As they left his lips, it was like pins popping my balloon of optimism. My heart had sunk.

"Surely it can't be that bad," I told myself to try to find some positive motivational sentiments from deep inside.

I re-read every detail on the Duncansby Head to Cape Wrath section of the Almanac. I'd torn these pages out of the 2015 version I'd bought on offer in a book store several years before this trip. The pages were folded in half and stuffed into my A5 Aquapac log book bag.

Anyone who has seen a Cruising Association Almanac will know they're not exactly pocket sized. Designed for use on a yacht navigation table, rather than a soaking wet Laser, even in the environment of a spacious and dry cabin they're considered bulky. There's so much detail in this sailing bible, it's impossible to fully appreciate how long it must take to create unless you've ever tried to produce something like this. I was appreciating every detail but almost wishing I hadn't read them.

It wasn't what I wanted to know. No-one was saying the right things about this particular part of the journey sitting right at my feet!

"It is beautiful. The cliffs are spectacular. When you pass this point you can see the end of the world. The orcas will probably guide you round and wave you on your way."

There were no such words coming off the Almanac pages. Maybe their contributor for Duncansby Head had a bad day when they sailed this passage? Perhaps they weren't a very competent sailor? Somehow, I knew this probably wasn't true.

I had some experience collating information from contributors. I'd spent five insane years of my life publishing a baby equipment testing magazine; a venture Emma and I started and ran together. Emma had dreamt up the idea, a directory specialising in reviewing and cataloguing the latest baby equipment. Like a What Car equivalent magazine for baby gear and it'd seemed a good idea at the beginning over a glass of wine or two one Christmas. We poured our limited budget and thousands of pounds of other people's money into this venture. So many hours, burning the midnight oil, checking every fine detail from freelance writers and consumer reviews. Having assembled a vast team of volunteer product testers across the country, we thoroughly checked and rated everything anyone could possibly ever need for a new baby or toddler. Our testers pushed prams over bumpy ground, stuck 10 different types of dummy in their poor child's mouths, tested sleep suits, garden slides, car seats and baby gyms and meticulously recorded the results against predetermined criteria. We tried out upside down cups, plastic spoons, baby slings that load from the top, bottom, side and back. We ate every flavour of baby food and developed ways of storing breast milk that would make your eyes pop.

We both worked a million hours on this project from our garage near Horsham where we lived at the time. Emma always seemed to be surrounded by throngs of pregnant mums testing equipment for us and writing reviews. She recruited a local friend, Jacqui Collis, whose desk in our garage was permanently deluged with piles of surveys and questionnaires. Meanwhile there was baby equipment packed to the ceiling in every one of the seven sheds dotted around our back garden.

Somehow eventually we wrestled our way into the baby magazine market. This sector is one of the most cut throat areas in publishing. Every major magazine publishing house had a baby title. We found ourselves competing against the giants of the media world. We tried all sorts of tricks, ducking and diving on a daily basis to stay alive. We even partnered up with a plethora of entrepreneurial mums setting up a national network of regional baby shows. These arrangements generally involved me spending all weekend with a team of helpers dishing out magazines in some far-flung location around the UK. I visited so many places. Slowly and painfully and very expensively we dragged our way up the slippery readership pole.

By some miracle, each month Emma interpreted the assortment of data and printed a highly detailed review of each product "on test" and handed out much sought after and celebrated Platinum, Gold and Silver awards. Oh yes, I was well versed with the time it takes to research the details for a publication of this type. I was also fully versed in the consequences if you get it wrong. Consumers, manufacturers, retailers and just about everyone you meet has an opinion. We would get bombarded with emails from disgruntled manufacturers if they didn't come out top.

I knew the Almanac was definitely accurate. I tried to persuade myself it was like that old adage about the weather:

"It's not cold, you just have the wrong clothes on."

In that case, even I managed to conclude that today was almost definitely the wrong type of wind for rounding Duncansby Head.

I wrote all my notes from the Almanac in my new log book. Up to this point, I'd relied on scraps of A4 paper to record my plans and journey but this was my new plan.

Duncansby Head Forecast

7am -	20 knots -	gusting	30
8am -	19 knots -	"	29
9am -	19 knots -	"	27
11am -	17 knots -	"	26
12 noon -	17 knots	"	27
13.00-	16 knots	"	29
14.00 -	16 knots	"	30
15.00 -	18 knots	"	27
16.00-	17 knots	"	25
17.00 -	15 knots	"	22
18.00 -	13 knots	"	20
19.00 -	13 knots	"	20
20.00 -	13 knots	"	23

West Going Stream Begins

HW Aberdeen   - 0105 (one hour 5 mins)

- 0120 (Sunday HW Aberdeen is 4.12pm

Duncansby Race

The race going west ←

Extends ENE towards Muckle Skerry on the SE going stream) at - 0105

Extends NW from Duncansby Head at - 0440

HW at Muckle Skerry = same as HW Dover

Dangerous races - North End of Stroma

Persistent race off St.Johns point. Forms at HW Aberdeen - 0150 - extends right across Torness. Heavy breaking seas.

Persistent race off St.Johns point. Forms at HW Aberdeen - 0150 - extends right across Torness. Heavy breaking seas.

    I was determined henceforth to record everything in a black book. I'd found on sale in a cafe I visited with Jeff back in Inverness. I'd scribbled these words down in the Sinclair Arms at Keiss last night thinking they might help me.

    Reading back through my notes, it certainly looks like I knew what I was talking about. In reality, I had little confidence in any of my plans being correct, except for the weather forecast which, looking out to sea, confirmed I was right. I was about 80% sure I'd identified the high water time correctly. This was 4.12 pm. Subtracting one hour and five minutes adjusting for the distance from Aberdeen which I deciphered from the Almanac, meant I had to arrive at Duncansby Head at the start of the west going stream by 3.07 pm to be precise. I had very little chance of remembering much else from the info I'd recorded and could hardly take the log book out of its waterproof bag once underway. I tried memorising times and places and then reciting them out loud. Staring blankly at my Navionics app, none of the names seemed to bear much resemblance to those in my notes. Nevertheless, I persevered for 20 minutes, perhaps more, scrunching up my eyes and trying to recall the details. My brain was so confused except for one thing, 3.07 pm was the time I needed to reach the Duncansby race.

My plan was to leave early in the afternoon, hoping the breeze might have moderated a little by then. It was forecast to swing west starting off in the south. Both were good directions for the rounding and if it went west, the cliffs might offer some protection. This meant pushing off the beach 1 hour and 45 minutes earlier to cover the distance to the headland. I had plenty of time so, packing up all my gear, I headed off in search of a proper breakfast and fresh water.

Richard and Regula were sitting outside their van eating breakfast in the rain when I passed them. I needed water. They instantly offered me croissants, coffee, toast, salami, ham and Nutella. I needed to fill up my water bottles first and accepted their offer but excused myself for a few minutes while I located somewhere with a tap. I spotted a row of small bungalows a few hundred yards along the single track that the Germans had driven down onto the beach. Picking the first house, I jumped over the small white picket fence separating the dunes from their garden and strode up to the front door. Knocking confidently, a Dutch lady came to the door and after a polite exchange took three of my bottles and filled them up. Her husband or partner, a large Yorkshireman, appeared. He started explaining about how they'd just bought the place and only paid £170,000 for it. And wasn't it a bargain with these stunning views out to sea and being so remote and quiet. I just agreed and all I could think about was my coffee getting cold and the toast would probably be burnt by now. Smiling, I hurried off back to find Richard and Regula.

I dined like a king, accepting everything they offered me. I was uncomfortably full when I returned to the tent. It took a long time to pack away all my gear and drag it out of the hollow in the sand dune. I had to position the boat close to the water's edge before loading in all my stuff. The MOD27 was now too heavy to drag far across the beach on my own.

There was still plenty of time and once I'd changed, I noted the time, it was 13.00 hours. I sent a Safety Channel message via WhatsApp over the mobile network and Spot X message via satellite.

These Spot X (of Canadian origins) messages cost 25 cents for each custom message so I'd barely used them on the whole trip. I felt today warranted a small fee. Completing all my safety checks of the boat, personal equipment and then struggling to fit the Spot X and mobile phone back into their water proof cases meant I was now scrambling to leave on time.

Finally, at 13.45 I was ready to launch. As I was pushing the MOD27 to the water's edge I saw something I always dreaded when launching. A lone surfer was weaving in towards the shoreline. It looked like he was standing up, twisting and turning to stay on the wave, jumping off when neck deep and paddling back out through the breaking surf. Last time this happened I was on Craig Ewan beach in Peterhead. It was like Groundhog Day.

I watched and waited, counting the rollers. It looked like sets of six or maybe eight. I was struggling to concentrate, the knot in my stomach from too much food and nerves was playing tricks on my mind.

"Wait until the flat spot after the sets have come in," I muttered to myself.

I waited and waited then, "Go go go!"

Pushing as hard as you can push a thoroughly overloaded Laser, I made it through the first two sets of breakers. The second wave made the rudder pop up so I suddenly had no steerage. Whipping around reaching over the back of the boat, I pressed it back into the water, my arm was fully submerged. As I turned to face forwards again, a wave broke over the bow and washed me off, capsizing the MOD27 and sending her careering back towards the shore on her side. In a frantic movement, I swam to the boat which was rolling over in the surf and by a miracle I stopped her from inverting and snapping the mast. After a lengthy battle, I dragged her on her side back up the beach. Gasping for air and coughing out the lung full of water I'd swallowed, I sat shivering on the shore, already freezing. Time was slipping away. The

MOD27 had survived a full roll with no damage aside from a small batten pocket tear. Nothing too serious.

My next attempt to get off the shore failed and, after three similarly unsuccessful attempts, I was getting desperate. The boat hadn't been smashed back as badly with the other aborted launches but I was getting tired. My current technique wasn't working, a new one was required. This involved wading out to my neck then holding onto the tiller, steering and pulling the sail in, lying on my stomach half on the boat, half in the water. By removing my weight from the boat, it floated higher over the waves, all I had to do was try to avoid winding myself as we bounced over the top of a crest and dropped down the other side. To this day, I've no idea how I did it but it worked! I succeeded in breaking through the curling surf to reach the relative calm of the smoother waves further offshore. It took me a good 10 minutes to recover, wheezing and coughing out sea water as I looked back at the foaming rollers exploding onto Keiss beach.

It was 2.15 pm, less than an hour to cover the 13 km to Duncansby Head. I was sure I'd be late for the tidal gate.

I needed to get going, hiking as hard as I could. The MOD27 made good progress along the craggy inhospitable coast. Leading up to Duncansby, the breeze was blowing off the cliffs, staying close meant it almost disappeared so I stood well off the land to maximise my speed. When the giant rock stacks appeared standing guard in formation just south of the headland, all I could see was boiling white surf.

Every fisherman I'd spoken with told me they stayed tight to the cliffs following the western stream round the headland. They said get in so close you can almost touch the rocks. Looking at the size of the stacks, I felt scared of what was to come. In some ways, the trouble getting off the beach had been a good distraction but that was in the past and all I could see were standing waves in a foaming white frothy sea at the base of the cliffs. Surely they didn't mean stay tight to the stacks? I didn't fancy it and sailed well clear of the stacks cutting back in once I'd cleared them. I was definitely in now. There was no going back judging by how rapidly the cliffs were whizzing by. I'd found the tidal stream. It felt so powerful, I was sucked in tight to the cliffs, the waves were shortening as I closed in on the awesome overhanging headland. As I approached the most north eastern point of the UK, the wind switched off, obstructed by the huge cliffs, yet still I was ripping along. The waves ahead looked different. I was scared.

What was about to happen next nobody I'd discussed this headland with had explained fully.

With no warning I was in it. Waves converged from all directions, overfalling and standing vertically in my path. I had no way of steering away, there was no wind down here. The tidal flow was ripping me round a matter of feet from the rocks. Out of nowhere, a wave scooped me up then catapulted me clear of the water into the air, only to smash back down onto another standing wave from the force of gravity. The hull juddered violently as it landed. It was all I could do to hold onto the toe strap with both hands to prevent myself from being thrown out of the boat. I balanced, crouching low in the cockpit as I was flung airborne again and again, feet from the water into the air, each time landing with a terrifying thud into the next confused wave. I couldn't believe the boat didn't snap in two. With every landing, I got more and more concerned until, as if by magic it stopped. I was round. Looking back, I could see the cliffs rapidly disappearing. I was moving as fast as a jet ski. I couldn't believe I was still alive. Never have I ever been through anything like that. It was like being in a washing machine with the spin option set to full speed.

Once I'd popped out the other side into the Pentland Firth, initially the waters were much calmer.

I did, however, experience a large set of long powerful waves building behind me surging past the cliffs as the breeze filled in from behind. Surfing down these waves, which were now becoming disconcertedly large and incredibly forceful, started to unnerve me. I was on red alert and scanned around, worried what might be in store for me next. Then in the near distance, I could see the water directly ahead looked very strange. As I got closer, there appeared to be a long chain of seahorses dancing in the water. Shortly after, it became apparent these seahorses were in fact waves. Surely not.

"WAVES! WAVES! WAVES! Bloody hell someone get me outta here!" I shouted at the top of my voice.

Aiming inshore, I could see a sandy beach and made a beeline for it, sailing directly across a series of treacherous rocky outcrops invisible to me but barely buried beneath the water. By a miracle, I'd skimmed across one of the rockiest beaches at full speed and narrowly missed hitting anything on account it was just high water. Landing on soft golden sand, I was safe. It looked beautiful. The picturesque dunes with marram grass patches growing up the steep sandy dunes with sheep dotted around grazing juxtaposed to the treacherous seas not more than 50 feet away. Once I'd recovered my composure, I surveyed the area for any sign of life, especially a cafe. I noticed a pop-up gazebo with a group of young men cooking on a BBQ and on the other side a few brave walkers were sliding down the steep dunes on their bottoms bouncing off the tufts of grass to slow their descent.

I was alive! I couldn't quite believe I'd made it safely ashore. I didn't much care where I was. I'd turned the corner of the UK; I was now heading west. I saw seals playing just off the bay. One, then two, then five or six of them. They were circling around the rocks scattered all around the edges of the bay where I was standing. I had an overwhelming desire for a coffee and looked around for a public kiosk, cafe or something. There was a sign planted in the hill which made reference to no BBQ s, camping or overnight stays being allowed by order of the landowner. Looking out to sea, there was no way I was going anywhere in a hurry. The tide was dropping and, in the short time of my landing, the extent of the rocks I'd miraculously missed was being revealed. The whole foreshore was now encircled with dark semi submerged boulder shapes. Further offshore, the foam from dancing seahorses was spectacular. There were giant whirlpools dotted around in between the breakers. I stood speechless, gaping in awe at the forces in play on the sea, wondering how on earth a plastic Laser would ever make it through this patch of water. I was so mesmerised by it, I spent ages just watching and filming the water.

The MOD27 was safe where she sat as the tide was dropping so I made my way up the steep grassy hills, avoiding the collections of sheep faeces that covered all of them. I managed to place my hands in these offerings from nature several times as I scrambled up the never-ending banks until finally I was standing looking out to sea. Now several hundred feet above the Pentland Firth, I could see for miles. What a sight! It looked incredible. Weird patterns dancing on the water, clouds above blowing ominously along. Islands in the distance suddenly being illuminated by the sun fleetingly poking through a small break in the black veil shadowing the land, only to disappear again in an instant. Further inland, a few small buildings stood defiantly in the buffeting weather. One looked like a farm building surrounded by fences to keep sheep neatly arranged in square patches across the range of grassy inclines.

A well-trodden coastal footpath followed the contours of the cliff line. I followed it in search of a coffee and food, hobbling badly. I just couldn't put any weight on my right leg. It was screaming out at me with every step. I must have torn something after landing awkwardly following the impact of one of those highland flings I'd experienced around Duncansby Head. I could only walk by keeping my right leg straight. Every time I bent my knee, it sent a writhing pain straight up to my hip. It looked miles to anywhere. As I stopped, looking around I noticed two fervently striding ladies both carrying large backpacks making their way towards me.

One of them, Karen, who was walking from Inverness to John O'Groats in aid of the RNLI, said to me,

"Are you Stick?"

I was in the middle of nowhere! How on earth did she know who I was? It turns out she was a volunteer coastguard as well as being involved with the RNLI. Karen had heard my daily contacts with the coastguard over the VHF radio. She and her friend were on the final stretch of a 146 mile walk from exactly the same place I'd sailed from, Inverness. We chatted about a few of the places we'd both visited and swapped appalling weather stories of torrential rain and freezing cold winds. I said I was looking for some advice navigating the next part of the trip and Karen pointed her finger to a house in the far-off distance.

"Ivor Thomas, the local ferryman and coastguard. He's your man," she said.

They were anxious to complete their walk as they had a reception party waiting for them so promptly waved goodbye and left me standing alone on the cliff looking quite limp, not sure of my next move.

Hungry and exhausted I elected to hobble back to the beach after Karen's encouraging words to ignore the signs about no camping. I pitched Ron's leaky tent just above the foreshore in a deep grassy area, semi-camouflaged in case anyone was looking out for illegal campers. There was recent evidence of sheep where I pitched the tent but I felt if they wanted to eat my sailing kit strung out on a complex washing line, crudely made from an assembly of my boom and mainsheet, they could help themselves. Two hours later, I was hunkered down inside the tent, sheltering from the rain, eating boiled rice and drinking coffee made with powdered milk. I'd saved a few biscuits which tasted the best a biscuit can ever taste. My phone was nearly flat so I plugged it into the mobile solar charge pack Ron had lent me and hoped it worked better than his tent. I started to write up my diary but fell asleep immediately, waking slumped over the first line I'd entered on the page.

Everything was soggy from the rainwater seeping through the canvas walls. My feet were wet as they'd been touching the walls of the tent then outside I heard animals, a group of extremely unhappy sheep were surrounding me. They seemed quite put out that I'd camped on their favourite grazing spot and were foraging through my stuff for anything edible. They were surprisingly unscarred of me when I popped my head out and shooed at them, ignoring me completely. I couldn't really care about them either so we all just carried on with our business – them eating grass and pooping all over my wetsuit and sail and me trying to make breakfast of porridge and coffee on a tiny gas burner.

Chapter 28

Ivor and the Merry Men

I had landed at a place called the Bay of Sannick, literally next door to John O'Groats. After yesterday's trauma coming into the Pentland Firth, I needed some expert advice so decided to follow Karen's suggestion and try to locate Ivor Thomas, the local ferryman and coastguard. According to Karen, Ivor was the man to ask. Apparently, his father had started the John O'Groats ferry company with a single speedboat in 1974.

It took me a long time to locate Ivor's house. My right knee was in agony. Every step was slow and meticulously placed to minimise the impact. I cautiously ascended the dunes and then followed in the direction Karen had pointed yesterday. It took a few wrong houses before finally locating Ivor's. His house stood high up in the middle of a grassy field that overlooked the Pentland Firth. From here, you could see for miles with breath-taking views. The house itself was a fairly normal 1970s style four bedroomed detached house. As soon as I knocked on the door, I felt slightly shy and awkward. I was just turning up unannounced on a total stranger's door step at 8 am in the morning. Wearing soaking wet shoes, bright yellow waterproof trousers and a worn-out 30 year old Henri-Lloyd sailing jacket, I must have looked like I'd just crept out from under a hedge. Which was almost true. What was I going to say? "Help!"

Ivor's wife answered the door, she was getting ready for work and clearly in a hurry. After I made a brief introduction, she passed me onto Ivor before hurriedly disappearing down the drive to climb into her car and make haste to her place of work. When Ivor appeared, he seemed very calm and nonchalant about a bedraggled and probably quite stinky stranger invading his breakfast table.

After inviting me into his house, pulling out some charts and sitting me down at his kitchen table, Ivor indicated I could stay by spreading out the charts on the table. This was my cue to peel off the waterproofs. I'd already made a puddle and deposited grass and mud from my shoes on his polished parquet hall floor. He didn't seem to notice and very calmly listened to my story of woe from yesterday's rounding of Duncansby Head.

Ivor had a fantastic bushy thick greying beard that had clearly been cultivated with some kind of industrial beard combing and trimming device over many decades to make it appear flat and long. His face was broad like a true Highlander with sharp darting, penetrating eyes. When he moved, it was in a slow deliberate manner. His demeanour oozed calm and seriousness, methodically moving around the room looking for bits of charts to assist me with my journey. A soft quietly spoken Scottish accent gained my full attention as Ivor explained about the two stages of tides along the Pentland Firth.

The first stage had to be navigated at high water which was around 2 pm. I had two hours to make it through the Men of May before entering the next tidal gate for the rounding of Dunnet Head. He worked out some target times for places to hit. St. John's Point was 3 pm and rounding Dunnet between 4.30 and 5 pm, to be safe. His advice was to stand well off the cliffs at Dunnet and be wary near Stroma, keeping inshore at this point. It all made more sense looking at a large scale chart, far more now than having looked at it through the tiny viewer on my mobile phone. The level of detail was very comforting. He thought I should make Thurso Sand or Scrabster, a further 12 miles past Dunnet Head.

Ivor must have spent an hour with me before realising he had to be somewhere with his daughter. I couldn't resist one last request and thoroughly enjoyed the luxury of using his Armitage Shanks porcelain. Ivor volunteered to drive me to the local shop two miles down the road and when I departed from the car waving and thanking him, he offered to pop along later to see me off the beach at 1 pm.

It wasn't until I got to the shop that I realised the only way back to the boat was a two mile walk along the same narrow road we'd just driven. My right knee was just not working any more. I could hardly bend it. Hobbling into the shop I bought the bare necessities but afforded myself the luxury of fresh milk as well as a bottle of water, conscious of the weight I'd be carrying. A pasty, various snack bars, baked beans plus bread nearly filled the two plastic bags I walked out with. It felt a long way to walk but there was no other transport option. I was hoping Ivor might return and pick me up. Sadly this didn't happen. A few lone drivers passed me by, waving at me instead of stopping. They probably thought I was a tramp or undesirable. By the time I eventually reached the tent on Sannick Bay, my knee had freed up a little. I was short on time now. I had to eat then pack everything away. Fortunately everything was as I'd left it when I made it back to the tent. I was carrying all my comms and safety equipment with me just in case.

Ivor appeared on the beach at 12.30 pm with his camera and a super long telescopic lens. I was just finishing eating so politely he said he'd return at 1.30 pm to see me depart. I thanked him again for all his help and then focused on packing up. As I was loading my gear into the MOD27, having just finished changing into my wetsuit, another man appeared on the beach.

Kevin was dressed in high vis wet weather gear from head to toe. It looked like he was working on the roads. Nevertheless, his rain wear didn't disguise his powerful physique hidden beneath. Kevin had been sent to find me by Donald Sutherland whom I'd texted last night to confirm I'd made it safely to the Bay of Sannick. They really cared about me it seemed. Kevin was a local fisherman and confirmed much of what Ivor had advised. He also contradicted some of his advice too but was non-committal when really pressed so I stayed with my original plan which I'd worked out to the Nth degree of detail with Ivor.

Kevin helped me to carry the boat to the water's edge. I was really grateful to him as my knee was in no shape for a lengthy hauling over the dunes. Above the bay, I saw Ivor standing with his camera. He could see I'd found fresh help and kept his distance, probably not wanting to crowd me. I rather wished he'd have come down to say goodbye instead of a simple wave from the cliffs. I pushed off with the help of Kevin. It was 1.45 pm.

If you're about to set off on the most famously dangerous stretch of water in the UK, with a wind forecast of force 5 to 6 on the Beaufort scale, your safety team can be forgiven for blowing a fuse if you forget to tell them what you're doing. In the scramble to get packed away and off the beach, chatting with Kevin I'd either totally forgotten to send my standard Safety Channel notifications before setting off or I'd sent them but there was no signal when I did so and they never made it to the intended recipients. Whatever it was, it made for a highly stressful day for those volunteering to look out for my welfare whilst juggling their own personal lives. It was a bad mistake. One which had consequences long term.

Sailing along the Pentland Firth turned out to be surprisingly comfortable. I hit all the target times within a few minutes of the plan and there was no drama. I even headed out across the Firth to the far side towards Stroma which Ivor had suggested might become bumpy. I found it better than staying close to the cliffs where the waves were much shorter. By the time I approached Dunnet Head from two miles out, I was feeling very confident. It was only as I rounded the headland that the westerly wind was fully exposed. As I came round, the breath was nearly sucked out of my body as I watched the most enormous waves approaching from directly in front of me. I steered directly up and over the first wave sliding down the back of it into a giant hollow. Facing the next wave was like riding an Alton Towers rollercoaster. They weren't breaking but they were just enormous and the wind was now absolutely honking. On my left were sheer rock cliffs for as far as I could see and, on my right, just massive grey and white rolling waves for mile upon mile. This was a solitary moment. I knew what needed to be done, it was just not very pleasant doing it.

I ground away the miles in deteriorating weather with poor visibility. After several more hours sailing in strong winds, I'd settled into a routine rolling up and down a continuous conveyor belt of big seas. The cliffs slowly receded and a large bay came into view on my left. I knew Scrabster was close so headed into the bay hoping to see a harbour. I couldn't see a great deal through the spray and rain that was sheeting down into my face. The tops of the waves were being blown off causing spray and poor visibility but in the distance it looked like there was a sandy beach. I reached towards it, grateful I was no longer heading directly into the wind. There was a long yellow sandy bit of bay but it seemed to have white caps breaking everywhere. It looked particularly unfriendly and again reminded me of Craig Ewan beach at Peterhead so I carried on. I'd no idea where the harbour was. Looking at the mobile Navionics app, after taking many attempts to unlock the screensaver by swiping it across my woolly hat, I finally pinpointed my position.

"Oh shit," I swore out loud.

I was on the wrong side of the bay. The yellow sandy beach was in fact the world-famous surf beach at Thurso. There was no obvious safe landing here, all I could see was foam. Reluctantly, after staring for several minutes squinting along the shoreline, I gave up. I now had to beat all the way across the bay, directly into the howling wind. It was almost two more miles to reach Scrabster harbour. I really had no choice. I phoned Emma who was relieved to hear from me as PY hadn't received any updates since last night and had been in contact with her several times. Both were clearly very anxious. Emma tried to give me some idea of the course to steer to reach the harbour. After the amount of miles I'd sailed that day a two mile beat was the last thing I wanted. I cracked open a tin of sardines and swallowed them all down in one mouthful. Then I stuffed down a muesli bar, again virtually swallowing it in one, washing it down with half a bottle of water and set off again. There was spray everywhere, the wind was blowing dogs off chains! The light was fading fast and I was miles from a landing.

"This is madness! What am I doing here?" I shouted at the top of my voice through the wind.

"What an idiot! Why am I doing this stupid trip?"

I kept on at myself for a while, berating my senseless adventure and beginning to believe I may have bitten off more than I could chew.

After an endless beat I eventually entered the commercial harbour at Scrabster. It's a large commercial port and was somewhat confusing in the dying light with no navigation aid. Another call to Emma who was trying to help me over the phone by navigating for me using Google Maps. She finally guided me into the small craft entrance.

It was almost flat calm inside the safety of the walls. I pulled alongside a floating pontoon and tied up. The harbour master's VHF channel was posted on a sign. The place looked deserted. I radioed up.

A really nice man was relaxed about me mooring on the pontoon and told me to stay wherever I wanted. After signing off I felt unsure about where I could safely camp. There was nowhere suitable. I couldn't camp on the narrow pontoon and it was late, 7.30 pm. The harbour was deserted aside from a lone man working on his boat. I approached him and asked if he knew where the sailing club was. He directed me back out the harbour round the wall near a beach under the cliffs. This meant sailing again, I really didn't want to go anywhere in the MOD27 but after consideration felt this was my best chance for a comfortable night's sleep and maybe even a shower. Almost immediately after leaving I regretted this move. It was still windy and cold outside the safety of the harbour walls. Following them along, I located the sandy beach where the sailing club launched from and landed on at low tide. In front of me was 200 metres of sand stretching out from the cliffs and in the half-light I saw a shallow ramp which I assumed was the Pentland Firth Sailing Club's slipway.

"Bollocks." My language was not improving and a further hour struggling to drag the boat over the sinking sand didn't improve my mood much.

There was nowhere to camp here either. The boat park was fenced shut, no life at the sailing club and the security looked decidedly dodgy. I needed to eat so, as quickly as I could, I hid all my gear under the cover of a boat parked close by. It was freezing but I changed outside on the hard stand in front of the sailing club only to be greeted by several passers-by with quizzical looks as I struggled out of my wetsuit, hopping around bare bodied and shivering in the freezing air. Two girls practising cross channel swimming stopped to chat briefly before departing hurriedly due to the onset of hypothermia. I was optimistically hoping they would say,

"Come back and stay at our place, enjoy a hot shower and meal, we'll look after you."

No such luck! There was only one pub close by I could see as I searched on my phone's internet. It was called Popeye's Upper Deck which looked promising for grub. Abandoning everything in a hurry, I limped off into the darkness, making sure to check landmarks in case I lost my way coming back in the dark. It was a short walk through the industrial buildings spread around the harbour before I emerged by a main road opposite the restaurant. Crossing the empty road, I walked into Popeye's and went upstairs to the Upper Deck restaurant. It was empty. It was now 9.10 pm. The lady on reception looked at me as if I should have known then politely explained that they'd finished cooking for tonight.

"Oh please no," I said out loud. "I'm starving. I've just sailed a 13-foot plastic boat all the way along the Pentland Firth and I must eat. Please can you find me something?" I almost had to beg.

She was a very nice lady and, after a short conflab with the kitchen, made up a table for me. I spread out my whole electrical suite plugging my devices into every available socket. A couple of pints of Guinness followed by haddock and chips and apple crumble with custard made me feel my happy old self again. Rather amusingly, a party of seven sailors who were on a trip back from the Orkney Islands with Go West Sailing trooped in five minutes after me and were now offered a table too. We all got chatting, had a group picture and a good laugh with all the restaurant staff. As we left the restaurant, the reality of returning to my gear and nowhere to sleep depressed me. I was disappointed no one from the sailing club had responded to any messages or phone calls. Jeremy Warren had spoken so highly of his experience at Scrabster when he and Phil Kirkland had circumnavigated the UK in their Wayfarer.

It took a while to find my way back in the darkness. I was faced with the prospect of pitching Ron's leaky tent somewhere. The concrete veranda of the Pentland Firth Sailing Club seemed to be the safest place. The sailing club had an overhanging porch above the main entrance which at least meant my tent would stay dry. Sadly the concrete floor had no give and my wafer thin mat provided little cushioning. During the night, there were lots of cars drawing up and then moving off loudly, wheels spinning down the bumpy unmade road. It seemed various nefarious deals were going on in the car park. I didn't get out of the tent to investigate so this was only my supposition. Not surprisingly, the next morning I awoke early. In the commercial harbour I located a fishermen's washroom. The showers were metered. Luckily, I had one spare pound coin in my lifejacket. This fed the meter, great value at £1 for 10 minutes' worth of hot water. Afterwards I revisited Popeye's again, this time for breakfast, arriving just as it opened at 8 am. To cheer myself up, I chose the biggest option on the menu, a full English, costing an indulgent £8.

The wet tent was starting to get to me so the waitress in Popeye's found the number for a local taxi firm. When the cab arrived, I set off in search of a shop to buy a new tent. First stop, Lidl, brought no joy. After a bit of circling, I eventually found a fishing and tackle shop. Although they had no tents, I came away with a groundsheet which I planned to use as a fly sheet and also three cans of waterproofing spray. Everything I had which was likely to get wet got sprayed at least twice including Ron's tent and my ancient Henri-Lloyd jacket. I hung everything in the porchway of the Pentland Firth Sailing Club and sprayed until no gas was left in any of the cans. Once the housekeeping had been completed and I was waiting for the spray to dry, I started studying today's journey plan.

One element of this part of the trip I've omitted to mention is a growing tension with PY and myself over the safety comms. I've no notes on the subject and only limited recollection. However, PY threw his toys out the pram about the lack of comms and my cavalier attitude to safety protocols and various other failures on the comms management front after failing to send in a log before travelling down the Pentland Firth. I had very little understanding of the effect my trip was having on people around me as I was so busy focusing on just keeping going. Clearly the relentless nature was taking its toll on more than just myself. I recalled Jeremy Warren's wife's reaction when I'd arrived three years earlier at his house to discuss the circumnavigating idea with him. I imagined she too found the whole episode nerve jangling. At the time I didn't appreciate how stressful being at the other end of an erratically updated monitoring station probably was.

Chapter 29

Radioactive... Oh Betty!

Running along the top of Scotland felt a dangerous place, more dangerous than any other so far. I couldn't quite believe that since turning the corner past Duncansby Head, the wind direction had changed to blow from the west with a hint of northerly. This meant I was beating into the wind all day. Again! My knee was causing me serious issues and I was effectively sailing most of the day one legged, hiking on my left leg. The thing I noticed now was the waves seemed so much larger; long, deep, rolling, ominous waves, dark in colour due to the continuous rain and grey skies above and the reflections off the towering black quartzite rocks lining the cliffs that framed the sea. I took a more conservative approach, working through my Navionics app trying to identify bail out options, agonising over contingency plans in the event the wind dropped. As the number of places to land were so few and virtually no people lived here, I decided to aim for an easy distance and a place called Sandside Bay next to Dounreay, infamous for its controversial nuclear test centre, a mere 14 mile beat from Scrabster.

Population densities in Scotland are the lowest in the UK, averaging 70 people per hectare compared to 275 in England. However, the top of Scotland is the lowest anywhere with as few as eight people per square kilometre. Sailing along the coast from Scrabster, there was nothing but mountain sized cliffs and the relentless rollers coming from as far away as Greenland. Luckily the wind was blowing mainly from the west. There is no land mass between the Arctic Ocean and the top of Scotland. Fishermen I met later told me this area really kicked up a proper sea when it blew a northerly. I didn't fancy hanging around to find out.

I felt uncomfortable with the ferocity of the sea and scale of the cliffs on the way to Dounreay. Weirdly, it was a great relief to see the large dome of the nuclear test facility that had formed the UK's centre of fast reactor research and development between 1955 and 1994 before it was decommissioned. Dounreay was an imposing sight, situated just before Sandside Bay. I sailed in close to the shore and stopped, standing up in the boat balancing in the rolling waves to take a few tourist pictures. Unknown to me, there was a three mile exclusion zone to all craft. After my trip, I researched the history of this area following a chance discussion with an old friend of mine over lunch who knew the owner of the estate that bordered the power plant and included Sandside Beach.

Over the years, there's been an ongoing clean-up operation to remove nuclear waste particles from the sea and beach. This followed an explosion back in 1977 that was only first reported 18 years later in The New Scientist magazine on 24th June 1995 by Rob Edwards. The headline read, 'Lid blown off Dounreay's lethal secret':

"EARLY in the morning of Tuesday 10 May 1977 there was a loud explosion at the Dounreay nuclear plant on the north coast of Scotland.

The UK Atomic Energy Authority, which runs the plant, had dumped at least 2 kilograms of sodium and potassium down a 65-metre shaft packed with radioactive waste and flooded with seawater.

The results were dramatic. The sodium and potassium reacted violently with the water. The explosion blew off the shaft's huge concrete lid, threw its steel top plate 12 metres to one side, badly damaged the 5-tonne concrete blocks at the mouth of the shaft, and blasted scaffold poles up to 40 metres away. An eyewitness reported a plume of white smoke blowing out to sea. And, as government watchdogs revealed for the first time last week, the ground around the shaft was littered with radioactive particles hot enough to injure and kill. Over the past 18 years, almost 150 such particles have been found on Dounreay's beaches."

The Independent newspaper reported on the 5th July 2002 reported that:

"A landowner has launched a lawsuit against the UK Atomic Energy Authority, claiming it has repeatedly contaminated his beach with radioactive particles.

Geoffrey Minter, who owns Sandside Bay near the nuclear installation at Dounreay in Caithness, said the action was a response to a fruitless five-year campaign against the authority. Mr Minter described his action, believed to be the first of its kind, as the only way to resolve the long-running dispute in the face of "spin, excuses and broken promises".

The authority said it would consider the issues raised by the petition before issuing a formal response.

The first radioactive particle was discovered on the beach in 1984. Seven years later Mr Minter bought Sandside House, an estate which includes beaches, a harbour and an 18-hole golf course.

Two further radioactive particles were found on Sandside Bay's main beach in 1997, and a further 17 since."

There have been other strange goings on at Dounreay. The sudden death of a man at the nuclear plant was reported to the police on 27th March 2006. According to the BBC report:

"The body was discovered by staff at about 1445 BST on Monday and the Northern Constabulary has been assisting the Civil Nuclear Constabulary.

Police at the time said enquiries were at an early stage but there did not appear to be any suspicious circumstances.

A spokesman for the UK Atomic Energy Authority said at the time it was cooperating with police and the incident had happened in an area not controlled for radioactivity."

Perhaps more mysteriously of all, much earlier on the 5th April 1985, anti-nuclear campaigner William Macrae was found dead in his car. According to Wikipedia this is what happened:

"On 5 April 1985 McRae left his Glasgow flat at 18:30 to spend the weekend at his cottage at Ardelve near Dornie, Ross-shire. He was not seen again until the next morning around 10:00, when two Australian tourists saw his maroon Volvo saloon car on a moor a short distance from the junction of the A887 and A87 roads Bun Loyne, Glenmoriston, Inverness-shire. The car was straddling a burn about 90 feet (27 m) from the road. The tourists flagged down the next car to pass, whose driver turned out to be a doctor, Dorothy Messer, accompanied by her fiancé as well as David Coutts, an SNP Dundee Councillor who knew McRae.

It was discovered that McRae was in the car. His hands were "folded on his lap", his head was "slumped on his right shoulder" and there was a "considerable amount of blood on his temple". He was not wearing a seat belt.

Another car was sent to call the emergency services. Dr Messer examined McRae and found that he was still alive and breathing. She noted that one of his pupils was dilated, indicating the possibility of brain damage, and estimated that he had been in that state for 10 hours.

McRae was removed by ambulance to Raigmore Hospital, Inverness accompanied by Dr Messer. After admission it was decided to transfer him to Aberdeen Royal Infirmary. At Aberdeen it was realised that the incident was more than a road accident; six hours after he had been found, a nurse washing his head discovered what appeared to be the entry wound of a gunshot. An X-ray confirmed that McRae had been shot above his right ear and a bullet was detected in his head. His brain was severely damaged and his vital functions were very weak. The next day, Sunday 7 April, after consultation with his next of kin, McRae's life-support machine was switched off."

At the time, the New Scientist magazine published a report into the incident on Newscientist.com:

"The investigation was headed by Chief Superintendent Andrew Lister of Northern Constabulary CID. Despite no weapon having yet been found, McRae's car was moved at 12:00 on 7 April. It later transpired that the police had kept no record of the precise location where the car had been found, and the position stated by them was later found to be 1 mile (1.6 km) in error, and was corrected by a witness who had been present at the scene.

A weapon was found the next day, in the burn over which the car had been discovered, 60 feet (18m) from the vehicle. It was a Smith & Wesson .22 calibre revolver containing two spent cartridges and five remaining rounds.

Although it was ruled at the time by authorities that McRae's death was undetermined, aspects of the investigation remain disputed, some claiming that the distance from McRae's car at which the gun was found and the lack of fingerprints on it rendered a suicide not credible. At the time of his death, McRae had been working to counter plans to dump nuclear waste from the Dounreay Nuclear Power Development Establishment into the sea. Due to his house being burgled on repeated occasions prior to his death, he had taken to carrying a copy of the documents relating to his Dounreay work with him at all times. They were not found following his death, and the sole other copy which was kept in his office was stolen when it was burgled, no other items being taken. Neither McRae's medical reports nor the post-mortem data have been released to the public and there was no fatal accident enquiry.'

Landing on Sandside Bay beach, I'd never have suspected such a dark and unsavoury past had been inflicted on this mesmerically beautiful bay. The sand was golden, fanning out with swirly patterns created by the ebbing tide. The soft sand dunes covered in marram grass formed a picturesque backdrop. Two ladies walking their dogs were all I could see in the way of life.

Anne Bennet and Sue Russell were on a road trip in their VW campervan with their two dogs, Finn a spaniel and Jack, a lovely old soggy wet black lab. Finn charged over to me as I pulled the boat across the flat sands on the fender. It was a slow process making my way up the beach, picking up one end of the boat and pushing it over the fender in a wheelbarrow action until it rolled to the back, at which point the bow passed its tipping point and dropped onto the sand causing me to fall over on nearly every occasion from the sudden jolt.

Finn decided he liked the look of the MOD27 and leapt aboard sitting proudly with his snout in the air, wagging his tail as if it was the best thing he'd ever done. Jack was less interested in the boat but charged around in circles at full speed, then changed direction and barged into me, looking for attention. I had to laugh, they were so funny together. Anne and Sue came over and after a brief chat they offered to help.

I put Anne in charge of pulling, attaching a long line to the plastic eyelet at the front of the boat. She pulled at full speed while I pushed from the rear. Sue was in charge of picking up the fender and moving it from the transom to the bow when the boat had travelled past its tipping point. The three of us were much more efficient than just me on my own and in no time, I'd covered the few hundred metres above the high tide line, reaching the soft sand dunes.

While all this was happening, Emma back in Eastbourne had managed to locate Betty. She was the receptionist in charge of the local golf club that was close by. Following a phone call, Emma asked Betty if I could use the club's shower. Betty explained there weren't any showers at the club but that I was welcome to use hers at her home. The instructions were for me to walk across the dunes to the golf club and rendezvous with Betty at 6 pm. She'd then drive me back to her house. Looking across the dunes, I could hardly see the golf clubhouse. It looked miles away. There was no way I wanted to walk that far with all my gear given the state of my knee so I dismissed the shower idea and elected to wash in the fresh water stream running off the land into the sea.

Anne and Sue had started cooking up a meal and invited me to share it by their campervan. A quiet night on the beach seemed the most likely format for tonight. Then, out of the blue, a car pulled up tooting its horn. Betty was standing on the door frame, yelling out at the top of her voice,

"Stiiiiick, Stick. Stiiiiiiiiiiiccckkkk"

It was a comical moment. This little lady of around 60 years old with permed white hair and a thick Glaswegian accent wasn't taking no for an answer. It didn't take long before her mission of rescuing me was completed. I felt slightly awkward as Sue and Anne had been so nice and as I walked past the bubbling broth cooking on their open gas burners, I felt a little ungrateful towards their kindness. Betty didn't give it air. She'd confiscated everything I had, hurriedly bundling it and then me into her Land Rover Freelander. Before I had a chance to say bye properly, we were off bouncing down the road in search of a warm bed and the hot shower I thought Betty was going to provide.

Betty's home was a good size bungalow with a beautifully manicured garden containing every incarnation of flower and vegetable you can imagine growing in it. On my arrival, I was greeted by John, her husband, and their two friends, Matt and Brenda, who were up visiting for a few days from Glasgow. Matt was draped in a striped blue and white chef's apron and was busily cooking freshly caught trout, tatties and vegetables on the BBQ.

I was instantly given a seat at their wooden garden bench table and within minutes a plate of food worthy of MasterChef and a beer were presented to me. I gratefully chomped my way through the mountain of delicious food whilst recounting stories of my adventures between food filled mouthfuls. Desert was toffee caramel pudding. I ate alone outside in the garden while they watched on and fed me more beer. After my demolition of their food was complete, I was escorted by Betty to her immaculately clean bathroom where I changed out of my wetsuit and showered while they all sat down inside to eat.

Afterwards we had a great laugh, joking and chatting into the night, while Betty raced around attending to my every need, even washing my wetsuit and making sandwiches for the next day. Then almost as suddenly as we met, I was whisked off again.

"Right, let's get you home!" said Betty.

I thought I was home for the night so this announcement was slightly surprising. Betty handed me a fantastic packed lunch for the following day, neatly arranged in a waterproof plastic bag and before I knew it, I was waving goodbye then back standing on the pitch black shoreline of Sandside beach watching Betty whizz off as quickly as she'd arrived. Watching her headlights disappear into the darkness I was almost in shock at their kindness and hospitality! It had all felt like a military precision planned pitstop. The only bit missing was the comfortable bed with Egyptian cotton sheets. Well, you can't have everything.

I spent nearly an hour groping around in the dark trying to find and then pitch my tent. There was no moon so it was difficult to see much. The sound of the gentle waves lapping at the shoreline provided a soothing ambience. This was the end of another amazing day. I was in total isolation, my only companion the white dome of the defunct nuclear reactor next door, just visible against the blackened skyline. Beauty and the beast!

After I'd returned from this trip, I had lunch with my old friends, Simon and Annabel Holly. Simon told me the story of Geoffrey Minter. It was after this meeting I decided to research more about Sandside Bay. I was quite shocked when I started reading through the online articles. I even made a phone call to Dounreay Nuclear Power Station. I was genuinely concerned that both my boat and myself had been exposed to radioactive particles from the beach. I emailed the Dounreay communications department and a day later was contacted by the head of PR, Sue Thompson. She said I'd nothing to worry about and the chances of coming into contact with anything radioactive were 1 in 80 million. To give you some comparison, the odds of winning the UK National Lottery are 1 in 13,983,816. Let's hope I'm not a winner!

Chapter 30

Flattened at Sango Sands

Armed with Betty's food parcel I stared out to sea, standing on the water's edge of Sandside Bay scanning the horizon. The sun was out and I felt uncomfortably warm in my wetsuit as the waves gently lapped at my feet. It looked beautiful in the bay. I hoped the forecast for the day was wrong; 29 mph winds and near zero visibility with rain and squally weather later. It certainly didn't look much like that from where I was standing.

As with most things, I was beginning to learn along this journey that nothing was ever the same for very long. One minute all was well, the next you were swimming. True to form, it didn't take long for the wind to build and fortunately, although there were some very large squalls throughout the day, they were blowing from across and behind, a broad reach the easiest point of sailing to ride these out. The day seemed to be never ending. My plan was to try to make it to Cape Wrath, the western most point at the top of Scotland, a colossus of a headland, the turning point before heading back south. I didn't fancy it at all. The only good news was it wasn't blowing from the north which apparently causes a much worse sea state. It was scaring me plenty from the direction it was blowing but I kept pushing all day, five continuous hours of broad reaching in terrible visibility and howling winds, whipping sheets of spray into my face, blinding me most of the time followed up with icy cold water running down my neck. I hated this place.

"I hate you Scotland," I howled in the gale. "Just because I'm English. What's wrong with us anyway?"

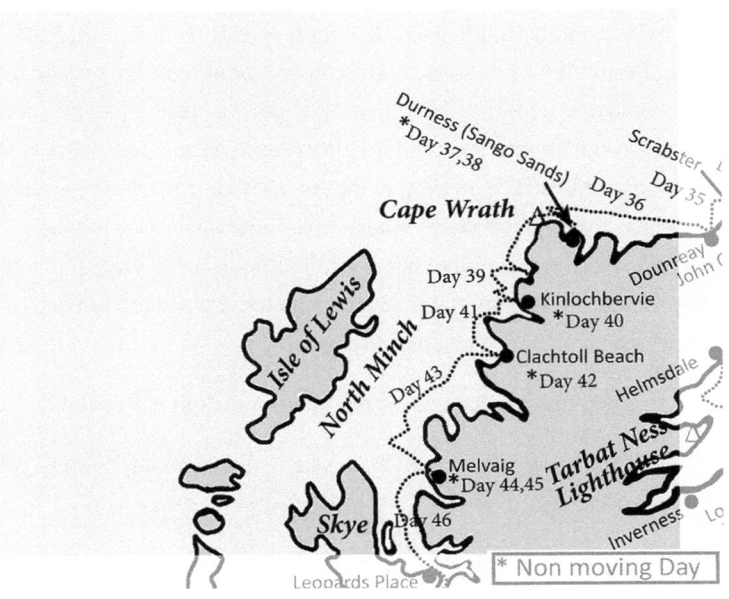

I screamed other various defamatory comments at the top of my voice. Nobody could hear and no one was interested. It really had nothing to do with Scotland nor its ancient rivalries with the English. It was just a really bad day and a tired over stretched Laser sailor with low blood sugar and severe fatigue from the relentlessness of this task. I kept on shouting most of the day until around 4.30 in the afternoon when I saw this amazing thing!

Throughout the day, the sky had been invisible through the grey spray and mist. As I was approaching Cape Wrath, the skies in the distance started to clear and a great shard of light broke through the cloud. It was like God shining a spotlight showing me the way to go. The wind was still blowing really hard but the sun, yes sun, was shining through the clouds, silhouetting this notorious landmark at the western tip of Scotland. Such a magnificent sight. It looked mesmeric. The sea felt like it was calming down too. It felt like I was being shown the way.

Before setting off, I'd agreed with PY that I'd make contact with him before rounding. PY was adamant that as soon as I passed the Cape, I'd lose all mobile and VHF comms for at least 25 km and my only contact would be via the Spot X which was proving to be sporadic and inconsistent with its updates (I later discovered a lot of this was down to user error). However, at the time, I didn't want to risk another explosion from PY about my gung-ho attitude towards safety so I stopped the boat and pulled out my full armoury of devices to try to make contact with him. After several minutes I managed to warm my fingers up enough to type out a text message.

Irritatingly he replied, "Give me 10 minutes - in a meeting"

"FFS" I shouted to myself. "Does he realise what the bloody hell I've been through all day?"

The sea was bouncing me around as I sat waiting for a call back, my sail noisily flogging in the wind while I sat freezing cold, drenched and deeply irritable. I calmed down after tucking into a tin of sardines and the last of Betty's biscuits and tried calling again. The phone wouldn't work through the waterproof cover. My fingers were just too cold and wet to activate the screen. By now, I was getting really angry with everything. I could see the sun blazing away over Cape Wrath and felt this was my moment. I was wasting time getting permission.

"Come on....bloody well hurry up with your effing meeting."

I was nearly about to set off again when the phone rang. I swiped the cover to answer but my cold fingers couldn't activate the screen so it just kept on ringing. Eventually it dropped to voicemail. I tried everything I knew to call back but to no avail. I just couldn't make the buttons work. In a really desperate moment, I did something I really didn't want to do. I unbuttoned the waterproof case and removed the Samsung Galaxy 8. This was very risky. I felt uncomfortable as the boat was lurching around in the waves and could easily have capsized.

With the waterproof case off, I finally got the phone to ring and got through to PY. Once connected, I tried to speak clearly and concisely, explaining the position and my desire to round Cape Wrath tonight as it looked perfect weather and the wind was a perfect broad reach. My lips were cold so the speech coming out of my mouth must have sounded slurred and barely comprehensible. I omitted the divine light shining a pathway for me from my explanation of the situation though; believing he'd really start thinking I'd lost the plot. PY was never one to be pressured into an impulse decision and went quiet for a minute or so. He pinpointed where I was and agreed it was achievable to round. He then pointed out that the nearest inhabited landing point was Kinlochbervie, some 45 km away. This involved beating directly into the wind on the other side of Cape Wrath. He then followed up with the weather forecast for the next few days which indicated gales, near hurricane force winds coming in. So, even if I made it round, I'd probably not make Kinlochbervie and end up sitting on an isolated beach, assuming I could find one, sitting on my own, eating tinned food and no beer for several days.

Not surprisingly, this news didn't improve my mood but I begrudgingly conceded the points PY mapped out before me and about turned. The nearest landing point was Durness, 10 miles back from where I'd come; 10 miles sailing into the wind.

By the time I reached Durness, two hours later, I was shot to bits. It was as much as I could do to stand up when I landed. The saving grace was the sun was now out and it was a beautiful sandy and sheltered beach.

It took me a while to get myself back into normal mode and I sat just staring blankly at a few holidaymakers messing about on the beach. An Indian father and his beautifully turned out three little girls caught my eye. They were perfectly dressed as if they were going to church. I could barely believe it when Dad appeared and instructed them to climb into a four man plastic kayak to go for an evening paddle. The only issue was they clearly didn't have a clue and the shore dump, which was deceptively strong, would instantly soak them as they pushed off. The screams from the girls were predictable. Dad ignored the protests and waded into the surf with his chinos partly rolled up round his ankles as a token gesture to the sea. After half an hour and a mammoth effort from Dad, everyone in the kayak was dripping wet from top to toe and the three girls were crying their eyes out. Reluctantly, Dad gave up and then had to climb back up the near vertical crumbling cliff with his now mutinous crew and the kayak to reload it onto the car roof. It looked like seriously hard work from my position. I couldn't see the fun in it myself. But who am I to talk?

My turn next. Unpack everything and drag the MOD27 up the beach using the fender. Nearly an hour later and a difficult scramble up the same near vertical sandstone cliff my Indian friends had ascended, I found it hard enough with my bags let alone a four man kayak. There were only people's old footholes to use, no steps or handrails. Tufts of hard bush or grass frequently came away in my hand as I scrambled up the cliff.

Finally I was standing at the top. Before me were a few static caravans and a plethora of campervans and tents dotted around. They were vaguely arranged on putting green length grassy pitches. These were dissected by a winding tarmac road that weaved its way through the campsite. It was a busy scene of activity. I followed the road to the main entrance and came across a small red brick building which looked like it might be the reception. In front of the building was a large sign with Sango Sands printed in bold letters.

Once in the reception area, a high desk faced me almost immediately I squeezed through the door. It was crammed full of leaflets and other stuff. Rosie on reception greeted me.

"Hello. Have you lost your boat?" she said with a cheeky grin.

"Ha ha" laughed Alan, the maintenance man leaning against the wall in the corner of the room.

Both were well meaning and I laughed with them, explaining what I'd been up to and that I'd parked my boat at the bottom of the cliff and was looking for a place to pitch my tent. They were lovely, they seemed to laugh and smile more often than they spoke. Alan took me over to the restaurant where he introduced me to James, the owner of Sango Sands. They couldn't have been more welcoming and friendly. James offered me a free pitch for my tent and a pizza and beer in their onsite restaurant.

I got chatting with him and one of the guests, a man called Mark. Well Mark did most of the talking. According to him, he was a fixer for the stars, arranging celebrity holidays. He apparently was on a recce for someone famous I hadn't heard of, in search of the perfect celebrity holiday location. As far as I could tell, this involved taking lots of selfies and drinking whisky and talking incessantly about people whose names meant nothing to me. I wasn't complaining though as I was now part of the research team and as such, a recipient of a portion of the holiday recce free drinks budget.

By 10 pm my wetsuit had gotten too itchy to hang around in the bar any longer in spite of the potent lubrication passing through my body. I bade farewell and headed off to the shower block where by 11 pm I'd changed into dry clothes and was thinking about sleep. It was pitch black. No moon at all. Apart from my spare clothes, I'd only brought up a wash bag, my bright yellow waterproof trousers and Henri-Lloyd jacket, the plastic ground sheet and my head torch with a dying battery. Crucially, my tent and sleeping bag were still in the boat.

"Shit! How stupid." I said to myself out loud.

There was nothing else for it. I'd have to climb back down the crumbly cliff to the beach. This was about a mile away from the campsite. When I reached the cliff, I started to pick my way tentatively down the footholes carved out by numerous tourists. They were tricky to navigate going uphill in daylight, going down was harder. Almost instantly I lost my footing, only just managing to keep hold of a spiky plant which fortunately didn't uproot and so saved me falling at least a hundred feet onto the rocks below. I retraced my steps and looked for an alternative route to the beach. Following the line of the campsite cliff edge I cautiously groped my way to a small lane heading downhill. Following this to the bottom, it pitched left which looked like it would lead to my beach. It was black as night. My head torch was useless. I trudged up and down the beach for nearly an hour trying to locate the MOD27.

"Surely she hasn't floated away," I kept asking myself.

I'd pulled her miles above the high tide line. I searched every inch and found nothing. It was well past midnight and I was knackered. I had no option but to return back up the hill to the campsite. It was way too late to wake James or Alan who'd said to call if I had any issues. I just felt I couldn't. So, back at the campsite I set about looking for somewhere I could bunk down for the night. The rain was lashing down and the howling gale that had been forecast was beginning to get going, smashing into the tents and campervans, buffeting them with brutal force on the exposed promontory high above the beach. I headed for the laundry room.

"Hmm not the comfiest bed I've ever slept in," I mumbled to myself.

So, I used my lifejacket for a pillow and the Henri-Lloyd, wet and not quite waterproof jacket and yellow trousers for the mattress. Final touches involved turning on two tumble dryers to warm up the room, closing the door and propping it closed by leaning a plastic school style chair with bent metal legs against it. I turned off the light and rolled up in the plastic tarp like a caterpillar. Bingo, job done, fast asleep in minutes.

No sooner was I dreaming of waves crashing over my head when I woke up startled by a loud crash and the sound of the metal chair legs scraping across the concrete floor. I sat up and banged my head on the underside of the table top. A woman was standing in brilliant light holding a basket of washing, poised to pour it into the machine when she stopped dead and let out a blood curdling scream, fleeing before I had a chance to open my mouth. Five minutes later, after I'd switched the light out and reset my chair's early warning system, settled down under the table like a caterpillar again and returned to a deep slumber, another interruption woke me.

Bang!

This time the chair flew across the room, crashing into one of the metal driers. A man wielding a truncheon length torch was shining it under the table into my face. Before he started to set about me, I managed to blurt out,

"I've lost my tent, it's in my boat. I've lost my boat on the beach," I garbled hurriedly without taking a breath, hoping this would prevent the torch landing on my head.

It seemed to work and he backed away. I continued to explain I'd sailed from Eastbourne and was circumnavigating the UK but had lost my boat in the dark and had left my tent in it. I'd camped in this laundry room as I really had nowhere else to sleep. He looked at me with an amazed expression on his face and after a few seconds said,

"I can't believe you've got this bloody far," in a sarcastic northern English accent before laughing out loud and walking out the door.

I smiled in a slightly pathetic, embarrassed way.

Now he'd established I wasn't the mass murderer his wife thought I might be, he turned round and took himself off to bed, calling back to his wife struggling through the door with the washing basket full of clothes.

"He won't trouble you. He can't even find his boat on the beach," he shouted as he walked back into the howling gale blowing outside.

To my surprise, his wife carried on filling all four washing machines in the room with clothes and then left me alone with a cacophony of swishing, gurgling and whirring noises for the next hour.

The following morning, I had a stiff neck and my back felt like it might snap if I stood up. The cold concrete floor had proven to be as uncomfortable as I'd expected. Stepping outside the laundry room, the whole landscape had changed. Where the previous evening, a neat arrangement of tents had been pitched equally spaced out, now all I could see were people picking through the remnants of their possessions. Flattened tents, broken poles and giant lakes festooned the short cut grassy cliff top. There wasn't a tent still standing.

Making my way over to see Alan and Rosie in reception to collect my mobile phone, which I'd left charging in their office overnight, I saw a long queue of bedraggled people holding an assortment of bent and broken tent poles. When I arrived, James was just dealing with multiple members of the queue at the same time.

"If you're looking for poles, we don't have any!" James said dismissively.

"No poles needed here," I replied from outside the reception.

"Yours must be the only surviving tent from last night," James said over the noise of vehicles streaming out through the exit in search of a non-canvas style holiday location.

"I've lost it," I replied to James.

"Lost what?" he responded quizzically.

"My boat, and the tent was still in it."

"Where did you sleep last night then?" James looked puzzled.

"In your laundry room," I replied

Rosie, Alan and James all paused then simultaneously burst out laughing as I explained about my mystery midnight guest and losing my boat in the dark. James said that the woman using the washing machines probably wasn't even staying there. Non-campsite guests often sneaked in at the dead of night to use the washing machines. It was quite a common problem he explained.

After collecting my fully charged phone and checking the weather forecast, I was in no hurry to go anywhere. Fifty knot winds and rain for the next two days as PY had predicted. Finding the campsite restaurant for a full English breakfast seemed the best idea I could come up with. I'd battle the hurricane strength winds and go back down the cliff to look for my boat afterwards. It was really nice to know I didn't have to go anywhere today and I enjoyed a monster bacon, sausage, egg, beans, black pudding and toast breakfast with several coffees and fruit juice. I felt ready to go and look for the MOD27 now.

The climb back down the cliff I'd ascended the previous evening was still tricky even in daylight. Picking my way carefully down the near vertical drop, I realised it was no wonder I couldn't do this in the dark. All became clear as I reached the beach. The reason I couldn't find the MOD27 last night was that I'd approached the northern end of the beach from the road. In the middle there was a giant rock promontory which separates the beach, forming it into two bays. I couldn't possibly reach the southern side from the road where the boat was as it was cut off by a giant rock outcrop stretching into the sea.

"No wonder I couldn't find it!" I mused to myself.

It took three days for the storm to blow itself out. Not fully, but enough to get going again. In my time at Sango Sands I'd managed to make a number of urgent boat repairs using some epoxy glue mixed with sand from the beach to bung up the worst of the gaping holes at each of the corners of the MOD27. I taped up the sail rips with the sail cloth I carried with me and I reversed the control ropes to spread out the wear where they ran through the pulleys. It wasn't pretty but would hopefully reduce the ingress of water and improve the hull's watertight compartment where I stowed all my gear.

The rain fell day after day as if a bucket of water was being poured continuously from the sky. After making my repairs, there really was very little to do aside from sheltering from the atrocious weather. Most of my time was spent catching up on my journal and drinking coffee followed by drinking beer in the evenings and chatting to the visitors and a few locals. I was keen to meet some fishermen who could give me some advice on rounding Cape Wrath and what to expect on the other side. The Sango Sands bar didn't disappoint.

It was late into the evening. I was due to depart the following day and still had little idea of what to expect at Cape Wrath, let alone having constructed a proper plan. I'd studied the tides and read a lot about the headland but it was just words on paper. I needed to find someone who had first-hand experience of this area. Luckily for me, propped up at the end of the Sango Sands bar were three local fishermen – John, Andrew and Murray. The youngest two I believe worked at the Eriboll Fish Farm in Loch Eriboll, mainly driving boats ferrying the vast amount of feed the salmon farms required to maintain their stocks. John was the most interesting having clearly lived through many a dark storm of his own and by his own confession been largely inebriated throughout much of his career. He was dry now and provided me with some helpful gems of advice about the surrounding waters of the Cape.

Andrew was the youngest and the easiest to understand, his accent being less broad than that of John and Murray and he had a dry sense of humour too. We'd been talking for several hours and it was getting late when Andrew suggested we carry on to another place they knew. My problem when I stand in a bar for too long is my common sense switch always lets me down. This occasion was no different. Really, I should have dragged myself off to bed for an early night in preparation for another long day tomorrow. Instead, I agreed to being whisked off into the night with a bunch of fishermen to go drinking. Fortunately John drove, following a winding road with high banked edges, a 15 to 20 minute drive to another pub I had no idea where.

Everyone inside the packed tavern knew each other and I was supplied with a constant stream of ale by my new friends. Andrew appeared to be having some issues with the young heavily tattooed bar lady. For reasons unknown to me, she was refusing to serve him on account of some previous misdemeanour. He wasn't entirely sure what he'd done but the bar lady wasn't having any of it and after an hour of cold stares and steely looks across a heaving floor, Andrew was growing thirsty. I think he'd been watching me. John drove us back to the Sango Sands bar. Several whiskies later, I bade them goodnight and squelched my way back to Ron's leaking tent where I bedded down for another wet night's sleep, falling asleep oblivious that most of my clothes were sodden.

Pushing off from Sango Sands the next morning was both a sad and happy moment. I'd had such a laugh staying there and it had been a good rest. I really enjoyed all the people but was glad to be moving again. After all, time was pressing, it was now Saturday 24th August, shortly the start of autumn would be upon me and the advent of the official UK stormy season.

Chapter 31

Dive for Cover – Kinlochbervie

Rounding Cape Wrath was reasonably uneventful if somewhat tedious. I seemed to get caught in currents going nowhere in little wind, standing well off the giant cliff face. After several hours my patience waned and to get round this massive headland, I elected to try to beat the tidal races by clinging inches from the cliff face, sailing amongst a minefield of collapsed slabs of semi submerged rocks beneath the waves. It worked but didn't improve my mood when it came to these traumatic headlands. I launched my usual assault of expletives towards the rocks whilst making no progress. The only positive was that the live firing range which extends four miles offshore wasn't active. When PY quizzed me before setting off, he nearly fell over when he found out I'd already been in contact with the range to check firing times. I was learning!

Sandwood Bay was my next planned stop off point but the shore break looked particularly difficult so I gritted my teeth and carried on, seeking out the safety of the well-sheltered fishing harbour at

Kinlochbervie. In fact, it was so sheltered I ran out of wind a mile out having to paddle the last mile in fading light through a narrow cliff-lined natural loch before finally reaching the safety of Kinlochbervie harbour slipway at 20.43.

The harbour looked deserted. Apparently it had benefited from a significant EU grant to upgrade the cold storage facilities and industrial fishing facilities. The moored up large fishing and transportation shipping seemed out of place in such an idyllic landscape. I tied the MOD27 up at the first slipway, leaving her floating amongst some weed-covered rocks and set off in search of a trailer to pull her up the concrete ramp. Fairly quickly, I found the perfect thing, an abandoned dinghy trolley. Not finding anyone to ask, I decided they probably wouldn't mind me borrowing it. When I had the boat safely at the top of the ramp, I surveyed the surroundings. There wasn't any life, not even a harbour master's office as far as I could see. Enormous concrete quays with a road running parallel were festooned with chiller buildings but nothing that seemed to resemble a shower block. I noticed a rusty looking Land Rover Discovery parked up nearby and squinting through my salt encrusted prescription sunglasses it looked like somebody was inside talking on a mobile. I walked towards the vehicle and made a gesture to open the window.

"Hello" I said smiling my best friendly smile.

The occupant looked a little unsure and hesitantly responded with a similar greeting.

"Would you happen to know where the harbour master's office is?" I carried on.

"He's gone for the day" was the short reply.

"I'm on a circumnavigation of the UK and I'm looking for a shower and somewhere I can pitch my tent for the night," I persevered, not able to gauge how my new acquaintance was reacting to my presence.

As I was speaking, I was becoming increasingly aware of the midges that had clearly decided I was very tasty. My face was being eaten alive. This was the first time I'd experienced the famous west coast midges. It was horrendous.

There was a pause and then the occupant of the car before me said, "I've got a dive cabin you can stay at just up the road."

He then blurted out a series of directions pointing up towards a hill and leapt out of the Land Rover. Before I knew what was going on, I'd loaded all my gear into the back of his car. Just as I was expecting him to offer me a lift he then unexpectedly climbed back in the car, waved towards the hilltop behind and said,

"You can walk. I don't want my car floor to rust from salt water. See you there."

He then reversed and raced off along the deserted concrete harbour road, leaving me standing wondering what had just happened. I hadn't fully followed what he was saying and now thought,

"Here I am in the middle of nowhere, being eaten by midges, in an itchy wetsuit, tired after a very long day and now with none of my stuff. What was I thinking?"

There was nothing else to do so I set off in the direction of the Land Rover, feeling decidedly uncertain if I'd ever see my kit again. I needn't have worried though as by the time I reached the harbour exit a 15 minute walk later, the Land Rover came skidding to a halt next to me.

"Jump in"

The driver introduced himself as Andy Jennings. He'd spread a plastic tarp over the seat and floor. He explained he was a member of the Cambridge University Sub Aqua Club and had transported so many divers around in his old Land Rover that the floor pan had rusted through from the build up of salt water. I didn't see that I was particularly wet and salty but accepted his explanation at face value, grateful I was to be reunited with my kit bag. The prospect of a night under cover in a dry bunkhouse safe from midges was great. What a fluke!

When we arrived at Andy's house, it was teaming with fellow divers, 11 to be precise. Andy and his colleague, John Baart, were leading a weekend dive expedition for their club. It looked like a well-practised set-up. I hosed myself off using the outside hose in the overgrown back garden then stripped naked and hung it all on the washing line before racing into the bunkhouse, which I had to myself, to escape the midges. The building could easily sleep six and was located away from the main house at the bottom of the garden. There were three sets of bunk beds, one on each wall. The timber clad building smelt musty but was essentially warm and dry.

Meanwhile, inside the main house a team of the divers was busily cooking a great feast of pasta and freshly caught scallops for evening dinner. When we sat down to eat, everyone was as hungry as each other. There was little conversation until a good chunk of the food had been consumed after which it became a raucous flow of intellectual banter and questioning as you would expect from mainly Cambridge graduates. Wine and beer flowed, conversation was excitable and by the time we'd finished eating, I was almost popping.

Andy and John, the two expedition leaders, told me an amusing story of how they'd lost their boat whilst out diving together. Apparently for some reason which I fail to remember, they both fell out of the rib. Neither were attached to the kill cord but fortunately as Andy fell into the water, he'd managed to knock the throttle back so it was just idling but still in gear. The two men were dressed for diving and although the rib was barely moving it was just fast enough to keep out of reach of them as they swam after it.

Andy told how both he and John decided the best course of action was not to panic. They were dressed in drysuits and would just hang about until a passing boat could be hailed and pick them up. They waited some considerable time before a lone yachtsman who was on the last part of a transatlantic crossing from Canada passed by and picked them up. They managed to convince the yachtsman to chase after the rib and after consulting some charts they made a heading. The yachtsman was absolutely adamant that the engine should not exceed 2000 revs or else it would probably blow up. Andy and John spent several hours slowly closing in on the rib which was heading directly for the cliffs. Their story sounded like a bit of cat and mouse game going on with the engine speed of the yacht as the two divers made more revs while the owner kept insisting they throttle back. Andy said they only narrowly averted disaster by reaching the rib when it was only a few hundred metres away from the rocks which would have smashed it to pieces.

What a lucky break meeting Andy in the car park at Kinlochbervie was! I considered the alternative prospect, a night sleeping in the fishing port being eaten to death by midges in a damp tent, scoffing a tin of cold tuna and chickpeas. Someone was definitely looking after me.

The following day there was literally no wind. The divers set off early in perfect flat calm sunny conditions and I stayed behind with Cathy, the wife of John Baart, one of the senior dive instructors. Cathy fancied a day off and I wasn't going anywhere in this wind. I hung around writing and checking the forecast, sunbathing and reading up for my next leg.

Cathy planned to go off for a long hike in the afternoon but before she left we had a deep conversation for several hours about some of my more traumatic sailing experiences. Quite unexpectedly, I started to cry in front of her when I was talking about a family incident from several years earlier that I'd recounted. My emotions were totally surprising to me and I thought she reacted well.

I was alone all afternoon in their house and started to feel I should try to keep moving. Around 3 pm it looked as though a breeze was going to come in so I packed up my gear and carried it all the way down the long winding hill to the MOD27. It was quite a trek and I was sweating in all my sailing gear by the time I reached the boat and the wind had disappeared.

I waited for some time to see if any breeze filled in and was just about to return to the dive lodge when a small rowing boat pulled into the slipway. Two men stepped out and quickly it became apparent the trolley I'd borrowed belonged to them. They were extremely gracious about the fact I'd stolen their trolley and that my boat was still sitting on it. They politely helped me to unload the MOD27 and I tried to repay the unsanctioned loan by giving them a hand up the ramp. After a chat, which inevitably came back to my circumnavigation, they offered me a lift back up to the dive lodge which I accepted.

Meanwhile, Emma had come back up to Scotland for a few more days, flying into Inverness airport where she'd left the van. She drove four hours across the country along some tiny mountain roads to find me, arriving just in time to join in with another big dive group meal, this time pizza, which carried on late into the night. During this evening I had an interesting chat with Mike Walker who was spending one year studying nuclear science at Cambridge on secondment from the US Navy. Born in Texas, Mike was one of the quietest people in the room but a fascinating individual who oozed self-confidence in an untypically American understated way. Andy told me later that Mike was the most accomplished diver amongst the team and was a serving officer in the US Marines.

My alarm clock was set for 4.45 am which felt like it was hardly worth going to sleep. By the time I'd managed to kick start my system with caffeine, carried out all my pre-launch tasks and rigged, it was close to 7.30 am. I berated myself for taking so long every day getting ready. I passed out of the loch entrance to be greeted by a brutal swell and 20 plus knots of breeze. The night before, Andy had mentioned something about going inside Handa Island or outside. I started to regret that I hadn't paid much attention to his words. As I approached Handa, it was blowing so much I elected to stay close in to the cliffs, seeking any shelter I could find. Handa Island is a picturesque but barren island, known for being a nesting site for important bird populations. It lies almost opposite Stornoway and there's a notoriously strong tidal race between the mainland and the island. If you make it through with the tide behind, the waves can literally wash you through. It narrows like the waistline of a supermodel and the birds surrounding you are equally as beautiful.

The puffins were my favourites, flapping and landing like they weren't really designed to fly at all, gazing at me bobbing up and down with the boiling sea sluicing me inches away from great slabs of granite often just barely below the water. I found myself frozen in fear yet mesmerised by the rawness of this place. In the distance, a sandy cove had two people doing something I couldn't make out. They looked out of place in this natural world. An array of birds swooped and divebombed all around, busily ignoring me and carrying on with their daily task of surviving.

I'd had enough of being pounded by freezing waves by midday and turned into a sheltered harbour inlet called Scourie. As I approached the shore, nestling between sharp granite rocks, a fan shaped sandy beach spread out invitingly before me. In the corner of the bay was a steep concrete ramp and above it stood an old boathouse, a picturesque scene you see in one of those Hollywood portrayals of a small Scottish fishing hamlet. The beach looked an easier landing option and was contrastingly still compared to the roaring torrent racing past the end of the cliffs protecting it. A cafe perched on the shoreline with a small car park. I rendezvoused with Emma and together we reunited for a full

English breakfast somewhat ironically in the heart of Scotland. By the time I'd finished the meal, the floor under my table was looking like a small pond. I awkwardly excused the mess and left, continuing to drip my way across the immaculately clean cafe to the exit. Part two of my day's journey continued in teeming rain. Eighteen more miles saw me beat past Stoer Head, following the contours of some of the craggiest rock faces I'd seen so far, only to arrive in the fading light and dying breeze on Stoer beach.

Chapter 32

Wet Wet Wet – Clachtoll

I'd landed on what looked like a private beach. It was a nightmare getting the boat up to the high tide line as the beach was strewn with large rocks and boulders everywhere. The light was fading, a fence surrounded the shoreline. I was concerned I was in some type of military exclusion zone or nuclear wasteland or maybe an area of unexploded ordnance. It was barely possible to see now. At the far end of the beach, I could just make out a small cottage with no lights on. Parked outside was a large silver Mercedes. A tiny track wound up the hill which I assumed must join a road but nothing was visible from the beach. My mind raced thinking perhaps this was an area for drug running or smuggling. Maybe someone was inside this remote cottage counting out money or bagging up cocaine. A remote corner of Britain out of sight from prying eyes. The darkness and a strange place coupled with barbed wire fencing were playing tricks with my mind.

Once I'd got the boat to where I thought would be the high tide line, scraping the bottom over so many sharp pointy rocks I felt sure she would get punctured. I checked my mobile phone which was virtually out of battery and had no signal on the Vodafone network. I carried a spare mobile connected to O2. This had one bar flicking in and out but it was enough to call Emma. She too was struggling to get a signal and it took a series of garbled messages and dropped calls before we worked out exactly where I was.

Forty minutes later she found the house. The van's headlights lit up the darkness as she bounced along the tiny track. If anyone was in, they'd have come out as the noise and commotion of the van would have alerted them to my presence. It was pitch black so I signalled to her using the torch on the mobile to attract her attention. I was in the van like a shot, stumbling over the giant boulders and clambering up the receding bank, hurdling the fence and legging it as fast as I could to get out of this spooky place. I didn't like it, there was a bad feeling here and I was freezing cold.

Emma had already located a campsite only two miles away. She drove me shivering in the front of the van through flooded roads in torrential rain, made worse by the pitch-black sky. Jim, the owner of Clachtoll campsite, greeted us as if he was expecting me to turn up. I didn't realise Emma had already told him what I was up to. He was so friendly and welcoming, allowing us to stay free for the night, parking us as close to the shower block as he could, reducing the distance we had to run in the relentless rain. It was like the skies were swimming pools emptying all over us. I just managed to stuff down a gourmet meal of pasta, mixed with tinned peas and mackerel that Emma cooked in the back of the van washed down with a beer before I passed out, exhausted again.

This leg of the journey, through the Minch, was proving so complex. I knew nowhere at all, could barely pronounce some of the Gaelic names and, when setting up each day, realised I was just guessing about places I might be able to land at. Having Emma in support was a real boon as at least I wasn't camping in Ron's leaky tent. That would have been a real test, maybe even a deal breaker. I often thought fleetingly to myself about giving up but used to hurriedly bury such demons with distractions or other thoughts. My body felt like cement. I was so stiff, nothing wanted to bend. My right knee was sending regular complaint notices to my brain which was doing its utmost to ignore the messages.

It was nearly the end of August and I was still so far away from home. The weather felt like October would in the south of England and the rain just kept on coming. All my kit was worn out. None of the boat's pulleys would turn properly, having been filled too often with sand. All my ropes looked frayed and I was constantly concerned about them snapping at a critical point. I felt so exposed here. There was nothing for miles and miles, no people to see and nothing else with me day in day out on the water. Why would anybody venture out in this weather in a boat unless they had to? Even the wildlife seemed to have given up except for the odd puffin that still bombed around at breakneck speed.

Planning my onward route from Clachtoll just looked like a world of headlands. There was Reiff, Altandhu, the Isle of Ristol, Laide, Mellon, Opinan and Cove which apparently had a World War 2 gun emplacement on it. These names meant nothing to me just reading them off my Navionics app. They were fingers of land sticking out into the sea. I could see the words on my route planning like 'the Summer Isles' which sounded friendly and warm. Dots of islands were spread out all over this area. It was going to be easy to mistake one headland or island for the wrong one. The forecast looked dire again for the next day. Windy, overcast and treacherous.

"So what's new?" I asked myself. "Just man up and quit bleating about everything!"

The next leg of my journey from Clachtoll winding down along the western coast involved navigating through some of the most stunning islands on this earth; the Summer Isles, only at the time, I just couldn't see much of them as they were shrouded in thick black clouds and I was being lashed by seaspray as I passed between them. Sailing in such poor visibility made the time pass very slowly. It was hard-going and miserable. At around 3 pm I made it to what seemed the largest headland of the day, Rubha Reidh, with a magnificent, sadly defunct, lighthouse perched on the top.

Sailing close into the rocks I found myself battling the tide. The number of submerged rocks close in was particularly unnerving, appearing seemingly out of nowhere. Surrounded by frothing, foaming water, swirling, breaking eddies that reared up unexpectedly over the whole boat, it took nearly two hours to get round Rubha Reidh, staying in close was my only option, dicing with the rocks to get into the back eddy under this onerous headland. I was going to have to stop very soon. The tide was surging against me as soon as I poked my bow away from the land and the wind was rapidly dying.

My original plan had been to head for Big Sands or Gairloch but I'd never make it that far. There was a real danger I could get swept back out past the Rubha Reidh headland if I didn't get ashore fast. A small lone cottage in the distance drew me in and as I neared, a tiny stone slipway revealed itself. Narrow yes, but it looked landable so I went in closer to investigate ending up driving through two narrow breakwater walls, framing the ramp crunching the MOD27 onto the concrete before leaping out and safely making her fast on the shore. The time was 17.20, another eight hour day and only 33 miles covered. It sounded such a trivial distance for the effort put in. I felt totally drained again as I hauled the MOD27 further up to the safety of the top of the ramp, perching her next to the tiny shoreside cottage.

I'd landed in Melvaig, best known as an ancient Viking settlement and in more recent years as a smuggling location. The many caves buried into the cliff faces provided a perfect landing and hiding place for contraband. There were cliff top croft houses dotted sparsely on the landscape. The cottage I landed beside was owned by Eric. It was the only one by the shore. Eric himself only stayed here during the summer months, choosing to spend the rest of his time living in Malaysia with his wife who sounded like she wasn't a great fan of his Scottish homeland, preferring to stay in Malaysia herself. Eric looked like he might have played rugby when he was younger. He had that distinctive hooker shape, short bulky torso, little neck and stocky legs. Although probably 10 years older than me, I was surprised how strong he was when he helped pull the MOD27 up his slipway. When Eric spoke, it was with a soft Edinburgh east coast accent. His words were delivered in a calm unflustered manner. Dressed in three quarter length beige shorts and a thin short-sleeved shirt, he wouldn't have looked far out of place in the BBC comedy series, "It Ain't Half Hot Mum". Eric seemed quite unphased at my sudden arrival. In fact, he gave the impression he was almost expecting me.

He told me of two fellow circumnavigators who had stopped in their kayaks the previous year at this exact same spot. I almost felt I was on the circumnavigator tourist trail after our initial chat which didn't last long on account of the rain thundering down out of the sky in bucket loads.

This was Emma's last stop with me in Scotland. We camped on the beach that night in the van surrounded by sheep grazing on the lush green grass by the water's edge adjacent to Eric's cottage.

The following day I tried launching from the ramp. The winds were gusting up to 35 knots and the sea was cascading through the tiny breakwaters designed to protect the slipway. Launching looked like it was going to be tricky, even with Eric and Emma's help. I felt a constant pressure to keep moving especially as this section of the journey was going so slowly. I felt I was making so little headway. Looking out at the sea, it looked horrendous. However, I convinced myself this next part of the journey was slightly more sheltered than yesterday. I calculated that if I reefed, I may be able to cope with the strength of the breeze. In an attempt just to keep going, I deployed my reefing system for the first time, using my specially made sail with the vertical top batten that Gary Smith from Eastbourne had sewn in for me for just such an occasion. The vertical batten allowed me to roll the sail around the mast to reduce its overall size.

Once the MOD27 was rigged with her new sail configuration, Eric helped me down the ramp. The winds were so strong the boat just kept getting blown over while I stood up to my chest trying to launch through the breaking waves falling over the top of the breakwater walls. After 30 minutes of trying I finally made it away and, as I cleared the breakwater smashing through a tidal wave that engulfed me, I knew this was a bad idea. I carried on for around five minutes but was being smashed by every wave which were short but nearly vertical. My progress was so slow and the effort so great.

"This is pointless, I'm going to wreck the boat and me if I carry on."

I was trying to convince myself it would be alright when an almighty weather bomb landed on me. I could see a dark stripe of wind streaking across towards me, approaching from a long way offshore. It was moving at an incredible speed heading down along the length of the Minch, the stretch of water I was on. I knew it would flatten me and headed into the wind as it hit. The top batten snapped instantly and I was amazed I didn't capsize. The sail flogged uselessly for several minutes before I decided this was insane. Returning to Eric's was a hairy experience, comparable to that at the Mull of Kintyre. The smaller sail seemed to make no difference as with every gust I felt the boat get picked up and scream off in a mass of spay uncontrollably heading back towards the concrete slipway. I made it back to Eric's but wasn't in control enough to land on the ramp, electing to risk the rocks and land on the shore next to it. Eric looked almost disappointed at my return so quickly. However, he helped me carry the MOD27 back to the top of the concrete ramp, tying the bow to a rock further up the slope using the mainsheet to stop her blowing away.

Gary, the local plumber and member of the Gairloch Sailing Club, was trying to fix Eric's water main and emerged from the cottage to investigate what was going on. We got chatting and as a sailor himself he understood the value of a hot shower as he watched my teeth chattering and body shivering away. He made a call on his mobile and then told me he'd arranged for both Emma and I to pick up the key from the local shop to use the sailing club's hot showers in Gairloch. This was an upgrade from the previous evening when I'd washed in the freshwater stream running outside Eric's cottage.

Our trip to Gairloch was so wet and cold that we decided to use the offer of a sponsored night's stay in the local hotel donated by one of my Eastbourne Poker Gang friends, Cobie Loubster. I'd been introduced to Cobie through one of Emma's friends when we moved to Eastbourne. Cobie was the local vet and hosted a weekly game of poker in a room above his surgery.

Cobie was the perfect host for our poker nights, supplying copious amounts of wine and snacks. We played on a special padded felt table, located in the large mirrored room that, prior to his occupation had been used as a dance studio, hence the mirrors. Below us was a room full of cages packed with ill or recovering pets. While the animals slept in a sedated state of semi-consciousness, we'd work ourselves into a comatose state too, sampling the delights of the wine selection contributed each week by the players. For the first six months I managed to give away all my money to most of the room's occupants. Slowly I worked out that stemming the volume of alcohol proportionally reduced my losses. After a year or so, I even started to make some inroads into my expensive poker learning curve. I was surprised to find one of the members of the Poker Gang was completely blind which initially I felt was rather unfair for him. That is until Giles, the unsighted member at the table, managed to win all my money at our first meeting. I quickly lost any benevolent feelings for him after this and decided he must have developed a cheat method using the braille cards we played with.

We were a rag tag eclectic mix of professionals and misfits. Rather like myself, all had varied anomalous backgrounds but united by a common goal of drinking more wine or beer than your competitors and arresting £15 off them, Thursday evenings became a permanent fixture in my diary. We had such a laugh I'd nearly always run late into the early hours, more often than not landing me in trouble at home. I'd grope my way clumsily up the stairs, crashing into a picture or vase or some other unsuspecting object as I tried to sneak into the matrimonial bedroom undetected. This was usually about as successful as my poker skills and often started a full-scale assault from Emma on how inconsiderate I was for waking her when she had work the next day, etc, etc.

Our time during this enforced stop in Gairloch was wet but thanks to Cobie, it was comfortable and warm. When I wasn't falling asleep, which happened frequently, we visited the local museum and learned about crofting. We spent time in the local cafe where I met a lone Irishman who had to cycle 140 km that day to make it to his next accommodation stop. It was still torrential rain and 40 mph headwinds. It made sailing seem safe. When I said to him that I couldn't believe he was going to ride in this weather he replied,

"Well at least I won't drown!"

Without hesitation I responded, "I'm not planning on drowning."

This statement I delivered with a speed and confidence that surprised me. The Gairloch Hotel stopover was needed. Emma and I had a lovely evening meal together, drinking beer in the bar and with me munching my way through a Cajun burger and sticky toffee pudding. That day, Rooster Sailing sent me a full set of new sailing kit and a replica Laser sail after responding to a nationwide appeal through my Facebook page. It was a welcome gift. My current kit was proving woefully inadequate and worn out. I'd been trying to figure out somewhere for it to be sent for about a week but couldn't pinpoint anywhere I'd be staying long enough. This had been the perfect opportunity.

The Gairloch Museum kindly agreed to receive my deliveries, we must have set this up before checking into the hotel as I can't recall why it didn't go there. Andy French, another follower, sent me a new windex and Max from South East Sailboats supplied a full complement of ropes to replace my worn-out control lines. Simon Ogden from LaserPerformance LLC, the boat manufacturers, also agreed to send a new sail and mainsheet ratchet block to replace the broken one I was using but there wasn't enough time to arrange delivery to Gairloch so they went to my home address and sat there until my return. Biddy, a fellow drinker from my local, The Eight Bells in Jevington, sent me £100 which I used to buy personal safety equipment later in the journey. PY had taken pity on me and sent up his personal tent and his ex-army bivvy bag which he described as fully waterproof. Nothing could be worse than Ron's tent. When I left Melvaig on the 30th of August, it felt like a brand new start. It was nearly the beginning of a new month, Day 44 of my trip.

"Where had August gone?"

While I was upgrading and renewing my kit there were changes afoot behind the scenes. PY was preparing to hand over the Safety Channel reins he'd so diligently manned with Emma. Rupert Bedell, Dave Freeman and Roger Glass were the new recruits. Emma was going home again. I'd be alone. Camping, running wild. I felt good about the new kit and the boat was holding up well. The changes to the support team weren't foremost in my mind at this moment but it would unnerve me later.

I had a decent sail again, warmer kit and new ropes. My mainsheet ratchet block wasn't working but I'd learned to live with it, my fingers had got used to gripping the mainsheet all day. The new windex from Andy was a relief, I'd been moving for a week or more without one and although not essential I found the downwind legs trickier without a wind indicator, especially when there were sudden changes in direction which seemed to be happening frequently on this coastline.

I woke at 6 am on Saturday. No one was able to take payment in the hotel at this hour so Emma agreed to phone in later with a card to check out. Arriving at Eric's via the local bakery, where I picked up a Scotch pie and sausage rolls, I noticed the boat was in a different place. Eric appeared from his front door as we drew up. It was teeming with rain again and he approached draped in a waterproof coat. Eric explained he'd just saved the MOD27 from being washed away in a high tide last night and managed to drag her back up the ramp on his own. I couldn't quite believe it. What a lucky break! Again.

I departed with Eric waving through a fog of rain from his house, kissed Emma goodbye and on the way to the boat felt an overwhelming sinking feeling in the pit of my stomach as I pushed off. I often got it before launching, I was usually OK once I was sailing. Emma had triggered it, just as I was about to launch

"You look so tiny when you're out there at sea. Like a dot on the landscape."

I didn't respond but it's surprising how even the most minor comments can unsettle and play on your mind.

Chapter 33

Leopard's Place

The plan today was to make it to Applecross. I left Melvaig in pouring rain but the good news was the breeze was behind me and I made good progress, surfing along at 8 knots. Applecross was a place people had mentioned a lot, of recent fame after a weekend visit by Boris Johnson, his wife and new baby seeking a remote location to hide away from the media glare during the Covid-19 pandemic.

I made it past Applecross without seeing anything of it, 35 km knocked off surfing along in a force 3 to 4 and even the rain had stopped. Things were looking up. I carried on until it looked like the end of the land before a vast expanse of open water appeared. I could make out buildings on the far side but the wind had dropped and I was unsure about the tides in this area.

The open water was called the Inner Sound, adjacent to Loch Carron, some 1 km past Applecross. I could see a large ferry ploughing across and it looked fairly innocuous. However, I wanted to check so, as I approached the sound, I pulled into a small seaweed strewn inlet of rock. Nestled behind the weed was a small croft house. It looked deserted but I wasn't certain. I pulled the boat up and tied her off to a rock then set about checking my Navionics app for my location, weather, tides and distance. I was in a place called Uags. I made a call to PY who was still just hanging on to his Safety Channel commitment pending his imminent break to go sailing himself at the Laser Masters World Championships in Holland. He agreed that the tides looked fine and after a short stop I decided to go for the crossing.

The passage through the Inner Sound took a while as the wind was now light. I aimed for the large bridge silhouetted dominantly in the bright blue sky, sitting 200 feet above the Kyle of Lochalsh. As I approached, the tide was sucking me towards the other direction of Loch Carron. It was pointless resisting so I turned and flowed inland towards Badicaul, another small inlet. There were a number of yachts moored at anchor but after a good search I couldn't see anywhere soft amongst the rock-strewn inlet to land. I considered tying up alongside one of the yachts. When I pulled alongside, the deck height was only just parallel with my head. Climbing aboard was going to be tricky but not impossible.

"Then what? Break into the yacht?" I thought to myself out loud.

Dismissing this idea fairly quickly, there was nothing else for it. Retrace my steps, hug the shore and keep out of the tide as much as possible. Once I made it to the bridge, the tide would split and whoosh me along; it divided between the Inner Sound and Lochalsh.

It took over an hour to crawl my way to the other side of the bridge. Once through it, there was an attractive frontage on my right-hand shore lined with canopied shops and hotels along the water's edge. A high wall protecting the structures from flooding prevented me from pulling in here. The other side of the loch looked very industrialised, full of large ships and vessels. I carried on until I came to a small harbour. I sailed in but there were no pontoon spaces free and the only landing option was a steep narrow concrete ramp, half covered in green slime at the harbour mouth. For the second time that day, I circled looking for somewhere. It's surprising how difficult I was finding mooring my tiny 13-foot boat.

There was a tiny collection of houses in one corner which looked similar to dolls' houses planted on the bank of the horseshoe shaped harbour. They looked pretty but their paintwork looked beaten and tired. Sliding off the side of the MOD27, I sank into the green weedy harbour, water up to my neck. I waded across a floor of slippery uneven boulders, through a tonne of seaweed before reaching the stony boulder-lined shore. I must have looked like a sea monster draped in red and green weed from head to toe as I emerged. I slipped and tumbled face down in the icy water.

Once ashore, cursing and removing weed that had stuck in great clumps to my body, I nosed around the houses packed tightly together but found no sign of life. The place was deserted and there was no obvious landing place, other than one of the house's front gardens, where I could park up and camp for the evening. I called out

"Hello! Hello!"

I felt awkward shouting loudly. No one responded. I was almost pleased, as I didn't think anyone would appreciate a bellowing Englishman hoofing across their lawn dropping seaweed and shouting.

"This place is no good," I told myself.

Even if I found someone to ask, I couldn't leave the boat anywhere, it was just rocks and weeds, so I pushed off back out into the main channel of Lochalsh and carried on moving away from civilisation. Soon it would be dark and I was sailing in a broad expanse of water, surrounded by nothing except rolling hills covered in dense woodland on both sides. Behind, rising as far as I could see, were jagged mountain tops. Far in the distance, I spotted a lone kayaker moving slowly towards the eastern shore. He was a long way off but even from where I was, it looked very low in the water. I changed direction and aimed for him, pulling in my sail to intercept him before he crossed the channel.

"He may be able to offer some advice on a place where I could stop this evening," I thought.

The kayak looked totally weighed down and in danger of sinking when I got close. As I approached, I could only see one head in spite of it being a two man boat. A jet black face with gleaming white teeth and a giant afro poking out of the cockpit greeted me with a wave. I hailed from a distance, asking him if he had any ideas where I might camp for the night. My new friend paddled towards me then reached out an arm, catching hold of my mainsheet at the back of the boat to steady himself. This was a particularly bad idea as it had the effect of speeding me up as he pulled the sail in harder to stay close to me. I nearly capsized on top of him. Shouting for him to let go, I managed to arrest the mainsheet off him, regaining some control. We then conducted a merry dance as I circled the kayak desperately trying to stop him grabbing the mainsheet again. He really didn't seem to understand the problem of doing so. It was a total Laurel and Hardy moment.

He was gesticulating in the direction of a large power pylon snaking its way across an otherwise unspoilt landscape in the distance and shouting. In a surprisingly thick Scottish accent he said,

"Aye hed fur Leppardman's Place o'er there. Leopards Place, aye unda tha pylon. That'll serve you tonight. It's a bothy unda tha pylon. O'er there."

As he pointed and shouted, his kayak visibly took on more water through the rear seat and I feared he may not actually make it ashore. I had my own mission of finding a place to camp so dismissed him as probably knowing what he was doing and cracked off the sail to head for 'Leopard's Place' as he called it, near the giant pylon.

Quite what Leopard's Place was, or indeed who Leopard Man was I hadn't a clue but it seemed like a plan which, in the absence of any other, may as well be explored further. I sailed for only 10 minutes before closing in on the pylon although it was still a long way in the distance half way up a hill. Immediately in front of me now was a shallow grassy shoreline with water so clear it looked like crystal.

I pulled the MOD27 up onto the grassy bank sitting some two feet above the water. It had reeds growing through the soft marshy soil underneath and was boggy to walk over. I set off in search of the "Leopard Man's bothy". After walking only some 10 metres, in front of me, almost invisible from the shoreline, was a stone-built structure with a corrugated sheet metal roof. These were partially covered in the same stones as the bothy walls. It had a narrow winding entrance which meant you couldn't see what was inside until you turned the corner.

As I ducked lower to get under the partially collapsed roof I approached cautiously, unsure what might be waiting for me inside. I needn't have worried as a collection of plastic water containers stacked in one corner was the only occupant. There was an open firepit under another stone-covered corrugated sheet. The middle of the bothy was open. It looked like storm damage had lifted the central sheet away offering a night sky view from the shelter. On the far corner of the floor was a rubber cushioned mat laid out for sleeping and a series of shelves created from the rocks to hold a selection of vessels like cups, a lighter, bits of tyre for lighting the fire and other odd trinkets that had all been reclaimed from rubbish, like an old soup can and baked bean tin. Someone clearly was or had been living here. The fire had some charred wood still on it although it was quite wet as the roof had been leaking directly above.

Well this was Leopard Man's bothy and I was going to be his guest tonight! As I returned to the boat, the midges started. I unscrewed my hatch cover and frantically searched for the head net I'd bought in Kinlochbervie. They were beginning to have a serious feed on my face and neck. I located the head net and pulled it over my head. This hardly improved the situation as I was now being eaten from inside the net by trapped midges. Running headlong into the stream next to the bothy I dived underwater tearing off the net to rid myself of these man-eating insects. Once in the stream, I stripped off all my wetsuit gear in the safety of the water, keeping my head mostly submerged as much as possible. It was certainly fresh but this was only temporary relief from those flying piranhas. I realised all of my clothes were still in the MOD27.

"Oh shit! Now what do I do?" I groaned to myself out loud.

Making a run for the boat where my kit was stowed, naked as a baby, I managed to outrun the midges until I reached the MOD27. Stopping was my weakness, searching madly, pulling out bags and tossing them wherever they fell while the midges tucked into my exposed flesh. I eventually located my towel, underwear, trousers and a clean top. By the time I'd struggled into my clothes and was fully dressed I'd now successfully invited midges into every orifice, devouring my soft white flesh like it was their last supper.

Returning to the bothy, I set about getting the fire lit to frighten off these unbearable pests. There wasn't any dry wood and lighting the fire wasn't working at all. Scrounging around, I found some drier wood supporting the mattress keeping it off the damp floor. Feeling a little guilty about breaking up the bed support, I succeeded in getting a flame, driven on by the ferocity of the midges biting. Once alight, the smoke drove them away. I was safe for a while. I recall John from Kinlochbervie telling me you can set your watch to the midges, emerging on the dot of 5 pm every day on the west coast of Scotland.

By the time I'd cooked my tinned pimento sausage in a tin and macaroni cheese on the open fire and washed it down with a can of lager I'd saved from the previous evening in Gairloch, there was not a midge to be seen. The air was completely still. Silent all around, the only sounds were animals moving about outside. Animals! What sort of animals lived on this island? Were they dangerous? I'd read about the endangered Scottish wildcats (Felis silvestris grampia, their Latin name) inflicting injuries on vets. Surely it wasn't an island of wildcats I started to wonder. Maybe the reason it was called Leopard Man's bothy was because there were leopards here or something that vaguely resembled them? Surely not. This is Scotland not Africa! I convinced myself.

Just in case, I spent some time building an animal obstacle barrier at the bothy entrance, making it secure. I then started wondering if Leopard Man would come home in the dead of night and seeing a stranger lying in his bed, draw his hunting knife and cut my throat like in one of those Rambo movies. My afro kayaker friend had mentioned something about him being an ex-SAS soldier. Settling down to sleep, I kept one eye open for the first minute before passing out with exhaustion after another long day.

As it transpires, I needn't have stressed, Leopard Man was actually deceased. Following a subsequent Google search later on in my journey I uncovered the full story. Tom Leppard, or Tom Wooldridge as he was christened, had lived as a recluse in the very bothy I was sleeping in. He'd lived on the Isle of Skye for 20 years after moving up from London. He'd served in the army, the navy and then had a stint in the Rhodesian Special Forces. It would seem Tom had adopted the notion that he was a 'Man Leopard'. According to several high-profile media reports I uncovered, he apparently patrolled the island virtually naked bearing only the head to his toe leopard spots tattooed on his body and a tiny pouch for his essentials. I found pictures online of him bathing in the very same stream I'd washed in. Tom was in the Guinness Book of Records as the most tattooed man. Local stories tell of him crossing to the mainland in his canoe once a week to collect his pension and drink a pint in the local pub before doing his shopping. Tom left the island in 2008 and ended his days in a care home for the elderly at a ripe old age of 80.

The following morning when I pulled on my brand new Rooster Sailing gear I smelt like a bonfire. Everything absolutely stank of smoke from the fire I'd kept alight all night. Leaving the Isle of Skye that morning felt like I'd just had an extraordinary experience. Isolated in such beauty, I felt blessed to have spent an evening in this mesmeric place.

Chapter 34

Magic Carpet to Portnadoran

My task now was to keep heading south. It was calm today and drifting along with the current, I passed down the narrow channel through the Kyle of Lochalsh. It was like riding on a magic carpet of bubbles. The further along the loch I travelled, the narrower it became and the higher the cliffs rose either side. There was little wind yet I was moving at close to 10 knots. I passed the local Glenelg Isle of Skye car ferry, consisting of one small green hulled barge with a bright red platform stuck on top, capable of transporting three or four cars at a time. The people onboard waved as I whizzed past and I watched the boat slewing sideways fighting across the tide towards the miniature white lighthouse next to the slipway. Behind it, a small turquoise hut with glazed windows across the top of the doors seemed to smile at me as I passed by.

Shortly after this point, a series of large whirlpools gripped my boat and tried to spin me round in the same whirling direction. I kept steering straight and weaved around the larger pools until the water opened up into a breath-taking wide expanse of sea again, surrounded by mountains on all sides. White clouds hung like smoke rings near to the summits, the sun poked through them and disappeared again. I savoured the heat as it broke through and shivered when it disappeared again. The day's journey was like changing scenes from postcards. It was beautiful!

As I exited the loch, I emerged into a busy shipping area at the mouth of the Kyle of Rhea. There were numerous large ships ploughing past so I elected to stay close to the mainland side of the ever widening loch. I was halfway across Loch Hourn, working my way along the shore, there was still very little wind and it was morning coffee time.

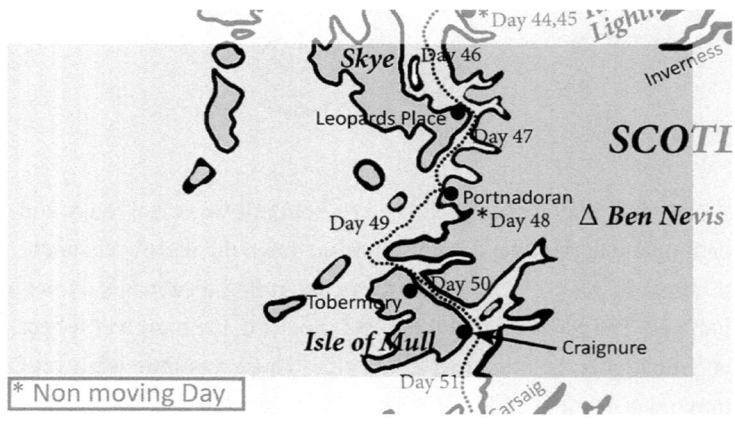

"Not much chance of finding a cafe here," I said to myself out loud.

Almost as soon as those words had left my mouth I sailed past a small inlet with a rocky beach and noticed a large modern wooden Scandinavian looking house perched on a long terrace overlooking the bay. I thought there was little point continuing in such light winds and I needed to fill my empty water bottles so I decided to pull in and investigate.

The bay had a wide entrance leading into a narrowing beach. After dragging the MOD27 up the deserted beach, I walked up towards the house across a grassy lawn. There was an old rowing boat artistically placed to add authenticity to what was clearly a modern addition to the landscape. As I approached the double set of large glass double sliding doors looking out over the tiny natural harbour, I noticed several bags of shopping left on the veranda, then boxes of beer, a six pack of Guinness and a case of wine.

"Hmm..they must be expecting me," I chuckled to myself.

Just as I was laughing out loud, a lady appeared at one of the doors, looking interested but not concerned at my sudden appearance

"Hello" she said in an English accent.

She had a shoulder length thick bob of blonde hair, half-moon glasses and a silver locket hanging on a chain around her neck, placed neatly over her navy blue crew neck jumper. Her face was pale with rosy cheeks and I guessed she was in her early forties. Her friendly face had a perfect second chin which appeared to symmetrically follow the contours of her jaw, drawing to an attractive blunt point when she smiled. It was a welcoming smile.

"Sorry to intrude upon you but I was wondering if I could fill up my water bottles?" I enquired.

"Of course," she replied slightly cautiously but invited me inside.

I was standing dripping on her mat in her kitchen area, conscious I probably still smelt like an old bonfire. There was a long pine island in the centre and a deep white butler sink on the far side of the kitchen. It was a very large room all clad in pine boards and, judging by the assortment of shoes and jackets lying around the house, was clearly home to many people. She made her way to the sink to fill up my bottles for me. While I stood on the mat I was greeted by a beige poodle dog that bounded over excitedly. Another lady appeared behind the dog.

I had landed at Dun Ban Bay, Doune. It transpired there was a group of 10 of them on holiday with their husbands and friends who were presently out in a motorboat on a diving expedition. We got chatting and I explained about my journey. In the process, I managed to somehow slip in something about why I'd stopped here, thinking it might be a cafe. Within a few minutes I was being served a cappuccino and chocolate biscuits. I could have eaten the whole tin but didn't want to appear rude so subtly managed to slip in four or five biscuits, eating them two at a time to disguise how many I'd taken, trying desperately not to look greedy. I don't think it worked.

My new friend, the dog, was very excited at my arrival. Whilst patting him, I chatted for nearly an hour about all sorts including the remoteness of this area. The ladies explained it was so remote from any medical services there that a Land Rover is permanently parked at the top of the hill. The keys are left in it for the community in the event of a hospital emergency. Glancing out of the window, I noticed the MOD27 sail was flapping. The wind had filled in so thanking them, I disappeared as quickly as I'd arrived.

On the morning Safety Channel briefing, I'd put down Mallaig harbour and Arisaig as likely stopping points today. The latter of these was still 30 miles away. This could take around five hours to reach, assuming the tide didn't turn against me which I believed it would do very shortly. I battled away most of the afternoon, often going sideways the wrong way in the tide, crabbing along a few feet away from the numerous lumps of vitrified rock protruding into the sea, keeping close inshore to stay out of the foul tide.

Around three o'clock my progress improved with a freshening breeze but with it came the rain, driving me south at around 8 knots with a northerly breeze behind me. By 5.30 pm, I'd had enough and made landfall at Portnadoran, a small inlet set deeply inside a plethora of large and very difficult to navigate boulders. They seemed to be an impenetrable collection of rocks just strewn all over the sea. The navigation was made more difficult as the breeze had continued to build and visibility became appalling with driving rain and a fog like cloud obscuring the lumps of rock dotted everywhere.

Pulling my boat into a small sandy area where I could see other small boats and kayaks were stored, I worked my way in pulling alongside a fishing boat with a long anchor line leading out to sea from one end and high up to the shore from the other. The sandy shore was soft and quite steep, making getting the MOD27 up as far as high tide mark hard going. After a long struggle I finally tied off to an anchor ring embedded onto a low wall.

"That's a Laser, isn't it?" an inquiring voice piped up from behind a rain soaked, wide brimmed leather hat said.

I acknowledged the person but paid little attention, thinking about getting my tent up in this weather as fast as possible, finding a shower and trying to figure out how I could keep everything dry in the process.

"I sail a Laser," the person continued.

I really wasn't in the mood to engage about the fineries of a Laser at this precise moment but somehow managed to keep myself from saying anything rude and just smiled and nodded.

Paul was my new first contact so in my customary style I asked him to pose with me on the shore for a selfie to prove I'd landed where I was. We both smiled inanely in the rain for our picture. I continued with setting up camp and went off in search of the campsite owner to investigate if they minded me perching on a patch of grass very close to my boat.

The campsite owner was a tough Highlander. She seemed about as miserable as I was with the rain. However, she kindly allowed me to pitch my tent on the grass next to her house for free and she let me use the shower which I had to feed with pound coins. Fortunately I still had a few pounds in my lifejacket for just such an emergency. I was also able to hang all my gear up in the shower room overnight which, although unheated, was at least dry.

Getting unpacked every time I landed was still taking me ages. The problem was that the tent was always in the wrong place inside the boat or the bags wouldn't squeeze through the tiny hatch, there was either too much air trapped inside one of the dry bags or they'd all got jumbled up inside. I'd often squeeze both hands through the hatch and, to get them out, I had to unroll one of five Rooster mini 5 litre dry bags, press any air out of them while they were still inside the hull and then force them one at a time back out of the hatch. My knuckles nearly always ended up bleeding after pulling all the stuff out. On this occasion, nothing was different. The tent was the last item to come out, somehow it had slid along the inside hull of the boat, probably when I was pounding into the waves headlong downwind. Then to extricate the tent, I almost had to insert half of my upper body and all of my arm stretching lying on the soaking wet deck of the boat squashing my cheek into the orange hull, extending my fingers until they nearly dislocated to grasp one corner of the tent bag and slowly draw it towards my hand before getting a firm enough grip to withdraw it.

This was the first time I'd ever put this particular tent up. PY had sent me his personal tent as he'd clearly got bored with me moaning about Ron's sieve of a tent. The rain was lashing down and the wind howling; neither ideal for the first time erecting a new tent. A lot of cursing later, it was up. There was barely any room for me once my gear was fully unloaded. The sleeping bag was just damp when I removed it from its waterproof casing but much drier than it had been after a night in front of the fire at Leopard's Place.

After showering that evening, I placed my gas burner cooker inside the fly sheet but outside the tent. It was a precarious set-up, balancing a tiny pot on top of the penknife size burner, itself screwed into a midget size gas canister. It was the smallest cooker I could find, often so small that I usually lost it and I regularly had to tip everything out of my dry bags to locate it. For £12.99 though, it had proven to be great value. I carried a spare gas cylinder with me in the boat but had only just changed it. They seemed to hold an incredible amount of fuel for their size. The trick was to cook the pasta first then add any veg or whatever I had to the same pan. I could only cook a cupful at a time so often did two or three brews. Water wasn't an issue here so coffee and a muesli snack bar made up dessert.

Paul, my new contact, had invited me over to his caravan for a beer and I really fancied one so I groped my way across a fence and along a long grassy pathway. Wearing my waterproof yellow wet gear and Henri-Lloyd top, I arrived at his in the pitch dark looking like I'd taken a bath. My dry shoes were totally sodden. Paul hung all the gear up and stuffed my shoes with paper, placing them in front of the gas fire burning away.

It transpired Paul was a Laser sailor and regularly visited this area for his annual holiday. He lived in Perth and worked at the Morgan car factory as a senior technician. He also had a son at Dundee University who was a similar age to my youngest son. Tragically, his wife Wendy had died suddenly five months earlier. This was his first time at the caravan on his own without her since they were married. I felt very sad for him, clearly he was trying to find a way to adjust to his loss.

The following day it was too windy to move. Paul came and found me hunkering down in my tent in the lashing rain. I was grateful for a dry refuge and Paul and I visited Arisaig and Mallaig harbour, driving around in his mustard yellow Camel Land Rover. That evening we talked about Paul's and his father's passion for Morgans, Rovers and Jaguars. We ate steak in his caravan and sampled some of Scotland's finest malt whisky. He opened his heart further about his father who was in palliative care suffering from dementia and cancer. His loss seemed a lot for one person to bear.

Chapter 35

Western Most Point Latitude 56°43.619'N/Longitude 006°13.567'W

I found leaving Portnadoran in the early hours of another dank, windy day, somewhat depressing. It took me just shy of three hours to get myself up, fed, packed and launched. This was so slow. Even after coming all this way, I still hadn't perfected a faster way to get going each day. I was cheered by the fact I was now approaching Ardnamurchan which is the western most point of the UK mainland. It was a landmark moment and the thought that I must have travelled over 1,000 miles in my tiny Laser to reach this point felt good.

"Only one more corner to turn after this one and it's homeward bound," I said out loud, trying to convince myself I was on the home straight.

My concerns about the weather had been raised another notch the day before after visiting Mallaig harbour and watching boat after boat being craned out for the winter. I was barely keeping ahead of the weather window which I felt the pressure of closing in on me as I moved into the month of September. Forecasts of gales sweeping in from America were inevitable.

The day's sailing started in 8 mph of wind, the sea was flat and there was a constant drizzle, visibility was murky. What I'd describe as a dank day. Despite its strength, I made good progress as the wind direction was south easterly. I needed to make it round Ardnamurchan by 2 pm. After this, the tide would turn and I'd probably not make it round at all until it switched back again six hours later.

Approaching the lighthouse which sits high up on a rocky peninsula, it looked ominous, silhouetted against a blanket of haar. Sailing very close to Samma Bay, keeping tight to the black fearsome rocks, I made it round just before 2 pm. The sea was pretty bumpy now with waves crashing back off the headland rocks. They did their usual washing machine impression, throwing me and the MOD27 up and down like a tiny matchstick. I banged my way around even taking time out to study the lighthouse standing defiantly on top of the rocky headland.

Built in 1849 by the chief engineer, Alan Stevenson, the lighthouse has a range of 18 nautical miles, sitting 55 metres above the sea. The structure of the tower is grey granite which stands 35 metres in height with 152 steps to the top of the tower. The bottom of the tower is surrounded by a high solid white wall standing at least 20 feet high all round. In the early years, a 50 foot section of this wall and 40 feet of the access road were washed away in a severe storm.

As I drew parallel with the lighthouse and rounded the western most point of the UK mainland, I felt the full force of the Atlantic. The waves had significantly increased in size and were now bowling me through a chaotic mass of foam and white water bouncing back off the cliff face. I wondered how much more punishment the boat would take. With every wave, the aluminium mast smashed up and then down in

Western Most Point Latitude 56°43.619'N/Longitude 006°13.567'W

its fibreglass slot. I was sure it would eventually punch a hole through the bottom, leaving me sinking without trace. After about half an hour, I'd made it into the Sound of Mull. Now the only issue was avoiding the massive container ships appearing out of nowhere. I cautiously kept close to the cliffs in order not to get run down and when the breeze was right, I made a dash for it reaching across towards Tobermory in the thick fog.

As I crossed, my phone rang. I managed to answer and Dave Freeman was on the line. As I reached along covered in spray, Dave gave me his full and detailed appraisal of the options I had available to me for landing. It was Dave's first day on the Safety Channel and unlike PY he started offering me detailed managerial advice on what to do and where to go. I half listened as I battled my way through the surf but barely heard a word of his comprehensive assessment. I gleaned Tobermory as a possible stop off but that was about it.

Following Dave's call, I felt I was being micromanaged, a feeling I don't respond well to and decided to dismiss his initial advice but as I approached Tobermory on the screaming reach I'd been enjoying, the wind evaporated and it turned into a very slow beat, fighting against the tide and very little wind. By now the phone had packed up with no juice left in the battery, eliminating my navigation aid. It was decision time so I heeded Dave's advice and headed for the large rafts of pontoons I could see in front of what I assumed must be Tobermory.

This day we'd both survived again and the MOD27 and I had covered another 60 km. Approaching the sheltered port of Tobermory, the cliffs rose like centurions behind the array of pretty buildings. A single near continuous, row of shops and houses were arranged as a horseshoe running parallel to the single lane road, painted in a bright assortment of pastel colours. The pale stone wall was all that held back the force of the sea from washing these buildings away.

I pulled into the large pontoon village at the far end of town and parked the MOD27 on top of one. There were so many pontoons and being late in the season, it was easy to find a reasonably empty one. Made of metal with a wooden slatted deck, the pontoons floated along above the water. It took quite an effort heaving the boat up and by the time I'd managed it, I was tired and couldn't be bothered to un-rig so I pulled the sail and mast out in one go and laid it down flat, lashing it a few metres away from the hull to the mooring eyes spread evenly along the rafts. The pontoon was narrower than I'd thought and I nearly fell in trying to avoid walking over the sail, tiptoeing precariously around the edge.

The first person to meet me was the harbour master, Joe. He was a jolly sort and was happy to partake in the usual selfie pose. His bushy beard disguised his youthful face. He directed me to the harbour showers which I was allowed free access to. Camping here was going to be quite an issue. It would involve a long walk up into a wood. I didn't fancy that idea so much and parked this problem for later. I half thought the harbour changing rooms would be a good shelter for the night until I read about the CCTV and security barriers closing after 9.30 pm. On my way into town, I searched for any redundant sheds or buildings I could bunk down in for the night. There was nothing obvious.

Fish and chips sold from the kiosk on the harbour front looked an easy option for grub so I sat in the drizzle on the bench opposite along the quayside. A half price punnet of blueberries and natural yoghurt I bought from the local Co-op provided dessert. A pint seemed like a good call after that but as I was heading towards the local pub, I passed a YHA building. For reasons unknown to me, I stepped in through the door and asked the man on reception if he had any rooms. He did.

"Good news," I thought.

Then he asked, "Do you mind sharing it with two ladies? It's a mixed sex room."

For a second, I thought he'd said it's a sex room. Where was I? It didn't look much like a brothel. Everything seemed quite pristine and above board.

"Sorry what does that mean?" I asked tentatively.

"It's a four person mixed sex room share. Bunks. Are you ok with that?" he asked.

I really didn't care, I just needed to lie down. Right now, the place was dry and warm, that was enough, who cared if I hadn't packed my pyjamas and dressing gown. Hopefully the ladies wouldn't mind.

The room was quite large. When I opened the door, it was empty. The beige walls had little personality but it was fine. There was a large Victorian sash window opposite my bunk. Crossing the room, I squinted out across the harbour and just made out my boat and sail still safely perched on top of the pontoon.

Plugging in all of my electrical kit, I used up all the sockets in the room.

"This place was a good call," I mumbled to myself.

I found a drying room where I could rinse and hang up all my wet weather gear and a kitchen to cook where you could help yourself to make a free cup of tea or coffee. I felt drained so took my tea upstairs and crashed out for an hour, crawling into the bottom bunk nearest the door. The other bunk bed was on the opposite side of the entrance door and it had someone's bag next to it. The single bed under the window also had luggage on so I assumed it was already occupied too. Both appeared to be female bags.

The sleep was short-lived because as soon as I'd conked out, the door opened.

Jolting upright in response I instinctively said, "Hello."

"Hi" replied a slim waisted girl with shoulder length, fawn coloured hair in her mid-twenties. She was dressed in a pair of skin-tight green joggers and a loose, long, faded long sleeved pink shirt. From her initial accent she sounded slightly Germanic but I couldn't be sure.

"I'm Anja" she said.

"Stick" I replied.

She stood, slightly guarded, chatting to me with the door ajar just in case she had to make a run for it. I was sitting up in bed with only a t-shirt and underpants on. As we struck up a simple question and answer type conversation, I was conscious my trousers were some way from my bed so I stayed where I was, not wanting to frighten my new roommate so soon. We talked about the usual things like what are you doing here? Where have you been? Where are you from? Our chat carried on for quite a while and I felt less awkward as Anja told me all about her day. She was on her own in Scotland walking the West and East Highland Ways. In Germany she worked as a forestry commission ranger, teaching woodcraft to young children. She told me that day she'd been out walking in the torrential rain. Reaching a swollen river, she made a decision to cross it by climbing a fallen tree instead of turning back and walking another 10 miles to go round it. She'd just made it across the river, narrowly avoiding falling in. It sounded very dodgy. When I was up in Gairloch I'd seen for myself how fast these rivers were flowing. If you fell into one, you'd have very little chance of surviving. From her voice, she sounded like she'd confirmed her belief in destiny. I felt a strange bond after this conversation as I too was feeling someone was looking after me.

Later that evening, I dressed and went downstairs to the kitchen. I chatted with my new roommate while I worked out my route plan for the next day and updated my diary entry. The other lady staying in our room introduced herself in the kitchen and we all had a grumble about the relentless rain in Scotland.

That night I barely slept. Whether it was the presence of two strange ladies sleeping less than 10 feet from me in the same room or my experiences of the previous few days keeping me awake, I couldn't tell you. I rose early the following morning at 5.30 am and was under sail by 7 am. One of the fastest exits I think I'd managed on the trip so far.

Chapter 36

Josh n' Craigy Fish

Leaving Tobermory was difficult. I'd enjoyed my new friends' company the previous night and could happily have stuck around for a day enjoying breakfast and looking around the harbour with them. I knew I had to keep pressing on. The forecast for the day was terrible after midday. My plan was to make it down the Sound of Mull before lunchtime, park up and aim to cross the infamous race at the bottom and cross to Oban the next day.

The start of my journey was very calm, near flat calm. After rigging on the pontoon, I waited for half an hour for some wind to fill in and got chatting to two yachtsmen. One called David offered me accommodation on his yacht, Goldfinger, which apparently was on a mooring somewhere near Oban. Regrettably I didn't write down the harbour name at the time so managed to forget what it was called instantly. He did, however, give me some advice for navigating through a short cut across the shallows out of Tobermory which resulted in saving me an hour off my journey.

By 9 am I was well underway, the sun had come out and the scenery was simply stunning, surrounded by grassy mountains with Ben Nevis in the background. There were inlets everywhere and I flowed along with the current, down the narrow sound taking in the scenery from both sides. I passed the fish farms, dodged the ferry and put my feet up relaxing, lying across the boat enjoying the glorious sunny weather.

Bang!

Out of nowhere, it felt like a giant hand just reached down out of the sky and picked me up tipping me upside down. In seconds, the sky had turned black and I was swimming frantically after the MOD27 in the freezing water. The boat was lying on her side being blown away from me in a hurricane force wind. I wasn't tied on and as I'd fallen over backwards out of the boat, I didn't have a chance to grab hold of anything. I could see the sail filling as it blew away from me. I felt my body and chest tightening and thought I might be experiencing cold shock. Staying calm, I concentrated on breathing and regulating my heart rate. I was still within swimming distance of the boat but because of the buoyancy bag and dry bag stowed in the cockpit the boat hadn't turned upside down and was being blown along the sound.

My hands were going numb as I thrashed around trying to take as long and smooth a swimming stroke as I could wearing a buoyancy aid. The problem with a lifejacket is it makes you float but swimming in one is seriously inefficient. Coupled with wet boots on my feet, I wasn't dressed to win any swimming records. My laboured front crawl did seem to be working though and after a few minutes I closed in on the back of the upturned hull and managed to grab a rope which was hanging under water using this to haul myself onto the centreboard.

"That was a close one," I thought as I pulled the boat upright.

The sail was flapping madly in this sudden squall and I headed directly inshore which was some distance away, uncontrollably surfing on a broad reach in towards the nearest shoreline. I was nearly bowled into the water again by another ferocious gust but somehow managed to wobble my way in, averting a repeat performance. I landed shortly afterwards on a rocky shoreline next door to the beach of the Craignure ferry terminal. Standing looking down the Sound of Mull, the Caledonian Ferry was slewing sideways, as she turned towards me she was being blown sideways and listing a long way over, aiming for the safety of the ferry terminal in the howling winds. I watched for nearly an hour as it tried to dock. It looked seriously dangerous for the winchmen on the landing jetty. The wind had come in almost to the minute of the forecasters' predictions, blowing 35 knots plus from nowhere.

How bizarre that exactly the same thing should have happened to me when I was passing the eastern most point. This was the second capsize of the trip, the first had been near Lowestoft and this near Ardnamurchan – east and west. Was this perhaps some kind of scent marking thing?

As I stood on the shore, it was as much as I could do to stand up and hold my camera phone while I recorded the ferry coming in. Ian, the site manager at Sheilings Holiday Park, approached me on the beach and offered me a hand pulling the boat up above the high tide mark. We grinned for another ridiculous landing selfie. When I explained to Ian that I was raising money for prostate cancer by sailing round the UK, he offered me a free space on the campsite. We wandered around for a few minutes barely able to stand looking for a spot, there were plenty to choose from and it seemed nearly deserted. The problem was finding a place where the tent wouldn't blow away. In the end he suggested I bed down in one of their marquees which were strapped to the floor with scaffold poles although these were still trying to uproot themselves. We both watched the top of a large tree snap off and disappear in the distance.

"You can bed down in here if you like."

Ian was pointing at a marquee held together with scaffold poles to stop it from taking off. Inside there were four bunks standing on a wooden floor. Certainly it was a lot easier than trying to pitch a tent in this wind and also I could spread out my gear for it to dry overnight. Plugs for the phones and space for my cooker. No breaking down time in the morning.

"Fantastic!" I exclaimed before Ian had a chance to change his mind.

The shower block was some way from the marquee but it was modern and the water was boiling. I spent a good half hour in there, stripping out of my wetsuit and reheating my frozen bones. I'd been lucky today. I knew the forecast was bringing gale force winds and I'd pushed just a bit too long. Had the MOD27 and I got separated I doubt anyone would have seen me and picked me up in that weather. It wasn't something I'd dwell on but another dent was made into my unconscious thoughts.

I'd no idea what to expect for the next part of this journey. The coastline seemed brutal and inhospitable. Researching routes for the next few days, I couldn't figure out any soft landings or simple passages. All the maps showed were cliffs, crags and tiny inlets, raging tidal races and numerous whirlpools. I was on Day 50 of this journey and nowhere near in sight of the end. Today I'd only managed to dig out 30 km and the weather was looking terrible for the next week ahead. I decided that I must try to find some local fishermen or boat people who could offer some advice so headed for the richest source of local information, the pub. Struggling into my bright yellow trousers and red waterproof top, I headed to Craignure Inn, a short but wet walk away.

Craignure Inn is described on its website as a small and characteristic island drovers inn. It's sited opposite the Craignure ferry terminal and looks out to the Sound of Mull, Ben Nevis and the

Highlands. When I entered through the pub's door wearing my bright outfit, every head turned and stared at me. Unperturbed, I strode to the tiny bar and ordered a pint of bitter and some grub. Two locals were bouncing off the ceiling and each other standing at the bar as I ordered from the polite young girl behind it. Joshing and laughing, these two seemed as likely as anyone to know if there were any fishermen around so I asked them straight out.

"Do either of you know if any local fishermen drink here?" I asked in the most non-southern English accent I could muster.

"Aye we ur fishermen" replied the taller of the two lads standing beside me, suddenly looking a lot more serious than a few seconds ago.

"Ah good. Well perhaps you could help me. I'm circumnavigating the UK in this small boat."

I pulled my phone out of my pocket and showed them both the picture of me standing next to the MOD27.

"I could use a bit of advice for my next stage down past Jura. Do you think you might be able to help?" I asked questioningly

"F**K OFF! F**K OFF!" the tall dark-haired fisherman said out loud. He continued to repeat this many times over.

"Whit urr ye saying. F**K OFF. Yer joshing me."

I took my beer and seated myself at a table near the bar. The two of them just kept repeating out loud,

"F**K OFF"

I got bored and waited for my food. Soon the tall dark-haired lad joined me and sat down. He was now genuinely intrigued and had come over to interrogate me. He started by introducing himself and his friend who was still standing at the bar.

"Craigy Fish n this is Josh," he said pointing to his drinking mate at the bar who was tucking into a freshly poured glass of whisky.

Neither of these two were very old, I'd say mid to late twenties and they were clearly well into a proper night's drinking even though it was only midweek – a Wednesday night. I opened the Navionics app on my phone and pulled out my notebook.

"So can you give me any tips on how to sail down through this lot tomorrow?" I enquired, pointing to a host of craggy islands and headlands.

"Aye dinnae dae it in that thing," Craigy Fish said laughing and pointing to the picture of my boat.

"Na seriously. Heid ben Lunga 'n' Scarba tis aff tae be blawin fae th' wast th'morra."

I looked at the words coming out of his mouth and tried to process what he was saying. The combination of several pints and a thick Scots accent made it almost impossible for me to understand.

"Do you mean here?" I said pointing to the islands of Scarba and Lunga on the map.

"Aye, whitevur ye dae, dinnae gang between th' Sooth o' Scarba 'n' North o' Jura. That's th' Corryvreckan. It'll swallow ye hail."

I was starting to get it. I think he'd said, "Whatever you do, don't go between the south of Scarba Island and north of Jura."

This, I surmised, was the location of the infamous Corryvreckan Whirlpool. I'd heard a little about this place from people I'd met along my journey. It's one of the largest permanent whirlpools on earth and one of the most dangerous stretches of water around the British Isles. It's said that at certain times the roar is so loud that it can be heard 10 miles away. At full strength, the currents can reach over 10 knots and produce waves over 9 metres high.

Using my Navionics app, notes, Google Maps and a lot of patience, I was beginning to piece together a plan for tomorrow. Josh and Craigy Fish, despite having oodles of excess fuel on board, turned out to be extremely helpful. A night of banter and drinking continued until I excused myself at midnight leaving them to continue into the small hours.

Reading my scribbled notes and the squiggles Craigy Fish had drawn in my notebook, afterwards I was only slightly surer of tomorrow's plan. It was still blowing and sheeting down with rain. I was pleased the marquee was anchored down to the floor with those enormous poles or it would certainly be halfway to Scarba by now.

Checking all my electronics were charging, I crashed out to the noise of the marquee walls billowing and the wind whistling through the trees and power poles above.

Chapter 37

Carsaig Caravan

Leaving Craignure, I really was none the wiser which way I was going today. Looking back at the Safety Channel message sent that day, I'd done a pretty good job of pretending there was a plan. Dave had been joined by Rupert Bedell who was serving his first full day on the Safety Channel. I almost felt I could say anything now that the chief scrutineer, PY, had left for a personal holiday.

Reading back through my black log book/diary, I found a squiggly drawing Craigy Fish had done in the pub the night before. It was annotated with the words, high nets and low nets. I had no idea what this was all about but it clearly had something to do with fishing and nothing to do with which way to go today.

Safety Channel:

"Weather concerns - westerly 18-29 mph 10 -11.00 then dropping 15-24 mph. Dropping more possibly later.. aiming to make through the Firth of Lorn race at the bottom of the Mull Sound. Heading inside

down to Crinan. Stopping to check the Jura race (similar to Pentland Firth) if tide looks good will continue to Lagg bay on the isle of Jura and make camp".

I can't remember much about this part of the trip. I recall passing two enormous lighthouses marking the entrance to the Sound of Mull as I moved south past them into the tidal race of the Firth of Lorn. I was aware of a much larger expanse of water with many big ships ploughing back and forth probably oblivious to my presence.

Most of the day I kept thinking, where am I? I was constantly checking my bearing and cross referencing it with the Navionics app. I was just conscious I was heading for the Corryvreckan but didn't really know where it was in relation to my position. It was pretty windy so stopping and checking the app continuously was very tricky. On a number of occasions, I nearly capsized looking up what island or headland I was crossing or passing.

The tides were flowing rapidly in my favour. Two lighthouses stand guard to the entrance of the water which flows between Luing and the Rubha Fiola, famous for a tidal rip leading down to the island of Lunga. I didn't know this at the time but the rip, known as the Grey Dog, runs at 8 knots (15 km/h) at full flood which it was as I traversed through the boiling cauldron. The water looked so angry it felt like it might bite. Perhaps that's why it's called this name.

At the island of Scarba section, there was a series of shallows which were more suited to white-water rafting than a Laser sailing dinghy. Emerging the other side was the southern race of the infamous Corryvreckan and I could now hear the roar. In the near distance there was another lighthouse parked on the south western shore of the next island. This place was known as Reisa an t-Sruith and apparently is famous for the presence of a colony of water voles. It marks the start of a submarine exercise area, not that any came to introduce themselves to me. There was yet another light beacon on a smaller island on the horizon. I didn't have a clue where I was. A stop in these calmer waters was needed. Sitting in the lee of Reisa an t-Sruith, I pulled out the phone and called Rupert. He'd been tracking me on the Spot X and Google Maps but neither were working very accurately. He wasn't sure of my precise location. He suggested I aim for a place called Tayvallich and a small natural harbour on Carsaig Island which is technically on the Scottish mainland.

Fixing an approximate bearing roughly towards where I thought Carsaig might be, double checking the Navionics app, it seemed I'd guessed correctly. I passed yet another large light beacon which sat up high on a rocky island in the middle of the sea. As soon as it passed my transom, the MOD27 was tossed into another set of rapids. I traversed these at great speed, hiking as hard as I could to escape the turbulent waters, appearing on the other side a few hectic minutes later relieved to still remain unscathed now in flatter water.

Ahead was a horseshoe shaped natural harbour. I guessed this was probably Carsaig Bay, a quick check of the app confirmed this. I'd used the phone so much today for navigation that by now my battery was nearly dead so stopping was essential to recharge. I couldn't risk running blind with no navigation aids in these treacherous waters. Once inside the bay, the wind died down and the drama of the past hours ebbed away as quickly as the tidal races I'd just been through. I continued into the bay and noticed on the southern shore there was a tiny river inlet with a low harbour wall. Inside were a number of small boats and a grassy bank which looked like the sort of place a tent could be pitched. The tide was out. All the boats were sitting on the muddy bottom tied with mooring lines forwards and aft. There was a trickle of water I managed to sail in on but was still 20 feet from the bank when I ran aground, jumping out of the boat and instantly sinking knee deep in mud. Pulling the MOD27 through the thick black silty mud took an age. I got within a few feet of the bank using the fender to make it across the final bit. Pushing the bow up onto the bank it got stuck halfway. I couldn't budge it.

The only way it was going to get up the bank was to find some help or unload everything. As there was no one around, the second option was the only choice. This involved removing the rig whilst still half way up the bank and unloading all my gear. When eventually the MOD27 was sitting happily on the soaking wet grass above the silty harbour, I was caked in mud with gear lying everywhere. Finding a large puddle on the grassy bank, I lay prostrate with my arms out wide, exhausted. The next five minutes were spent rolling around like a dog, ridding myself of the stinky mud and sea salt.

"What a day! Again!!" I said out loud.

Around me were piles of old windsurfers, small dinghies and old kayaks that looked like they hadn't moved for quite some time. There was also an old windsurfer that carried the same Laser logo as mine. I didn't know Laser ever made windsurfers. It must be very old. Around me were a series of static caravans laid out in slightly untidy rows running up a sloping grassy hill. There were a number of farm buildings with an assortment of old rusty pieces of machinery lying in and around them.

Camping on this stretch of grass wouldn't be ideal. It was soaking wet underfoot. After sorting my bags and stuffing them into the cockpit, which I had sluiced down with rain water to remove the worst of the mud from, I set off to find the land owner and scout out a better overnight pitch for the tent.

There was no one around. It was like a ghost town. Then up the hill in the distance, I saw a small white house nestled into the hill. It was up a gravel track so, with nothing to lose, I made my way towards it. Outside the open five bar gate lay four collie sheepdogs. I'm quite used to dogs as I've owned several myself but sheepdogs are usually very protective. I have a collie cross called Bruno who is actually more of Heinz 57, made up of bits of every type of dog imaginable. I thought about him when the four dogs got up and started walking slowly towards me. Out of nowhere, one of them raced over and started bouncing up and down barking excitedly. This set the rest off and now if anyone was within two miles of here, they'd know a stranger was present. My Bruno usually behaved very similarly to this with unknown visitors, terrifying them with his bark before licking them to death once he knew they were friendly. These dogs behaved the same. Barking in unison, they were noisy but encouragingly they didn't bare their teeth. The oldest dog looked like it only had one good eye and was circling and barking madly at me as I walked slowly towards the front door of the house.

A tall elderly man with a Father Christmas beard appeared from under a carport at the side. He looked suspiciously at me as I approached him with his posse of barking dogs snapping inches from my heels. He must have thought what an unusual person I was as I stood in my wetsuit still smeared in mud and dripping wet.

"Hello," I said, smiling my best smile and trying to look as unthreatening as possible.

The expression on the face of the man standing before me looked blank and unamused by this rude interruption. Persevering...

"Sorry to intrude, I'm sailing around Britain and have just landed in the harbour. Would it be alright if I pitch a tent on the grass down there?" I asked, pointing to the grassy bank in the distance as if it were the most normal thing in the world.

"How long for?" was his blunt response in a thick west coast Scottish accent.

"Only tonight. I'll be off early tomorrow morning," I smiled again as the words left my lips.

"Sailing round Britain you say," he seemed to be warming to the idea.

"Yes that's right," I replied and started my story of how I'd set off from Eastbourne on the 17th July and had just been past the Corryvreckan today and made landfall here in Carsaig as I was tired, thirsty and hungry.

"Well you'd better come inside and my wife will fix you something to eat and drink."

The dogs had calmed down a bit now but followed me inside until Duncan dispatched them with a short sharp command that I couldn't understand. The sun was blazing through the clouds directly onto the farmhouse. A warm feeling went through my body sitting in the kitchen as my host formally introduced himself

"Duncan Shaw and this is Moira, my wife."

"Neil. Neil Peters," I replied.

"Do you want a sandwich, tea and cake?" Moira enquired as I pulled up one of the small wooden kitchen chairs set out in the middle of the small room.

I nodded, "Yes please."

The dogs stayed outside the back door guarding, just in case any other circumnavigators arrived to gate-crash our tea party, splaying themselves on their sides and bellies, absorbing the rare heat of the Scottish sun.

The kitchen had a stone red-tiled ceramic floor, a bit like the Esto Clinker tiles we used to sell at my first ever job at Fulbora Marketing in Epsom, Surrey. I got a position as Marketing Assistant straight out of school after passing my A levels. I was supposed to go to Wales University to study Humanities only no one told me what Humanities was at the time so I decided to become a marketing expert instead. The firm actually specialised in flat roof and drainage equipment so you could say I started my career in the gutter.

I well remembered these small square ceramic tiles that I was now dripping all over. They measure 100 mm square to be exact with 10 mm wide grout between each tile. I stood at the Ideal Home Exhibition for 10 solid weeks back in the 80s. I know everything there is to know about this flooring. My employer had partnered up with a conservatory company for the show. We supplied the ceramic floors free in return for one of our marketing people attending the show free of charge. I was that person. I studied the tiles closely and noticed they weren't laid quite evenly. When I dragged a chair across them, the scratching noise made your teeth stand on edge. Any droplets of water usually seemed to multiply on these surfaces making them treacherous to walk across. Underneath my chair a small lake was forming from my dripping wetsuit. Neither Duncan nor Moira seemed to care much about the mess when I mentioned it, offering to stand outside.

The sandwiches, tea and cake kept coming. I must have eaten five, maybe six, pieces of cake and drank a pot of tea. Duncan became more and more inquisitive about my journey and he insisted I go to meet Dennis, a friend of his who'd sailed across the Atlantic four times. I asked if I could plug in my electronics and we dotted these into the multiple plugs around his kitchen.

Duncan then disappeared and I heard a revving noise as he disappeared into a shed emerging on a weather beaten two-seater John Deere quad bike-cum-pickup truck. We both clambered into the front and bounced off down the bumpy track in search of Dennis. The dogs started barking again and chased us down to the end of the drive before peeling off to resume their guard posts on the driveway.

Dennis' house looked like it was in the final stages of building. It was a modern high roofed bungalow with a large glass frontage and open plan interior. The plot was tucked neatly away on its own at the end of another bumpy road. I was introduced to Dennis by Duncan whose enthusiasm was ebullient, grinning from ear to ear as he explained what I was doing. It was as if something inside had been ignited in him, like unearthing a piece of buried treasure. Duncan did mention later that evening over dinner that his wife Moira had had a stroke last year so I can only imagine this must have been a difficult year for the two of them. I'd like to think my unexpected visit provided a ray of sunshine in his life.

Dennis and his wife welcomed me inside and immediately he went off in search of his charts. His wife offered me some more tea and cake which again I accepted. We rolled out the charts on his dining room table and he started pouring over them like he was suddenly in charge of a new expedition. We analysed the next stage of my journey down past the island of Gigha and round the Mull of Kintyre. He produced tidal charts with currents marked and talked about overfalls and the optimum tidal state to round the Mull. His advice was to do this as close to slack water as possible which we calculated as being 3.30 pm. He slightly worried me with a few stories of sailing this route in a 36 foot yacht and raised an eyebrow when he discovered I was in a Laser. He suggested the weather forecast the day after next was more favourable and hinted quite strongly I should wait.

There was a lot of talking and so much detail my brain just couldn't absorb any more. It was 7 pm and I was still in my wetsuit. The sugar rush from all the cake was wearing off and I was flagging badly. Duncan was keen to buy me dinner in Tayvallich and wanted to whisk me away before we missed last orders but not before Dennis went scurrying through his garage that was packed to the rafters with everything you can imagine, including half a boat chandlery's worth of bits. After five minutes or so, he emerged triumphantly holding three assorted mainsheet blocks with various ratchet arrangements. I'd mentioned to Dennis in passing that the ratchet switch on my own block had broken. After a bit of fiddling around with a Hobie Cat set of multiple blocks and trying to separate one out from the three joined together by a steel plate, I suggested it only needed a ratchet and no cleat. At this point, Dennis abandoned his Hobie Cat blocks and re-emerged with a perfect replacement to my existing block, complete with working ratchet.

On the way back to Duncan's he said that he'd just bought an old caravan for his campsite. It didn't have a boiler but there was running cold water and a shower cubicle I could use. I was welcome to sleep in it overnight if I wanted, instead of pitching my tent.

"Yes please" was my instantaneous answer. Anything would be more comfortable than the tent pitched on soggy grass.

After collecting all my gear and moving it to the caravan on Duncan's beaten-up John Deere buggy, I had a fast shower in the caravan which, although freezing, washed off the salt and freshened me up. By 8 pm I was tucking into a curry and a pint in the Tayvallich Inn. Duncan had fish and chips. We talked about some of the places I'd been to and Duncan's dogs, Moira's stroke and the caravan park he runs. By 10 pm, I was spent when my head hit the pillow in the caravan, falling asleep instantly.

Chapter 38

Madness at the Mull

The 6th of September will forever be etched in my mind. This was the maddest day of my entire journey. It started well. I woke in the caravan early. Duncan told me he'd only just bought it and fortunately for me hadn't even had a chance to clear out the cupboards. Scavenging for any food, I found a tin of baked beans and a bottle of ketchup. I still had some bread, sausages, eggs and bacon in my supplies. By the time Duncan arrived to pick me up at 7.30 am in his John Deere buggy, I'd already had another freezing shower, eaten a full cooked breakfast and a bowl of porridge, drunk several coffees and packed everything ready for the off.

I was pushing off the grassy bank in the MOD27, this time into some water instead of black silty mud as the tide was right in. I left at 8.38 am, close to the start of the ebb tide.

Waving goodbye to Duncan, who I left standing alone again to continue his normal daily business on the bank, I headed out into the horseshoe bay. It was windy but quite sheltered at first. However, as soon as I turned south outside the cover of the headland, the breeze kicked in from the west south west. This was just in front of me, or on the nose in sailing speak. I had to beat out to the end of the headland before I could get a better angle for reaching down the Mull.

I had Rupert, Dave and Emma tracking me today. I checked that my Spot X tracker was set. The VHF radio I used daily to contact the coastguard wasn't working. It had had a very limited signal all the way along the west coast of Scotland. I tried again once I'd broken the cover of the cliffs surrounding Carsaig but still couldn't get any response on channel 16. My mobile was showing limited coverage as well with only one bar so it was unlikely even if I knew the phone number for the coastguard that I'd get through.

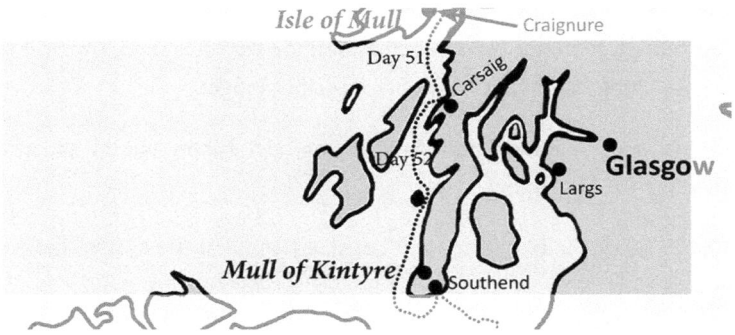

I wasn't too worried as I was beginning to have more confidence in the Spot X tracker. We'd ironed out the earlier glitches and I believed Rupert and Dave would have eyes on it during the day. Just as I was readjusting the position of the tracker, which I kept in a waterproof bag attached to the outside strap on my life jacket, I was hit with an almighty gust. The boat was simply bowled over and I found myself groping for the mainsheet so as not to lose contact with the MOD27 as I fell backwards into the freezing water. My whole body and head were submerged and I surfaced, slightly shocked and gasping for air.

"What just happened?" I gasped as the cold water filled up from my neck seal. I couldn't believe it.

Once the boat was righted, I hurriedly scrambled into the cockpit. I was quite close to the rocky high cliffs running parallel and was drifting alarmingly quickly towards them. In my haste to get back onboard I must have snagged the Spot X lanyard and snapped the plastic eyelet. I didn't realise it was missing until I went to check it was still working a few minutes later. All I found was the empty lanyard. I had no way of tracking the Spot X myself and even if I could, time was really tight. If I stopped, I'd miss the tidal gate at the Mull of Kintyre. I couldn't afford the time to go searching. Chances are it would be washed up on the beach somewhere further south along from Carsaig.

Losing the Spot X was a problem. I had to let the Safety Channel know or else they might think I was in trouble and contact the coastguard. It would keep tracking until the batteries died. I wasn't sure for how long but at least 24 hours, possibly longer.

I stopped again and pulled out my mobile. Typing out the shortest message I could saying

"06/09/2019, 09:36 - Stick: Juzt capsized and lost the spotx. track on google only"

I relayed this message via WhatsApp, hoping they'd receive it once my mobile picked up a signal. The breeze was noticeably increasing, still blowing from the same direction only harder. Half an hour later the same thing happened again. A blast of wind came out of nowhere and flattened me. This time I was quicker and made it onto the centreboard, avoiding falling into the freezing water. Pulling the boat upright, I stepped into the cockpit and gave myself a dressing down.

I was pushing too hard I thought. Dennis' comments last night were praying on my mind. I kept thinking of his face when he recounted his experiences of rounding the Mull of Kintyre himself, only he did it in a yacht. He was adamant I must make it there by 3.30 pm to catch the inner ebb tide. He said otherwise I'd probably not get round or worse, the sea would become unstable. Whatever that meant. He was really saying wait another day for better weather to make this passage. I couldn't wait, I was running out of time.

After the second capsize, I eased back a fraction but was still moving at good speed. The breeze had swung round slightly more from the west which had improved my performance and stability. I checked the WhatsApp messages on the Safety Channel and Rupert had confirmed I was tracking and had been calculating my speed and position using Google Maps. He sent me the following message:

06/09/2019, 11:07 - Rupert Bedell: Revise projection, you are currently travelling 17km/hr, will pass Mull at 2.30pm assuming current pace.

He followed up a few minutes later with another encouraging message:

06/09/2019, 11:09 - Rupert Bedell: 60km to Mull at 11.05am. You've done 30km so far today.

30 km in two and a half hours with a Laser loaded with 60 kg of luggage felt like a good achievement. I smiled and was beginning to enjoy myself screaming along, up and down some amazing waves. I was alone on the edge of the Irish Sea, cliffs on my left and islands on my right. This was going to be an epic day I told myself. Little did I know how epic at this stage.

I passed inside the Isle of Gigha and crossed towards the shoreline to seek some shelter to stop and eat. I was down to my staple diet of tinned mackerel and muesli bars. The waters around the island were deceptively calm as they were sheltered from the westerly winds. Although I didn't stop for long, it was a welcome break. I'd considered stopping overnight on Gigha as someone had told me it's an incredible place. It was still early though and I was making good progress so pressed on. I checked the Navionics app and could see the headland at the Mull of Kintyre was 42 km away. At my present speed, I should make it to the start by around 2.30 pm. The headland is then 12 km long until you round it and then another 6 km to reach Southend Bay beach, the likely end point. Along this stretch, Rupert had identified one bail out point, Machrihanish beach, which was 16 km short of the headland.

I dithered for 10 minutes or more thinking about waiting until tomorrow but decided to go for it. If I got round Kintyre and made it to Southend, I'd have sailed 100 km today. I set off again from Gigha and as soon as I made it clear of the end of the island, the full force of the Irish Sea and unabated breeze blowing from the west hit me. The MOD27 took off in a plume of spray. After the initial shock of the increase in pressure, I settled down into a comfortable position and blasted my way towards the great stack of rock I could see in the far-off distance. I was moving too quickly to even attempt to retrieve the phone and check my position. This was compass bearing time now and just keep holding on and sailing as fast as possible.

Passing a wide inlet which I'm pretty sure was Machrihanish beach meant I was fully committed to making the Mull of Kintyre rounding. Looking at the surf piling into Machrihanish, I doubted I'd ever get off any beach with this wind direction if I landed there. It was getting really breezy now but Rupert had reassured me the forecast was only between 17 and 20 knots. It felt stronger than this but I was still in control and the direction was perfect for a fast rounding. Given my current speed through the water and the following tide, I guessed it was only going to take a few more hours to complete the day's trip.

These next hours proved to be the longest I can ever recall in my life. I think looking back at the Safety Channel tracking, I must have entered the Mull of Kintyre overfalls around 13.30, two hours earlier than Dennis had calculated I should be there. As the cliffs grew in height on my left, the seas seemed to follow suit. The breeze also felt fresher and the sea was being blown off the tops of the waves I was rolling up and down on. It was fast and furious sailing but nothing I hadn't already experienced along the top of Scotland. Then from nowhere, a wave came from behind me and smashed across the MOD27, nearly washing me clean out of the boat.

"Holy shit. What was that?" I shouted out loud, trying to regain control and spinning round to see if there were any more waves coming like it.

I carried on but was wary of what might come next. I regularly craned my neck round, checking behind me for other similar rogue waves. Just after a really good long scan of the sea behind, another massive wave hit me from the front, dropping vertically on top of me and again nearly washing me backwards out of the boat. I managed to keep my feet firmly wedged under the toe strap and clung on, emerging through the surf. Now I was facing a giant water slide that opened up in front and pelted straight down the trough catapulting towards the bottom of this enormous wave. I was sliding so fast the boat reached its maximum hull speed. My sail moved into the centre line of the boat, flapping uselessly and the rudder had little or no effect. Once at the bottom of the trough, I felt vulnerable. I'd stopped and needed to get some speed up to avoid being blown over. I eased off the sail and bore away from the wind. I was moving again only to look up and see not one breaking wave forming but two on top of each other both the size of a house.

"OMG!" was all there was time to say.

These waves were terrifying. I was finished if this landed directly on top of me. I could see a wall of water building higher and higher. The top wave crest was already breaking. It must have been 100 metres away but was so wide there was no escape. The only option was to harden up and try to climb the face of the wave gaining as much speed as possible before doing it. I sailed parallel with my sails eased for as long as I dared, hiking as hard as possible to gain maximum momentum. As the wave was nearly on top of me, I sailed straight up its face and made it over the first crest only to feel the impact of the second crest drop directly on top of the mast. To this day, I've no idea how but, by some miracle, the MOD27 punched through it and I kept her upright hurtling down the other side once through.

After this encounter, I headed out to sea to escape as far away from the cliffs as possible. The wind strength had gone bonkers, it was absolutely howling and the prospect of heading further offshore wasn't something I wanted to do. Given my present circumstances, it seemed like the least bad option. At least if I was beating into the waves, I had a better chance to see the double stackers rolling in from a way off.

Heading out, all I could see were rows upon rows of massive double stack sets of waves, with breaking crests lining up towards the cliffs. I swerved around them, sailed over them and at one point sat stationery head to wind hoping to ride out the storm with my sail flogging. This was even worse than sailing over them as there was no way of avoiding the really big breaking crests. In the process of my sail flogging, all the battens snapped they were shaking so violently.

The next hour I spent heading up and bearing away, weaving and ducking around the really big, breaking double, occasionally triple, crested waves. I was hanging on for grim death to avoid capsizing and being washed out of the boat. The odd wave caught me out, smashing down onto my head, shaking my nerves as I grimaced through this latest torrent. The further offshore I sailed however, the more regular the waves became. They were still enormous but at least they were consistent and predictable. The cliff line seemed to extend forever. After more than an hour, I was nearing the end of my resilience when the end of the headland came into view. Most headlands I'd rounded during this journey, except for Cape Wrath and Duncansby Head, are quite short. Once you get round them, the wind and the sea state tend to flatten off pretty quickly. The Mull of Kintyre was not behaving in this way. Looking at a map from plan view, the headland is shaped like a giant penis. I was entering the helmet phase of this rounding but rather than getting easier it was actually getting more problematic.

To avoid the overfalls, I was several miles offshore. Rounding the bell end of Kintyre, I had to sail downwind on what is called a dead run. Any sailor who has sat in a Laser, or any sailing boat for that matter, will know that sailing dead before the wind is regarded as the least stable direction, especially in large waves and strong winds. As I bore off onto the run, I careered almost vertically down the first wave with the bow inches from burying itself into the face of the wave in front. My speed downhill was so fast it was a bit like sticking your head out of a car window on the motorway. The wind generated from the forward motion (apparent wind) had the effect of making the sail go limp, sliding forwards so fast there was no longer any sideways pressure. However, as soon as I reached the trough at the bottom of it, I urgently needed to power up again or the boat would literally trip up and capsize as the sideways forces came back into play.

I narrowly avoided a capsize on the first wave. I surfed down and ended up facing head to wind sitting in the middle of the boat with the sail flogging itself to death at the bottom of the trough. I survived three or four waves and each time I ended up spinning up head to wind. By now, I was really scared as I turned to see row upon row of giant, double crested waves lining up behind me. My adrenaline had been mostly used up and my energy tanks were empty.

In the distance, a large patrol boat was standing off watching. It was dark blue and unmarked in any way but looked like a navy or coastal patrol boat. I tried to contact them on channel 16 on my radio. I wanted to be rescued. I'd had enough of this. After several attempts, there was no reply. Perhaps the radio wasn't working or they didn't know it was the tiny white sail boat attempting to hail them.

Another wave narrowly missed and then another large crest crashed onto the deck. This decided my next course of action. There was nothing else for it.

"Grit your teeth and carry on."

As I sailed on, the patrol boat looked like it had changed direction and was heading towards me. The next minute, the patrol boat was careering headlong down a steep wave. I was open-mouthed as the whole boat disappeared into the waves in front. I waited, watching to see if it would come up. Time seemed to be moving in slowmotion then I saw the bow emerge, punching through the wave like a dolphin. That was it for me. There was no way on this earth that boat would be able to help me because even if it got close, I'd be smashed to bits if it tried to come alongside.

"Oh f**k here we go!" I shouted at the top of my voice, "Never give up! Never give up! Never give up!"

This motto morphed into a song – the Mull of Kintyre by Wings so, in the middle of the largest gale ever, plummeting down the face of the most horrendous waves the Irish Sea could muster, I sang my heart out to the words of Paul McCartney's longest ever UK Number 1 hit. I hated this song when it first came out and now I hated it even more. I didn't even know any of the words past the first line. Every wave I successfully managed to negotiate I'd turn round and swear a string of expletives at.

"Ha, come on...is that all you've got?" followed up by me belting out the same line of my song at the top of my voice over and over.

"Mull of Kintyre, oh mist rolling in from the sea."

Gradually, bit by bit, the 6 km downwind leg got shorter until the best sight I've ever seen appeared slowly into view. A sandy beach. Without hesitation, I aimed directly for it, driving straight up the sand, capsizing on the shore and falling backwards into the gentle shallows lapping the shore of Carskey Bay.

I'd made it!

I'm alive!

It was a miracle.

I sat there for several minutes just staring out to sea. From this sheltered beach no one standing here would have believed a word of my story. The sea looked quite inviting from here, there was even a ray of sunlight trying to poke through the clouds glistening across the bay. My hands were shaking. My teeth started chattering uncontrollably and I felt very cold. I'm not sure if it was shock or cold from the sea but a drink would help. Retrieving my water bottles, downing what was left of the first one and half of the second, I thought I must warm up and jogged up and down the beach for a few minutes before returning to the MOD27 just before she floated away in the surf. Whilst dragging her further up the beach, a group of geology or geography students on a field trip watched me struggle. None of them came to help.

The team had to be notified I was safe. My hands were shaking so badly I could only type a very short message on the Safety Channel which read,

06/09/2019, 15:26 - Stick: Landed

That was the best I could do for now. Holding the phone and shaking violently, I misdialled Rupert's number several times before it eventually started ringing.

"I'm alive," I started as soon as he picked up.

"Ah that's great" said Rupert in his spritely Irish accent, sounding surprisingly upbeat.

"No I'm alive Rupert. I'm alive," I repeated sounding really weird as my lips weren't moving correctly because I was shaking so violently.

"Ah yeah, I can tell," he quipped, amused at his own joke.

"Anyway," he carried on, "You'll have to get back in the boat, you're two miles short of Southend. I've called ahead and they're expecting you at the Argyll Arms. There's no accommodation but my credit card is behind the bar and they have hot food and beer."

I was listening to Rupert talking but thinking with every word that came out of his mouth,

"I'm not getting back in the boat. I'm not getting back in the boat. I may never get back in the boat."

I then blurted out down the phone, "Rupert I'm not getting back in the boat, there must be something here."

"Aah no. Fraid not. It's only two miles along the coast. You'll be fine."

We chatted a little but I can't remember saying much. He seemed very excited about how far I'd sailed but couldn't chat any longer because he was at work and had a meeting.

I'd calmed down a little and was shaking less after talking to Rupert. It was about half an hour later, bracing myself, I pushed off from the beach again. As soon as I moved outside the cover of the headland, the full force of the wind kicked in. The waves were much smaller inshore but the gusts were still bowling along, striking randomly out of the blue all the way round the coast to my destination, Southend. The saving grace from that day was that I landed for a second time on a beautiful sandy beach with no rocks and a gentle sandy slope. I'd travelled exactly 100 km since leaving Carsaig!

If this was a Laser racing event, the hardest part of the day would be over after coming ashore. On my round Britain adventure, very often I found the after sailing trickier. You had to figure out where to sleep, eat and wash. With no support, this becomes another big mission.

Standing on Dunaverty beach, I was alone with the wind still howling and rain falling mercilessly from the sky. Close to where the MOD27 was parked I saw a square flat roofed building. It looked a bit like one of those World War 2 pill boxes used to house anti-aircraft guns. Upon further investigation, I discovered behind the open metal door there were two urinals and a toilet cubicle. The floor had the same red ceramic tiles as Duncan and Moira's kitchen. On the wall there was a hot air hand dryer. Unfixing the wedge jamming the door open, it sprung shut behind me. I pressed on the hand dryer which immediately improved the room temperature. I rummaged in my dry bag and located a roll of duct tape. Ripping off two lengths I stuck them across the knob which kept the blower going permanently.

The best thing about Scottish public loos, unlike most English ones, is they have hot running water. The hand basin was small but would be fine for a strip wash. Removing my clothes, I stood naked inside the Dunaverty public loo, lathered up from head to toe, rinsing off by cupping my hands with the warm water. Afterwards I blow dried myself under the warm air dryer. It was lovely!

A barbed wire fence high up on the beach bank bordering the caravan site above where the MOD27 was parked provided a ready-made washing line. I strung my gear out to rinse off in the rain. Hopefully no one would steal it. There were no signs of life so I assumed they'd be fine. Dressed in full waterproofs with electronics, valuables and head torch stuffed in my pockets, I set off in search of the Argyll Arms where Rupert had left his credit card behind the bar for me. It was nearly a two mile walk to the pub. I thought I must have gone the wrong way at one stage because there were no pubs and very few houses here. I almost missed it because the Argyll Arms looked just like a house. It was a large 1900s style house with most of the original period features removed or ruined except the original slate grey roof. A

'For Sale' sign propped up outside the front entrance was an interesting feature. Unusually, there was no pub name sign on the outside and it was empty inside except for three large screens blaring out Coronation Street at full volume to keep themselves company.

When Rupert had enquired earlier in the day, all their accommodation was fully booked but they were open for dinner. The barmaid greeted me and was nice enough. She suggested shepherd's pie, chips and peas followed by a tart with custard for pudding. I'm not sure there was any other option but right then even the table mats looked appealing.

With a full stomach and two pints of beer inside me I could only see one other customer. He looked like a walker but I was in no mood to talk to anyone this evening. Enquiring again if they had any rooms available when the barmaid re-appeared from one of her many fag breaks, I received the same reply Rupert had on the phone.

"No, we're fully booked," she said quite curtly.

The barmaid was sporting purple hair and a multitude of unusual tattoos. She had a body with so many piercings it looked like she might deflate if you removed one. The landlady appeared from the kitchen for a brief chat. She was friendly enough and I guessed she was the cook. When I mentioned I'd been sailing today she said,

"What? In this weather?"

I smiled. "Do you have a bottle of water I can take back to my tent please?"

"Where are you staying?" she asked.

I was getting closer.

"I'm not sure. My boat is on the beach at Dunaverty," I replied with a crestfallen expression.

I was really labouring the point but she wasn't forthcoming in offering me a bed or even a sofa to sleep on. However, she seemed to take pity on me and offered me a sparkling bottle of water on the house.

Trudging back in the rain, everything looked different. Those of you who know me can vouch for my poor sense of direction. Sailing round the UK is quite easy to navigate, you just keep the land on one side and keep going straight. But trying to find your boat in the pitch black while it's pouring with rain, no street lights and a head torch with dying batteries is a much harder task. Three wrong turns later and I luckily stumbled upon the caravan park entrance above the beach where the MOD27 was parked. Tiptoeing my way past the maze of caravans brought me back to the barbed wire fence where my wetsuit gear was hanging up.

The prospect of unpacking everything and pitching a tent in the dark was more than I could face. PY's bivvy bag was supposed to be waterproof according to him and my sleeping bag stuffed inside would be warm so there was nothing else for it. Set up camp under the urinals in the public loo. At least I knew the floors had been washed recently.

With the door wedged closed and the hand blower taped on using the piece of duct tape I'd saved from earlier, the toilet soon heated up. I recorded the day's video log there which was pretty creepy as the only light was from one of the battery pack torches my friend Cobie had sent me. That's how the most dramatic day of my journey ended, fast asleep under the urinals in Southend.

Chapter 39

Meltdown at Portpatrick

The main upside of bedding down in a WC is at least you don't have far to go! However, in Scotland make sure you vacate the premises by 7 am to avoid being caught by the cleaners. It was 7.15 am and sitting on the deck of the MOD27 munching breakfast, muesli with water, it was amusing to watch the bemused janitor trying to understand why his door wedge was no longer jamming the door open and all the windows were closed. He looked suspiciously at me sitting on the beach before packing away his cleaning equipment and driving off.

The sky was a beautiful bright blue and the sea was calm but there were some ominous black clouds in the distance. Dog walkers were starting to fill up the beach. One inquisitive spaniel came over to me and jumped onto the MOD27, wagging its tail at a thousand miles per hour then jumping down and running round in circles excitedly.

What I'd found each and every day of this journey was that you could never know what was coming next. What starts off badly often turns out fine and vice versa. Just because yesterday had been a bad day didn't mean today would be any better or any worse, you just never can tell. I thought long and hard about my planning on this trip and tried to think how I might have made things easier. It wasn't great at the beginning but I was much better now. The only method I found totally foolproof was to make an outline plan and then improvise.

Portpatrick was today's planned target point. Everything started comfortably enough, launching into a flat calm sea in warm sunshine and light winds blowing from the west making for easy sailing on a reach again. There was a large bay to cross called the Firth of Clyde, the gateway to Glasgow. The nearer option would have been to cross over the Irish Sea to Northern Ireland. There were a number of sailors from Ballyholme Sailing Club in contact offering me a warm reception. I just couldn't face the Irish Sea today after the events of yesterday. My nerves had taken a real hammering. Crossing the Clyde was actually three times further across open sea than hopping across the North Channel to County Antrim on the Northern Irish east coast. Somehow it felt safer to stay on the UK mainland side.

Within 15 minutes of launching the first difficulty came in the shape of McCosh Rock. It looked like a tidal flow was racing over shallow ground directly in my path. Keeping well south of this area, I skirted around the most ferocious looking water. In the near distance, several smaller and one large island passed. Winds were still very calm but the tidal flow was sweeping us along at a good rate. Staying well clear of any obvious obstructions around the islands and the bubbling whirlpools which seemed to be eddying around the rocky outcrops, I pressed on across the Clyde.

There were a lot of very big ships moving around but nothing seemed close enough to me to be of any concern. Today seemed to be going far too easily with nothing untoward happening. It wasn't until within sight of Ballantrae on the southern side of the Clyde, approximately eight miles out, when the wind died. I was sitting in the middle of the shipping channel. Stranraer, a large ferry terminal, was close and the tide was pulling me towards this direction. Several hours were spent standing up rocking the boat and flapping the sail backwards and forwards, trying to make some progress. I only really succeeded in making myself hot and sweaty in the midday sun.

Drifting towards Loch Ryan, south of Stranraer, the Stena Line ferry emerged and seemed to be aiming directly for me on its route across to Ireland. Tracking its movements for 15 minutes it looked to me as though we were on a collision course. Grabbing the radio on Channel 16, I tried calling them up.

"Stena Line Ferry, Stena Line Ferry, this is Pevensey Laser"

"Stena Line Ferry, Stena Line Ferry, this is Pevensey Laser, the small sailing craft directly on your bow. Over"

This is probably not the correct protocol to use when addressing a commercial ferry. However, given the lack of wind and their size, I wasn't really that bothered. They responded but it took a minute or so before the captain came on the radio.

"This is Stena Line Ferry. Confirm if you are the small yacht off my starboard bow."

"Stena Line Ferry, this is Pevensey Laser, that is correct. Please advise what course you wish me to steer. Over"

The Irish captain seemed slightly irritated with me judging by the tone of his voice when he replied,

"Whatever course you want. We'll pass you in two minutes and then head right for Belfast. Out!"

I watched the ship steam past miles clear of me and the bow wave which inevitably followed seemed to take minutes before it reached me.

After this incident the wind started to fill in and it looked hopeful that I'd get ashore somewhere before nightfall. A call to Dave Freeman manning the Safety Channel delivered a bit of a bombshell. He advised the nearest soft landing was 10 miles away. Given my boat speed was only one or two knots, that meant hours bobbing around in the dark unless the breeze increased.

"10 miles? Oh shit," I bleated down the phone.

Because there had been no shop at Southend yesterday, I hadn't been able to get any food. I was down to four Club biscuits for food for all of today and I'd already eaten three of them. There was a quarter of my water bottle left to drink and I was getting a headache. I usually did by the end of a day baking in the hot sun.

Hanging up on Dave, who proved remarkably resilient to my pleadings for him to provide a miracle landing point in a pile of impenetrable rock cliff faces, I felt really grumpy. I started wafting the sail violently, shouting and yelling at the top of my voice. Clearly this wasn't going to help.

"Get a grip" I told myself out loud.

Someone must have been listening because within 10 minutes of my mini meltdown the breeze filled in. The MOD27 was on the move again and going at a good 4 to 5 knots. Ten miles should be possible to cover in a few hours. My mobile was nearly out of battery and I was anxious about needing the Navionics app to find my way to Portpatrick so to conserve juice I switched it off, conscious of the Safety Channel losing my Google Maps tracking.

The next three hours steadily improved with a fresher breeze and calm seas. Passing the cliff line, it was shocking to see how much abandoned fishing gear was snagged on the jagged rocks. It was littered everywhere along this coast, more than anywhere else on this journey.

It deeply saddened me to see the contrast of such a beautiful wild landscape being ruined by man's impact on our planet.

Pulling into the harbour entrance at Portpatrick just as nightfall was beginning was a welcome relief. Safe inside the harbour, there was a hive of activity going on along the quayside. The pubs were heaving with people and music was playing. It turned out that night was the first Saturday of the annual Folk Festival. There was a sandy beach below a small low wall at the town end of the outer harbour directly in front of the busiest pub. I didn't fancy camping there or leaving the boat for the local drunks to push her off for a midnight play.

Carrying on navigating round the many harbour pontoons, I aimed for the far corner of the inner harbour where the local lifeboat was moored. This looked like the safest distance from the crowds and had its own slipway bridge up to the top of the 30-foot high harbour walls surrounding the boats. Pulling alongside the back of the lifeboat, I decided to leave the MOD27 tied up in the water that evening. The pontoon was way too high to drag the boat up on my own so I left her floating in the water. She'd be safe here in this sheltered spot. Just to make sure, I tied my fender onto the side of the jetty, unstepping the mast and rolling up the sail, before stowing it under the walkway where there was a low void making a perfect store.

Robert, the harbour master, had his phone number on the board outside his office. Everywhere was locked. Calling him, I was disappointed to discover the shower blocks were all locked for the weekend due to the Folk Festival. Covered in salt, itchy and irritated by this news, I sat down on top of the harbour wall with my legs dangling in the water. I was mentally and physically exhausted from the past two days. It was a dejected moment.

Calling Emma to tell her about the day, she leapt into action to try to help by sending a Facebook message pleading for anyone to provide assistance. While I was strip washing in the disabled toilets on the quayside, with the cleaner repeatedly banging on the door to ask if anyone was inside, one person responded to Emma's message.

Simon from a bed and breakfast in Portpatrick responded to Emma's appeal. She called me at 10.30 pm when I was sitting in the pub having just made it in time for last food orders. I was contemplating my night's sleeping arrangements. The best option I'd come up with was sleeping on the metal quayside in PY's bivvy bag, next to the boat.

"I've found you somewhere," Emma blurted excitedly down the phone. "This really lovely man called Simon has offered you a room at No.4, his B&B. He's got an empty room and is happy for you to use it. The keys are in the box on the wall. Just punch this code in and let yourself in. He said he'd see you at breakfast. No charge."

Emma told me this so quickly she was barely taking a breath between words. I couldn't believe it. What luck. No.4 was just around the corner from the Waterfront Hotel where I was eating. It turned out to be a great night's sleep. Quite a contrast to my previous evening in the public toilets. How bizarre this journey was becoming.

Meeting Simon for the first time the next morning, I was self-conscious and a little awkward at first. Simon was running a business and was busily cooking breakfast for his paying guests, all of whom were neatly sitting in the dining area at the rear of his house. I popped into the kitchen, squeezing past the table where they were all sitting, to say hello. My plans were to eat elsewhere as I didn't want to impose on Simon's hospitality and it wasn't really part of his offer. The bed alone was a fantastic gesture of human kindness to a total stranger.

While Simon was cooking, we got chatting a little about what I'd been up to. Simon asked me what the best bit of the journey so far had been. I started off saying the people but before the words were fully out of my mouth, I found myself sobbing my heart out in front of him whilst poor Simon was trying to cook a posh full English breakfast for his table full of expectant clients. It was a surprising reaction for us both to comprehend. Excusing myself fairly swiftly, feeling a little embarrassed, it was time for me to reset my emotions and start focusing on what lay ahead for the rest of the day.

As it turns out, no sailing. The forecast was very light and from here there were some big decisions to make on which way to go, either inland towards Liverpool or across the Irish Sea to the Isle of Man. Neither option had been investigated at all so today I designated a rest, repair and research day. The sun was glorious and it felt amazing just lying back on the jetty next to the MOD27 absorbing the heat, safe in the knowledge I didn't have to go anywhere.

Checking over the boat, it was clear she'd been through a major battle but was largely unscathed aside from broken battens and shockingly a torn kicking strap pin. This item is essential for keeping the boom under control when sailing downwind. Had the pin snapped round the Mull of Kintyre, I'm not convinced you'd be reading this tale. The top of the pin is made of solid stainless steel. I can't imagine the forces needed to tear this off. Fortunately for me, it didn't completely separate, approximately 1/10th mm of metal was keeping it together.

My supplies of replacement parts were limited but surprisingly there was a kicking strap pin in my spares bag. All the sail control lines looked decidedly tired so as South East Sailboats had sent a complete set of spares in Gairloch, I used this opportunity to renew them all. The new sail that Rooster had supplied had no red or orange triangle on the top like my original. After yesterday's events, it seemed prudent to colour this in the same way as the first sail so at least I could be seen. A local hardware store sold me a can of red aerosol paint which I proceeded to cover the top triangle of the sail and half of the RNLI's shiny pontoon with overspray. Simon was extremely generous letting me stay a second night before I planned to move off early on Monday morning when the weather forecast was blowing from the north north west at a decent rate to push me south, east or west, whichever choice I'd make tomorrow.

Chapter 40

Across to Man to Meet a Poole

During my sojourn in Portpatrick, my attention had turned to the next stage of rounding Britain. This was a watershed moment. There were three choices. Head south through the Mull of Galloway and turn inland towards England and then run south and turn west back to Wales. Looking at the map, there were some extremely large sections of open water to cross even if I played it conservatively. The extra distance hugging the coastline of north west England was hundreds of miles longer.

The other option was to keep going south, sailing directly across the Irish Sea, 45 km of open water to the Isle of Man, hoping the weather was kind so it would be possible to get off the other side. At least once on the island there were options to cross back east into England, west to Ireland or south to Holyhead in Wales. All three of these looked shorter routes than navigating round the complex tidal patterns of places like Barrow-in-Furnace, Blackpool and Liverpool with all their commercial shipping movements. Or through the Menai Straits between the Isle of

Anglesey and Wales with its infamous tidal flows, reversing currents and whirlpools. However, the Isle of Man required large expanses of open water to be crossed, in all directions.

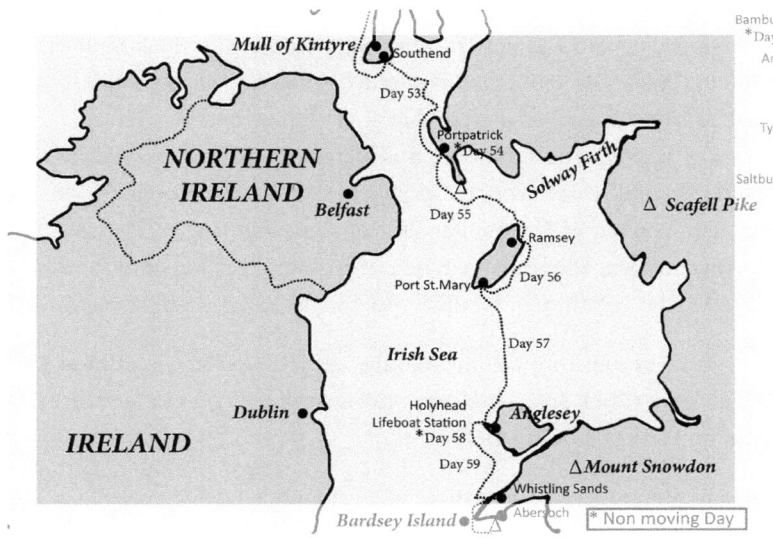

I had very little idea what to expect along any of these routes. My only experience sailing in the north west of England had been attending the 24 hour Southport relay sailing race, held on a three foot deep lagoon overlooking Southport beach. My first proper club, Island Barn Sailing Club, in Walton-on-Thames in Surrey, had entered a team for this event when I was only about 17 years old. During it, I managed to restyle my nose on the boom of an Enterprise sailing dinghy by not ducking fast enough at 2 am in the morning in a howling gale. I recall whilst sailing looking out from the shallow man-made lagoon and wondering where all the sea had gone. All that was visible was mile upon mile of sand, stretching as far as Blackpool. How would it be possible to haul a Laser on a fender over that distance of sand? Southport is famous for swallowing cars up on its soft wide beaches with reports of hundreds of cars getting stuck daily in 2019. These sands were treacherous and unpredictable. Usually my timings were out and it would be easy to arrive at the wrong state of tide.

With this in mind, my plans had started to hatch at Portpatrick. Researching sailing clubs on the Isle of Man, Donald Edwards' name had popped up. He was down as the training officer at Manx Sailing Club in Ramsey. Looking up his phone number on their website, I called Donald. We had a great chat about Lasers and his view on crossing the Irish Sea in one. He was incredibly relaxed and laid back about the whole thing. Very reassuring in fact, almost encouraging. Reflecting on our call, I discussed the options with Rupert. He was significantly less enthusiastic. Being of Irish origins, Rupert was fully versed in the volatility of the Irish Sea and his exact words were

"On no account are you to cross the Irish Sea to the Isle of Man. On NO account Chief. Just work your way around the coast to the Isle of Whithorn and chip away at it."

"OK Rupert it was just a thought," I responded defensively.

The rest in Portpatrick did me the world of good. It also bought me time to think. Until now, I'd been charging headlong into each day, trying to deal with whatever obstacles came along, busking my way around, making it up as I went. Now there was time for a period of consideration. Looking at the forecast for the next week, it looked terrific for a very fast route south, blowing mainly from the north switching to the north west. There were some very strong winds forecast in Ireland, 30 plus knots. The eastern side of the Isle of Man was more protected and the forecasts here were 10 knots less than Ireland.

The day came, pushing out of the harbour at Portpatrick quite late at 11 am to catch the tide heading south, my plans for an Isle of Man crossing looked to be scuppered. The forecast had changed and I feared being stuck in the middle of the Irish Sea becalmed; a more frightening prospect than gales to me. There was nothing to be done other than head south to the Mull of Galloway and see what happened after that. The Isle of Whithorn was looking like the most likely destination now.

The cliffs were similar to those near Kintyre with the Mull of Galloway being the southernmost point of Scotland and the Rhins of Galloway peninsula on the very tip is one of the best kept secrets. It's 318 miles from Land's End and 285 miles to John O'Groats from this point. I was nearly half way down Britain now and I wanted to get home. Approaching the peninsula became a struggle, the tides are notorious around this finger of land. The lighthouse sits a long way up, to see it from sea level you get a stiff neck with the top sitting 99 metres above sea level. Gauging my progress against this landmark, I didn't seem to be getting anywhere, fighting the foul tide whipping around the peninsula. Heading east seemed futile, I was clearly fighting a battle I couldn't win, at least not for some time. Entering the tidal race flooding south towards the Isle of Man, I was being sucked along out to sea. The breeze was better off shore too, blowing from the north west unimpeded by the high cliffs. This was the perfect direction for a fast blasting reach across to the Isle of Man. It was a shorter way home. My mind was made up. Nature was determining my destiny. To the Isle of Man it was.

The Safety Channel was adamant the Isle of Man should not be attempted so I felt I'd try it for a while before telling them. I kept hearing the words of Rupert in my ear as I set off...

"On NO account..." Rupert rarely ever used such forceful language.

Sailing fast now, clear of the headland, I ignored his comments, all I could see was open water. I'd assumed the Isle of Man could be seen from Scotland but not even a dot was visible. Twenty minutes into the route, I checked the heading was correct. It felt like I was heading the wrong way. The Navionics app showed I was perfectly on track. Still nothing was revealing itself on the horizon. Nerves came into play and I had a change of heart. Rupert's words must have penetrated my conscience.

"This is mad. What am I thinking? This sea is the Irish Sea. Turn around."

I spun round and started to retrace my steps then hesitated and turned back to sea again. The next few minutes I kept on changing my mind, sailing backwards and forwards several times before finally deciding to contact the coastguard and file a passage plan to the Isle of Man. At least this would provide me with a little reassurance.

"Coastguard coastguard, Pevensey Laser Pevensey Laser, radio check. Over"

"Belfast coastguard, Pevensey Laser you are loud and clear" came the reply.

"Coastguard coastguard, Pevensey Laser, I'd like to file a passage plan. Over"

"Belfast coastguard, Pevensey Laser, go to Channel 27 and stand by"

I waited for the coastguard to come back.

Squinting at the horizon, trying to see the faintest dot that would at least give me some reassurance that the Isle of Man was even out there, I waited patiently for the coastguard to respond on channel 27. When they did, I recorded my approximate position and filed a passage plan for Port Ramsey, Isle of Man. One unusual thing happened, which no other coastguard around the UK had so far done when I'd filed previous passage plans.

The operator said, "Are you being supported by another vessel?"

"Negative," I replied

"You are aware of gale warnings in the Irish Sea?" they asked me in a slightly concerned manner.

"Negative," I responded again but continued with, "How strong are the gale forecasts?"

"Gale force 6 to 7 Irish Sea." The coastguard said this in a surprisingly insistent manner leaving me in no doubt I was ill-advised to proceed.

"Roger that, I'll call in on the hour with a position update. Many thanks, Pevensey Laser out"

"Good luck. Belfast coastguard out"

This seemed very unusual. Normally, the coastguard expresses no opinion and just records the information. I recall early on in the journey trying to get an opinion from the Thames coastguard when rounding Dover and none was given. It was entirely neutral, in fact I'd go as far as to say devoid of all opinion, just statements of fact.

I checked my weather app again and couldn't see anything suggesting more than a force 5.

"Must be localised," I thought.

There was no point wasting any more time, sheeting in the sail I set out to sea again. The further offshore I sailed, the more the waves grew in size and the breeze filled in. This was quick. The MOD27 was skipping along as if she'd just come out of the starting blocks. Constantly checking the boat, nothing looked like it was about to break so I carried on, following the compass heading of 140 degrees. The Isle of Man must come into view soon. When I'd radioed the coastguard, I'd agreed to do an hourly check in and give an estimated speed and distance travelled along the compass bearing. I'd no idea if they were tracking this but at least if something did go wrong it would narrow any search and rescue area down a fraction. PY had always calculated the distance a search and rescue team would need to look based on my Safety Channel notifications. The size of the search area was way too scary to remember. This one went into the box labelled Not Required. I hoped!

When I first spotted the island, it was a tiny speck. It was difficult to make out but the clouds hanging above suggested to me there must be land underneath. The furthest a human eye can see at sea level is 20 miles. That is assuming perfect visibility, bright sunlight and a flat even platform. It was 24 miles in a straight line to the nearest point on the island from Scotland. Having been sailing for two hours, I should have expected to have seen something by now. This must be it. The Navionics app suggested it was and the compass heading was still constant. Unless there were large tides influencing my heading, that must be land. Another hour and the island was looming large, features were beginning to become distinguishable, landmarks would soon be possible to see. I hoped.

It was getting quite late in the day, past 5 pm and the winds were easing. Now instead of any concerns about a gale, my biggest worry was the wind dying as the evening drew in. Getting within five miles of land, the wind was seriously dropping. The marooned feeling was beginning to sweep over me like a mist rolling in across the sea. What ifs and doubts were starting to invade all positive thoughts. The last hour of this journey was slow-going but by this time I'd reached the land and was following the shoreline south.

Rounding the top of the Isle of Man, approaching the Point of Ayre Lighthouse from the west, I stayed in close, feet from the shingle beach. I was fighting the ebbing tide running round the headland against me. It was an incredible feeling seeing the waves breaking on the shingle shore knowing that if I wanted to at any minute I could land. I felt safe again.

Donald had been in contact with Rupert by phone and was teeing up a welcoming committee at the Manx Sailing Club. The Safety Channel was on red alert by the time I checked in. Within the camp there were still mixed feelings about this crossing mainly because it meant a 45 mile crossing to get off the island. That was a problem for another day. Today, as I pulled into the slipway in Ramsay, I'd completed an Irish Sea open water crossing of 24 miles. It felt good. Really amazing!

David, Donald's father, greeted me first on the slipway. Donald was on his way but held up with childcare at home. David was hobbling down the slipway with a dodgy hip. He'd borrowed an abandoned, rusty old boat trolley from the dinghy park. Not quite the red carpet reception one would hope for after such a crossing but very welcome nevertheless. He helped me up the wide concrete ramp. Shortly afterwards, a posse of people arrived from the Manx Sailing Club. Keith Poole, the Commodore, had been plucked out of his local watering hole. Others present were Niamh, Keith's wife and May Shiu Chan, Vice Commodore and head of the local medical practice.

Keith was a larger than life character, dressed in a cream gilet, blue shirt and navy trousers. His hair was neatly flattened. The cameras were out and he walked across to me in front of the MOD27 to pose for a photo shaking hands. In the process we smiled and throughout the smiles he was muttering,

"You're f**king nuts. You're f**king nuts. You're F**king nuts"

I kept smiling and accepted this as a compliment.

That evening, David and Donald looked after me in the local pub. I ate fish and chips at Donald's house and I met Aifric, Donald's wife, who explained some of the history of the Isle of Man.

According to Aifric, the Isle of Man has the oldest government in the world, meeting annually on the 5th July to set the rules. The Parliament was started by the Celts who were succeeded by the Vikings who sat to resolve disputes and appoint successors. She explained the process can be traced back over a thousand years of unbroken existence.

A new member of the team had joined the Safety Channel to fill PY's absence. Rarely have three additional people been needed to fill one man's boots. I'd recruited Roger Glass when it became clear there was a need for the normal members to be able to carry on with their daily lives while I tried to end mine. Roger had agreed to help out when we were short-handed. What no one had advised Roger of the rules on the Safety Channel. Well, PY's rules which were no emojis, thumbs up, holiday pictures or any unnecessary clutter that would reduce the level of importance of the channel's primary function of safety. As PY regularly pointed out, every message sent on this channel set off a ping alert on his phone so he wanted minimal messaging.

It was, in PY's words, "a Safety Channel not a chat show."

The number of pings going off on PY's phone today would probably have sent him over the edge. The rest of the team clearly weren't on the same strict code of discipline as PY wanted them to be. It cracked me up to see so many thumbs up and smiley faces. Now PY had left for a few weeks, there was a whole new protocol. I chuckled at him grumping around in the back of his campervan in Holland if he was still tracking my progress. The accounts back from the event suggested he was having a terrible time at the Laser World Championships, racing in light and tricky winds, his least favourite conditions. I could feel his groaning at the euphoric and excited behaviour of his understudies on the Safety Channel. I suppose humans just can't help being human!

Chapter 41

Aground at Port St Mary

After the exhilaration of the previous day, crossing the Irish Sea for the first time in a Laser, I felt I'd earned an easier day today. I'd sail as far south down the island as I could to set up for my biggest open water crossing back to the mainland at Holyhead on Wednesday. David Edwards had let me stay in his lovely house the previous night and together we worked out a route plan for the next two days. We looked over the charts until the early hours of the morning with the assistance of a glass or two of single malt whisky.

Setting off from Ramsey, the number I was aiming for today was 3 pm. By now, my strategy each day was to fix on a tidal change time and use this as the number to focus on, breaking the journey into achievable chunks. Today, 3 pm at Langness Point was the figure that was relevant to my ultimate target destination, Port St Mary, a distance of 50 km, the same distance as the day before.

Because today's route appeared less dangerous, I was lulled into a false belief that this would be an easy day. Leaving Ramsey, that was definitely my thinking although David had mentioned the tidal race around the southern headland of Langness Point being impassable if I didn't make it by 3 pm with 5 knots of tide against. The significance didn't register. I felt like I was going for a relaxing cruise along the east coast of the Isle of Man. A sightseeing tour of the island, passing Douglas, the capital city, and then popping round the corner to Port St Mary where Jenny Neale, the coxswain of the local lifeboat and one of Donald's contacts, was going to meet me and put me up for the night.

All started well, a comfortable reach past the Queen's Pier which stretches 2,160 feet into the sea at Ramsey. With the wind coming off the land, the flat seas and the sun in the sky made for a relaxing start. However, very soon after leaving, the wind backed and turned the route south into a beat, sailing into the wind nearly the entire length of the island. An estimated journey plan of 50 km became at least half as much distance again, if not more, due to the zigzagging nature of a sailing boat. Not only had the distance increased but the energy levels required to beat were significantly more than either reaching or running.

I arrived at the approach to Langness Point at 2.55 pm. It had been flat out hiking to make it in time yet already the tide felt like it was on the turn. Hugging the headland to try to find a back eddy to help me round, I punched through the tide eventually making it out onto the southern coastline at exactly 3 pm. Crossing Castletown Bay with the full force of the fetch rolling across the Irish Sea was exhilarating. Fighting the tide this side was less problematic as once again I was surfing at full speed.

Port St Mary is the southernmost port on the island. It has an outer and inner harbour and has one of five RNLI lifeboat stations stationed there. The RNLI has its roots firmly embedded in the Isle of Man. Sir William Hillary of Douglas is largely credited with founding the

National Institution for the Preservation of Life from Shipwreck, later renamed the Royal National Lifeboat Institution. He'd witnessed the destruction of dozens of ships from his home on the island and got involved in rescue attempts himself so Hillary appealed to the Navy, the government and other 'eminent characters' for help in forming 'a national institution for the preservation of lives and property from shipwreck'. With the support of London MP, Thomas Wilson, and West India Merchants' Chairman, George Hibbert, the Institution was founded as a charity on 4th March 1824. The name was changed to RNLI in 1854.

My contact Jenny Kneale was not only a coxswain of the Port St Mary lifeboat but also a formidable Laser sailor. She runs the 7th Wave sailing school in nearby Port Erin, living locally on the shore of Purt Verk. As I approached the outer harbour, I was unsure exactly where to head for so called Jenny on my mobile while still at sea. Picking up the phone she seemed busy with other things and was quite vague but told me to call back when I was a bit nearer to the harbour walls. I just kept going straight for the centre of the harbour. Approaching the large outer wall, the waves increased in size making it difficult to call again until I could find shelter. I came into the yacht anchorages. Once inside the outer walls, conditions were much calmer and I called Jenny.

"Just head for the lighthouse," she said, "I'll see you there" and hung up quite abruptly.

A small tower resembling a lighthouse was perched on one of the harbour walls. The tide was very low as I approached and I could see this was an inner harbour. The miniature-sized lighthouse had a red band around its waist and I assumed Jenny must mean this one and aimed directly for it then,

Clonk!

Below the boat there was a loud smack. I'd sailed directly into a large underwater rock which luckily didn't shatter the centreboard as I was only moving slowly. Nevertheless, the impact was enough to jolt the MOD27 to a near standstill.

"Shit" I swore, pulling up the daggerboard as quickly as I could.

There was nearly no water anywhere and I was surrounded by submerged rocks. It was still 20 metres or more to the shore. Hurriedly releasing the rudder tie down to prevent the blade from breaking off if I hit anything else, I skidded in towards the beach. It was so rocky there seemed a real risk of puncturing a hole in the hull or breaking the daggerboard tip off which was still partially submerged to stop me sliding sideways. There was nothing else for it. I was going to have to swim or wade in the rest of the way. Dropping into the green water I sunk up to my chest. Underfoot were large uneven boulders and sharp rocks covered in slippery weed. Half swimming, half walking the MOD27 through the last bit, I saw Jenny standing watching on the shore.

Dressed in her RNLI jacket and boots, she looked concerned as I struggled to keep the MOD27 from capsizing, swinging violently in the gusts popping over the top of the harbour wall. I felt really grumpy and irritated. She could have told me about the rocks. I smiled through gritted teeth as she helped me ashore. No point falling out with your host when you first meet them, I told myself.

The rocky beach was dried out and covered in slime and harbour silt. After a lot of faffing under Jenny's advice, I abandoned the MOD27 on the filthy black silty mud, 20 feet short of the shore. I struggled but finally unstepped the rig and deposited it on the beach then unpacked the essentials I'd need that were stored inside the rear hatch. I then attached one very long line to the bow and fastened it onto a mooring buoy. The problem with this was, as the tide came in, the boat would swing and smash into all the other boats in the tiny harbour. These were all fixed with two lines, one to the stern line and one to the bow. Jenny didn't seem too bothered about this and helped me haul my gear further up the beach which I discovered was right in front of her house. However, I was quite concerned about leaving the MOD27 so poorly secured.

Inside Jenny's house it was cosy with low ceilings and an artistic welcoming shabbiness. Sitting down at the table in her single living room and kitchenette, Jenny served up coffee and cooked a bacon sandwich while we chatted. I was starving and destroyed everything in front of me. Her friend Dewan came round to investigate. My initial irritation soon dissolved and the conversation flowed very naturally. Seeing I was still shivering, Jenny dispatched me to her bathroom to warm up. I was unsure about changing before securing the boat but she insisted it would be fine. After a long hot shower, when I returned downstairs in dry clothes and a warm jumper the MOD27 was parked outside her cottage. It was like magic. Jenny and Dewan had brought the boat up, parked her on two tyres and packed everything away for me. That evening Jenny brought out her charts, cooked shepherd's pie followed by the most amazing strawberry and chocolate sponge and then gave up her sumptuous double bed so I could have a good night's sleep.

Just before dozing off, I picked up a book on the bedside table with an intriguing title "Against Birching". I later discovered the book was a very brave political stand at the time and owes its existence to the author, Angela Kneale, Jenny's granny. Angela believed in the power of the pen and was one of a very small and courageous group of women on the Isle of Man who campaigned against the use of judicial corporal punishment. The birch was only banned on the Isle of Man in 1976, 28 years after the UK outlawed its use. I felt honoured to be in the company of such people.

Rising early with the sun streaming in through the curtains, I thought at the time I couldn't have chosen a better day to sail the 42 miles across the Irish Sea to Holyhead. Changing into dry clothes I ventured downstairs. There was no one around so using the quiet time, I plotted my route for the day.

Steer 170 degrees was my only plan. Head on that bearing until reaching land. Don't fall in and don't break anything and I'd be back on UK mainland soil again, having cut out 230 miles or more distance by sailing straight past the south west of Scotland and the north west of England. Simples!

High water was at 10.37 am so I didn't have to leave until around 10 am to follow the ebb south. Jenny had left the house early and returned with two bulging bags of shopping.

"Breakfast," she responded to my questioning eyes as she squeezed through the narrow cottage doorway. Bacon, egg, toast, porridge, coffee, fruit juice and even a packed lunch, including a pile of protein and Snickers bars. She refused any payment.

By 10 am I was ready to go, dressed in my wetsuit and fully loaded. I'd invited Jenny to join me in her Laser Radial at breakfast but she was concerned she might slow me down. I wouldn't have minded being slowed down if she wanted to ride shotgun. This was going to be quite a moment so any guests were welcome to join in.

The night before, Roger O'Gorman (one of the G7 Laser gang), had been in contact with me via our WhatsApp group. Amongst the euphoria of making it successfully across to Ramsey, he merely said,

"Yes well done but you've still got to get off the island," in his Irish, intellectually understated way.

"Have you sailed this route before?" I asked Jenny as I was about to push off into the harbour.

"Not in a Laser," she replied quite nonchalantly. "The worst bit is likely to be the first bit," she added encouragingly as I stared out at whitecaps breaking near the harbour walls.

Aground at Port St Mary

"It's the bar just outside the harbour. The waves kick up over it, usually about 2 or 3 metres. Once you're past this bit, it'll be fine," Jenny smiled confidently.

I pushed off into the stillness of a sheltered harbour but after sailing 50 metres I turned round to fix the rudder down and promptly capsized with a sudden gust of wind unexpectedly dropping over the harbour wall.

Jenny had her camera running and I could feel her lens burning into the back of my head as I scrambled back on board after pulling the MOD27 upright.

"Not my best start of this tour," I thought, feeling quite embarrassed.

A second gust nearly caught me off guard again but once past the harbour walls, the moderate west south westerly breeze was less gusty. I just focused on riding over the steep rolling waves building all around the harbour. Once past the bar, Jenny was right it was much easier. The waves were large but reasonably predictable. Focusing on the compass aiming 170 degrees, I looked ahead. This was some sight. All that was visible was a wide-open expanse of sea. Wave after wave piling in from America.

The sky looked a hazy blue through my salt obscured Oakleys which I'd miraculously managed not to lose. The lenses were beginning to delaminate and the arms were slightly cracked but otherwise they were still good for 10 miles visibility if it was a clear day. There was nothing but the sea. I kept staring, trying to see something, a ship, island, bird. Nothing! Sucking in hard, I took a slow deep breath to settle the nerves.

"Here we go," I quietly mumbled to myself.

Jenny stood on the outer harbour wall taking pictures with her telephoto lens. I regularly craned my head around for the first few miles checking I could still see her. After a while, the harbour walls disappeared from view and then finally the Isle of Man. I could see no land in front or behind. I was alone with the sea.

170 degrees became my obsession now. That and the hourly VHF contact with the Belfast coastguard to give them an approximate position. Everything was going well. The boat was moving well. Occasionally I'd get soaked by an unusual wave dropping onto me somewhat irritatingly from behind with the direction of the waves coming at me just in front and to the side. It was an awkward angle, hampering my speed, which I estimated was only 6.5 knots. In reality, with the tide behind it was more but I couldn't tell. It felt uncomfortable. If I was racing, I'd be weaving up and down the peaks and troughs. I wasn't racing. I was trying to steer an accurate course so the MOD27 and I didn't completely miss Holyhead and carry on out to sea – next stop Dublin or Wexford in Southern Ireland.

The Belfast coastguard was very reassuring as I plotted each hour using the Navionics app, this time stopping to take an accurate fix reading off the screen of my Samsung Galaxy and calling it in. At 20 miles offshore, almost halfway across, I was on the radio to the Belfast coastguard who were in the middle of explaining they'd be handing me over to the Holyhead coastguard when the radio died.

"What? What's happening? Oh come on. Don't do this, not here."

I shook the radio, pressing the on/off power button repeatedly. Nothing, it was dead.

Scanning around for some reassurance of other life, I was disappointed there was only sea. The waves were increasing in size and the sky felt like it had suddenly turned a dark steel grey colour with banks of ominous clouds setting up on the horizon, like a pack of wolves stalking a lone elk. There was no sign of the bright yellow sun and blue sky of Port St Mary any more. I was starting to have one of my "What am I doing here moments?" again.

No mobile signal, no Spot X tracker, no VHF radio.

These moments are really bad news when I have them. I've spent years trying to figure out how to control them. First my stomach tightens, then the butterflies kick in. I can feel myself losing control of rational thought. Decision making becomes appalling. I used to get these feelings a lot when I found myself standing in front of the class trying to recite my times tables and in more recent years when I found myself unexpectedly leading a Laser race at a high profile event. Everything would be fine until my conscious self took over from my subconscious self. Inevitably, instead of carrying on instinctively as before, which is why I had found myself in that position in the first place, I found myself freezing, making unbelievably bad choices and panicky decisions. On a few occasions, I've even been known to fall out of the boat in a race when I was a leg ahead for no known reason.

"Keep breathing, just keep breathing," I told myself.

"1,2,3,4,5..." I started counting the breaths in and out, in and out.

"Relax. All is well. Nothing has changed. The boat is fine, nothing broken. I'm fine. The sea is great. The breeze is fine. We're all fine."

"Talk yourself into a positive mind set." My self-help strategy was working.

I kept repeating these phrases and carried on the same course, 170 degrees.

"Nothing had changed!"

It took a good 10 minutes into this "moment" before I felt I was starting to function OK again.

"All good. The land will be in sight within an hour. I'll probably get a mobile signal shortly after that, 10 miles off shore," I carried on talking to myself out loud to block out negative thoughts. It was working.

Settling back into a rhythm, I even started weaving and surfing up and down some of the larger waves, deviating from my rigid 170 degrees course. Then the singing started. This time the theme tune to M.A.S.H., 'Suicide is Painless'. As per usual, I couldn't remember any of the words so I just repeated the same three words continuously to the tune, singing at the top of my voice, surfing through waves, dropping off the top of a crest and racing down its back. It was getting windier and here I was all alone, just the MOD27 and me. Nothing else to worry about, just focusing on the task of sailing a tiny plastic boat the wrong way round the United Kingdom. A meaningless, pointless task in the scheme of the world. A pinprick of insignificance but right now providing a feeling of total euphoria to the person sitting in the boat.

The radio had packed up at 13.00 and I'd been out of sight from land for two hours. In the far-off distance, it looked like it might be a land mass. There was a large clump of clouds hanging on their own in a continuous line on the horizon. The time was 3.30 pm.

"This must be land," I told myself.

Over the next hour, a dark shadow started to appear on the sea. As I closed towards this, it was becoming more distinguishable.

"I can see land, can't I?" I was sure it was land.

Nothing changed very quickly but slowly the shadow had edges, then a top. Squinting through my glasses, I started to make out the shape of a cliff and a hill top. It's quite incredible how reassuring seeing land is. Somehow, psychologically the sight of land makes everything feel safer. In reality, it often makes things more dangerous. As you approach the shoreline, suddenly tidal forces, headlands and other unknowns like submerged rocks come into play. This is far more dangerous than the open sea where there's nothing to hit but it feels like it ought to be safer. It somehow addresses an insecurity in the human psyche which has its roots on land. There was a reason we crawled out of the sea and evolved on land millions of years ago.

I needed to urgently let the coastguard know I was OK. Opening the Navionics app on my Samsung whilst bouncing through the surf getting soaked proved tricky. I gave up trying to open the app but needed to get a message to the Holyhead coastguard that I was OK. It worried me they may have put out a distress call after I'd failed to check in for the past two hours. The phone screen just wouldn't open in the right place and, not wanting to lose any time crossing, I didn't want to waste valuable time stopping to sort this out. In the end, I got the phone book to open and just hit the last number on my recent calls list.

Jenny answered. "Hello?"

Jenny wrote...

Just after 3 pm my phone rang... it was Stick! The line was a little broken but I heard his message "Lost comms with coastguard, VHF died, can you call Belfast coastguard for me". I duly did, the lady in Belfast Ops room asked if I was his designated person ashore. "I guess I am, I hadn't met this fella until yesterday, but it was me that helped him out to sea today" I replied. We were all happy to hear the update "10 or 12 miles off Holyhead". What a trip!! 30 odd miles in five hours in a Laser!!

Jenny had told me when I approached Holyhead to stay west of the Skerries and keep the tall chimney on the left. The Skerries is a group of rocks infamous for shipwrecks and terrible seas. According to Karl Brady's book, Shipwreck Inventory of Ireland: Louth, Meath, Dublin and Wicklow, there are 210 recorded shipwrecks from Balbriggan and Loughshinny with 100 of these lying off the Skerries. I was wary of these rocks after the conversation last night so gave them a very wide berth only to realise I was fighting the tide and losing distance keeping so far west. Surrendering to the tide but keeping south of the Skerries improved headway. I was being whisked just clear of the ferocious breaking overfalls, moving towards the safety of the harbour arm.

Entering the outer harbour, I saw the search and rescue helicopter conducting a training exercise with the RNLI lifeboat. I hoped this wasn't for my benefit. Keeping the chimney in line, it seemed I'd made it, having past the Skerries and now within reach of land. I made calls to Emma and messaged the Safety Channel once the seas had calmed down as I got nearer the shore. Everyone seemed relieved I was back in comms, a nice feeling to know that somebody cared.

On the way into Holyhead, there's a long harbour wall they refer to as the breakwater. It's actually the longest breakwater in the United Kingdom at 1.7 miles. Turning the corner, I found myself having to tack into the wind back and forth along the narrowing harbour entrance. It seemed to go on forever. Quite a let down after what had been my biggest milestone so far. A 'megaplasmic' moment. Slogging slowly towards the harbour against the tide and wind was a total anti-climax to the day's events. It took another hour to cover the last 1.7 miles.

I called Jenny again as I thought I must be in the wrong place.

She wrote, *around 5 pm my phone rings again.... "Where is the RNLI station in Holyhead?"*

Now I'm in Shoprite trying to act as a Holyhead pilot for a chap in a Laser. I hope he found Holyhead Lifeboat Station and had a good night's rest before carrying on the next leg.

I wrote, "Thank you, Jenny."

Chapter 42

Holyhead Whip

Arriving at a location where someone was waiting to greet me was pretty unusual. Throughout most of my journey I'd landed at impromptu places based on the tides, wind, fatigue or hunger. Holyhead was different. For almost the first time, a support chain was starting to emerge through word of mouth or deliberate efforts, mainly from Emma and the other members of the Safety Channel sending out appeals on the Facebook page. This was beginning to gather momentum and my journey was attracting a sizeable following. Offers of support and, most importantly, accommodation were starting to come in quite regularly.

Jenny had set up a rendezvous for me in Holyhead through the lifeboat network. She referred to it as being passed down the line. Standing on the concrete ramp shared by the Holyhead Lifeboat Station and Holyhead Sailing Club, or Clwb Hwylio Caergybi to give it its proper Welsh name, was Tony Price, the local lifeboat coxswain. Here is a person who oozes warmth. He'd lived in this area both man and boy. Of medium height and stocky build, Tony had one of those smiles that peeled open and stretched from ear to ear making you feel instantly at ease.

"Welcome to Wales," was Tony's first line as I pulled into Holyhead.

"Wales!"

Yes of course. I hadn't even thought about this. I'd been so focused on getting here, I'd bypassed the English border at sea and was now out of Scotland rejoining land in Wales. How fantastic that felt. Today was the 11th September. It had taken 39 days to get round Scotland, crossing out of England on the 4th of August.

Someone had looked after me again today. Wales is sometimes referred to as a land of poets. I'm not sure Dylan Thomas would necessarily have thought of singing Suicide is Painless repeatedly all the way across the Irish Sea but somehow it seemed a fitting way to enter Wales, a country where song and verse are so entwined in their culture:

O let us see another day!
Bless us all this night, I pray,
And to the sun we all will bow
And say, good-bye – but just for now!
From 'Under Milk Wood' by Dylan Thomas

When you've had one of the most epic days of your life, usually afterwards you would think having a rest would be in order. Today, Tony was so enthusiastic he wanted me to meet the crew who were all assembled in the lifeboat station and stood in a circle waiting to greet me. Tony introduced me. Slightly caught off guard and still dripping in my wetsuit on their polished wooden floor, he said.

"So tell us what you have been doing and why."

"A presentation?" I said, thinking does he realise I can't quite believe I'm still alive.

"Just a few words for the boys and girls," Tony replied

Never knowingly short for words, it took me a few moments to get my head together before dropping into my usual blurb about circumnavigating the UK, raising money for Prostate Cancer UK, leaving Eastbourne on the 17th July, 56 days ago.

"Wow 56 days ago. Really had it been that long?" I quizzed myself under my breath.

The crew was a great audience and following a round of applause one of the lifeboatmen came forwards and presented me with £30. He said they'd had a whip round to buy me dinner and some beers at the sailing club restaurant next door. I couldn't quite believe it but accepted it gratefully. My personal funds were nearly exhausted so this was a welcome surprise.

Tony had made up a bed for me in their training room with a duvet and pillow. What a welcome to Cymru. The Welsh language name for this country fittingly translates to 'friends' or 'countrymen'.

The following day's forecast was for 29 to 39 knots of wind, making it another red zone day. I thought I'd utilise the workshop facilities in the lifeboat station. The next day was spent resealing all the splits in the hull, of which the corners were the main culprits. The local chandlery was stuffed full of gear. I bought a new VHF radio after a deep intake of breath when seeing the price. I also bought a praddle to replace the one Ditta had given me in Stonehaven and a special hook for the outhaul, both of which I'd lost in Carsaig.

Late into the afternoon, Tony came and found me to give me a full tour of his childhood spots. He showed me where he swam, fished and messed around growing up. We looked at the wrecked yachts from the March 2018 storm Emma when the harbour and 80 boats were destroyed.

As we drove over the hill to the other side of the island Tony quipped, "This is our mountain. Only it's not a mountain."

Then later, as we drove along valley road he followed up with, "This is our valley. Only it's not a valley."

The port seemed to be the cause and the cure for the Isle of Anglesey's modern decline. It was sad to see the longest breakwater in the UK, an incredible feat of engineering which took 28 years to build, costing the lives of 40 men and employing 1,300 men to build it, in such a sorry condition. In its heyday, a standard gauge railway had carried seven million tonnes of stone along the 1.4 mile track from Holyhead Mountain before loading directly into the cargo holds of massive ships. Closed down in the 1980s, the track now looks overgrown and abandoned. What a waste!

I really enjoyed the two nights in the lifeboat station. It was certainly a break my body needed and it gave me a good chance to plan the next five days. Setting off early on Friday 13th, I felt better prepared than at any point. New kit in my VHF radio and Tony had given me a spare battery and a detailed briefing on rounding South Stack and heading for Bardsey Island. The forecast looked great although the breeze was only light winds, a northerly with sunshine.

As I was packing up to leave early that morning, Tony appeared. I mentioned I needed to pick up some food but was short on time. Next minute Tony was whizzing off to the Co-op and returned minutes later with a bag bulging full of food for the day. He refused to accept any money. Tony went over the need for me to get round Bardsey Island before the tide turned around 3 pm.

Anglesey had shown me warmth and humanity, more than I could have ever imagined.

Chapter 43

Friday 13th, Whistling Sands

Somewhat ironically, Friday 13th turned out to be a thoroughly uneventful day. After pushing off from Anglesey with Tony still enthusiastically waving me off, I made it safely round South Stack at 10 am. In a gentle breeze, I reached all day in beautiful sunshine and clear blue skies. In fact, it was so uneventful that I nearly fell out of the boat on one occasion as I nodded off with my body lounging across the hull and legs skimming across the glistening soft lapping waves. The sun seeped into my bones. Aches and pains that had plagued me throughout my journey through Scotland seemed to have miraculously disappeared. The glint of light reflecting back off the electric blue and white surf seemed to breathe new life into me. I could barely remember the date I'd left Eastbourne. I wasn't even sure what day it was now. Time had seeped away like water running back through the beach. Since crossing the border into Scotland, I could only recall a handful of days when the sun had been this warm. By 5 pm, Bardsey Point was clearly in view but the tide had turned and after battling against it for nearly an hour I elected to give up and head back towards an incredible sandy bay called Porth Oer, also referred to as Whistling Sands. I'd passed this half an hour earlier but assisted by the tide it only took half this time to retrace my steps. Approaching the bay, I took aim at a large boulder lodged deep in the sand in the centre of the horseshoe shaped beach. It was such a gentle landing that if I'd been asleep, it wouldn't have woken me. I'd made it half way down through Wales. As I stepped off the MOD27 standing on the golden yellow sands, life felt wonderful.

Whistling Sands reminded me of my childhood holidays with my family at Criccieth in North Wales with the miles of sand and secluded bays hidden in the granite cliff line. People busied themselves like ants moving back and forth in a way that only made sense to them. I felt like I was looking down on the world, as if I was no longer a part of this random activity called normal life. On the beach, I sat for ages watching a column of ants scurrying across the sand, foraging for food. Flies devouring the remnants of some child's ice cream. The detail made little sense to me anymore. It was like a strange dream. I'd never believe my own stories about crossing the Irish Sea, rounding the Mull of Kintyre in breaking overfalls and 40 knots of wind, being launched into the air around Duncansby Head, running away from a pod of orcas to find the safety of shore in north east Scotland. These moments seemed surreal, already make-believe fantasies that someone else had told me about.

Whistling Sands was different. The wet, rippling sand under my feet felt real. The deep, sandy bay looked like paradise. It was near deserted. The sun was still warm but would soon be dropping. Scanning around, I could see a few people making their way walking up a long inclined slope at the far end of the beach. They must be a long way off as they looked like tiny coloured specks against the backdrop of the cliffs they were ascending. I was in Wales proper now.

My two day stay, hunkered down in the lifeboat station on Anglesey, was technically my first Welsh stop but this felt different. I was alone again, away from the company of people. Running free, I had no one meeting me in Whistling Sands. I craved the isolation after having been surrounded by so many people the previous few days.

Where I'd landed, there was a small rock planted in the centre of the beach. I'd been drawn to this approaching the bay. Strange how objects can act like magnets when you see them far offshore. Entirely unknown landmarks become the focal point. For reasons I can't explain, I was pulled into this rock.

When I left Anglesey it was Friday 13th August, unlucky for some but I'm sure in my case it was lucky! I was originally planning to sail to Abersoch which I'd previously visited twice, the first time racing my first Laser aged 17 at the Laser National Championships. I remembered how I broke my mast at deck level on the way out to the start of the first race. Lots of people asked if I was OK as they raced past me to the start line. Three hours later I was picked up by a rescue boat drifting miles out to sea. As I'd said at the time that I was fine, no one thought to report my incident to race control. On my second visit to Abersoch, I recall spending an unusual week crewing for someone who's name I forget in a squib. This is one of the strangest looking boats with ochre-coloured sails and a blobby shaped hull which just looks all wrong. I can't remember how I ended up sailing this boat for a whole week with a virtual stranger but I do remember spending the evenings learning to windsurf on the most beautiful sandy beaches.

Abersoch, or more crucially South Caernarvonshire Yacht Club, was once the main dinghy sailing centre in North Wales, staging all the major championships. This position has been eroded over more recent years with the new Welsh National Sailing Academy and Event Centre in Plas Heli in Pwllheli now competing for the major championships. This is on account of the Welsh Government throwing millions of funding into the building of a purpose-built location. It's certainly an impressive facility. I'd sailed here too in a Laser Masters event fairly recently. On that occasion, we'd no wind so members of the G7 spent an evening in the local town racing our bikes up and down the front after which PY and I went off strutting around a local bar or two till three in the morning. I narrowly missed getting involved in a scuffle with the locals. This is when PY explained to me about his pre-emptive strike technique. He told me to raise my hands to give the impression of surrendering but really it's just a way to wind up your backswing. I didn't need it, deploying my mouth instead.

I'd arrived at Whistling Sands because of missing the tidal gate for rounding Bardsey Island. The wind was dying and after fighting the tide for more than an hour, the race between Bardsey and the mainland looked unwelcoming, especially at the end of the day. It was pointless struggling on. I'd never make it round the headland. Scanning the horizon, there was little choice other than to turn back with the new tide to the bay with the rock.

That's how I met Diana Harvey. After dragging the MOD27 and all my gear across the light, golden sand to the safety of the cliff line, I noticed a set of three caves nestling in a remote corner of the beach. It looked like a sheltered location, less exposed than the centre of the beach where the MOD27 was now parked. I struggled with my cooking kit and camping gear across the sand heading towards the caves. Approaching, I noticed an elegant elderly lady sunbathing in the mouth of one of the caves. I set up my cooker close by her in the entrance of a smaller, less sheltered cave and started cooking chickpeas and rice. At this point, I realised I was nearly out of water. There appeared to be nothing resembling fresh water close by so I boiled the rice up in the juice of the chickpea tin.

Diana watched me cooking for a while then, as the sun dipped behind the cliffs, she packed her chair and rug and made her way back up towards the slope which I assumed was the way out. We smiled at each other but said nothing. As soon as she'd vacated the cave, I moved in. It looked perfect for sleeping in. My only concern was would it flood when the tide came in. It looked like it might as there was dried seaweed inside. The tides were pretty strong today but I wasn't sure how high. The comms here were non-existent so there was no way of checking. I'd just have to risk it. It felt pretty dry inside, however today had been a scorcher so the cave could easily have dried out in the sun. Laying out my bivvy and sleeping bag, I stowed my kit bag then set off in search of water.

After walking several miles in a vain search for water, I gave up. The National Trust Cafe at the very opposite end of the beach to my cave clearly had water but was locked down like it was Fort Knox! The blue pipe into the cafe looked very tempting. I did consider cutting into it but vandalism wasn't really on my agenda. Although I'd eaten the chickpeas, which had liquid in the tin, I was still seriously thirsty. Both my water bottles were now empty. Plan B evolved slowly at first. Surely it hadn't come to this. There must be somewhere I could find fresh water, after all, only a few days ago I'd been complaining about how much rain there'd been. I scoured the cliffs for any small crevices and cracks that might have been storing rainwater. There were none. Trudging back to my cave, I could hardly swallow, my mouth was so dry. To make matters worse, now I also needed the toilet. I tried thinking of something else. Perhaps there was a pub nearby? Looking at the nearby landscape, I felt this very unlikely. I'd watched Bear Grylls on TV once explain how it worked. In the wild, to survive, you must drink. If there's no fresh water the next best thing is to consume your own urine. It slows down dehydration!

I managed to nearly fill one bottle without too much trouble. It looked surprisingly clear, given how dry my mouth felt. Closing my eyes, I went for it! It tasted surprisingly like water, warm but nowhere near as bad as I'd expected. I finished off the lot, ate a small oaty bar to remove the aftertaste and almost instantly fell asleep inside the cave. I'd done it. Another first today.

As I woke early with the sunrise, a warm sun blazed across the glassy bay. I was now really thirsty so got up straight away and set off again in search of water. As I left the cave, I realised last night I'd been lucky, the sea had come to within a few inches of the cave's mouth at high tide. The water had been lapping at my feet but I was too tired to wake up. I couldn't have cared less if it had flooded. It would probably have been a welcome relief.

Packing my empty water bottles and phones into a small dry bag, I set off across the wide sandy beach once again in search of water. Foolishly, I didn't put on any shoes and when I reached the road, which was the only way up the cliff line, it was covered in tiny sharp stones. I tiptoed tentatively along the tiny grassy edge but I found this was full of stinging nettles, thorns, dog turd and an assortment of other objects far from ideal if you're trying to tackle it in bare feet. I really couldn't face walking all the way back to the cave to pick up my shoes so carried on. At the top of the hill there was a public toilet, my feet were cut and burning by the time I found it. I was several miles from where I'd camped. The door was unlocked. Inside was a urinal, toilet cubicle and a tiny stainless steel sink with the smallest tap I think I've ever seen. It was designed in such a way that a water bottle wouldn't fit underneath. I improvised by cupping my hands and pouring water into my bottle, balanced precariously on the narrow stainless steel basin rim. Above the sink a large sign read,

"Do Not Drink"

Surely it couldn't be worse than urine. I downed half a bottle immediately then carried on with my painstaking hand filling technique.

By the time I'd trudged back to the cave, my feet were on fire. The hot tarmac stones were even more painful coming back down the hill. I was cursing for not wearing shoes. I walked into the sea and felt the stinging of saltwater on fresh wounds. My pain eased as I stood admiring my surroundings. I noticed the same elderly lady from the previous evening was now sitting in the adjacent cave to the one I'd slept in last night. She'd obviously come to secure her usual spot only to find I'd rudely taken it. I apologised when I returned but she was fine, so I set about cooking packet rice and coffee on a small burner. We got chatting whilst I cooked and ate. I told her about my journey and she told me about hers.

Her name was Diana. Her partner had been taken ill with Parkinson's some years ago and she was now his full-time carer. Whistling Sands, Porth Oer was a respite break for her from the strain of caring full time. What they were both battling through sounded terribly sad. She was clearly well-educated and thoroughly versed in the raising of children and grandchildren but this caring task appeared to be taking a larger toll on her than anything she'd previously experienced.

Diana emailed me a few days later and said,

"This is one of the best holidays for some years for me, and for many reasons, particularly this amazing sunny weather, day after day! Everything is sooo beautiful, and the peace and tranquillity really feeds the soul"!

I smiled and felt lucky for what I have.

Chapter 44

Commodore's Reception

Whistling Sands was such a beautiful beach I stayed a while the following morning waiting for the cafe to open at 10 am on the far end of the beach. I had a swim before packing up. The favourable tides weren't with me until 12 noon so there was no hurry. The sun was already hot and once I had loaded the MOD27 I decided it would be easier to sail the mile along the beach to the café, landing the boat right outside and dragging her up the sand just high enough for her to be safe from the last hour of the flooding tide. I left her capsized, lying on her side with the sail still rigged.

The cafe had a pretty wooden veranda overlooking the sea. The large glazed front door was open and inside there was a small queue of customers. Entering the cafe in my wetsuit, I joined the queue buying cappuccinos and bacon rolls. As I stood in line, a damp patch formed around me as I dripped my way towards the teenage girls serving behind their Formica counter.

"Large cappuccino, two bacon rolls, three bottles of water, three muesli bars, a piece of chocolate cake and an orange juice please."

I felt weirdly awkward. My dress sense and the snail trail of water oozing out of my boots onto their pristine white floor seemed oddly out of sorts with this well-heeled clientele. The young girl serving looked at me in the same way my teenage children would have, a sort of co-operative agreement whilst harbouring silent judgemental thoughts about my clothing and the mess I had made.

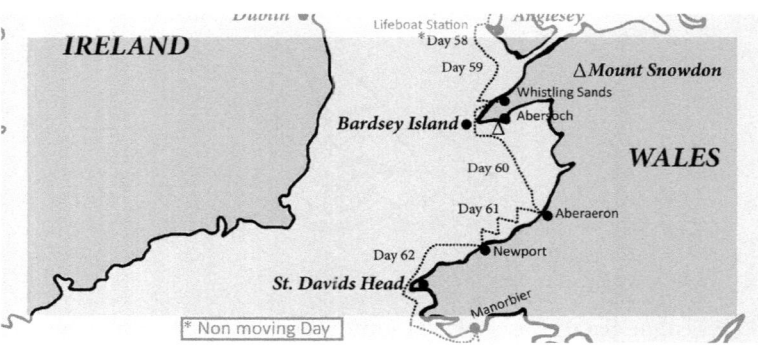

"What a weirdo," I could feel the thought seeping out of her brain into a speech bubble above her head as she looked at me dressed in my frogman's uniform.

Taking the goodies and devouring the chocolate cake and coffee at the nearest table while I waited for the bacon sarnies to cook, I glanced out the window and noticed the MOD27 beginning to float very slowly away on the encroaching tide. The water was lapping at the transom. I dithered about going outside to pull her further up the beach but dismissed it as being unnecessary. The timing of the bacon sarnies was now critical. No point wasting my energy levels dragging the boat up again. I felt myself willing them to cook faster. When the food finally arrived, presented in a plain white paper bag, I swiftly scooped it up and hurried to the exit, emerging onto the veranda in front of the beach.

As I walked down the steps, the MOD27 miraculously uncapsized herself and was sitting bolt upright as if to say, "I'm ready."

Incredible timing. She stood bolt upright, lifted by a gust of wind that caught under the sail as I emerged from the cafe door. Memories of the film Herbie Rides Again came to mind when Herbie the VW Beetle has a mind of its own and frequently drives itself to get Jim Douglas, his driver, out of trouble.

With a small crowd watching, I stepped casually onto the now upright dinghy, drifting out with the tide as if this was the normal way a circumnavigator launches, casually tucking my newly acquired bacon sarnies into my life jacket, knowing that as I did so all the tomato ketchup squirted out the top of the paper bag smearing all over my life jacket. Not wanting to spoil the illusion and disappoint my gawking onlookers by stopping to lick it clean, I brushed back my hair in an overly dramatic fashion smearing red sauce over my face and disappeared into the distance, wiping ketchup all over the decks as I pulled in the mainsheet and set sail. I really wanted them to cheer me but knew there was an air of indifference from my spectators, looking at me like I was some strange eccentric. Sadly no one was on the beach providing expert analysis and an over excited commentary. Where was John Motson, the famous British football commentator, when you needed him?

The first part of the day's journey was tricky. Tony from the Anglesey lifeboat station had talked about Bardsey Island which stood some 3 km off the Lleyn Peninsula, my first headland of the day. The tidal flows are fierce round here. The dangers seemed to be masked by the blazing hot sun and crystal clear water. I was wary as I approached the large block of rock standing isolated just off the coast.

Bardsey Island is described as a rocky melange of sedimentary and igneous rocks including some granite. It is approximately 1 km wide, narrowing to 300 metres at the thinnest part, and 1.6 km long. It stands

48 metres tall at its highest point overlooking Bardsey Sound. The tidal flows around this rocky outcrop were not represented in any local tidal references I could find at the time but I read a published research article whilst compiling this book entitled, Bardsey - An Island in a Strong Tidal Stream. Underestimating Coastal Tides Due to Unresolved Topography by J. A. Mattias Green and David T. Pugh which reads,

"The curvature of the streamlines as the flow is squeezed through Bardsey Sound and swings up around the peninsula, leads to the enhanced generation of non-linear higher tidal harmonics due to curvature on the reversing tidal stream curves. This contributes to the large M4 amplitudes around the island and headland."

Or, in plain English, lots of non-intelligible confused, somewhat uncomfortable rapids, whirlpools, overfalls and generally nasty waters.

I sailed through this area and sighed a deep breath of relief once on the other side. Now just the small matter of crossing Cardigan Bay of which the first name to appear on my Navionics app further inshore was called Devil's Ridge, followed by the Devil's Tail. Needless to say, I elected to stay well offshore away from these areas.

Steering a compass heading exactly south 180 degrees sailing directly for Fishguard, I was a long way out. Not being certain how far the breeze would carry me, I was fetching along at a decent pace most of the day. By mid-afternoon, it was clear there was no way Fishguard would be achievable during daylight hours so my plans changed. Aberystwyth was half way along the bay. By now though, I was so far offshore I'd have to sail eastwards almost as far as I'd sailed south.

There had been some chatter ongoing during the day with the Safety Channel about possible options of assistance from locals. One follower of my journey based in Eastbourne, Peter Dickens, had passed on my details to a friend of his in Wales called Wendy Price-Jones. It was unclear to me where Wendy lived but the Safety Channel advised me she was happy to help and had offered to meet me wherever I landed and would then look after me.

I googled Wendy's location and came up with a load of places which didn't seem to be anywhere near my present location. I must have misspelled it. Doing google searching on a tiny mobile screen whilst surfing along at 9 knots in a Laser is always difficult but in Wales the spelling of place names and also the number of different places with similarities added a new dimension of difficulty. It took over an hour with numerous messages bouncing back and forth before it was resolved. Emma, manning the Safety Channel, was getting increasingly frustrated with my lack of knowledge of my whereabouts and likely time of arrival. She was juggling a number of other volunteers along the Welsh coastline and not surprisingly was clearly struggling to pass on any meaningful information as I'd no idea where I'd end up.

I finally found Aberaeron on Google Maps which was Wendy's location and realised the other place, Aderdaron, was miles north of me. I was now in danger of overshooting Wendy. It was getting late and I was still so far offshore I could barely see land. She sounded perfect and the idea of a comfy bed for the evening became my top priority. New mission: find Wendy.

Easing out my sail and steering more easterly in towards the shoreline, 160 degrees at first then 140 degrees, I headed towards Aberaeron. I was screaming along now, surfing down some really big waves, enjoying some of the best sailing conditions of my trip. Wendy here I come.

When Aberaeron finally appeared in view around 7 pm it was a sight to behold, the most picturesque harbour town you can imagine with pastel coloured Georgian town houses neatly arranged along the harbour frontage lit up by the bright blue summer sky. Yachts were neatly moored at anchorage and then in front of me was Wendy, standing waving her arms above her head enthusiastically with a beautifully warm welcoming smile. Her face was framed by a carefully carved blonde bob haircut and her pink alpaca jumper looked like it had been selected from the same colour palette as the houses.

Standing behind Wendy on the concrete slipway were some of the local Aberaeron Yacht Club members including the Commodore, Nick, who was wearing a very smart suit. Nice of him to dress up for me I thought as they all struggled with me to pull the MOD27 up the very steep ramp on a borrowed cradle trolley that looked like it had originally been designed for a lifeboat to launch on.

Nick then explained while I was unrigging that it was the Commodore's Dinner that evening, due to start in half an hour. He offered me an impromptu invitation to be their guest. Wendy wasn't attending but offered to pick me up after it was over and take me back to her house later that evening. I insisted she joined for a drink around 9 pm and she agreed.

Covered in salt and tomato ketchup, Wendy showed me to a multipurpose disabled toilet come shower room to clean up. Strangely, the shower was directly above the toilet so I had to sit down. However, the on button was located three quarters of the way up the wall making it impossible for anyone disabled to switch it on as it only lasted for 30 seconds after pressing the button. Having a shower was a serious workout with me repeating a series of squats to keep the water on each time the timer ran out. I wasn't complaining though as it was warm and clean.

My only dry clothing was a pair of shorts and a Rooster polypro sailing top. Everything else was wet. Wendy offered to take all my clothes to her home and dry them so that's how I attended the Aberaeron Commodore's Black Tie Dinner in shorts and a lycra top.

The evening was a grand affair with most of the yacht club in attendance. I was plied with beer and wine all evening and invited to give a short presentation about my journey and Prostate Cancer UK which I was supporting. Wendy joined me near the end of the evening and we had a bit of a giggle whilst the official photographer took a panoramic photo of all in attendance. Wendy and I managed to appear at both ends of the table in the picture by running around behind the cameraman whilst he panned the camera through 180 degrees.

I'd had an interesting conversation earlier in the evening at the bar with one of the visiting yacht club members who was clearly an expert in the local waters. After mentioning my experience round Bardsey Island that morning and asking about any possible suggestions for rounding St. David's Head further along the coastline, he pulled out a napkin then I experienced a Bob Ross painting moment, watching mesmerised while he proceeded to draw the most detailed map whilst standing at the bar. The map was a work of art, detailing the obstructions, obstacles, tidal rips and overfalls to watch out for. By the time he'd finished this work of nautical genius he'd worked his way through nearly half a pack of paper napkins and presented me with a set of illustrated charts that Captain Robert Fitzroy of the Beagle would have been proud of.

The yacht club's raffle raised hundreds of pounds which they generously donated to my prostate cancer fund. By the time my head hit the pillow at Wendy's house that evening, I went out like a light. This had been another big day, covering over 60 miles and most importantly having avoided any self-ingesting requirements this evening to quench my thirst.

"Thank you God!" I thought.

Chapter 45

Torpedoes at Fishguard

Aberaeron had been a great call. Wendy had looked after me like royalty and even took me to the Harbourmaster Cafe on the front the following morning where her friend's cafe cooked me the most enormous full English breakfast and donated this free. The best Welsh full English I can remember. The next step of my journey was bringing me closer to the most feared crossing of all, the Bristol Channel, notorious for its massive tidal range of between 12 and 14 metres, making it the world's second highest tidal range, exceeded only by that of the Bay of Fundy in Canada. Is this dangerous? I assumed yes.

I'd sailed across the Bristol Channel twice in a tall ship called the Donald Searle when I was 15 years old. My memory of this experience was vague but I do recall being the person they sent to the top of the 24 metre tall mast to keep look out and check the mast wasn't going to hit the Severn Bridge as we entered Bristol. I remember thinking we were going to hit all the way until, within a few metres of the bridge, it seemed to miraculously elevate a foot or two above my head. The navigator had judged the tides just right for us to clear it. To be fair though, I've no idea what I might have done had he miscalculated. The discussions and workings out that preceded my high level experience were detailed and numerous between the ship's skipper, navigator and first mates. There were extensive calculations to determine heights of tide, depth of water, rate of flow and time of arrival. It sounded so complicated. Fortunately, my Laser was unlikely to encounter any bridges but the tidal flows would certainly pose a challenge.

Almost the first thing I'd considered after dreaming up my initial idea of undertaking this journey was how to cross the Bristol Channel. A range of water which, if I sailed straight across the mouth at its widest point following the rhumb line directly towards Lundy Island and onwards to Hartland Point in North Devon, would be in excess of 40 miles, a distance I'd already covered in a day previously. Somehow, staring at this vast stretch of open water seemed more onerous than anything I'd experienced before. I've no logic to explain this but for the whole trip, the Bristol Channel was always going to be my biggest mental test.

That was for another day. I still needed to make my way along Cardigan Bay's extensive coastline. It would be a beat all day today down to St David's Head sailing directly into a south westerly wind. I was cursing sailing so far eastwards yesterday. Had I carried on my track and skipped Wendy, I'd have been on a much faster course today across Cardigan Bay to St. David's Head. I knew full well that it would have meant sailing very late last night. However, I afforded myself the fantasy that it would have been a better choice than bumping along into the wind over tide conditions I was finding deeply unpleasant at this moment.

I'd found myself doing this a bit during this trip, the 'if only I had' moments of reflection. These are bad signs for a circumnavigator. You really have to work at removing these negative thoughts from your mind. As soon as regret and contemplation of things that have gone wrong creep into your mind, they become very destructive to morale. I forced this current negative thought out of my mind and concentrated on finding as comfortable a position in the bumpy conditions as I could then struck up my favourite song, Suicide is Painless, in full voice followed up with a few Welsh Rugby songs using my own made up lyrics. After half an hour of belting out songs at the top of my voice, I was feeling really jolly happy.

The Safety Channel was busy that day with numerous offers of accommodation ahead. This cheered my mood. As per usual, the tracking wasn't really working but looking ahead Fishguard was a place that kept being mentioned. I searched and this seemed to be the most likely place to stop. The breeze was only running at 10 knots so progress today was slow. By 4.30 pm, I was starting to struggle for speed. The tide was turning against me and the likelihood of reaching Fishguard looked less and less likely with a dying breeze. I identified Newport as the preferred stopping point for the night. There were a number of messages back and forth trying to identify which Newport I was referring to. At first the Safety Channel thought I'd miraculously managed to leapfrog all the way down to Cardiff where Newport Town is located. After sorting out the right Newport, just north of Fishguard, Emma made contact with Roger and Gale on Facebook who'd offered a bed for the night. Incredibly, they responded quickly even though Roger was out in his fishing boat. The message came through that he'd drive to Newport and meet me there, sending a warning that it would be low water when I arrived.

Newport Bay dries out to a trickle of water so access is severely restricted at low water. I ignored this warning as I figured a Laser could get in pretty much anywhere so elected to go for it. When I arrived at the channel entrance of Newport it was nearly 6 pm. In front of me was a large wide sandy bay with a small estuary river meandering in towards the tiny harbour and boat club. The entrance was marked with some very small green and red buoys, almost toy boat size. I was now proceeding very cautiously as the bottom was brushing on my daggerboard. With the rudder and daggerboard half up, I made my way gently along the windy silty channel. The wind was behind and quite light so it meant I could skid across the shallows with no rudder blade or daggerboard in the water. I had a few close scrapes when I nearly got stuck but made it to within a few hundred metres of the pretty harbour slipway before running aground.

Roger was waiting. He'd brought his Laser trailer and trolley and was instantly enthusiastically racing around to assist in any and every way possible. Roger himself sailed a Laser and had a daughter he'd travelled around the UK with visiting various Laser events so he knew what to do. He was full of energy, dressed in his mustard yellow fishing trousers and wellies as he'd just come straight from his boat. He waded into the water to meet me and we loaded the boat onto the trolley before hitching up to his car and dragging it the rest of the way up the ramp.

Roger's car was full of fishy things, not really surprising as his business was lobster pot fishing. Over the course of the evening, I discovered all sorts of interesting facts about pots, crabs, lobsters and the like. Gail, Roger's New Zealand-born wife, cooked a meal of chilli con carne and rice, large enough to sustain Lazlo for a week followed up with rice pudding, cheese and biscuits and plenty of wine. Roger quizzed and questioned me about every fine detail of my trip. He excitedly ran off to fetch pictures of him sailing his yellow Laser and his daughter in her Laser. We talked about everything that evening. So many stories recounted. Gail sat there like a verbal shock absorber, recounting the stories at a reduced pace as Roger dashed off to find something else to show me. The contrast between Gail and Roger was magical to observe with her being the picture of calmness moving at a quarter of the speed of Roger. He was so enthusiastic he just couldn't sit still.

We discussed logistics for re-launching the next day. Roger had his Spanish lorry driver turning up to collect his freshly caught lobsters at 6 am. I'd never seen a lobster boat in action and asked if I could come along and see how it all worked. He was happy to take me. The lifeboat station was next door to his boat. He suggested I could look at the charts in the lifeboat station while I was there. He seemed to think St David's Head and after this past Solva were tricky and potentially treacherous. Roger himself confessed he didn't know these waters very well but he had a friend who did. Without allowing me to speak, he leapt into action and called up one of his sailing contacts living in Solva, Piers Beckett, the father of Olympic Laser hopeful Michael Beckett who, as it happened, I knew.

"Fishy here," Roger blasted, laughing down the phone.

A burst of narrative followed about my journey and how I was staying with him that night and I needed some advice on the best time to leave and where to go when I got as far as Solva. The conversation was like the rattle of machine gun fire. Questions being launched in short sharp bursts from Roger followed by a considered series of agreements as he listened to the answer coming down the phone.

"Yes yes. Oh! Yes yes. Ok. Ok. Well Ok. Oh! and what about ..."

The conversation continued for a while until Roger stopped abruptly and handed me the phone. Piers was on the other end. He spoke with a great calmness, confident in the information he was imparting, very succinctly and in easily digested snippets. He outlined a few key places where, if the tides and winds were with me, he suggested I just keep going for as long as possible. One timeline was passing through Ramsey Island at St. David's Head. We agreed I needed to make it there before the flood tide at 5 pm. If I passed it, he recommended carrying on for as long as possible.

I was trying to establish how far I should go to set up for my following day to minimise the crossing distance for the Bristol Channel but felt little wiser after the call on this particular point. I did, however, learn about the firing range at Castle Martin extending 3 nautical miles or about 3.4 standard miles offshore at St Govan's Head, but remained blissfully unaware of the prohibition on landing at Manorbier where there was an anti-aircraft artillery range.

The evening meal was significant and I felt dead tired almost as soon as the last mouthful went in. An early night and another early rise tomorrow before a big day again. The pace was becoming relentless. I was starting Day 61 tomorrow. Would I ever get home?

In the morning, Gale passed me a packet of sandwiches and Roger packed his fishing gear into the car. Together we set off to the local lifeboat station where his lobsters were and where his boat was moored. There was a hive of activity when we arrived. The Spanish driver was marching up and down, fishermen were hauling out a giant wooden box on wheels submerged in the harbour which contained hundreds of live lobsters. There was some discussion going on about them smelling of diesel. I witnessed the fishermen picking up the lobsters one by one and sniffing them, holding them inches away from the ends of their noses and quizzically looking at each other, conversing then returning the sniffed lobster to the wooden box before selecting another and another.

There was some concern a diesel spill may have tainted the lobsters. It seemed to get resolved because before long the entire contents were being loaded onto the giant refrigerated truck soon to be bound for a plate in Spain.

Roger explained that the best priced lobsters were sized to fit onto a dinner plate. The large ones were valued less than those that were plate size and then the ones that had only one claw were worth less still. The lobsters with least value were what he referred to as 'torpedoes'.

"Why do you call them torpedoes?" I enquired.

"Well that's because they haven't got any claws, so they look just like a torpedo," Roger replied somewhat dejectedly about the limited value of a clawless lobster.

I assumed these must have lost their claws in a fight and started to wonder how a torpedo caught its food if it had no claws. None of these questions got asked.

Following my brief introduction to the world of pot fishing, Roger raced me back to the MOD27. High water was at 9.05 am so I needed to be underway by then to gain the maximum favourable current for the day. It took me an hour to get going, pushing out into the estuary around 10 am, later than I'd hoped. My body felt as stiff as an iron bar. The relentless strain on my muscles was causing me numerous physical issues daily.

The first tack I made in the estuary resulted in my back refusing to bend and then getting stuck under the boom trying to cross the boat, resulting in a slow motion, rather gracious capsize to windward, depositing me head first into the freezing water. Not quite the start I'd hoped for. I felt embarrassed as Roger was clearly watching when I righted the boat and clambered back on board.

After this far from ideal start the rest of the day went well although passing Strumble Point I encountered some big waves but nothing terrible. St. David's Head went without issue, making sure I avoided the frothy areas of water that looked like they probably had some ominous undercurrents caused by partially submerged rocks. I passed numerous whirlpools swirling viscously in clumps like a field of wild mushrooms spawning in the most unexpected places. I was used to dodging these bad bits by now and navigated through these with no scares. Blasting along the Pembrokeshire coastline in an increasing breeze with some incredible scenery felt fantastic. I was smashing this leg. Crossing Bridies Bay around 5 o'clock I passed through an extraordinary passage between a series of rocks called Crab Stones, located between Skomer Island and the mainland. Here, the tidal flow was ripping along at 8 or 9 knots. It was full of whirlpools, back eddies and mystical jet black pools that looked like they would reach middle earth. Safely through, I was on a roll. I felt this could be a chance to go for Lundy

Island right now, hole up overnight and then make it across to Devon the following morning. My adrenalin was racing. I called Rupert on the Safety Channel.

"Rupert I'm through Rook passage, thinking of going for Lundy tonight."

"Ah hold on chief. Let me just check."

Rupert was pretty whizz with Google Maps and it didn't take him long to dismiss this idea as being over ambitious.

I conceded quite easily and made a plan with him to head for Tenby. We identified this as a good place to set up for an early crossing of the Bristol Channel the next day. I whizzed past Milford Haven looking out for the standard hazard of multiple BFS associated with large industrial ports and reached my way along the coast following the shoreline closely. I came to an abrupt halt at Castlemaine. The red flag was hoisted with a six foot black ball hanging underneath. This must be the firing range

I called up on the radio and made contact with the firing range officer. He explained I couldn't pass until 5 pm. It was 4.45 pm when we spoke. I asked if he could make an exception and he curtly refused. The next 15 minutes dragged but I consigned myself to the wait, eating a muesli bar and a pepperami snack I'd stashed in my life jacket and then drinking half of my remaining water. At 5 pm I radioed again and this time the duty officer gave me permission to carry on. I do wonder if I hadn't brought a radio and had no way of contacting them if they would just stop firing when they saw a sailing dinghy crossing. It seemed a risky strategy. The wind was slowly beginning to die as I passed the range. Tenby was beyond me today so Rupert and I had another call. He identified a pub, the Castle Inn at Manorbier, only 5 km from me.

I was only making 5 knots now so this was nearly an hour away. The breeze seemed to be dropping all the time, compounded by the feeling that the tide was starting to turn against me. By the time I made it onto the beach, the sun was setting as I drifted into a most extraordinary small sandy bay with an 11th century Norman castle set up high on the cliff. This was Manorbier.

The shoreline was still. I let the MOD27 drift onto the sand whilst messaging the Safety Channel to let them know I'd landed. It was now 7.30 pm. Wading calf high to the shore, in front of me was a gentle sloping beach. Fifty yards inland, a two metre high sand dune with large clumps of marram grass poking through overlooked the bay. As I unrigged, a man approached and showed me a picture he'd taken of me sailing silhouetted by the sunset behind. It was an incredible shot. Paul Hinks, the photographer, chatted with me. I asked him about the local pub and he mentioned I'd need to hurry if I wanted any food as they stopped serving at 9 pm. We exchanged numbers so I could get a copy of his photo and then I set about pitching my tent and getting changed out of the wet gear. The only fresh water in sight was a stream running down into the sea so all of the gear went in. Myself included. A fast pack up of the valuables, electronics and my journal and I set off into the pitch black night along a tiny sandy path in search of food and power.

The path weaved through a wood coming out at the top of a steep hill after a series of turns had been negotiated, wiggling left then right. Or was it right then left? I arrived at a tarmac road. I stopped to ask for directions from a lone dog walker and after five minutes found the Castle Inn. Once inside, I went straight to the bar and ordered food.

"Sorry we stop serving food at nine," the young barman said in a flat, not terribly polite manner.

"Oh come on. It's only one minute past nine," I said in a rather feeble pleading voice.

"Sorry the chef's finished," he repeated

"I've just sailed 90 miles today from Fishguard in a small dinghy to get here. I've hardly eaten all day. Surely you must have something I can eat. Please!"

The young man told me to wait and he'd ask. After a few minutes he returned and told me,

"Chef said that they have lasagne, salad and chips."

"Done" I snapped instantly.

"Take a seat and I'll bring it over."

I scanned around the pub for electrical sockets and deposited all my devices around the pub. Several pints later I also asked if they might be able to make me a packed lunch for tomorrow which they agreed to and then I proceeded to empty the snack basket sitting on the bar counter filling up with anything I could find for tomorrow's journey. Whilst in the pub, I received a message from Paul who I'd met on the beach earlier asking if I needed anything.

I replied, "A cappuccino and bacon sandwich at sunrise tomorrow morning please."

He answered instantly, "What time?"

I sent an immediate reply, "5.30 am"

"See you there," came the response.

I wasn't holding my breath. A drunk local was beginning to get lardy and his constant overly loud shouting was starting to irritate me so I left as soon as all my batteries were fully charged. Once outside, it was pitch black, there were no street lights anywhere. I wandered around for half an hour thinking I was heading back to the beach before realising I'd taken a wrong turn. After retracing my steps back to the pub, I finally located the sandy footpath through the woods down to the beach. The time was 12.06 am.

When I arrived at the sand dunes it looked as if someone had been rummaging through the tent. I wasn't certain but usually I leave it zipped up and it was open. There was the faint scent of weed in the air. Checking my bags, there didn't seem to be anything missing but for the first time on this journey I felt uneasy. The night was still and the gentle lapping of sea breaking onto the shore was the only sound.

Settling down to sleep I thought I heard a rustling sound outside the tent. Grabbing my head torch and poking my head outside of the tent I scanned around. It took some time for my eyes to adjust but there was definitely some noise coming from the nearby woods. Very slowly I climbed out of the tent, shoving my shoes on and circling around behind the path that approached the woods. After waiting and listening for several minutes, the noise was gone and after 10 more minutes I heard and found nothing else so returned to the tent, zipped myself in and crashed out. It was now 1 am. I needed to be up in four hours' time.

The alarm was blaring away. I barely stirred but something inside me was pressing the wake up button. Oh man what a way to prepare for the biggest day of my life. Groaning and creaking with stiffness, my first thought was to get out of the tent and change as quickly as I could. Yesterday evening I'd left all the sailing gear spread out on a plastic tarpaulin so it didn't get covered in sand. There was no hope it would dry out so I hadn't bothered making a clothes line. Picking up the wetsuit first, it felt cold and dripping wet. If someone had filmed the next bit it would have made a great Charlie Chaplin scene. Firstly I stripped naked before attempting to pull on the wetsuit. It felt horrible. I was determined not to get sand on the inside though and was hopping around on one leg, trying to stay on the tarpaulin whilst pulling on the wetsuit. I fell over several times but just about kept on the marginally less sandy tarpaulin. It was pitch black and freezing cold. I started laughing at the absurdity of it all.

"What was I doing? I must be mad. No! I am mad."

I started singing a made-up tune whilst hopping about on one leg, struggling with the wetsuit.

"I'm mad. I'm mad. I'm f'ing bloody mad."

Once dressed, the next task was to pack up the tent and stuff everything into the MOD27. By now, the sun was just starting to appear with a tiny ray of light. Looking across the bay, it looked like a figure was walking towards me from the far end of the beach. It was still very dark so I wasn't sure at first.

"Surely not. It can't be. It is. Really. Ha ha! It is!"

"Cappuccino?" asked a voice as it approached me.

"You're joking" I said.

"Morning. Bacon sarnies too."

It was Paul Hinks, the man who'd taken the photo and messaged me last night at the pub.

"Paul. Wow that's fantastic. Cappuccino and bacon baps. You top banana," I eulogised.

This was a good sign. The gods were going to be with me today. If you'd asked me at the time, I probably would have said Paul was Jesus. This was such a nice thing. A total stranger. A randomer who'd literally said a few words to me on the beach the previous day, turned out of bed at 5.30 am in the cold dark morning to bring food and drink. It must have taken him half an hour or so to make the bacon rolls and coffee let alone walk to where I was staying so he'd probably had less sleep than me.

We both ate and chatted a bit as we watched the sun rise very slowly from the horizon. By the time I was packed up and ready to go, the sun was just throwing enough light to see the way out of the bay.

As I was departing, Paul threw in a quick comment along the lines of…

"I don't think you're allowed to land here. It's a prohibited military artillery range area for small craft."

Smiling to myself as I sailed off the beach, I thought how effective a Laser sailing dinghy was at evading the British military's defence systems. I'd come within a few hundred metres of a nuclear plant in Scotland undetected and now into a prohibited military firing zone.

Chapter 46

Put the Bentley Back in the Garage, Uncle Francis

Rupert had told me the day before that I needed to get going very early to make it across the Bristol Channel as the forecast was for the wind to drop right off around 2 pm. The tides were favourable early. I calculated they would wash me in towards Bristol initially then out to the Irish Sea later. Feeling more comfortable about heading inland first prompted my decision to leave so early.

Sailing out into the Channel, a number of large ships were silhouetted in the distance against the early sun. The water was calm and the breeze a healthy 10 to 12 knots. Setting a compass course of 140 degrees, I aimed for open water. There was nothing on the horizon to measure the effect of the tides against. Just sea for as far as I could see.

Studying the tidal range in the pub late last night, I thought there was a typo on the charts I was looking at. It said the tidal range was

12 metres at Bristol. I actually thought it should have read 1.2 metres. It took several takes and careful reading before to my horror it was correct.

"12 metres," I said out loud to myself in a disbelieving voice.

I'd no idea what this strength of tide would do to my course planning. I'd no idea at all. This was more than anything I'd encountered, ever. I spent the first two hours repeatedly checking my track on the Navionics app. I couldn't see Lundy Island but was aiming for it. I felt at least if I needed a bail out option, Lundy was about halfway across.

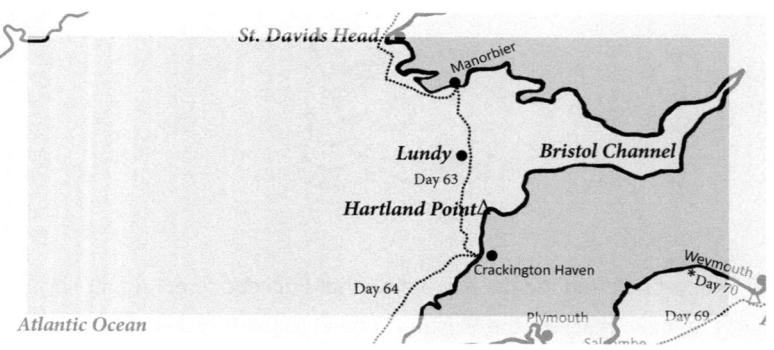

Two hours into the journey and there was nothing that looked like land. Perhaps the Navionics wasn't working properly. It showed I was on the right track. Surely I'd see the island from where I was. Doubts were creeping in like never before. Fear of the fear was starting to play its tricks on my mind. I checked the app again. I was definitely on 140 degrees. It looked right. I checked behind and couldn't see any land for reference behind either.

"Just keep plugging away. It'll come good soon," I told myself.

This positive thinking wasn't working too well today. I scrunched my eyes into tiny balls straining for any hint of land. Still nothing. The wind was steady and the sun was already quite warm. There was nothing to fear. The boat was all fine. I was all fine. Yet my anxiety levels were racing.

"Come on Lundy. Come on where are you?"

Another long 10 minutes passed. I checked the Navionics app again. It was there right in front of me on the map. Why couldn't I see it?

Perhaps the tide had taken me so far out I'd bypassed the island. Perhaps the mobile GPS signal didn't work accurately in the middle of the Bristol Channel. I was by now a long way off shore. My heart was beating fast. I started focusing on slowing down my breathing.

"In out. In out. In out. Slow everything down. Breathe and relax. Sing. Yes, sing."

"I am sailing

I am sailing

Home again

'Cross the sea

I am sailing

Stormy waters

To be near you

To be free"

Rod Stewart's 'I am sailing' song was all that came to mind. I'd belted out the only verse I vaguely knew of this song at least 30 times before a dot appeared. There it was. Lundy Island. It looked like a tiny rock at first but slowly it grew out of the sea. I was a long way east. The tide must have pushed me in towards Bristol as I'd expected. I corrected my direction slightly, using the Navionics app to confirm the bearing.

The island gradually, very, very slowly got bigger but I couldn't seem to reel it in. It was like nothing was moving. I was definitely moving at a good speed. I'd had a similar experience when crossing to the Isle of Man. It seems that as soon as you can see land, you believe it will only be a matter of minutes before you reach it. Sadly, in both these cases that wasn't happening. Lundy seemed to take an age to reach. The wind was already beginning to weaken in strength. Rupert had told me 2 pm before it changed. It was only 11.30 am and it was down to 5 knots.

My anxieties now switched to losing the wind before I made it to Lundy and getting swept out to sea as the tide changed, being whisked past Lundy, helpless to do anything about it, being carried along on the ebbing tide. I focused on sailing fast, hiking out hard and working the boat through every wave.

The cliffs of Lundy were very striking when I finally closed in on them around midday. I sailed past the North Lighthouse. It seemed to be quite low down close to the water, set deep into the edge of the cliff. Surrounding the northern end were plenty of partially submerged rocks. I gave these a wide berth but with little wind found myself unable to effect much change in direction. The east side of the island crept along, passing Gannets' Bay which didn't look like it had any bay from where I was sitting. There were sheer cliff faces. Nothing looked like it was landable. The water had become much more confused and felt like it was more tidal as I battled to make any progress around the cliffs. It was all painfully slow getting past the first headland. I was starting to regret coming in so close to the land. I should have stayed out in the open channel where I was sure the tidal influence was less. Certainly the hazards were less.

As I was thinking this, a much more violent set of waves started throwing me around in a confused way. Vertical standing waves. I was concerned it was a hidden reef or underwater rocks so changed course, heading east offshore from this extraordinary rock in the middle of the sea. My instincts were right. I was directly over half tide rock. Fortunately for me, it was high tide. As I changed direction, the breeze improved a little giving me more momentum to work my way around the more violent wave patterns appearing in front of me

The only landing jetty on the east side of the land came into view. It was a long way off. From where I was sitting, the shore dump looked terrible. I was keen to land and take a look around the island and considered the options. Even if I could get ashore safely, there seemed nowhere sheltered to relaunch. Getting off again would be impossible. A jetty with a few boats moored looked the best chance. I couldn't really see how this was laid out and it was rammed full of other boats so I dismissed this as a bad idea and abandoned my tour of Lundy, vowing to return one day as a tourist, continuing on my course due south.

It seemed I was going to make it to Devon. The breeze picked up after I cleared the southern tip of Lundy and I calculated it was only 18 km to reach Hartland Point, the nearest land in a straight line south. Originally my plan was to get across and land further into North Devon somewhere like Woolacombe. Checking the map, now this made no sense. It was miles too far east. South was best for both wind direction and distance. I was heading south. 180 degrees on the compass. West Devon here I come.

Unknown to me at the time, my family had been keeping my Uncle Francis up to date with my whereabouts. He was excited about my journey and lived somewhere near Woolacombe. I'd never visited him there as he'd moved to the West Country relatively recently. He'd arranged to make up the spare room and I believe even asked his daughter Katie to come over and dust off the historic Bentley, one of his many vintage cars. There was a plan to locate me and bring me back to their home for the evening in style. Sadly his eyesight had started to fail him in recent years so he needed a chauffeur to drive him around these days. When we were kids, I couldn't believe it when he showed me his two Formula 1 style racing cars parked in his garage. I think they were

Formula V or Formula Ford cars actually but they looked seriously fast to me.

The number of people I must have disappointed by not stopping off to see them along the way was growing daily. It just wasn't feasible to make a plan and stick with it. If the winds were good, I had to keep going. Right now, the wind was getting better and better and the waves were fantastic. Long flowing giant rollers, pushing me south, surfing in brilliant sunshine and a fresh tailwind. Sailing doesn't get any better than this, or faster.

I passed Hartland Point and kept going south. There was a sense of immense satisfaction in me. The Bristol Channel was behind me, I was now into the Atlantic Ocean leading me south, onwards to Cornwall. Was this really happening? One minute I was in Wales and the Irish Sea, the next stop was Cornwall. It was correct. The Navionics confirmed I was now running parallel to the Cornish coast with one of Cornwall's most famous surf beaches at Bude seven miles inshore on my left.

Ron tells a funny story about his landing on Bude beach. It didn't end well for him here, pitch poling his boat up the shore to count as one of several places around the UK where he broke his mast landing. This was now going to be the next big challenge; where to land along this exposed surf beach land.

I parked the landing issue into my box labelled, don't worry about it yet, and carried on sailing for two more hours. The miles were getting eaten up, I was really enjoying this day more than any so far. As it got later, I racked my brains for places I'd visited along this stretch of north west Cornwall, trying to think where a landing might be possible. Two places sprung out of the map at me, Boscastle and Crackington Haven.

We'd had a week's family holiday at Boscastle in the summer of 2005, the year after the terrible flooding wrecked the town and made national news for the speed and ferocity at which it arrived. Staying in a farmhouse near the main town, I recalled visiting the harbour one day and, although it was 14 years ago, I remembered thinking at the time this place was incredibly well protected from the south westerly swell.

Crackington Haven I dimly recalled visiting too but my brain was a bit foggy on the detail. I had a hunch this bay was also quite sheltered. Time was running on and I'd been on the move for nearly nine hours. The lack of sleep last night and the previous days' efforts were suddenly catching up. I made an executive decision to make a course directly inland for Crackington Haven, the nearest of the two, and chance my luck.

The prevailing wind was blowing from the north east so coming in to the shore was easy. Once I identified the cliff line and bay, I literally cruised in under the protection of the cliffs and stepped out of the boat, letting it sail in the last few feet and plop gently on the soft sand. Tiny waves lapped at the shore as the tide slowly receded. It was close to low water when I landed. The boat seemed safe enough as I set off in search of water. I'd done it. 115 km in one day, from Wales to Cornwall in a 'oner'. Bristol Channel eat yer heart out!

Chapter 47

Julie Seaweed and Friends

Crackington Haven at low water is several hundred metres of flat sand. Getting the boat all the way up the shore would be a long and tedious job using my fender roller as the trolley. I felt finding food and water would be a good use of time while I waited for the tide to turn, harnessing nature's power to help wash the MOD27 up the beach.

Standing slightly dazed on the beach enjoying the late afternoon heat of the sun and taking in the busy seaside surroundings, a lady draped in seaweed appeared next to me. She was with another lady paddling on the water's edge. As they were my first contact, I asked them both if they minded posing for a quick selfie to prove I was here. I was unaware at the time they didn't know each other. Amanda and Julie introduced themselves. Amanda was friendly but it was Julie who did most of the talking. She called herself Julie Seaweed and I soon discovered she had a seaweed obsession. Her body was draped in a mass of slimy seaweed. If you can imagine King Neptune's wife, Julie could have been her.

We chatted a bit and when asked where I was staying, I mentioned I had a tent and deployed my pregnant pause, lost soul technique. Julie was the first to break the silence and offered me a patch in her garden to put up the tent if I wanted to.

"Yes please" I replied as slowly as I possibly could, not wanting to appear over eager and rude but equally not wanting to pass up on her generous offer.

We arranged to meet at 8 pm in the local pub which Julie pointed out to me. This would give me plenty of time to sort my gear out. Thanking her, I carried on with my business of finding food and somewhere to park the MOD27 for the night. The options were limited; the only place was by the entrance road on a really difficult rocky beach. I'd need some help carrying her above the high tide line.

My arrival had aroused quite a lot of interest. Two more people approached me and started chatting as I walked up towards the narrow beach road. Phil and his wife Robbie started to enquire where I'd come from. They didn't believe it when I said Wales. This started a load more questions and before long Robbie was opening packets of various types of biscuits for me. Phil then noticed the MOD27 was starting to drift away in the tide. She was a good 200 metres away from where I was standing. Like a rocket Robbie, dressed in a wetsuit, ran off to catch her while I tried to find somewhere safe to stow the three dry bags I was carrying.

"Chuck it in the garden here," Phil said pointing at the house on the front. "It's OK, no one's here, it's a holiday home," he continued.

Robbie, Phil and myself heaved the boat up the beach, carrying her across the rocky final 20 feet to a safe high water mark. The gear all got thrown over a wall into some unsuspecting person's front garden. There was no fresh water to wash on the beach but outside the adjacent house I spotted a shower. I tried knocking on their door to ask permission to use it but it appeared to be empty so I figured they probably wouldn't mind if I borrowed their cold water and stripped off naked and showered whilst a steady stream of beachgoers filed past. No one seemed to notice. If they did, they weren't particularly interested.

A few pints of Betty Stogs and steak and ale pie with chips at the bar were had at the local inn with Robbie and Phil before Julie arrived. She then whisked me off to her very unique cottage. The route took me uphill along a wooded narrow track along a lovers' lane. It was a fair old walk, Julie had a bad hip so it took a good half hour to get there. Her cottage was nestled amongst a bower of trees opening out with a wooden veranda and a stunning view across open fields full of sheep precariously balancing on a steep grassy slope. It was a beautiful setting. No sooner had we arrived when she asked if I wanted to join her for a drink with her friends Pete and Helen Gilmour (brother of Dave Gilmour from Pink Floyd) who were staying nearby in her brother's chalet. I felt, "not really" wasn't an option. We trundled off back down the lane and appeared at another tiny chalet cottage seated under a similarly picturesque tree lined landscape.

When we returned to Julie's home, inside there was seaweed hanging up drying everywhere. The tent idea had been discarded hours ago and she offered me one of her beds for the night. The room I was shown looked a little like something from the Bayeux Tapestry with elaborately embroidered drapes and throws. The dark French oak furniture was crammed into every nook and cranny and it felt like I really was in Neptune's castle.

My seaweed experience was only just starting. When I awoke the next morning unfamiliar cooking smells were wafting through from the tiny galley kitchen. Julie was making me a seaweed breakfast. Another first for me. The seaweed porridge was particularly good. Everything seemed to move at half speed in Julie's world and by the time we'd packed away breakfast and I'd loaded my gear and the sandwiches that

Julie had made for me, the time was already approaching high water at 8.55 am. I needed to get going as the ebb tide would turn in half an hour.

Back on the beach, Robbie and Phil were waiting to see me off.

"What time do you call this?" asked Phil.

"I know, it's a slow start," I replied.

"Where are you hoping to get to today?" Phil enquired

"I'm really not sure, I think Penzance if I'm lucky."

I hadn't done any preparation for today. By the time I'd got back to Julie's last night, I was asleep within seconds. There was little time to prepare at breakfast and I was now standing on the beach getting ready to launch. To where? I had no idea.

I hopped over the low wall onto the lawn of some poor unsuspecting, but crucially absent, holiday cottage owner's garden. My gear was all still where I'd left it. Word had got round and a small crowd gathered to see me off. This made changing into my wetsuit in the public space slightly awkward. Once the visitors clocked what I was up to, they politely averted their eyes until I emerged in full sailing pantomime uniform.

Getting the boat back into the water was a lot easier than taking her out. The tide was all the way in so it was only a few yards. Robbie and Phil helped carry the MOD27 across the boulders spread over the beach. She weighed a tonne with all the gear stowed. It was a struggle but rigging in the morning sunshine again attracted a small crowd. I stood in the shallows in the brilliant sun, a light breeze whispered across the water which looked glassy smooth. As I turned to wave for a picture, a small but surprisingly powerful wave washed in innocuously and bowled me and the boat over, capsizing her and sending her back up on to the rocky beach. I was wet and a bit shaken but scrambled up and grabbed the boat. Dispensing with the pleasantries now, I focused all my attention on getting out of Crackington Haven without any further incidents. Not until I reached the bay entrance did I turn and wave to the posse of onlookers.

Chapter 48

Dr Bottom

Part of the problem with covering so many miles in such a short time frame was my information was struggling to keep up. I'd done no planning for this part of the journey and was completely winging it. There is only so much Navionics can tell you when you're surfing along in waves, trying to read a tiny screen getting covered in water.

Exiting from Crackington Haven there was little wind and I drifted along with the tide. This gave me a chance to check out place names and look for stopping points along the way. One person I thought might be a useful source of information was another Laser Master sailor, Denzil May, who we'd nicknamed Dr Bottom on account of his job as a specialist colorectal surgeon.

He was from down this part. I didn't know exactly where but I knew it was along this next bit of coastline. I checked Facebook and had already received a message from Denzil with his contact number. Adding this to my phone book was to prove a crucial decision for later in the day. For now, I concentrated on keeping moving and checking I was covered in sunscreen. Yesterday my face had felt like it was going to crack as I'd forgotten to apply any. I rummaged around for something to eat in the small blue bag I carried in my cockpit containing snacks, sunscreen and a small bottle of water.

"Water! Where was the 1.5 litre bottle I'd loaded this morning?"

It was missing. I must have lost it when I was rolled in the surf launching. I now only had the single bottle containing a third of a litre for the whole day unless I could find somewhere to stop. This was not good. It didn't look like the sort of coastline there were many stopping points. I'd just have to be careful. There was a bit of water left in my other bottle from yesterday but it was only a third full.

After drifting for several hours in the blazing sun, the breeze finally started to fill in. It was around midday. I'd travelled only a few miles but was now surfing along at an average speed of 9 knots. The conditions were very similar to yesterday and the miles were being munched away. After passing Tintagel Head, the coast curves eastwards. The most direct route south was out to sea towards Trevose Head where, after this headland, the coast straightens out again.

There's an old sailors' saw that goes,

"From Padstow to Lundy Light is a sailor's grave by day or night."

Looking down 45 metres above Padstow bar is the Trinity House Trevose Lighthouse. Sited on the towering granite cliffs, it was first built in 1847 with an oil lamp backed by reflectors. There's an upper and lower light, the highest is positioned at 204 feet and illuminates 274 degrees of the compass and is visible for 19 miles. This stretch of coastline is notorious for sea mists which can dim even the most powerful lamp. Historians find it difficult to understand why a foghorn wasn't installed and commissioned until 1913. The first horn built measured a whopping 36 feet long with an 18' x 2' foot aperture.

Sailing towards this landmark went on for several hours. I made sure I kept well clear of the headland to ensure I passed it at a safe distance. I tracked the time at 1.58 pm.

The drinking water situation was pretty bad. I'd barely a quarter of a bottle remaining and my mouth was feeling constantly dry. I could feel the sun crisping my skin through the crust of salt slowly encapsulating my body. These were great sailing conditions though and I didn't want to waste time looking for a stop off just for water. I was simply going to have to put up with being a bit thirsty. As the crow flies, I set a course aiming directly towards St. Ives, 50 km from my current location. At the present speed, I felt this might just be achievable as an overnight stop. The ETA was 7 pm according to my crude calculations. It would still be light until around 7.30 pm so there was a bit of margin.

By 5.30 pm, I was getting tired and still 20 km short of St. Ives. Aside from a dribble I'd been nursing in the bottom of my bottle, I was out of water. Rupert on the Safety Channel had been in contact with Denzil but told me he thought St. Ives would be too far. I was starting to agree with Rupert and thought it a good time to call Denzil for some advice. He'd sailed these waters all his life, his father was a yachtsman and Denzil had grown up on the water. I regarded him as an expert sailor. I felt sure he'd be able to suggest a stopping point for the night close by.

Denzil answered the phone quickly. He wasn't working that day fortunately. I asked about places to stop and everywhere I suggested he said, "No".

"Are you sure there is nothing for 20 km?"

"Nothing" was Denzil's blunt Cornish reply. "You'll never get off tomorrow if you try beaching anywhere before St. Ives."

"What about Portreath?" I pressed him, hoping he may have overlooked this place.

"No chance. The swell's too big."

I thought back to how powerful the tiny waves had been in Crackington Haven that morning. I was surfing along in 3 metre waves whilst talking to Denzil on the phone. He was right. Unless I could get into a harbour, I'd never get out through the surf again once I was on the beach.

"Ok thanks I'll let you know when I'm close." I hung up.

Twenty kilometres is a long way when you've been at it all day, especially after the last few days.

"I must keep pushing while the weather is on my side," I thought and knuckled down for two more hours.

"It's only two hours, that's nothing," I kept telling myself.

I broke into my last tin of mackerel and drained every drop of the tomato juice they were swimming in. This felt better. Time passed slowly. The silhouette of Godrevy Lighthouse was now visible, standing proudly on its isolated rock only three miles from St. Ives on the far side of the bay. I called Denzil again. I needed to stop as soon as possible now. My body was shutting down and the concentration was going. Every now and again, a partially submerged rock would appear in the middle of the sea and scare the bejeebers out of me as I narrowly missed it, oblivious to the danger until it had passed me by.

"Denzil. I'm approaching the lighthouse before the bay. Can I go inside it and try to find somewhere to stop. I'm knackered and out of water?"

"No! Don't go inside its full of rocks. The only possible place is Hayle, there's a river creek in the middle of the bay, but it's not much closer than St. Ives. Once you're past the lighthouse, it's only a few miles. I can swim it in 20 minutes."

"Oh! OK, sounds good...shit! Denzil what's with the steep waves out here. Shit! Rocks they're everywhere. I'll call you back."

I hung up, stuffing the phone down my lifejacket. I'd entered a dangerous reef called The Stones which extended outwards towards St. Ives from Godrevy Lighthouse. Many ships have been lost here. The rocks were whizzing past and almost invisible from the surface in the maelstrom waters. Standing waves were breaking over the bow. I had to get out of here. Changing direction, I headed directly out to sea, narrowly missing a set of razor-sharp looking granite boulders barely below the waves. The waves were breaking from the side which I successfully managed to surf down rather than bury my way through. Ten minutes of total madness stopped as quickly as it had started. I was now in the bay. The one Denzil can swim across in 20 minutes.

St. Ives harbour lights were visible on the other side. The light was starting to disappear. It was nearly 7 pm.

"Not far now." I could picture the pint of beer waiting for me on the quayside and called Denzil again.

"Denzil. You didn't tell me about the submerged rocks," I started.

"What rocks?" he replied

"The ones after the lighthouse."

"I didn't know there were any. We don't normally sail that far out."

The wind was dropping alarmingly quickly. There was only half an hour of favourable tide left before I'd be sucked back to where I'd come if I couldn't get ashore soon.

"Where should I aim for?" I asked.

"The main harbour straight ahead. I can see you," he replied.

Within five minutes of hanging up on Denzil, the wind completely switched off. I was 1.6 miles from shore. A long way to swim. Standing up, I rocked the boat backwards and forwards trying to make my own wind to propel me along the final mile and a half. It was slow going and hard work. I pulled out the paddle and splashed my way towards the harbour wall. I could see Denzil drinking a pint standing on top of the entrance but wasn't making any progress. It could only be a few hundred metres. The tide had turned though and I was battling to make any forward progress. I saw a local lifeboat crew driving into the harbour and tried radioing them on channel 16 to ask for a tow. No one replied!

At exactly 7.49 pm, I finally made landfall by dragging myself along the harbour wall using a combination of wafting the sail and paddling in succession. I parked the MOD27 on a small sandy beach close to the Sloop Inn and watched Denzil laughing at me as I tried to drag the boat above the high tide line. Flicking the mast out in one, Denzil helped me roll up the sail before we dumped it in a big heap partially hidden around a corner in the sand. Everything of value was stuffed in one bag and the rest stuffed underneath the sail. We headed directly for the pub.

I had two pints running simultaneously, one filled with water, the other beer, four pints in and it was time to go. Denzil's house was half an hour's drive away through a series of complex country lanes, barely wide enough for the giant VW Tiguan he was driving at worrying speeds around blind bends. A fellow Laser sailor who knew Denzil well said he only had one speed and that he regarded second place in a race as 1st loser. Reading back through my log book about my next day's planning, I wrote in my journal

"No time to make any, too busy talking."

Dinner and wine finished around midnight. I was propping my eyelids up with matchsticks for much of the evening but made it through to the end without passing out. We talked about so many things. One of the most notable stories Denzil told me was when I quizzed him why he had specialised in bottom surgery. He said he found it fascinating and highly rewarding. Aside from the lifesaving colon cancer work, another of the operations in Denzil's extraordinary range of skills is removing artefacts that have become lodged in a patient's bottom; a great choice of subject I explored with him in some detail over dinner.

He mentioned one particular instance when an elderly gentleman with an RAF style moustache and blazer presented himself to Denzil holding a briefcase. Putting the case on his table he opened it to reveal a full suite of adult sex toys. There were nine neatly arranged items and one empty slot. The patient said very plainly and eloquently,

"One of these appears to be missing!"

Denzil went into great detail about some of the specialist surgical tools he'd designed to assist him. The most impressive of these I thought was the conical foam roller clamp. This allowed a soft wide end foam item to be squashed small enough so the item can be extracted the same way it went in!

So you can see there really was very little time to talk about the less important stuff like sailing around Land's End the next day.

Chapter 49

Hiding in a Mousehole

The following morning was another early rise. Denzil had to be at work by 7.30 am. We had a whirlwind drive back along the same perilous lanes he'd navigated the night before. I was dumped out of the car followed by a quick good luck, after which Denzil disappeared in a cloud of dust. I needed to make a plan for the day so I found the nearest coffee shop to the boat and chewed my way through a bacon butty washed down with a cappuccino whilst studying weather, tides and bail out options around Land's End.

By 9 am, I was afloat. I was apprehensive about the day. Although the forecast was as good as I could ever have hoped for, Denzil had sown enough doubts in me last night about this infamous headland to make me nervous. Passing the first big lump of rock at Clodgy Point, I again passed boulders of granite nearly fully submerged strewn randomly and often a long way off shore. All day, rocks haphazardly appeared right in front of me in the middle of the sea, seemingly deliberately scattered to catch out unsuspecting seamen.

There was very little wind to start with and I drifted along quite slowly for the first few hours. The bright blue skies and moderate winds made the landscape clearly visible and the water bright and clean. I couldn't have asked for better weather.

When I write about the places I passed on this leg, rather like most of the way around the UK, at the time I was usually unaware of the names of most of the landmarks and place names. This section of the trip was no different, in fact it was worse than normal as I'd had so little time to study before setting off. For the purposes of this book, I've revisited my Navionics tracks and added in the place names for reference.

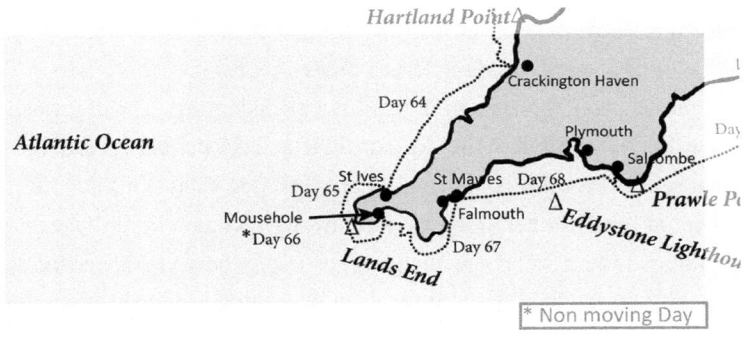

The cliffs looked sharp and jagged. They emerged from the sea forming a landscape that looked like it had climbed up out of the sea, as if laid down as a mass of broken bits. Approaching Cape Cornwall, the first of several large lighthouses, the wind started pumping over the cliffs as the headlands lowered but I felt very comfortable, there was nothing very testing at this point of the rounding. I'm not sure what I was expecting but it seemed too easy. My guard was still on full alert waiting for the moment when everything started to go crazy.

There were no obvious bail out options here with solid cliffs and rocks strewn all along. In the distance, another very tall lighthouse with a flat top came into view. I wanted to see a sign with Land's End written on it. No such luck. It stood off the coast on a pile of rocks about a mile off the land. Towering above the sea I assumed this must be Longships Lighthouse, Land's End. I tried checking on the Navionics app but the screen was too small to read the detail and it seemed safer to concentrate on the sailing rather than the tourist trail. The sea became much more turbulent as I passed by but still nothing like as bad as many of the many other headlands I'd sailed around.

John Rushkin said of the seas around Land's End,

"It is an entire disorder of the surges."

The Victorian art critic was referring to the relentless driving forces of the Atlantic Ocean breaking on the granite fissures and rebounding back into oncoming waves, causing confused and chaotic waters. Strong tidal currents and numerous broken reefs make this a very dangerous place for seamen. I just wasn't sensing this. The day was beautiful, not a cloud in the sky, sunshine and crystal clear, relatively calm seas. According to the coastguard, I passed Longships at 13.02. A person I met further along the journey, who's name I didn't catch, standing at Land's End saw me pass by. Funny how you are oblivious to people on the land when at sea. You're much more visible than they are.

Once past the lighthouse, I hardened up coming onto a beat, sailing into the wind as I turned north east. This was the last corner of the UK and I was definitely round it, that much I did know. Far off in the distance, out to sea I passed another lighthouse standing defiantly on a large rock. This was Wolf Rock Lighthouse which sits on a pinnacle of rare granite constantly swept by the sea. Before this lighthouse was constructed in 1861 it had posed one of the most formidable obstacles to shipping for centuries.

The tide was ferocious around this area, I was making little headway so elected to head in tight to the land. I found if I got in right under the cliffs to within a few metres, the tide went slack and, in some instances, created a back eddy which propelled me forwards. It was a nerve-racking tactic but seemed the only way I was going to make any progress. Rocks below and above the surface were dotted all around. Often, I was corralled in a crop circle of boulders with breaking waves crashing over them and had to make a hasty exit back out to sea to escape.

After doing this for a while, prompted by a near miss with a submerged rock, I found a new sailing technique. By slightly heeling the boat over as I sailed, I could look down under the water behind me at the underside of the boat where my centreboard was sticking out. This way I could actually see through the water at the maze of rocks below. When I encountered a higher rock, I'd pull the board up quickly until I passed over it and push it back down once I'd sailed past. Often I was within inches from these rocks and the cliffs.

The technique of looking behind and downwards proved to be really tiring but was the only safe way I could think of to pick my way around this treacherously uneven coastline. On a few occasions I was concentrating so hard on looking through the water behind me that I nearly ran straight into a giant granite boulder directly in front, narrowly avoiding crashing into it by roll tacking off instantly the other way.

I sailed like this for five hours. My craned neck was screaming with pain by the time the waters appeared to have become less rocky. I was ready to stop so when I spotted a tiny opening appear in the cliffs, I went to investigate. Stopping to check my position, it looked like it was a small harbour called Mousehole. My target plan was to head for Mounts Bay Sailing Club where I had another contact from the Laser Masters circuit, Nick Stotten, who I was hoping would put me up. This was too far, I was broken and needed food and a rest.

Sailing through the tiny entrance, I'd arrived at the picturesque harbour of Mousehole, pronounced 'mowsal'. It was like stepping through the looking glass in Alice in Wonderland. The entrance is only wide enough for one large boat to pass through at a time; 11 metres wide to be exact. It faces east north east providing protection from the prevailing south westerly swells. Nevertheless, the harbour baulks (large wooden beams) are laid down across the entrance in November, staying permanently in position until spring which is known locally as buttoning down.

Once through the sheer rock walled entrance, Mousehole opens out into an oval shaped harbour, providing a picture postcard setting. Stone cottages line the harbour walls rising up the small hill in narrow rows behind. A string of small boats of all shapes and sizes attached to great lengths of seaweedy mooring lines stretched all the way up to the top of the harbour wall with both bow and stern lines attached to every boat, making it look like a spider's web. On the south side was a small sandy beach. I aimed for this end and drifted onto it with the shelter of the walls assisting me to make a very delicate landing.

Stepping out onto the sand, I said out loud, "Wow what a place."

Just the most perfect bolthole after a tricky day on the water, I stood taking in the surroundings. As there was no wind in the harbour and the tide was out, before unrigging I thought I'd go to buy a pasty at the small shop directly opposite where I'd landed. Tying the MOD27 to a mooring line attached to the wall, she floated perfectly upright as if showing off, saying look at me, standing on guard in the shallow waters of the windless harbour.

When I returned to the beach, munching my pasty, a man with an extra-long telephoto lens was taking pictures. He asked if I minded having my picture taken standing next to the boat. Two posers on tour. We got chatting and he introduced himself as Tim Green. He was visiting Mousehole for the weekend from Bicester in Oxfordshire. He had his wife Becs with him and their two dogs, Stanley, a 2½ year old cocker spaniel and Jess, a 13 year old springer. The dogs were very friendly, busying themselves around the boat.

On top of the harbour wall directly opposite the beach was the harbour office; a small wooden, slightly tired looking building. There was a man inside who directed me towards the public harbour shower cubicle. It was £2 for a shower which had a meter into which you fed coins. Stripping off inside the changing room I was really pleased there was a hot shower here. The cubicle was tiny for changing in and it was a real struggle to get my wetsuit off in the confined space. To turn the tap on I had to be directly under the shower rose. I couldn't wait to get the salty water off my crusty face.

"Aaah"

Freezing cold water poured out of the rose. I leapt out thinking if I let it run a bit longer it would warm up. It became apparent after 30 seconds or so that whoever was in charge of the showers had forgotten to switch on the immersion heater.

"Urrrgh" I felt robbed.

The money had been accepted but no warmth was in evidence. Gritting my teeth, I leapt back in, jiggled around for little more than a minute and then towel dried off with my handkerchief size chamois.

When I emerged, dressed in normal clothes with a bag full of rinsed but soaking sailing gear, I felt a plan was needed. I hung all the gear on the boat, now sitting high up on the beach then, grabbing my valuables, tent and sleeping bag, trudged off along the high street in search of somewhere to sleep.

It was a town. I hadn't thought about this when I landed. Towns don't have many camping spots in them. Wandering aimlessly around, unable to locate anywhere suitable to pitch a tent, I eventually stopped to ask a local elderly man if he knew anywhere, like a field nearby, where I might pitch a tent for the night. Pointing at a near vertical incline, he directed me up the hill and said,

"There's a campsite half a mile away up there. I'm not sure it'll be open now though as it's close season."

It didn't sound promising. With little obvious alternative I started walking towards the hill then seemingly from out of nowhere, Tim Green the photographer appeared.

"Hello. I've just been back to the harbour looking for you," he said, slightly out of breath as if he'd been running.

"Oh really? Did you forget something?" I asked.

"No no. It's just we're staying here in a small cottage and it has a spare room. Becs and I wondered if you needed somewhere to stay tonight."

All those atheists reading this book, please answer this question. Do you believe in God yet?

Well, as you can expect, my answer was 100% in the affirmative and, given the choice of walking half a mile uphill to pitch the tent in a campsite with no facilities open or the option of Egyptian cotton sheets on a double bed at a boutique 5 star holiday cottage, which would you choose?

So that's how I spent my evening in Mousehole, babysitting Stanley and Jess, watching a bit of telly with my feet up and a cup of coffee. Becs and Tim had already booked a table at the local gastronomic restaurant and were out until 11 pm. I sneaked a quick pint and a fish pie at the local pub, the Ship Inn, which was packed so I left soon after finishing eating. We chatted until late when Tim and Becs returned and had breakfast together the next morning.

Checking the weather forecast in the morning, it was clear that today was a non-moving day. A weather front had moved in producing gale force winds, gusting over 35 knots. Looking out from the top of the harbour, I couldn't believe how lucky I'd been with the weather yesterday. The sea looked horrendous. It was literally a sea of raging white caps.

I lingered at the cottage using the Wi-Fi until Tim and Becs were packed and ready to go home. I left the house when they did and watched them drive off into the distance back to Bicester. Standing outside as the cleaners went in, I felt a bit lost. I'd just been made homeless. Not quite sure what to do next, I loitered on the garden wall outside in the narrow street. I was still in range of the house Wi-Fi and checked the forecasts again, uploaded a few social media posts from the previous few days and sent a few emails. The cleaners left and gave me an odd look as if to say,

"You still here?"

Then I remembered Denzil had passed me Nick Stotten's phone number. He lived somewhere in or near to Mount's Bay. I thought I might call to see if he could meet up, perhaps even scrounge a bed for the night. His phone went to voicemail. I left a message and went in search of a cafe to write up my journal and make a plan for the next few days.

The phone rang just as the crab sandwich went into my mouth. I didn't recognise the number but assumed it must be Nick.

"Hawroo," I said unintelligibly whilst trying to swallow the crab sandwich down in one. It was Nick.

"Of course it's OK to stay the night."

After a brief chat, he offered to come to pick me up but said it would be an hour or so before he could make it over. While I was waiting, it seemed like an opportunity to carry out some repairs to the MOD27's sail. The top two batten pockets were ripped and I was trying to apply sail tape to them when Nick arrived. He jumped into action and helped stick tape all over the sail. It was looking pretty tired and by the time we'd finished it looked like it had zits dotted all over it from the patches we'd applied. I guess it had come almost halfway round Britain. This was my second sail, supplied free by Rooster Sailing when I was staying in Gairloch. It had definitely seen some very testing winds and on the whole was in remarkably good shape, all things considered.

Nick did try to convince me to sail the few miles across to Mount's Bay Sailing Club after we'd finished the repairs. I couldn't see any advantage in doing so. The angle would have made tomorrow's sail a beat if I left from Mount's Bay whereas leaving from Mousehole it would be a faster reach to The Lizard. Not only that, it was blowing dogs off chains outside the harbour plus I was now into a comfortable mindset for the day. No point ruining it by getting cold and wet for no reason.

It was a Friday and Emma called me to say she was planning on driving down. After checking Nick was OK with this, she drove the six hours from Eastbourne and joined Nick, his wife and me just in time for a fish and chip supper. We snatched a few hours together and had a good laugh that evening.

Chapter 50

At Last, The Lizard

When I'd arrived at Denzil's in St. Ives, I thought the Lizard Peninsular was somewhere close to Land's End which I could knock out in a day. Denzil questioned this but didn't say I was delusional at the time, even though he clearly knew a lot more about the local geography than I did.

Studying the map of this area for the first time briefly before departing that day, I started to realise the distances involved. Although it was actually 50 miles from St. Ives to The Lizard, by moving through an arc of 270 degrees following the headland, it was inevitable a lot of the passage would be sailing into the wind; the slowest direction for a sailing boat. Also, because of tacking, this effectively doubled any straight line distance you drew on a map not accounting for avoiding any obstacles I might encounter like reefs or wrecks along the way.

The wind direction had swung following the weather front that had blown in yesterday to a more south easterly direction. It was 20 to 25 knots, less than yesterday but near my top end. Today would at best be a tight fetch to The Lizard or more likely a one tack beat. I knew so little about where I was heading again. I was totally outrunning all my information. Fatigue must have been having some impact on my ability to plan. It was as much as I seemed to be able to do to check the weather, tides and look for a few target locations to aim at.

What I wasn't aware of is how dangerous the Cornish waters I was in really are. I only found out for example when writing up this account that there have been more than 6,000 wrecks off Cornwall's shores – with the coast around The Lizard peninsula dubbed 'The Graveyard of Ships'.

The Lizard is not named after some legendary beast, as I'd thought. The name actually comes from the Cornish, lezou, or headland. The Lizard is, in fact, a peninsula and the southernmost point of the United Kingdom. It sticks out into the Channel so far that it's the biggest shipping trap in British waters. So many ships have fallen victim to The Lizard's cliffs and underwater reefs that the Admiralty advises navigators to keep three or more miles off in any kind of rough weather.

There is also a reef full of treacherous rocks called The Manacles lying just off The Lizard peninsula. Over a thousand lives have been lost from more than one hundred ships wrecked here. Many of the well-known wrecks are in the central group of rocks where depths are less than 6 metres for an area of 300 metres by 200 metres. Before setting sail, I was blissfully unaware of any of this information.

Nick drove me back to Mousehole. It was a 6 am rise in order to catch the best tide. By the time I'd rigged, changed and sent the seven point plan to the Safety Channel, it was 8 am. I calculated Lizard Point must be rounded by 12.30 or I'd struggle to get round. Nick said the tides were ferocious once running against me. It was going to be tight. I guesstimated it was 18.5 nautical miles from Mousehole tacking inshore to reach The Lizard point. If I sailed at 5 knots, my normal upwind speed for a Laser in nearly any conditions, I could make it in four hours. Every minute I left after eight o'clock would be critical. After a hurried scramble, rigging and getting off the beach, I waved bye to Nick and squeezed out through the tiny Mousehole harbour entrance. Appearing through the entrance, I promptly got smashed by a combination of waves and ferocious gusts. By some miracle, I managed to keep the MOD27 upright. In front of the harbour entrance is a small island known as St. Clement's Isle. The strength of the winds and size of seas instinctively set me off on a course for the lee of this island to get some protection. Once past, I aimed directly at St. Michael's Mount and Marazion, a place I knew well from previous Laser sailing championships. One thing you can always rely on in Mount's Bay are waves. Usually, they are my favourite part of sailing but heading into them today was not pleasant. Breaking over my back they were running down my neck, making me shiver despite hiking flat out in the howling wind.

As I got closer to the shore of Marazion, the land protected me a little from the worst of the gusts and I ground my way, zigzagging painfully slowly along the peninsula. It was straight into the wind. By midday I could see the headland. I was tired and cold. Four hours of continuous beating in 20 knots is hard work. I was having to fight my way through rough water. The tide would be starting to turn soon. I couldn't check the Navionics as my hands were too wet and cold. It was pointless anyway. I probably wouldn't be able to see much even if the screen did open.

Pressing hard for the next 30 minutes I could feel the breeze easing off as I came under the lee of The Lizard. As it did, it became apparent to me the tide had already turned inshore. Measuring my progress against the land, I was making little headway. Most tides turn slowly at first and grow stronger then weaken and speed up again before slackening off as they turn again. This is called the rule of 12ths. Sometimes a tide will turn first inshore or first out to sea. I gambled that the tide in this part would turn offshore later. Heading away from the shelter of the cliffs, I went more in hope than any belief of catching the last of the favourable tide.

This decision may have been a life saver as I unwittingly missed most of the dangerous inshore hazards. At 12.40, finally crawling my way safely past The Lizard headland, I was able to ease out my sails and reach for the next point now skimming along on a much more comfortable, less physical angle.

"Phew I've done it," I said out loud as the mobile rang.

Emma had been watching me from the shore and called to say so, offering encouragement. She was puffing, running along top of the cliffs trying to keep up with me but I was now travelling too fast and had left her behind.

I started to relax and followed the coastline, gobbling up the miles passing across a wide open bay, around a headland and past a very pretty looking fishing village called Coverack. Today was going well. The winds had moderated, the mizzle from earlier had cleared and I was heading east towards the English Channel. It was the home straight. I was so happy. Nearly home!

I'd learned along this journey that when I start to relax and feel all is going well, this usually is one of the most dangerous times. Somehow my brain just doesn't seem to remember this rule.

I was singing one of my terrible songs, enjoying the scenery, watching the compass heading occasionally, but generally sailing by line of sight for the next headland. Underneath me the water seemed to have gone very dark. I thought nothing of it until a granite rock with water just washing over its surface loomed ahead. I steered in shore to avoid it. Then another rock appeared and the sea started to become very confused. What was happening? I carried on but shortly more rocks appeared and the waves were so steep they broke over my bow. I needed to get out of here and quickly. It was really scary. I felt trapped in a blockade of razor-sharp rocks with the sea washing violently around and over them.

Changing direction and heading straight out to sea, I tiptoed my way through obstructions, breaking waves and whirlpools for the next 10 minutes. Even when it seemed that the worst was behind me, I carried on for another 10 minutes. Only when I finally felt safe again did I stop. I ate a muesli bar in one and downed half my water bottle. My heart was racing as fast as a Formula 1 car and I was shaking. That was a close one. I'd just sailed straight into the middle of The Manacles.

After my Manacles' experience, I checked the Navionics app for a good few minutes, trying to see if there were any other surprises in store for me. After I was satisfied that I was in safer waters, I set a course for Falmouth, sailing straight across Falmouth Bay towards the castles of Pendennis and St. Mawes sitting opposite each other at the mouth of the Fal estuary. Both were built by Henry VIII to protect the country from invasion by the French and Spanish with gun emplacements overlooking the port of Falmouth entrance.

I aimed directly for the St. Anthony Lighthouse sitting as a beacon on top of St Anthony's Head, 22 metres above the sea. Apparently when it was first built, below the white light a red fixed light shone directly over The Manacles to warn shipping of the dangerous reef. It was too late for me to find this out now but I steered through the two castles and found myself entering another picturesque natural harbour on the eastern side of Falmouth at St. Mawes.

A shallow bay with a steep ramp leading up the cliff below the Tresanton Beach Hotel came into view. It looked promising as a possible overnight stopping place. A few small sailing dinghies were parked quite precariously on a narrow, steeply inclined path. I decided this would do for me. Borrowing a trolley from one of the boats, I hauled the MOD27 over the slab granite shore and parked her amongst the other boats on a thin strip of grass where it looked like it was just above the high-water mark.

After my Manacles episode, I felt a beer was needed. Emma had caught me up in the van and together we went in search of a pub. We didn't have to go far, a few hundred yards along the harbour wall was The Ship Inn. Outside, leaning against the wall, a few sailor types were drinking pints of beer. Stopping to ask if they knew of a shower I might use, two of them recognised me and knew all about my journey. Following this introduction, free beer flowed continuously from my new found friends the names of whom, Dan, Ben, John, Mike, Kieran, Jena and Tom, I wrote down at the time. Dan lent me his towel and showed me the sailing club's shower, accessible from the outside through a series of steps and doorways.

We spent the night in the van parked up on the road after filling up on burgers and chips at The Ship Inn.

Chapter 51

Salcombe Salute

Since leaving Scotland from Portpatrick on the 9th September to arriving at St. Mawes in Cornwall on the 21st September, I'd covered 372 nautical miles (688 km/428 miles). These figures are based on a conservative estimate taken from the Navionics tracks which were slightly incomplete due to my mobile phone battery dying on a few occasions. For the statisticians, I'd averaged 7 hours 46 minutes sailing time per day for the past 13 days with two non-moving days in this period due to bad weather. My average speed through the water was 4.2 knots. It doesn't sound very quick when you write it down on paper but it was quite good when compared to other circumnavigators. Jeremy Warren told me their Wayfarer dinghy, Hafren, was averaging 3.5 knots per hour so the MOD27 was a whole 0.7 of a knot faster.

All of these stats would count for nothing if I couldn't make it home to Eastbourne. The weather window looked like it was starting to close in with long range forecasts showing deep low pressure systems starting to build up over the Atlantic. There was no time to take the foot off the gas. If anything, it needed to be pressed to flat out. Not that I felt it wasn't already.

The plan sent to the Safety Channel that day was dead simple. St. Mawes to Salcombe in a 20 knot southerly breeze. Should be fast, broad reaching all the way I thought. Leaving St. Mawes, I was in a real muddle. Some mornings everything seems to get forgotten or gets in a knot. This was one of those mornings. I put it down to the uncomfortable night spent in the back of the van parked on a slope in the road. Emma kept rolling into me every time she turned over, added to the fact I may have drunk a few more beers than the standard athlete would have with my new St. Mawes sailing friends.

Pushing off from the shore, I'd forgotten to send out my Safety Channel plan and hadn't registered my new personal locator beacon (PLB) with the coastguard. I spent an age bobbing up and down on the water trying to make contact with them to file my passage plan and left Emma to deal with the PLB admin. By the time this was all done, it was 9.30 am. I'd started getting ready that morning at 7.30 am.

"Two hours wasted, I needed to get a wobble on," I told myself in no uncertain terms.

It was another big distance that day, close to 100 km to Salcombe harbour. I saw a yacht motoring past towards the river estuary mouth and started following her track. When she rounded the headland, it looked like she was heading in the direction of Salcombe so I set off on the same heading. It was pretty much straight across heading east to Salcombe.

The yacht was just a little faster than me while she was motor sailing but once her engine was switched off, I started reeling her in. The breeze was blowing east south east making it quite a tight reach to Salcombe. I followed the tracks of the yacht in front which was heading in the direction of Plymouth taking it north of Eddystone Lighthouse, one of the most famous lighthouses in the British Isles, if not the world.

The present lighthouse is the fourth incarnation to be sited on an extensive rocky reef lying 14 miles south of Plymouth Sound. Standing 49 metres, it can be seen up to 17 nautical miles away. First constructed to warn shipping of the treacherous underwater reef with swirling tides and extraordinary high seas in strong winds, it's home to literally hundreds of shipwrecks. A famous quote from Christopher Jones, Captain of The Mayflower, said,

"If any vessel makes too far to the south...she will be caught in the prevailing strong current and swept to her doom on these evil rocks."

Obviously I was blissfully unaware of these words as I tailed the yacht threading her way through the surfing waves aiming directly towards Eddystone rocks. After two hours chasing the yacht, I finally overtook her. We waved at each other as I pulled ahead and even managed to have a chat on the VHF radio and exchanged email addresses. Shortly afterwards, I noticed she peeled off northwards. I assumed this was because she was heading into Plymouth. I do recall the sea starting to churn up a bit more where she veered off but thought little of it.

Surfing up and down, making great speed through the waves, something in me was nagging away about the lighthouse. Why is there such a giant construction in the middle of the sea? There must be a reason for it, I mused to myself, feeling a little puzzled at the sudden departure of the yacht. Straight was the most direct and shortest route for Salcombe which, although I was many miles off shore, seemed safe enough for now.

Carrying on for another hour, the lighthouse loomed large. I needed to make a decision which side of her to pass. By sheer luck, I chose north based entirely on the wind direction, forecast to blow more from the west later. I calculated if I sailed in towards the land on a tighter angle now, the breeze would free off as I approached Salcombe and keep my boat speed higher. It was a longer route but I didn't want to get caught approaching Salcombe on a dead run, not knowing what the wave patterns around the entrance would be like, so this is how I accidentally swerved one of the most notorious shipping hazards in Britain. It was only when I started reviewing my journey afterwards that I discovered the detailed history of this infamous place.

The Eddystone Lighthouse was the first ever constructed on a rock at sea in 1695 by a flamboyant, eccentric entrepreneur called Henry Winstanley. Following pleading petitions to the Crown to do something about the red rocks near Plymouth, an initial payment of 1 penny for every tonne of cargo passing by was awarded to Winstanley upon completion of this impossible task. This first tower lasted eight years before it was washed away in the great storm of 1703. Winstanley happened to be in the lighthouse at the time and perished along with everyone else.

Three further towers were subsequently constructed. John Rudyard designed the first replacement built of timber in 1706 which stood until it caught fire on the 1st December in 1755, burning to the ground. A lightship stood in place until John Smeaton's tower was illuminated in 1795. This time it was made of stone in the shape of an English Oak tree. Trinity House lit up the present-day lighthouse in 1881. It dwarfs Smeaton's Tower which was dismantled and reassembled on Plymouth Hoe where it can still be visited today.

I passed well north of Eddystone and then eased off onto an even faster reach, sitting alone miles from anyone, weaving up and down waves in the electric blue sea. This was such a great day again. I was on track to make it into Salcombe by around 3 pm, possibly my fastest day's sailing. As I should have known by now, relaxing still 10 nautical miles short of my destination was a bad idea. Rather than go through the palaver of checking my Navionics app, I relied on line of sight and compass readings, aiming directly at Salcombe, or so I thought.

Salcombe Salute

It was when I arrived at the headland, which I thought was the entrance to the Salcombe channel, that it looked a bit different to the maps I'd studied that morning, not that I'd ever approached from the seaward entrance before. Finally checking the Navionics app, I realised this wasn't Bolt Head at the mouth of Salcombe but Bolt Tail, five miles further west along the cliffs.

"What an idiot!" I shouted to myself.

I now had to beat five miles into the wind along what looked like a seriously rocky cliff line. It also meant I'd be an hour later than I'd told Tim Law who was sailing out in his Laser to meet me at the Salcombe Bar. There was nothing else for it but knuckle down and grind out the last few miles. The seas around the cliff line were confused and I was bounced around, narrowly skipping over hundreds of submerged rocks along the way. On one occasion my board touched a rock and nearly capsized me only a few metres from the cliffs. Rounding Bolt Head was especially turbulent but I made it onto the approach to Salcombe Bar now screaming along on a very broad reach, occasionally a run. In the distance I thought I could see the tip of a white sail.

"Yes it is! A Laser sail! I'm sure of it!"

The waves were getting so large we'd take it in turns to disappear from view before reappearing simultaneously riding the top of a wave. I'd recognise Tim's sailing style anywhere, he was beating out to me through horrendous looking surf.

"That must be the bar," I thought

It looked awful and, to make things worse, I was approaching on a dead run with the wind by the lee with cliffs on the same side causing all sorts of weird wind oscillations and flat spots. Tim waved me towards the westerly channel marker buoys lying uncomfortably near a group of very large rocks. He'd turned onto a run back in and guided me along the narrow channel trying to avoid the worst of the overfalls kicking up off the bar. I had a couple of close shaves flying straight down the face of a near vertical wave. We were both put through the ringer and a capsize here would almost certainly have resulted in a broken mast or worse. We made it through safely and were greeted by another Laser, a club mate of Tim's, Esther McLarty, a leading urologist and prostate cancer expert. It felt like a Salcombe salute and was a very gratifying feeling after another long and arduous day sailing. Unknown to us as we arrived in the calmer waters of Salcombe harbour, Tim's wife Bernadette was still battling her way back through the bar in Tiger, their small wooden open motor boat. She'd come out to greet us but had experienced some difficulties with the engine. Bernadette was also struggling with her own personal health battle, having recently had surgery to rectify an erratic heart valve, making her feel exhausted and unwell.

I spent the evening with Tim and Bernadette devouring the largest shepherd's pie I've seen and retired early to bed. Everyone was feeling exhausted after the episode at the Salcombe Bar.

Chapter 52

The Way to Weymouth

Tim and Bernadette Law had looked after both myself and Emma (who'd driven up from Mount's Bay) royally for the short period of time we'd been in their company. Emma was heading back to work that day but got up with me at 6.00 am. She planned to accompany Tim and escort me out past the bar in Tiger. I discovered how dangerous this entrance was last night. Thirteen lifeboat men lost their lives here in 1916 after both lifeboats, one called Emma and the other William (bizarrely, the name of my wife and eldest son) were capsized by a massive wave. I hoped it wasn't a bad omen.

Tim had laid on a full English breakfast, Bernadette had forced herself up, still feeling very unwell and made me a packed lunch. It was the full red carpet treatment. In return, I'd accidentally managed to pull the shower head off their wall in the luxurious ensuite bathroom we'd been allocated. I fessed up and Tim laughed it off very graciously.

The previous night we'd calculated that for today's journey I needed to be at Portland Bill just outside Weymouth by high water minus one hour. That meant arriving at 12.30 pm to have the optimum conditions for rounding the Bill and mitigating the notorious Portland Race. In strong gales, the area can be torn by high and unpredictable breaking seas caused by the Bill connected to Chesil Beach extending 18 miles into the English Channel. This has the effect of both the flood and the ebb tides swirling in its shadow. Arriving at slack water was the best chance of reducing this effect. It was going to be tight, probably impossible to make that distance in the time. The mouth of Salcombe Harbour to Portland Bill in a straight line across Lyme Bay is 60 miles (96.5 km or 52 nautical miles). I'd have to average 17 mph (14.7 knots) to make it to Portland Bill for slack water. This was faster than any journey I'd made so far and I knew it was an unachievable number. I put this out of my mind. I'd just have to deal with what I found when I arrived.

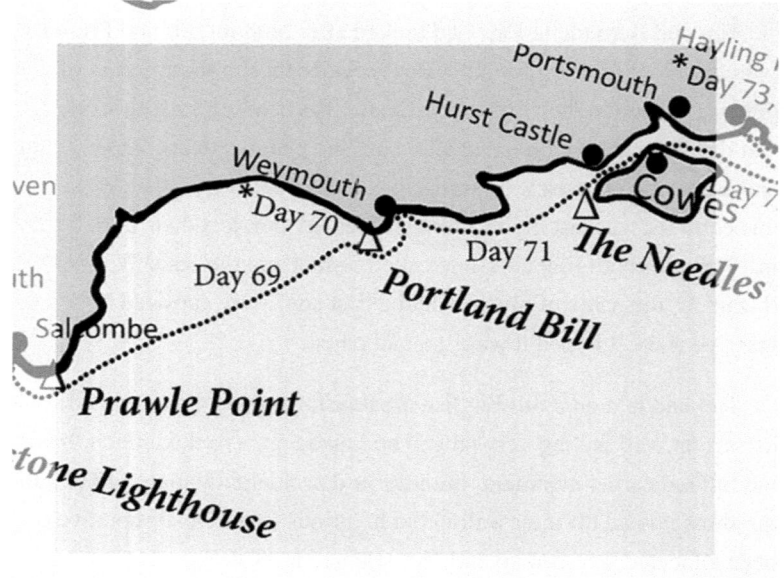

"Surely Portland Bill can't be any worse than other stuff I've had to deal?" I thought.

When we arrived back at the MOD27, the river was glassy calm. We were held up for 15 minutes waiting for a local fishing boat to unload crabs on the launching jetty. I was irritated by the delay, conscious of the deadline I was up against. We finally launched at 7.30 am with Tim and Emma guiding me along in Tiger, instructing me where to go to avoid the strongest tide. We parted company as I headed east onto a broad reach at Prawle Point at the end of the estuary. The time was exactly 9 am. I'd taken an hour and a half to beat my way out of the river.

The early forecast was the perfect wind direction for that day's run, blowing south south west. However, the visibility was poor and the wind strength was already building to around 20 mph. My concern was that by 1 pm the forecast was showing a significant increase in wind speed, gusting over 35 knots, probably just about the time I'd be arriving at the Bill.

I had to get going.

After half an hour, I checked my speed and was averaging 10 knots through the water. It felt like I was sailing flat out. I was never going to hit the 12.30 pm high water target. I passed Start Point by 9.20 am and continued straight out across Lyme Bay, sailing 17 nautical miles offshore (19.5 miles, 31 km) at the farthest point, aiming directly at Portland Bill. As I headed out into open water past Torquay and the mouth of the River Exe at Exmouth, visibility was down to barely more than 500 metres. The weather had closed in, the wind strength was building and the swell was already between three to four metres.

The crossing felt really fast, despite the large swell. I was still 6 nautical miles away from Portland Bill at 1.40 pm. Screaming along on a tight reach with spray everywhere, the wind was absolutely howling. The sea state was very similar to the Mull of Kintyre and visibility was appalling. Wind records show peaks of 38 knots at Portland Bill around the time I was approaching.

I kept a mile off shore around Portland Bill, sticking to the advice I'd been given by both Tim and Jon Emmett, who was sailing out to guide me into Weymouth in his Laser. I hoped! Although the sea state and visibility were terrible, everything was going well. However, as I aimed for what I thought was Weymouth harbour I had to change direction onto a dead run before the wind. Aiming at the cliffs thinking it was Weymouth, I cut inshore looking for shelter from behind the Bill. In doing so, I inadvertently sailed directly across the Shambles Bank. I only realised when I saw the yellow buoy with a cross sitting on top violently bouncing around. This looked like a definite no-go area. I was confused, where was I? This didn't look right. I stopped to try to check my position on the Navionics app when a near vertical wave picked me up and surfed me into the back of the wave in front. I capsized the boat. As the boat catapulted over in a cartwheeling motion, I just hung onto the mainsheet. A series of waves came crashing down on me, bowling us along upside down. I'd swallowed a lungful of water but clung to the upturned hull. Lying on her side, waves were now pounding down on top of the MOD27 and me. It took a Herculean effort to right her using brute force to spin her into the direction of the next wave. As it passed underneath, another wave approached towering above. Trying to avoid it, I scrambled into the cockpit, grabbing the tiller just in time to steer directly down the face of this near vertical standing wave. I'd saved a second capsize but only just.

I was so disorientated that I sailed further in towards the middle of the Shambles Bank thinking Weymouth harbour was just on the other side. Another giant wave broke over the transom of the MOD27 and spun me round, capsizing us again. This time I just saved her from inverting and righted her quite quickly by leaping onto the centreboard as the boat went over with a massive wave crashing over the top of me as I spun her into the wind.

The Shambles, I've later discovered, has been referred to as 'the blood of butchery', an area notorious for its horrendous Grove Point overfalls. The shallow waters and strong currents around Portland Bill create a break on the tidal flow both ways making all the water cascading through stand up vertically like soldiers. I'm told that in calmer weather, the fishing boats deliberately motor across the Shambles to scrub the barnacles off the bottom of their boats on the seabed. However, I didn't see any trying that trick today; not entirely surprising given it was blowing 38 knots.

As I tried to right my upturned sailing craft, the waves continued to tower frighteningly above me. They were the size of a house. Once I'd managed to recover the boat and get sailing again, the shallow water made the waves so steep and close together that it was like climbing a rope ladder to sail up their face only to slide down the back, a bit like dropping down a pole on the other side. I spent half an hour fighting my way across this stretch before I made the very reluctant decision to head back out to sea into the violent wind and try circling around this area, heading away from the cliffs.

I was less than 150 miles from home, I'd survived sailing around all of the notorious black spots of the UK mainland, around Dover, John O' Groats, Duncansby Head, Cape Wrath and Land's End. I'd crossed the Thames Estuary, the Humber, The Wash, the Forth, the Moray Firth, sailed through the Pentland Firth past the Men of May, around towering waves at Dunnet Head, across the Clyde. I'd rounded the Mull of Kintyre and past the Mull of Galloway, sailed across the Irish Sea to the Isle of Man, sailed straight across the Bristol Channel and right on down to Cornwall. I'd encountered numerous obstacles, rapids, whirlpools, dangerous rocks, cliffs, high winds, low winds, hailstorms, too much sun, pretty much everything that nature had. I'd survived it round the island of Britain. Yet here I was within touching distance of home, sailing along the south coast, a stretch of water I'd convinced myself was friendly because it was where I came from, as if this were a good reason for it to be any safer than the rest of the places I'd been in the UK. I was in trouble. I'd covered enough miles now to recognise the signs. I really was in big trouble.

I managed to get into a safer location where the waves were less steep and were no longer overfalling, just east of Portland Bill. Spray whipped off the tops of the sea. All I could see were white caps everywhere. I pulled out my spare phone. I'd carried two Samsung mobiles on separate networks since western Scotland as well as a VHF radio and the Spot X satellite tracker. By now I knew that I wouldn't be able to open the screen on my primary phone, the Galaxy S8. This required a finger swipe and electrostatic charge to fire up the screen. My hands were soaking and cold, a poor combination for opening the S8. My spare phone wasn't quite as sensitive and I managed to call Emma who was manning the Safety Channel at the time. At 3 pm I made contact.

"Emma" I yelled down the phone bellowing over the roaring noise, trying to be heard. "I can't work out exactly where I am," I continued.

I wasn't really sure if she could hear me. I could hardly hear myself, the noise of the wind and breaking waves were deafening.

"I've rounded Portland Bill but can't locate Weymouth harbour. My Navionics won't open, vis is terrible. Can you see on the Spot X tracker where I am?"

Emma had never heard me ask this before in all the past 70 days. She could tell my voice was expressing a level of difficulty she hadn't heard from me. She could probably hear my shortness of breath down the phone or my raised voice or simply the howling wind and roaring noises emanating from the sea. My sail was flogging to death while I bounced up and down, the sea smashing into my back while I was trying to communicate with her. It was pretty hopeless. I waited for what seemed a lifetime but she responded, sounding very faint,

"Aim east of the headland then north"

Then the line cut out. She rang back several times but it was getting more difficult to stay upright and hear anything she was saying at all. I was balancing on the edge of the boat, the cockpit awash with water. I just couldn't hear anything above the noise of the sail flapping wildly in the storm.

Emma tells me she then called Tim's friend who was in charge of running the Weymouth Olympic Centre. She'd insisted he send out a rib to find me. She waited for what seemed like ages and then called them back with an increasing sense of desperation as she hadn't heard confirmation. When she made contact again, they said it was too dangerous to launch.

Emma's retort was insistent that, as the premier sailing centre in the British Isles with all the necessary equipment and facilities to hand, they took immediate action.

"That's ridiculous, just get on with it. He's only just outside the harbour and he's in danger!" she impressed the urgency upon them.

Jon Emmett, my host in Weymouth, was my next call. I tried Jon several times but got no answer. Maybe he was on his way out to meet me I thought as his phone dropped straight to voicemail. Jon later told me he was on his way out to find me which is why he couldn't answer his phone.

I could vaguely see a headland north east of my position. It was difficult to be sure through the spray, mist and rain. I had to do something so, sailing on a broad reach, I headed away from the sharp overfalls I'd just nearly drowned in. This felt safer, a more stable sailing angle than previously. It was a longer route but I felt in control again. I'd need to gybe. This would be risky and could easily result in another capsize. I made the gybe, just staying upright, wobbling violently coming out of the manoeuvre as a new wave smashed me from behind. Closer in, there was some shelter from the wind under the cliffs. Heading towards them for the first time, the violence of the storm subsided a little as the cliffs now shielded me from the full force of the gusts.

Sometime later, I don't recall how long, I saw the shape of a large grey inflatable rib heading out towards me. According to my Safety Channel notes, I was spotted by the rib at 10 minutes past three. I'd made it nearly all the way round Britain without any outside on the water assistance. I'd sailed close to 2,000 miles in the MOD27. This tiny fibreglass dinghy had nearly carried me the full 360 degrees of the UK mainland. Even if they offered me support, there was no way I was going to accept any help but welcomed the reassurance they were on hand if I really needed it.

The only previous occasion I'd come close to getting help was in Scotland when I ran out of wind. I'd managed to attract the attention of a local crab pot boat using my VHF, requesting a tow to the local harbour about two miles away. They agreed to the tow but only after they'd hauled up their pots. It took them an hour before they came to me by which time the breeze had filled in and I'd carried on without their assistance.

Today, less than 150 miles from home, wasn't a day I'd be accepting a tow but I felt relieved and reassured by the rib's presence. I'd reached a place where there was civilisation. Shortly afterwards, I was greeted by the two people manning the rib. I waved back gleefully. Then a tiny Laser sail appeared on the horizon in front of Weymouth harbour wall. It was heading towards me making slow progress sailing directly into the violent wind. I recognised the body shape in the boat as Jon.

It's a funny thing about the Laser sailing dinghy. Everything on the boat is identical to the next boat. It's what's called a one design class which means there are strict rules ensuring the boats are all the same. However, every boat looks slightly different when it's being sailed. The Laser exaggerates your sailing style, making it a little bit like a fingerprint. Every person has their own unique look and way of sailing the boat that to the trained eye gives away their identity.

When you regularly race against the same people, you begin to be able to recognise them even when their face and sail numbers aren't visible; the way they sit, the angle of their head, how they hold the tiller, how far in or out of the boat they sit, whether they move backwards and forwards, where they look, the movement of the boat through the water. Some people look as still and smooth as silk while others look manic and constantly move in and out of the boat. I recognised Jon's sailing style from half a mile away. His boat always looks like it is slightly healed and down at the bow. He never seems to move much and the top of his mast seems to have an automatic twitch, flicking every time he goes over a wave. That was Jon for sure!

I started to feel exhausted now. I'd sailed over 115 km (71 miles), this was to be the longest day of the entire trip and one of my toughest experiences on this never-ending journey. Only the Mull of Kintyre and Duncansby Head had tested me as much as today. My legs and arms now felt like lead. My back ached. My right knee was screaming with pain again, the meniscus tear on my right knee that I'd been nursing since arriving in Scotland had been sorely aggravated again.

Tony, the coxswain at Holyhead lifeboat station where I'd stayed for two nights due to bad weather, told me,

"When people are rescued, often after they've spent hours, if not days clinging on for their lives they then give up as soon as they think they'll be rescued. Usually their bodies just shut down. They become helpless. It's like a switch. They move from survival mode one minute to limp torso the next, frequently unable to stand, raise an arm or help themselves any more, when the rescuers arrive".

My situation now reminded me of one of those wild animal chases you see on a David Attenborough documentary when the leopard finally catches and pins the antelope by the back legs, bringing it down after an epic pursuit. The antelope looks immobile, dead even, before the leopard has moved in for the final kill and sunk his teeth into its neck.

I don't know how but I made it back towards Weymouth harbour. I was following Jon now. He'd waved at me then promptly turned around and sped off back to harbour at a much faster pace than I could go. He was sailing unhindered by the 60 kilos of gear I had on board and was clearly less fatigued than me. I'd just crossed Lyme Bay in a 'oner' through a raging storm, didn't he know. I watched Jon pull away from me speeding into the distance, feeling slightly irritated but also impressed by his downwind technique. He weaved in and out of the waves. We were dead running now, by the lee; that's when the wind blows from behind you but slightly on the wrong side of the sail. It can be more stable when sailing dead downwind in lots of breeze but requires full concentration. In this case, the wind was blowing over the cliffs and across my left ear as I sailed on starboard tack. My sail let out, forming a 90 degree angle to the direction of the wind pushing me along. I was heading straight towards the harbour.

The grey rib was leading me in, Jon was a long way in front. I tried to get my radio out to ask the rib if we could come through the first harbour entrance. This required me to fix the mainsheet in a cleat on the deck so I had a free hand to operate the radio. Almost as soon as I did, a large gust hit me. With the mainsheet cleated, I had no ability to loosen my sail to spill wind. This is how you control the power of a sailing boat, a bit like applying the brakes in a car. As a consequence of not being able to adjust the mainsheet I was bowled into the water again, clutching the radio in one hand as I capsized, falling out the back of the boat.

This was all I needed. I was knackered, my arms felt like lead weights. It took a long time to get back upright. There was no strength left in my body.

My hands scrambled for the radio and shoved it back into my life jacket whilst swimming after the boat. When I reached the centreboard which was poking out of the hull, I didn't have enough energy left to climb up so using my feet on the underwater hull, I swam the hull round into the wind and pulled on the mainsheet. A gust of wind got under the sail and righted her as I gripped the bow as hard as I could, incredibly righting the boat. Getting back into the cockpit took forever and I was seriously struggling for breath by the time I was safely back on board.

I was annoyed, I'd hardly capsized all round Britain and now I had to do it on my way into Weymouth, home of the British Olympic Sailing Centre, where all of the UK's best sailors train. I checked, I still had everything onboard and when all was accounted for set off towards the harbour again. The boat screamed away in a plume of spray even though I was trying to reduce my speed. I didn't want to dump her in again. Too late, another strong gust caught me off balance. I was too tired to react quickly enough and again I went in, this time capsizing at the edge of the harbour. Thankfully I avoided falling into the water by rolling over the hull and landing on my back on the outstretched centreboard. I groped my way back into the cockpit as it came back upright and lay face down catching my breath.

"This is the last capsize of the day for me," I told myself.

Cautiously, I sailed along the harbour wall and finally the main harbour entrance appeared. I'd taken a cursory look at coming through the first harbour entrance I'd encountered just before my last capsize. A number of naval ships were moored in this section of water. Across the entrance a long thick rope was draped with the obvious aim of dissuading unauthorised visitors going in here. A small sign hung below the rope and although I couldn't make out exactly what the writing said, I surmised it meant, no entry. Again, I felt irritated. I wanted this episode over! It was a nice sheltered entrance instead of another half a mile sail along a 20 foot high solid wall, creating wind shadows and violent sudden squalls.

I entered Weymouth harbour at 3.31 pm having covered 71.8 miles (115.5km) in 6 hours 35 minutes. I calculated my average speed was 11.2 miles per hour (9.7 knots) including four capsizes and stopping to make two phone calls. This was the longest distance I'd covered in one day and probably the fastest too.

Chapter 53

"Double Dinner"

As a top flight coach of an Olympic Gold medal athlete, there's not much Jon Emmett doesn't know about Laser sailing. However, I do now feel I have the edge when it comes to circumnavigating the UK in a Laser. Jon recognised the distance I'd covered today. He understood the physical drain on my body from such a feat and knew the process to aid my recovery. Get warm and dry, then eat and drink quickly. Once he'd helped me up the Weymouth slipway and we'd showered, he drove me to find my first dinner at Subway, not necessarily my first choice of restaurant but plenty of protein and carbs on offer. I gratefully accepted Jon's generous offer to buy me what he called "my first dinner".

My sail was in shreds after the past two weeks and most of my patches had failed today. After making a call to Steve at Rooster Sailing, who offered me a free replacement, we struggled to figure out the logistics of how they could get it to me before leaving tomorrow. I parked Steve's offer and Jon took me to a sail loft he knew called Moat

Sails. Offering up my damp rag of a sail with another broken batten from that day, they smiled and promised to fix it all by morning.

We headed back to Jon's home where on arrival I sat down for two minutes on the bed and promptly fell asleep. Jon had arranged to meet Anja, one of his students, that evening for a debrief from their day's training. After waking me up several hours later, we made our way into town to meet Anja. There was plenty of confusion as the pub we were supposed to meet at was permanently closed so, following a number of unanswered messages to Anja, we eventually met up at the local Wetherspoons. After our second dinner here, Jon and Anja discussed sailing stuff which sounded highly technical to me. While they chatted, I busied myself looking up my journey plan and the weather forecast for tomorrow.

The weather looked even worse tomorrow than it was had been today with winds building all day, showing 44 knots from 2 pm on the Predict Wind and WindGuru weather apps. I'd need to be off very early again tomorrow morning to miss the worst. Checking online, I noticed the Lulworth Range was firing tomorrow. Making a note of the phone number, I decided to call them first thing in the morning to let them know I was passing.

The evening was surprisingly relaxing, Jon produced a microphone and interviewed me for the Laser Association broadcast at the back of the pub. After finishing my second dinner and having drunk two pints of beer, I was ready for bed again.

Back in Jon's flat, he showed me his bathroom, or drying room I think he called it. The room was like a shrine to the wetsuit. Opening the door, I was taken aback by the heat emanating, it was a room sized oven. The thermostat felt like it was set to 90 degrees. Neatly laid out on hooks and hangers before me was an array of wetsuits. It looked like there was one for every day of the week. I added my own collection of gear to the display and felt safe in the knowledge that I'd at least start off tomorrow in a dry suit.

Walking through Jon's flat I noticed dotted all over the walls were tiny post-it notes, planted neatly in rows. Apparently, Lily, Jon's Chinese wife, who sadly was away studying, was very keen on them. It was sort of post-it note art.

Following such a long day today, I worked out a plan to sail a short hop to Poole harbour tomorrow and meet up with a few of the Poole Sailing Club's Laser sailors. An old friend of mine, Richard Lott, had offered me a bed at his mum's house next door to the sailing club. Richard was now living in New York where he was running North Sails in America. We'd been in contact via messenger over the past 24 hours and Vanessa, Richard's sister, had been liaising with me about the logistics.

I first met Richard at a Europa Cup sailing event in Workum, Holland. He was a bit of a Laser celebrity at the time and sailing full time in the summer whilst studying as an accountant. I was a newbie to the Laser scene and only a part timer, grabbing the odd trip to a Laser regatta between work commitments. I seem to remember during this regatta that Richard wore two holes in his instep from wearing tiny lightweight rubber shoes that provided no protection when hiking out on his feet, resulting in third degree burns.

In those days, we all wore water bottles in weight jackets carried on our shoulders. These added leverage to keep the boat flat which made us go faster. There was an overall weight limit for your kit, including weight jackets, so other clothes were often sacrificed. It got so ridiculous we were nearly all racing in a pair of speedos, carrying the maximum weight water jackets permitted. We would shiver our way round a course almost hypothermic in order to gain the tiniest weight advantage. Not surprisingly, weight jackets are now banned for modern sailing athletes.

Richard and I became training partners when we both moved into the Olympic Finn class. This is a heavier boat, in some ways quite similar to a Laser but with a lot more powerful sail and technically more sophisticated. We enjoyed a memorable six week winter regatta tour in Miami back in 1991.

I always recall we were both eating permanently when we sailed the Finn as it was all about weight, strength and fitness. Being heavy was a massive advantage, the minimum competitive weight requirement back then was 90 kilos. Our American routine was to go to the gym early morning and evening every day and in between we'd eat, sail, eat, drink, eat, eat, sleep. We'd search out the best value, all you can eat restaurants in Coconut Grove and eat until we felt sick. There would be pasta and bacon, pancakes and maple syrup, scrambled eggs and milk, loads of milk for breakfast, then a gym session followed by bacon and eggs for elevenses followed by sailing for three or four hours and a burger and chips for late lunch, anything we could eat for teatime, doughnuts or something similarly dreadful, then all you can eat in the evening followed by another evening gym session. To finish off, we'd go down to the local bar to sink more beer than we should have and talk nonsense. We were proper athletes!

Accommodation was a sleeping bag on the floor at Richard's mate, Tom's house. He was working in Miami running a 50-foot racing yacht for some millionaire. As part of the job, he was given a free condo to live in with his German work colleague. I can always remember the look of horror on his housemate's face when he walked in to the smell of fried onion rings and garlic steak, a fridge full of food and two bodies snoring in front of the telly on his living room floor. We stayed there for six weeks. I forget Tom's flat mate's name but by the time we left, Tom's relationship with him was so bad he'd padlocked his bedroom and gone home to Germany.

The following morning, Jon was up and ready for me, tutting at how long it was taking me to get my gear together. We had to collect my repaired sail from Moat Sails and Jon had another training session with Anja. The Moat Sails guys had done a good job of patching up the sail and supplied me with a new batten to replace the snapped one. There was no charge!

It took four people to lift the fully loaded MOD27 across the concrete hardstand and down the Weymouth slipway. Jon and Anja had agreed to accompany me out to the edge of the harbour. Before leaving, I sent the usual Safety Channel plan which was to reach Poole harbour by 2 pm, hopefully missing the 40 knot breeze coming through in the afternoon.

The three of us set off sailing downwind in a zigzagging formation. The wind was already pretty strong, even in the harbour. Afterwards, Jon said he'd nearly capsized on the way out. I was thinking this was definitely more than was predicted. Regardless, I carried on past the harbour walls and waved goodbye to Jon and Anja. The sea was seriously lumpy as I made my way out from within the safety of the walls, aiming towards St. Alban's Head.

My route took me straight across the Lulworth Ranges, the military firing ranges located between Wareham and Lulworth in Dorset. I'd only been on the move for 15 minutes when a powerful speedboat came racing over towards me. It had the name 'Smit Frome' emblazoned down one side. It blocked my way and then pulled alongside. Easier said than done given the way the waves were breaking.

"We're firing," the man dressed in a dark waterproof jacket said.

"What does that mean?" I asked innocently, shouting as loudly as I could so he could hear.

"That means you'll have to sail five miles offshore over there," he said pointing directly out to sea where there was a mass of breaking white caps.

"Do you know what the wind speed is like out there?" I said.

"It's showing 29 knots at St. Alban's Head," he replied

"It looks like it's worse out there," I shouted back, bellowing at the top of my voice so he could hear me

"Why do you think we're in here?" he answered, laughing.

They were sitting in a military spec 30-foot high-powered motor launch with a cabin. I was sitting in a 13-foot fibreglass open sailing dinghy. The irony didn't seem to register with him.

He instructed me to return to the harbour and reluctantly I swung round and headed back in. It took me over an hour to make it back sailing into the wind. As I entered the shelter of the harbour walls, Jon and Anja were whizzing back and forth, tacking and gybing. I sensed a look of disappointment from Jon wondering what I was doing back so soon. This was further reaffirmed at the slipway when we met.

"What are you doing here?" he asked.

"They sent me back," I replied.

"Who did?" questioned Jon.

"The MOD firing range blokes," I responded.

Jon didn't seem over keen to see me but nonetheless he very generously took me back to his flat for a second night. He was eating to a training plan, rice and ready meals which he ate continuously. I sorted myself out for food with fish and chips and spent the rest of the time catching up with my diary and plans for the next day.

The forecast was terrible. It was blowing over 40 knots in the morning with the tail of a hurricane coming over from America. There appeared to be a small weather window at 12 noon. Checking the live firing timings at Lulworth, these were scheduled to take place again tomorrow between 12 noon and 5 pm. Both Jon and I stared in detail at the weather forecasts. There was no way I could leave any earlier, it was going to be absolutely howling through the night and was only dropping to around 25 knots after midday. We agreed to leave the house at 11.15 am the next morning.

I woke around 8 am. Jon was up at 6.30 am and had left the flat to do Pilates at his local gym. I walked into town and bought supplies for the day and ate a terrible breakfast at a tiny cafe. The coffee tasted of dishwater and the bacon roll looked nothing like it should have. How wrong can you go with a bacon roll? Apparently very.

I was feeling apprehensive about just about everything today. Nothing seemed right. The firing range officer I'd spoken to wasn't very reassuring. As advised by Roger, my policeman mate helping out on the Safety Channel, I told them I had to pass close to the shore today as it was my only safe passage option. Roger had researched this and sent me a plan of the range area. It extended five miles off shore. There was just no way I'd be able to cope with the sea state and the winds that far out today. It looked bad enough closer in where the cliffs offered some protection from the gale. The range officer was having none of it. Eventually he told me I'd have to radio HMS Sutherland on VHF channel 74 when I was under way but he wanted me to steer a course of 130 degrees. I'd argued for an age with him that 110 degrees was my only safe course and even that didn't look terribly wise looking at the weather forecast detail anyway!

Jon dropped me off at the slipway and we went through the same process of changing and rigging as yesterday. By 1 pm, the wind had definitely dropped a little but it still looked like it was howling even in the sheltered harbour. I sensed a pressure to move on and I wanted to get going. Anja was training again today so once again the three of us launched and sailed dead downwind towards the harbour mouth. It was windier than yesterday, lumps of wind were coming through in streaking gusts which lifted the boats up, making them take off, sending spray everywhere. I was slower than the other two as my boat was nearly twice the weight so I exited the harbour with them sitting waiting for me to pass. I waved to them both and, as I encountered the first waves outside of the walls, I knew I was in the Red Zone.

Chapter 54

Red Zone!

I was being battered by the force of the waves, so powerful they rinsed my ears out through the woolly hat pulled tightly down over my head. Torrents of icy cold sea water smashed into my face with disturbingly large waves roaring all around.

Perched on the edge of the boat's deck, clinging on with one hand, radio in the other, the sail flogging deafeningly in the raging winds while the sea engulfed my cockpit, I was shouting as loudly as I could, knowing that I was dangerously close to the Lulworth Ranges used by our Majesty's navy for frequent, active exercise

Roger Glass from the Safety Channel team had done some research into the logistics of crossing the Lulworth Ranges. Internet searches suggested that the sea danger area extended to six nautical miles offshore between Lulworth Cove and St Alban's Head. Vessels must keep out of the area at firing times and there is a published document that details the firing times of the Ranges. One might expect this to be a few hours a day but not so, the Ranges can be open for live firing both day and night. Needless to say, this was the case when I needed to cross.

The wind and sea conditions today were extreme, in excess of 30 knots and forecast to get worse. There was also the prospect of the tail end of that American hurricane routing towards the UK. For me to take MOD27 six miles out to sea in a south westerly gale with a forecast to increase could only be considered, even by me, un-seamanlike. Sea conditions close into the shoreline were much friendlier.

So, by phone, I'd contacted the Lulworth Ranges duty officer before I set off and explained that it wouldn't be possible for me to safely sail six miles out to sea and I'd have to cross the range area as speedily as I could. It was a poor line and difficult to hear his exact response. However, according to Roger, an experienced police officer with a forensic mind, there'd never been a successful prosecution in relation to making a safe passage across the sea part of the Ranges. I believed it was a good decision in the circumstances and I had, after all, had the decency to tell them.

Even so, my 1970s, 13-foot Laser sailing dinghy was no match for these gigantic seas. Above my head, military ordnance was whooshing past. The VHF radio was glued to one ear while I was bellowing into the microphone trying to communicate with the warship, HMS Sutherland, which was responsible for sending the barrage of colossal shells rocketing overhead. Shells! And no, not the type you collect in your bucket on the beach while eating ice cream and making sandcastles. These were the type of shells that are so frighteningly loud they make you feel physically sick as they pass. These are the sort of shells you see in active war zones reported on the 10 o'clock news. It's difficult to appreciate the force of these from the comfort of your living room. As they whizzed past, I visualised replays of live news footage showing shells dropping directly onto the roof of an Al-Qaeda complex instantly pulverising it into a pile of rocks in a 30-foot crater.

Well, I was definitely appreciating the significance of shells right now. Howling at the top of my voice down the radio and screaming into the microphone:

"WARSHIP SUTHERLAND!
WARSHIP SUTHERLAND!
THIS IS PEVENSEY LASER.
PEVENSEY LASER…"

I Paused Then Tried Again…

"WARSHIP SUTHERLAND!
WARSHIP SUTHERLAND!
THIS IS PEVENSEY LASER.
PEVENSEY LASER"

Pevensey Laser was the call sign I'd used for the past five years. During the summer months, I would sail up from my home club, Pevensey Bay, to Eastbourne Sailing Club to compete in their Wednesday evening racing. I used to think this trip was a really brave adventure, launching and landing on my own, usually sailing around half a mile offshore, coming back in the dusk, rounding the Sovereign Harbour where the waves usually kicked up and produced some unpredictable overfalls. I'd carry a handheld VHF radio with me during these trips to contact the Eastbourne race officer to tell her I intended to compete and notify my sail number. This saved having to beach at Eastbourne and brave the rolling surf and shore dump, just to fill out the race entry form. I found the radio reassuring in the event of equipment failure sailing back in the dark.

I used the Pevensey Laser call sign for my round Britain trip although my boat was named MOD27 due to this combination of letters and numbers being moulded onto the foredeck. When I set out, I'd considered changing my call sign to MOD27 but then thought better of it as it would be too confusing for the coastguard and any rescue services I might need to call in the case of an emergency. Right now, though, I thought this call sign could have been quite useful.

I continued blasting away into my crackly VHF radio

"MY POSITION IS 50°32.524'N. 0°16.692'E. I REPEAT. MY POSITION IS 50°32.524'N. 0°16.692'E

PLEASE CONFIRM

AM I IN RED ZONE?

I REPEAT

AM I IN RED ZONE?

I AM HEARING INCOMING FIRE"

I was repeating this several times before releasing the transmit button which was firmly depressed on my handheld VHF radio. I waited for a response.

A crackly, official-sounding voice replied, squawking unintelligibly over the radio. The voice was barely audible but I just about gleaned from the muffled noise that they were instructing me to stand by while they plotted my position. The sail was flogging and the boat was pitching violently up and down. I was having trouble just sitting in the boat as soon as I stopped sailing. The waves were breaking over me from all directions, a bit like someone throwing a whole bath full of water every few seconds, making me slide around the cockpit, hanging on with every blow – a sitting target. At least when I was moving, I could steer up and over the crest of the breaking waves.

Bouncing around in the middle of the Lulworth Ranges being shot at is not something I'd expected to happen to me off the beautiful Dorset coastline. It certainly wasn't something I'd even contemplated when setting out on my journey. After battling my way around most of the UK, by this stage I sort of did know what I was doing but this was something new. After sailing so far this was my first experience of communicating with a warship, let alone one that was in the process of a live firing exercise! Further explosions erupted, now from the shore some two miles away and again the force of the noise made me nearly dive overboard. Later, I discovered that this was caused by Challenger tanks firing at a target out to sea which sounded like it was just a few feet from where I was struggling to keep my tiny Laser upright.

Chapter 55

Flying Cowes

The experience of the Lulworth Ranges and HMS Sutherland launching cannon fire in my direction had really shaken me. Now I was clear of it and through the most exposed seas, I stopped to consider my options, sheltering in the lee of the giant cliffs in Durlston Bay.

Poole harbour was really the wrong way although I still had the offer of staying at Richard's mum's house which was appealing but felt like the wrong move. Eighteen miles east were The Needles on the Isle of Wight and then Hurst Castle. Lymington Yacht Club lay just next door. Dave Freeman, another of the Safety Channel volunteers, lived at Lymington. This was a possible target. My very old sailing mate, Nick Mason, was also nearby, sailing at Cowes on a yacht with a group of his ex-police colleagues. Cowes was 30 miles away. I might just make it before dark if I was lucky. The wind had dropped a little since rounding St Alban's Head but it was still blowing around 20 knots from the south west and the tide was with me so a run to Cowes would be pretty fast. Nick Harrison, another Laser legend, and I had chatted the previous day about stopping with him in Stokes Bay near Gosport but I'd totally forgotten about this conversation in the chaos that had just happened.

I decided to just keep going as far east as I could. Fortunately, my impromptu pause at Weymouth had given PY the chance to figure out how to get the third Spot X tracker finally working properly so at least the Safety Channel could see where I was, the first time they'd really had any reliable positional tracker on me since I lost the first Spot X at Carsaig just before the Mull of Kintyre. That seemed like a lifetime ago now.

Heading out into open water crossing towards The Needles Lighthouse was pretty hectic. Outside the cover of the cliffs above Durlston Bay, the sea state and wind strength deteriorated. I slightly regretted not hugging the shore and dropping into Poole harbour. I found out later a number of the Poole Sailing Club's Laser fleet were planning on sailing out to meet me but had turned back as it was too windy.

In the middle of the sea, Richard Lott called me from America. He was checking if his 80 year old mum should expect me. I managed to answer the call and relayed the news I was going to miss her just as a wave dropped directly on my head, making breathing and speaking on the phone quite tricky. Richard understood and hung up. As I expected, getting to The Needles was fairly quick but time was running on.

It was nearly 6 pm when I approached Hurst Castle. I'd only ever previously been through the narrow channel in a yacht but knew the tide behind me was good news. However, some advice on which side of the Solent to pass seemed important. Nick was my next call. It was still 12 miles to Cowes. Lymington seemed the better overnight option. There was something in my mind that kept telling me Cowes was the right place to stop though. Maybe it was because I felt it would be my penultimate day tomorrow.

"Nick?" I calmly enquired down the phone.

"Number 1," was his immediate and familiar answer.

This greeting was normal whenever we communicated. It's something which has hungover since we knew each other during our teenage years. To be frank, we had a lot of hangovers when we were younger. I was quite feral as a teenager, living with my grandparents from the age of 17 as my parents had to relocate for my father's job. At least that's what they told me.

Nick's became my second home most weekends, sleeping on his bedroom floor at his Mum and Dad's house in Worcester Park. Here, we would drive our cars too fast and usually end up drinking too many pints of Young's Ramrod Special at The Plough on Friday and Saturday nights. On Sundays, we then went sailing with thumping hangovers at Island Barn Sailing Club near Hampton Court.

I made my decision within a second of Nick taking my call.

"I'm coming to Cowes and I'll be with you in approximately one hour. Which side of the channel is best to pass Hurst Castle?" I blurted out.

Nick was with a few other sailors at the time and, conferring with each other, they all agreed I should stay in tight to the Castle wall.

"Ok thanks. See you soon," I said before hanging up.

The run past Hurst Castle was bumpy, keeping very tight to the wall whooshed me through with the tide spitting me out the other side into a chaotic mass of confused water. There was an overwhelming sense of relief after clearing this final hurdle. Cowes was all downhill now. Passing Yarmouth, for the first time I dared to actually believe I was going to be home soon. Cowes has a favourite place in my soul and I was really looking forward to meeting up with Nick and sharing a few beers with him there tonight. As I sailed past Newtown Creek and approached the beach huts neatly lining the shore of Gurnard, I knew the end was close. I could relax at last. I was getting home. This was my swansong. Tomorrow night I'd be in my own bed in Eastbourne.

By the time I arrived at West Cowes Marina and the Island Sailing Club's pontoon, it was virtually dark. Nick guided me into his location on the jetty with his mobile phone torch shining at me in the gloomy light. I couldn't see his face until I was only a few yards out. Grinning from ear to ear with a few of his mates from the yacht they were racing on, he said,

"Over here Number 1"

Those familiar words felt so good. A friendly welcome from someone who knows me for who I am, warts and all. No polite conversation required here.

Pulling the boat onto the jetty took six people. The MOD27 had taken on a bit of water and I was tired. I wondered if perhaps I had a bullet hole in the hull but on close inspection there was no evidence of any.

That evening in Cowes, I let my hair down more than usual. The Island Sailing Club sponsored my shower, Nick and his crew treated me to beer and a curry. The accommodation supplied was a comfortable bed in a rented house they were staying in nearby. By the time I finally went to bed, it was nearly time to get up again. A good night but in the morning, reality sank in.

There was still 100 km to go to Eastbourne. The forecast looked hairy with 28 knots blowing over Bramble Bank and 30 knots at the Chimet weather station further along the coast near Chichester. It didn't really register with me that today could possibly be a non-moving day. Despite the news that Nick conveyed, there was a rumour their racing today might be cancelled due to the wind strength. They were sailing 38-foot long yachts! I was surprised.

We all dined out at the local cafe for breakfast. Nick and his crew departed to check the status of their race while I focused on formulating a plan for the day. I posted this on the Safety Channel from the comfort of the cafe. During a call to Emma, she told me they weren't ready for my return so Newhaven seemed an appropriate place to aim for today. I could hole up at Nick Bush's house whom I'd already made contact with. The plan then would be to sail a short triumphant final leg back to Eastbourne on Saturday morning and wave at my new posse of followers. There was talk of the BBC coming along with a camera crew. It all sounded very exciting.

Nick lived near Newhaven. I knew him, his older brother, Olly, and Dad, Geoff, from Weirwood Sailing Club. Weirwood was the first club I'd joined after resuming Laser sailing following a 15 year break. I'd spent these hectic years raising my kids and starting various business ventures when there was just no spare time for Laser sailing.

My Weirwood Sailing Club experience started after a particularly draining five years when Emma and I had been fully committed to the consumer magazine publishing business. After four long years, our baby and toddler gear magazine was available on the shelves of nearly all the leading newsagents and most of the largest supermarkets.

To cement our advertising relationships, every year I'd charter a Sunsail 38-foot yacht for Cowes Week. We'd plaster our logo over the side of the boat and the crew would be issued with corporate gilets with the slogan, 'Let's make babies', emblazoned on their backs. I'd invite all the advertisers to come to have a near death experience racing with us. A rolling crew of seven joined us on board each day. Most had never set foot on a yacht, let alone race one. Occasionally I'd convince my unsuspecting sailing friends like Simon Mellors, who we called The Colonel, to come to help out if it was particularly windy. After a day's experience they rarely returned. More often than not, I was skippering and barking instructions on my own. I carried a whistle to attract the crew's attention then try to point or use sign language for the unsuspecting guests. My voice would normally fail after a day of shouting so the whistle proved very effective during the week-long exercise.

The first year I invited a new group of advertisers daily. Everyone was very excited and would normally stay on for a big night out in Cowes Yacht Haven, partying hard into the night then sleeping on board. Cowes Week is one continuous night and day party. In the first year, I made the mistake of allowing the new crew to join on the same day the current crew were leaving. This meant we'd all go out drinking after a hard day's racing. The problem I had was there was never any down time for me as a skipper and host to rest. It was like a seven-day, 20 hour a day "saildrinkathon". Whilst this was fantastic fun and an incredibly successful advertising sales strategy as we booked around 50% of our annual ad revenue during this week, it left the skipper (me) hanging.

I developed a special survival strategy to get me through the week. After we landed following a day of racing, I'd set the guests off in the direction of the main bar in Cowes Yacht Haven and then head off for half an hour on my own in the other direction with the excuse I had to complete some paperwork. I'd decamp to my favourite bar and decompress in a corner in the Vectis Tavern. This was one of the locals' pubs in Cowes and I deliberately chose it so I didn't meet any other yachties. I found solace in the strangest place. Sipping coffee, I'd stare intrigued at a queue of teenage girls playing a computer quiz game in the pub. There was always such a long queue for this machine. One day I went over to see what they were doing. The girls were trying to rearrange a picture that appeared whole then split into multiple bits. To win the game, they had to reassemble the picture in 60 seconds. When I looked more closely, the picture was of men with no clothes on. There were two picture sets, one male and one female. For some reason the pub's youngest customers loved it, especially the girls. I nicknamed this game, 'bits n' tits'.

The following year, I switched all new crew to morning arrivals which meant by the evening my guests were more tired than me as most had woken at 4 am to meet us for breakfast at West Cowes Yacht Haven for an 8 am briefing. I found myself with more time to hide in the Vectis Tavern these subsequent years. We had an incredibly good run, entertaining clients for five years. Only on one occasion did we have any hospitalisations and that was a gate crasher who filled a slot on the yacht when a guest had failed to turn up.

Alex Hall, Jeremy Clarkson's first wife, arrived on board after one of the guests had met her in the bar the previous evening. I spent most of the day shouting at her to keep her head down. It always seemed inches away from the boom every time we made a manoeuvre. Coming in at the end of a windy day, poor Alex finally succeeded in knocking herself out, literally. As we were about to pull into the jetty at West Cowes, the boom swung across the boat catching her squarely on the side of her head, sweeping her unconscious towards the water. I caught her flying head by leaping through mid-air, leaving the wheel and diving like a goalkeeper to prevent her from going overboard. When I picked her up, I fully expected her head to split in two, such was the force of the impact. Fortunately, all was well.

The 2007 financial crisis put paid to baby and toddler gear. All our profits had been eroded and with the major retailers like W H Smith cutting hundreds of titles, one Christmas Eve Emma and I both looked at each other and decided it couldn't carry on. We and our other investors took a significant hit that year but for us, despite the financial loss, it felt like a sea anchor had just been pulled up. After this, we both decided we wanted to get back to doing things we really enjoyed. Emma focused on gardening while I returned to Laser sailing.

I recall visiting my local sailing club, Weirwood Reservoir, for the first time. Chris Fyans, Vice Commodore, greeted me and after a short chat enthusiastically showed me to a rotting old green Laser in the dinghy park. He said it was mine for £25 despite there being a lot of missing bits. That was about all the money I possessed at the time.

I rummaged through my loft and found an old sail and some sailing kit, most of the rest I scrounged, begged and borrowed. Chris proved to be a real ally helping me get back on the water and even encouraged me to attend a few local competitions. On one occasion he even towed both our boats to Wraysbury Lake Sailing Club, an hour's journey around the M25. We took off in his 4.0 litre open top Wrangler Jeep. This sounds simple enough, except that Chris had the world's most ridiculously oversized tyres fitted to his ancient old Jeep. If you exceeded 50 miles per hour it felt like the vehicle was suddenly sailing through rolling waves. With no warning, the vehicle would violently yaw across the white lines with alarming and unexpected frequency. Chris's reaction to my heightened levels of anxiety and whitening knuckles clutching hold of the door handle was a mixture of disdain and disapproval at my lack of backbone, issuing a sort of mumbled dismissal followed by mutterings of everything is fine.

If you ever met Chris, on first impressions you could be forgiven for thinking he was some sort of eccentric misfit, dressed in open-toe sandals, shorts and a polo neck T-shirt most days of the year. I was surprised when I discovered he was in fact an eminent member of the shipping community and regularly attended arbitrations and tribunals as a judge or expert witness. My favourite and most endearing characteristic of Chris was his absolute desire to do anything I ever suggested, confidently delivering his usual line of "Go for it".

Whenever we travelled there was always a 'Safety Beer' involved which automatically qualified him for membership to our dysfunctional G7 sailing group. Had Chris been alive when I set off, I feel certain he would have followed my every mile around the country in his bright orange rib, laughing at my misfortunes every inch of the journey. Very sadly, Chris died from a sudden heart attack whilst riding his bike shortly after his 70th birthday, 18 months before my trip began. His final WhatsApp message sent to me the morning of his death was a photo of a newspaper article written about a single handed sailor who had circumnavigated the UK in his yacht, stopping off at every port in the land to drink a pint of beer.

My first outing in the green machine at Weirwood was racing on a Sunday morning dressed in my Henri- Lloyd 1980s one piece, not quite waterproof spray suit and matching turquoise and red lifejacket. It did the job but I looked a bit like Lady Diana. I was back on the water in a Laser after 15 years that was all that mattered! It was like I'd never been away. Fully pumped on the start line, according to PY's account, who was introduced to me that day, I treated this experience like the opening race in the Olympics.

Shouting "water" at every race mark, which is an ancient rule to get any boat nearby out of the way, I huffed and puffed my way round the course quoting rules that were quite obsolete and alien to most of those sailing competitively in the year 2007.

The Laser bug had bitten again and I raced the green machine for a whole year until she split open and virtually sank in an open meeting at Oxford Sailing Club. The event was sailed in quite extreme conditions. Simon Barrington, a fellow Weirwood Laser sailor, commented in his usual perfectly deadpan Aussie way,

"That green boat should never have left Weirwood."

As with most things, Simon was right, it was just the way he usually pointed out the obvious that sometimes rubbed people up the wrong way. As I loaded the poor old green machine back onto my borrowed trailer to be reburied back in the Weirwood boat park, I felt a sense of loss. That was the start of my Laser Masters adventure which led to my present situation, contemplating the last leg of my UK circumnavigation in Tiffany's Cafe on Cowes High Street.

Chapter 56

Watch Out for Bill

Nick said all yacht racing was cancelled due to gusts of wind exceeding 25 knots at Bramble Bank. I didn't really take much notice of this fact, carrying on regardless, first checking all my gear then making my way down to the Island Sailing Club to get changed into my wetsuit. By the time I appeared on the jetty, Nick and a few of his crew had come down to help me off. The MOD27 was lashed onto the top of the visitors' pontoon. When we dropped her in the Solent she was facing the wrong way which required an immediate gybe in order to set off in the right direction up river. In high winds this is usually a tricky manoeuvre so I was surprised how calm the wind seemed, given all the hoo-ha going on in the background about the weather and the cancelled yacht racing.

Before departing, I sent the usual Safety Channel message and set off on the nose of midday. Word had spread and a reasonably large crowd had assembled to see me off. Many of the passing yachts returning to harbour from the cancelled racing waved and hailed as

I passed. It felt like this could be it. I'd been instructed not to get to Eastbourne until Friday as Emma had been working hard to arrange a proper homecoming. Newhaven would be easily achievable today, giving me the whole of Friday to make it back to Eastbourne.

Before departing, I recall chatting to one of Nick's friends about the trip back and casually asking if he thought there'd be anything in particular I should avoid. He said there was nothing likely to cause me any problems but mentioned it might be a bit lumpy around Selsey Bill. I'd sailed this route earlier in the year from Eastbourne, delivering a yacht with a friend of mine called Geronimo who was now skippering Punta Del Este, one of the Clipper Round the World yachts circumnavigating the globe.

I'd first met Geronimo two years earlier when he came into my workshop unannounced in the middle of winter. He was a professional skipper, born and raised in Spain. His day job was delivering yachts all over the world for their owners but he told me the time had come for him to settle down and buy a house with his long-term girlfriend in nearby Hastings. Because he'd been at sea most of his life, he said he owned nearly nothing. That day, he bought all sorts of odd bits of vintage junk I had lying around, including an antique set of crown green wooden bowls and a pair of vintage leather suitcases plus, of course, a few doors. Afterwards we stayed in touch and I even invited him to come Laser sailing with me at Pevensey. He never quite made it but out of the blue one evening I received a phone call.

"Hi Stick. It's Geronimo, do you fancy coming to Cowes with me tomorrow morning? I've got a yacht to deliver from Eastbourne."

As it happens, I was free the following day. The only issue was I'd just loaned my waterproofs and lifejacket to my youngest son, Freddie, who was sailing in Southampton that weekend. I pulled together what spare wet weather gear I could find, nothing terribly appropriate for the forecasted conditions though, but went to meet Geronimo nonetheless.

The arrangements had been pretty sketchy so I didn't know what the boat's name was but I did know which pontoon it was moored on. I arrived at 7 am just before Geronimo and could only see one boat that looked like it would need a pro delivery team. It looked like a Jeanneau or Beneteau 40-footer.

"Nice!" I thought, "This is going to be fun."

Geronimo arrived shortly afterwards and punched in the gate code to let me in. We both walked towards the pretty blue hulled 40-foot yacht then unexpectedly Geronimo jumped on board a tiny Westerly bilge keel boat that looked as though it hadn't moved for 10 years, if not more. The top sides were covered in bird poo and the cockpit was even worse.

"Is this her?" I asked, shocked at the state she was in.

"Yeah, quite pretty isn't she?" Geronimo replied, half smiling.

Because I'd lent Fred my lifejacket, I was hoping the yacht would have one on board I could use. There was nothing! In fact, there was no safety kit on board as far as I could tell. Not even a danbuoy to throw in case anyone went overboard. This felt quite dangerous to me and I started checking all the shackles and rigging fixtures, finding two that were decidedly dodgy and tightening the capstans with a rusty old pair of pliers I'd found on board.

Geronimo seemed oblivious to the risks and general unseaworthiness of the craft and carried on as if everything was perfectly OK. Having retreated to my van, I pulled out a dinghy buoyancy aid I'd stuffed in a box full of spare kit I kept in the back. These are not really designed for offshore sailing but it was all I had. I also stuffed a Stanley knife, screwdriver, roll of duct tape and a few spare shackles into my pockets. By the time I'd returned, Geronimo was beaming from ear to ear. Somehow, he'd got the engine to fire and surprisingly she sounded quite smooth. I can recall passing out through the harbour lock where a few onlookers stood open-mouthed looking down on us from above. They may have been thinking the boat was some sort of wildlife decoy designed to attract seagulls. A number of buckets swooshed down the decks had made little impact on the stains but at least it was less slippery.

Surprisingly, we didn't sink, it was a reasonable tail wind and we threw up the sails to speed up the tired little engine, two of which ripped fairly quickly. Aside from a bit of minor sail failure, that we pretended hadn't happened, I don't recall anything very worrying about the journey as we entered the eastern Solent at Selsey Bill. In fact, I remember feeling everything had gone very well. When we met the new owner in Cowes later that evening, he admitted over the dinner he paid for that he was too nervous to sail her down himself as he wasn't sure of his new purchase's seaworthiness.

So you can understand why I feared nothing about the last leg home. I'd sailed it before, the only leg on this entire journey I had previous knowledge of.

After leaving the Island Sailing Club's pontoon, I turned right out of the Cowes River, past the Red Funnel ferry terminal and started my final leg home, running parallel to and close inshore to the Isle of Wight. Passing Osborne House, Queen Victoria and Prince Albert's holiday home, everything seemed good. It was breezy and the wind direction was quite southerly so the land sheltered me while I stayed close to the island. Nick was following on their yacht, filming from the bow. The breeze was OK initially. It wasn't until I ventured further offshore that I realised how windy it really was. Crossing out into the middle of the Solent at Wootton Creek, I got walloped. Catching me off guard, I bowled into the water, gasping and spluttering to the surface, hanging onto the mainsheet for dear life. That wasn't in the script. Fortunately, Nick had stopped filming at this stage and his boat was turning to make its way back into Cowes.

Righting the MOD27, sitting in the cockpit wiping the salt out of my eyes, I was surprised at the violence of that gust. It felt a bit like my Mull of Kintyre experience. The wind just dropped straight down off the island. Continuing on past Spithead at Ryde, I started to feel very very small and extremely vulnerable to large shipping movements. There was so much shipping. It was all around me, not many pleasure craft but row upon row of large commercial ships. Visibility had deteriorated too and this made reading the navigation buoy names nearly impossible. I aimed directly between the two large forts that were clearly visible guarding the entrance to the Solent. Apparently, these were dreamed up as part of the 1859 Royal Commission when fear of invasion by Napoleon III led the British Prime Minister, Lord Henry Palmerston, to commission sea-based defences to defend the Portsmouth dockyard. These were easy targets to steer for and were pretty much a straight line for Eastbourne.

Clearing the east end of the island exposed me to the full force of the raging southerly wind. The waves were really building now and unexpectedly one hit me from a strange direction. I was washed out of the boat just as I sailed across Bembridge Ledge. I just managed to cling onto the MOD27 as another wave dropped on top of the now capsized hull. Climbing back in, I carried on. The further I went outside of the island's protection, the more chaotic the seas became and the gusts combing the water were ferocious, piling in erratically, sending me racing off in a plume of spray. Watching the mast bending like a banana in the force of the wind, it was a wonder this tiny boat was still in one piece. She'd covered so many miles and none of those had been very kind. What had I done to deserve this today? So close to home, battling through another weather system equally as powerful as any of the entire trip. I couldn't check the Navionics app; it was just too hairy trying to stay upright. Massive ships were everywhere. I was certain they couldn't see me. One super tanker passed within what seemed like touching distance. It was going so fast. I must have been travelling at 10 knots maybe more, it sailed past me like I was hardly moving.

Approaching a large concrete looking tower, I was confused. Why was I so far out to sea? Then it occurred to me. The tide must be whooshing me out. I sheltered in the lee of the tower and tried to get my bearings. This wasn't easy with waves batting me around like a ping pong ball. I needed to get closer to shore. This felt seriously dangerous.

It turns out the tower I'd sheltered behind was the Nab Tower. The wind and visibility had quickly deteriorated and were now just terrible. There seemed to be buoys everywhere which looked to me like the main deep-water shipping channel. I couldn't be sure as it was impossible to get the Navionics app open while the sea was smashing me around so violently. I needed to find shelter so decided to aim for the mainland shore. I was way too far out to sea for the conditions and my confidence was rapidly draining away.

Approaching a red buoy, I sailed directly across behind another huge ship, straight downwind, and promptly capsized on the massive red navigation buoy. Struggling in the water, I could make out another ship looming up on me at an alarming speed. It took a long time to right the boat in the confused waves. When I did eventually get the MOD27 upright, the ship was already turning straight at me. This was madness. I'd never cross in front of her in time so reaching towards the ship, heading back the way I'd come I made a decision to sail alongside her hulking great starboard side and slip across behind her. As she got close, the sky went dark casting a shadow over me, a tiny dot on the water probably invisible to the captain in charge. Containers were piled 10 high on her deck and the speed at which she passed me was truly alarming. That was enough to make up my mind. I needed to abandon today and look for the closest soft landing.

The gusts were so powerful, the only direction I was able to stay upright was on a broad reach. This meant heading backwards away from the tower towards the mainland. My sail was flapping violently as I spilled as much of the wind I could to try to slow down. I reached for 7 mental miles, barely able to see anything in the ferocious waves and spray. Finally I found my way into a more sheltered area where I surfed in on a giant wave and rode it high up onto a shingle beach, capsizing the boat on the shore to stop the sail ripping in the violent winds. I dragged the MOD27 as high as I could up the beach on my own and collapsed lying spreadeagled on the stones. Staring up at the sky in a glazed daze, I said out loud

"What on earth just happened? That was madness!"

It was as if someone had just sneezed from the heavens directly on the tiny patch of water I was in. I was very lucky not to have been run down by that turning ship. My hands were shaking so violently I couldn't use the phone.

I just sat shivering not fully aware of what was going on for minutes. My trance was interrupted by a small black and white cocker spaniel that came racing up to me and jumped on my lap before instantly running off again. Shortly afterwards, the owners, a young couple appeared walking along the beach. I stood up and asked them where I was.

"Hayling Island," the man replied.

I was amazed. How had I got here?

"Do you mind taking a photo?" was my next question. "My hands are shaking too much to hold the camera" I continued and explained what I was doing, still trying to always get a picture of my first contact on landing to prove my location.

I offered the phone to them and Becky, his wife or partner took it from me.

The three of us grimaced in the gale and then Tim helped carry the MOD27 to the top of the beach. We both struggled with the weight across the soft sand but finally left her parked up next to a small clump of beach huts. Becky and Tim asked if I needed anything. I could see a cafe nearby, thanked them for their help but declined their offer and headed over to buy a toasted cheese and tomato sandwich and a cup of coffee.

That was really very scary. I thought I'd been through the worst weather in Scotland. I never expected the Solent to produce anything as bad as this.

I picked the phone up and my hands were less shaky now. Steve from Rooster Sailing was near Hayling Island I recalled.

"Steve, it's Neil"

"Neil, hello, are you alright?"

"Yes I'm fine but I've landed on Hayling Island. Wind's gone bonkers and I had to bail out today. I just wondered if you could help me out?"

"Sure, where are you exactly?" Steve asked

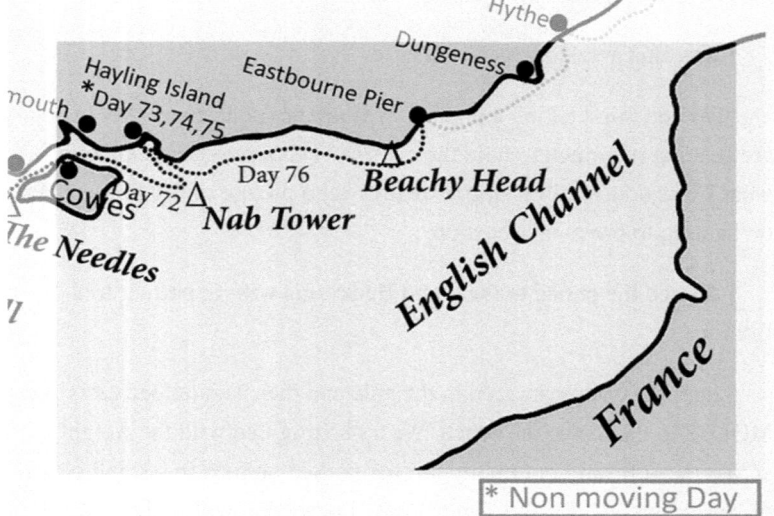

It took me a while to pinpoint precisely where I was. I should have known as I had sailed here so many times but I was clearly in shock and the answers were very slow coming. Steve figured out where I was exactly, after a game of guessing the landmarks. He arrived within an hour and helped me to finish off packing up. I felt calmer now I had someone who knew exactly what to do. Steve took me home to his house in Waterlooville where, after a hot shower and food, we sat and analysed the day's wind and the next few days' forecasts.

Chapter 57

Five Day Finale

Hurricane Lorenzo, also known as Storm Lorenzo for Ireland and the United Kingdom, was the easternmost Category 5 Atlantic hurricane on record. Lorenzo developed from a tropical wave that moved off the west coast of Africa on 22nd September, growing larger in size over the course of its development. On September 26th it rapidly intensified into a Category 4 hurricane which weakened into an extratropical cyclone as it moved quickly towards Ireland and the United Kingdom and became the first named storm of the 2019/20 European windstorm season. Yesterday I'd been caught directly in the line of this weather system, the first wave of the storm to hit the UK.

Through late September and early October, large swells were generated by the hurricane's massive wind field, impacting much of the Atlantic basin. The French ship, Bourbon Rhode, capsized amid the violent seas on 27thSeptember and of its 14 crew members, three were rescued, four drowned and the remaining seven were presumed dead.

I'd had a bad night's sleep at Steve's, waking at 4 am, having had a nightmare and struggling to get back to sleep. Steve and his wife Sarah had been up since 6.30 am to practice their morning Pilates routine. By the time I staggered downstairs at 8.30 am, Steve had been pouring over several of the wind apps. It was Friday 27th September. Talking over the options whilst demolishing a cooked breakfast of poached eggs on toast, we both agreed today was a non-moving day. There was nothing on the charts suggesting anything less than 40 knots of wind. Looking forwards for the next five days, it looked like this was actually a conservative top end wind strength. So much for getting home by Saturday.

I accompanied Steve into his office at Rooster Sailing and met a few of his work colleagues. We had a chat together on camera about my adventures and Steve posted a series of these on his website and YouTube. I really didn't know much about what I was doing or saying at the time. I got a few of the place names wrong and was slightly muddled about some of the details. There'd been so much to take in and remember and without referring to my notes, I found I often just went blank. My emotions were raw and on one occasion I just managed to stop myself crying uncontrollably in front of him on camera.

It felt odd being in a workplace. I accompanied Steve for a lunchtime meeting with someone who was hoping to advise him on establishing a European set-up in Ireland in view of the impending export issues that Brexit might bring. It felt surreal listening to a normal business discussion again.

The next two days, Saturday and Sunday, I spent time checking weather forecasts, driving back and forth to my boat at Hayling Island in Steve's van to make sure it hadn't been removed or stolen and looking longingly out to sea hoping the weather might break. At one point, it looked like there might be a small weather window on Saturday late afternoon but it was still showing 30 knots at Chimet, the closest weather station to my location.

Emma decided to drive down to see me at Steve's for the weekend now that all her plans for a big Eastbourne homecoming had been scuppered. That afternoon I used the van and drove over to visit one of my oldest sailing friends who I'd known since my early twenties and who we'd always nicknamed the Colonel, and his family in nearby Southsea. He'd given me a very good tip early on in my adventure advising me to run at 70%. At the start of the journey, I was maxing out close to 100% and found I'd hit a serious energy lag after doing so for several days. The idea of maintaining a steady 70% worked really well, especially through the difficult northern areas of the UK.

Returning to Steve's for a meal with Emma and Sarah that evening, we chatted about nothing else other than the weather and getting home. On Sunday, waking early after another uncomfortable night with backache, I checked the weather and Chimet was showing 50 knots. Another non-moving day. Emma and I spent most of the day hopping between breakfast and lunch venues, spending most of the afternoon camped in a pub called the Bat & Ball Inn near Hambledon, famous for fielding numerous cricket teams against the England national team. My brother's wife, Annette, was passing nearby and joined us for a coffee.

That evening, Emma drove home and Steve, Sarah and I debated the chances of getting off very early on Monday morning when there seemed to be a small break in the weather. The tides weren't ideal as I'd have foul tides for most of the way but at least the wind seemed sailable. It was going to need a big effort to make it in one day. I was 51 nautical miles (94 km) from Eastbourne and only had three hours of tide with me if I got underway by 7 am. After that, I'd be fighting it for the largest part of the rest of the day.

Steve had taken over the role of planning and he insisted I wake at 5 am in order to be ready to leave by 7 am. Everything was laid out ready to go as soon as I was awake. Sarah had made me a packed lunch of cheese and pickle sandwiches, pepperami sticks and honey and oat bars plus I had one of my mackerel tins. I'd unloaded everything to Emma last night for the final push so I was running with zero gear. We'd calculated I needed to average 6 knots in order to arrive at Eastbourne by 4 pm.

Rigging the next morning at 6 am on the beach, it was freezing cold and pitch black. I spent ages fiddling around sending the Safety Channel message, logging onto the Spot X where I shared my live tracking location publicly for the very first time. Then I spent 15 minutes trying to overcome my poor VHF reception and communicate with the coastguard to file a passage plan. I pushed off at 6.50 am on Monday 30th September. This was Day 76. There was hardly a breath of wind and as I tried to waft my way through the shore dump, a wave broke over my bow and filled the cockpit with icy water.

"Great start!" I said out loud to myself.

The first two hours I drifted with the tide making hardly any progress. I'd only got as far as the West Pole channel marker, 2.7km away. Around here, at the entrance to the channel into Hayling Island and the Chichester Harbour Conservancy, there are numerous sandbanks and shallow waters with strong tidal flows. With very little wind, I was at the mercy of these tides. Fortunately for me, they pushed me across the channel to the South Cardinal marker of the Chichester Bar off West Wittering. This bar is a series of shallow sandbanks that kick up some serious overfalls, especially at low water with a southerly breeze. Although there was little wind, the sea state started getting quite bumpy and I felt my anxiety levels rising. The feeling of trepidation I'd experienced so many times before came flooding back. A tense hour passed making little headway, inching my way towards Selsey Bill. I only had one more hour of fair tide under me, if I was lucky.

When the tide turned, I'd wash back into Chichester harbour unless the breeze filled in. It was difficult to identify landmarks this far out to sea. A sound I dreaded came into ear shot. Breaking waves, roaring as they crashed into each other no more than 500 metres from where I was barely moving. Looking back at my track, I was well north of the channel markers for the Looe Channel, crossing an area marked on my Navionics as The Mixon. This area has shallows which at low water dry above sea level and by some fluke I'd just missed two of these drying out areas. Navigating mainly by instinct, I swerved around the areas where I could literally see curling waves breaking. Usually, shipping passes through the Looe Channel past Selsey Bill to avoid this area. No one had pointed this out to me.

Once I'd crawled my way past the Bill, I headed in towards the shore with a sigh of great relief. If the wind didn't fill in, I wanted to be able to land before the tide turned. I certainly didn't want to go through that area again. It wasn't looking good though, the wind had virtually evaporated.

My old neighbours and friends, Dave and Lesley-Anne Methley from Horsham, now lived very near Selsey. I called them.

"Hello Neil," Dave shouted down the phone. It was a good sound.

"Fancy a coffee?" I replied.

We discussed a few possible spots where he suggested I might land. I was struggling to identify them on my Navionics app but agreed to try to aim for Pagham harbour. The breeze was barely moving. I was slowly making my way towards the harbour and about 15 minutes had passed since talking to Dave when I felt a south westerly breeze blowing in across the hairs on the back of my neck. It was like someone had pressed a switch to turn the wind on. Up until now I'd been sailing into a south easterly head wind, now it had filled in from behind I should start moving much faster. Heading back out to sea, the breeze was freshening all the time. I called Dave back to cancel coffee.

I was constantly checking my speed. It was at 5 knots sailing away from Selsey Bill. At this rate, I might make Eastbourne by 7 pm. As I made it further offshore, the breeze increased. The boat's speed was up to 7 knots and I was now surfing down waves. Although I was fighting 2 knots of tide, there was progress at last.

"This is going to be a long day," talking to yourself is the first sign of madness. I was fully certifiable now.

Sarah's packed lunch was demolished in no time. I was starving and ate nearly everything she'd given me, saving only two oaty bars and my mackerel tins for later. I reset my course to 015 degrees and aimed directly for Brighton. I was sailing a straight line as far offshore as I needed to minimise the distance. Landmarks were indistinguishable this far offshore. Ominous black clouds chased me towards Eastbourne. Storm Lorenzo was making a comeback, exactly as forecast.

I sailed directly over Bognor Rocks and dodged my way around numerous obstacles on this wreck-strewn coastline, keeping a bearing of 015 degrees for the Brighton i360. By the time I drew parallel with this architectural eyesore, I was screaming along with a force 5 gusting 6 driving me home. The seas had built and I was weaving in and out of crests and hollows, enjoying the freedom of having lost the burden of my luggage. The MOD27 was purring along. On the horizon, I saw a large tall ship sailing boat that was also heading east. I aimed directly for its transom. Gradually, hour by hour, I closed on her. By the time we passed Newhaven, I'd caught her up and waved as she peeled off towards the harbour.

Unknown to me at the time, Ollie and Nick Bush were trying to launch their Lasers from Seaford beach to join me for my sail past Beachy Head. Sadly the surf was now too large for them to get off the beach. Then the best sight of all. Legacy, the Eastbourne Sovereign Sailing Club rib, appeared from out to seaward of me. What a great feeling that was. Gary Smith and Mick Whitmore drew alongside and we all laughed as the seas smashed into us, both boats sliding up and down the increasingly large waves. Shortly afterwards, Jason, a kite surfing friend of mine, who did make it off the beach at Seaford joined me, darting off and circling backwards and forwards as we headed for the final headland of Beachy Head. Fifteen miles to go!

The last part of the journey was as hard as any other bit of the entire circumnavigation. Approaching the Beachy Head Lighthouse with its iconic red and white stripes visible from miles away was deceptively reassuring. As we closed in, the waves became as steep and deep as nearly any on the trip. It was blowing a full force 6 by now and I was dead running around the headland. Sailing the final leg towards the pier was particularly tricky, running by the lee, sliding down towering waves with the wind dead behind, exactly the same as I had when entering Weymouth. Several of the support motor boats that had braved the weather were struggling with the ferocity of nature's free rollercoaster.

I locked myself into a position in the MOD27 where my centre of gravity was low and centred in the boat.

"Just keep plugging away. I'm nearly home," I kept telling myself.

It was precarious sailing but many of the ribs were also finding the conditions challenging. My cousins, Gemma and Sarah with her family, skippered by Ollie, an expert local helm turned back in their rib as they got completely swamped by a large wave over the bow. Jason the kite surfer bailed out before rounding Beachy Head after getting into difficulties in the conditions.

The MOD27, a £50 Laser built in the early 1970s, was performing magnificently. She felt sure footed in the enormous seas, was still holding together and bowling me along at 10 knots plus. When I passed the pier a large crowd of friends and family had gathered and cheered as my circumnavigation was completed. The time was 6.15 pm on the 30th September. Exactly 76 days, 6 hours and 15 minutes after leaving Eastbourne on the 17th July.

Gary and Mick raced over to me in Legacy and swerved, sending a cascading tidal wash over me then swiftly followed this up by spraying a bottle of champagne over my face and passing me the remainder. I scrambled around in the safety kit dry bag I had onboard and pulled out my handheld flare. I thought I may as well set it off to see if it worked. In spite of being out of date, Aaron who supplied it from Simpson Marine was right, it still worked. The bright orange glow fizzed and flared, spitting red hot sparks into my face.

The final sail into the beach was a show-off moment. I gybed and narrowly avoided spoiling my final landing with a capsize before surfing flat out down a wave and sliding half the way up the beach. Falling out the back of the boat, I was relieved to have made it back in one piece. Ron was one of the first people to greet me on the beach and a posse of Eastbourne and Pevensey Bay Sailing Club members, friends and family made my homecoming a moment to remember.

It was done. Today had been the longest nonstop sailing day of my entire journey at 12 hours 20 minutes. Eastbourne Sovereign Sailing Club opened the bar and all my visitors gathered around. My adventure was finally over. I'd often thought in the last week it would never end or that I might blow it like so many other moments in my life where I'd snatched defeat from the jaws of victory. I'd come close rounding Selsey Bill, the day I abandoned my course ducking behind a giant container ship in 35 knots of wind. I'd done it. Circumnavigated the UK mainland in a £50 Laser.

I'd laughed a lot and nearly died a few times! If you ask me why I did it, the only answer I can think of is, because I could!

Appendix

Three Years on

Readjusting to normal life was a significant challenge when I first came home. I found my adventure dominated daily thoughts. It took two weeks before I could even bring myself to go back into the workshop. And when I did it felt like an alien space I'd left behind in another life. Gradually reality crept back into my world. Bills needed paying and the pressure to pull my finger out and get stuck back in to work became impossible to ignore. I sleep walked through the first three months, aching to be doing something more adventurous.

Emma was extremely tolerant during this phase as she could see I was suffering. I'm no expert but I think I was displaying many of the symptons of PTSD. Waking up in cold sweats in the middle of the night, having nightmares and some very dark thoughts during my lowest mood moments, most out of character for me. I was lucky enough to be invited to give a few interviews and talks which allowed me to relive some of the best and worst moments but as soon as these talks were over I usually felt worse. It was like everything was pointless. Then followed a succession of Laser masters events where I started racing again and hosted a few talks. These I truly enjoyed as it allowed me to engage with like minded people who understood the significance of my challenge. During these presentations I often found myself welling up and on one occasion crying in public, emotions I never expected to feel. Afterwards I usually felt very low for weeks on end but found it difficult to understand why.

The most exciting opportunity post trip presented itself around Christmas 2019 when the Laser Masters Worlds organiser in Australia invited me to give a talk in Melbourne. They offered a free boat for me to sail in The Worlds and free accommodation. I simply had to get there. I became more motivated to sell a few doors and set about planning the trip. En route I made a whistle stop visit to Will my eldest son working and living in Hong Kong. At this time a strange report was filtering out of China about an entire city locking down due to a virulent deadly bat virus. Events unfolded slowly and it seemed incredulous to me anything like this might ever happen to us in Europe. The term pandemic started to be mentioned increasingly more frequently on the news. It wasn't a word I really comprehended and I excitedly carried on with my travel plans, oblivious to this unfolding disaster. Until that is in Australia when the government shut everything down and the event got cancelled four days after I arrived. All non nationals could be seen scrambling to get to their nearest airport and get home. I didn't take this very seriously at first. That is until Jon Emmett messaged me to get to an airport and go home. Quite surprisingly his prod registered and I acted. Miraculously I got the last standby seat on the last plane out of Melbourne back to London before all flights were cancelled and the borders closed. I was clearly being looked after again!

Three years on I am firmly back into the same routine as before I left. It is like nothing ever happened. I still hunger for a new adventure and have been scheming about everything from taking my Laser around Australia to sailing through the North West passage in a two man sailing dinghy. Watch out for the sharks, crocs and polar bears they say. You just never know what the next chapter in life will be? In the words of Morgan Freeman narrating in the film The Shawshank Redemption. "You either get busy livin' or get busy dyin'."

Parts of the Laser (ILCA*) Class dinghy

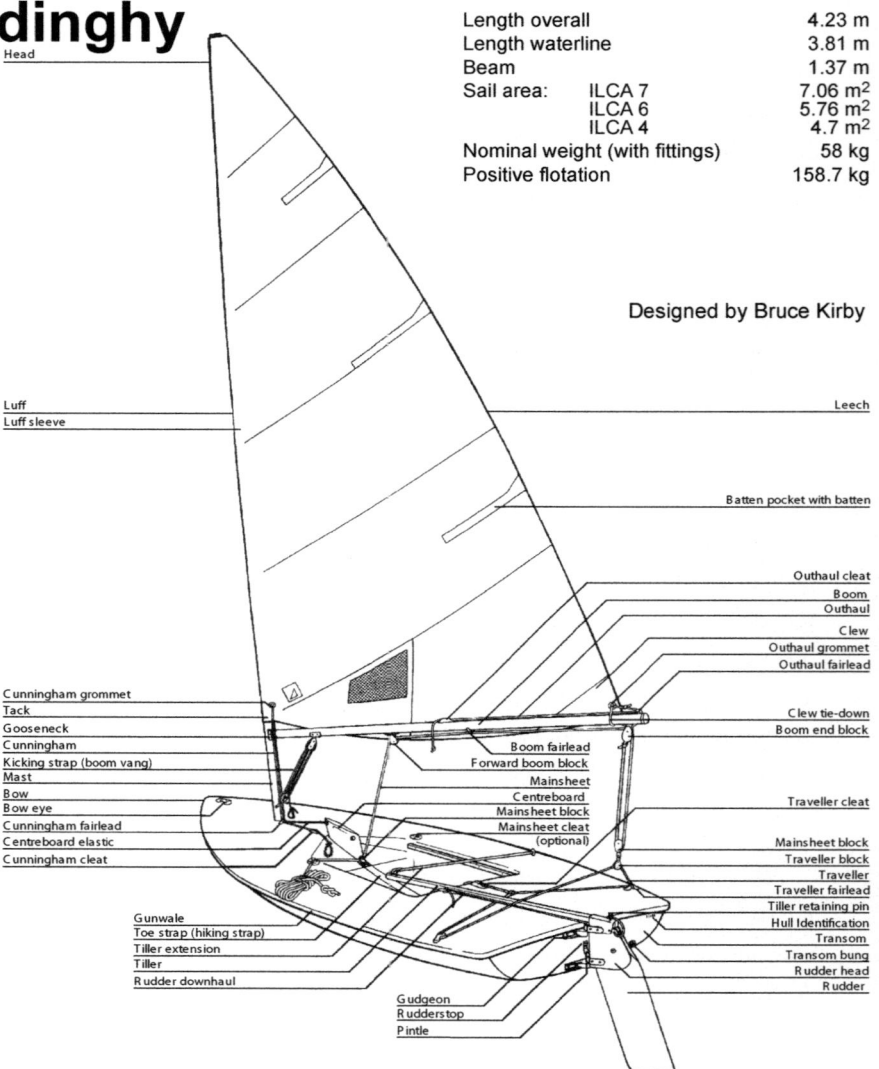

*ILCA is the new name for the Laser which changed on 25th April 2019.

Kit List

Item	Size	Qty	Brand
Dry bag	5 Litre	4	Rooster
Dry Bag	10 Litre	1	Rooster
Dry Bag	20 Litre	1	Typhoon
Tent	1 man	1	supermarket special
Bivvy Bag	1 man	1	Army issue
Sleeping Bag	1 man	1	Adventure 3 Season rating
4mm foam mat	2m x .3m	1	unbranded
Plastic ground sheet	4m x 3 m	1	Generic brand
Micro towel (chamois)		1 1	Amazon
Head torch		1 1	Amazon
Tooth brush		1/2 1	Wooden
Tootpaste	Small	1	Colgate
Soap bar		1 1	Tesco
Wetsuit Long john	6xl	1	Rooster
Wetsuit Shorts	Medium/Large	1	Rooster
Wet suit vest	Large	1	Rooster
Wetsuit Bolera Top	Large	1	Rooster
Poly Pro Fleece	Large	1	Rooster
Wet socks	11 (UK)	1	Rooster
Wet boots	11 (UK)	1	Rooster
Waterproof Top	Large	1	Rooster
Bouyancy 50N	50N	1	Rooster
Wooly Hat	floppy	1	unknown
Cap	Peak	1	various
Gloves Thermal	large	1	Rooster
Gloves Summer	large	1	Rooster
Waterproof offshore Jacket	Large	1	Henri Lloyd
Goretex Hi Vis Waterproof Trousers	Regular	1	Port West
Shore shoes	11 (UK)	1	Soft trainers - Sketchers
T-shirts	large	2	Cotton
Roll neck jumper (light weight)	Large	1	Base layer
Marlborough Wool Jumper	Large	1	Top jumper
Socks	11 (UK)	2	Warm thermal
Training trousers	Medium/Large	1	Trek
Belt	Rope	1	Dynema
Pants	Medium/Large	1	M&S
Shorts	Medium/Large	1	Quicksilver
Compass		1 1	Silva Racing Elite
First Aid pack		1 1	Small kit
Sail repair tape		1 1	1 metre strip
Knife / combi		1 1	Unknown
VHF radio		1 1	Ntel x 1, Icom x 1
Mobile phone		1 1	Samsung Galaxy 8 (vodafone)
Mobile phone		1 1	Samsung 5 (EE)
Plug Triple		1 1	240 v plug
Samsung charger and lead		1 2	240v Samsung
Battery back up 12v charger pack		1 1	2000ma
Solar battery back up 12v charger		1 1	2000ma
SpotX tracker and satellite text		1 1	SpotX

The Amazing Adventures of Stick Daring Part 2

Item	Size/Type			Brand
EPIRB		1	1	Epirb distress signal
Hand held flares	Handheld		3	Unknown
Mini flare pack and launcher		1	9	Unknown
Waterproof phone holders	Mobile phone size		3	Rooster
Waterproof radio bag	VHF size		1	Aquapac
Waterproof A4 bag	A4 size		2	Aquapac
Fender		1	1	Fender Oval
Praddle		1	1	Hand held
Gas cylinder	small		2	Gaz
Gas cylinder top for cooking	micro		1	unknown
Mini double saucepan stacking set			1	unknown
Combi pot, cup and spork	Small		1	unknown
Candle & inner tube rubber	Small		2	unknown
Lighter gas	small		2	Disposable
Flint striker	small		1	Mountain warehouse
Water bottle	1 litre		2	Rooster
Mini dry bag	1 Litre		1	Rooster
Masthead float inflatable	15 litre		1	unknown
Head torch and spare battery		1	1	Mountain warehouse
Mitosyl cream zinc		1	1	Mitosyl
Suncream factor 50		1	1	Generic brand
Mini screwdriver phillips and slotted head		1	1	Generic brand
Pinsers		1	1	Generic brand
Insulation tape green		1	1	Electrical tape
Sewing kit		1	1	Sewing kit
Control Lines		1	1	Control lines various
Midges Net		1	1	Generic brand
Plastic bags clip bags		1	5	Ikea
J Cloth		1	2	J cloth
Food packets	Noodles		2	Noodles
Food packets	soup		2	Soup
Food tin	Chick Peas		2	Chick Peas
Macrel Fillets	Tins		4	Macrel
Sardines	Tins		2	Sardines
Oat bars	Oat bars		4	Oat bars
Hot Chocolate	Hot Chocolate		2	Cadbury's
Mini snack bars Meusli	Meusli bars		15	Meusli
Coffee	Small dry bag		1	Coffee
Tea	Tea bags		1	Tetley Tea bags

Dedication

For Emma, Pete and all The Safety Channel

Glossary of Terms

Block

A pulley through which a rope is threaded to make pulling in and out easier

Boom

The horizontal length of tube extending along the length of the hull holding the bottom of the sail attaching to the mast at the gooseneck and the mainsheet in the middle and back of the boat

Capsize

When a boat turns over onto its side or upside down, often referred to as "turning turtle"

Centreboard

The retractable board in the centre of the boat which is raised and lowered to increase lateral resistance and prevent sideslip.

Compass

A magnetic instrument with a pointer which shows the direction of magnetic north and bearings from it.

Cunningham

Rope used to pull down the front of the sail to flatten or depower the sail in strong wind

Ebb tide

The tidal phase during which the water level is falling

Flood Tide

The tidal phase during which the water level is rising

Gooseneck

A fitting used to attach the front of the boom to the mast

Hiking

Hiking is leaning or sitting out in a sailing dinghy, to counteract the wind's pressure, thereby preventing the boat from capsizing.

Hikers

Pads protecting the underside of the thighs to make sitting out (hiking) more comfortable.

Hull

The hull is the body of the boat. It is sealed to prevent water from transmitting its way through and keeping your boat afloat.

Kicker or Kicking Strap

A series of ropes and blocks attached to the boom to control the height of the boom; stop it flying uncontrollably into the air

Knot

1 Knot = 1.150 MPH, 1.852 KM H, 0.514 Metres per second, 1.687feet per second

Laser (ILCA) sailing dinghy

The Laser (changed its name to ILCA on 25th April 2019) is a single-handed racing dinghy. The biggest attraction of the Laser dinghy is that it is protected by strict one-design class rules, which means that no changes are allowed to the boat unless they are specifically permitted in the rules. The result is that all Laser boats are virtually identical whether they are brand new or 30 years old, making it the sailor that wins the race, not the boat. The Laser is a challenging boat that rewards athleticism, subtle steering and trimming techniques, as well as tactical excellence. It is a single-handed Olympic class boat for both men and women and is sailed at club, national and international levels. With over 220,000 boats in 140 countries, it is the world's most popular adult and youth racing sailboat.

Hull weight: 58.97 kg

Mainsail area: Standard Rig (ILCA 7) 7.06 m2 (76.0 sq ft)

Designer: Bruce Kirby

Beam: 1.39 m (4 ft 7 in)

PHRF: 217

Year: 1969

Laser Standard rig (ILCA 7)

The largest rig of 3 sizes and the original 1970 sail design. The mainsail area is 7.06 m^2 (76.0 sq ft).

Mainsail

The sail rigged on the mast to propel the boat. There is only one sail on a Laser.

Mainsheet

Rope attached to blocks on the boom used to adjust the main sail in or out

Mast

The two-piece top and bottom section of tubing, which holds up the sail. Mounted vertically in position by being slotted into a tube inside the boat deck.

Outhaul

The rope attached to the bottom corner of the sail closest to the rudder (Clew) used to pull tight or loosen the sail.

Overfalls

A turbulent stretch of open water caused by a strong current or tide over a submarine ridge, or by a meeting of currents.

Port

The left-hand side of a boat when looking forwards from inside the cockpit

Rudder

The blade in the water at the rear of the boat used for steering

Spot X

Electronic tracker and two-way messaging device

Starboard

The right-hand side of a boat when looking forwards from inside the cockpit

Tiller

The stick made of aluminium or carbon fibre attached to the rudder used for steering

Tiller Extension

A length of narrower tube made of aluminium or carbon fibre to extend the length of the tiller

Toe Strap

Is a piece of webbing strap anchored at each end to a fixed point on the dinghy. Toes are hooked under the strap when hiking out to prevent the sailor falling in.

Traveller

A rope located across the top aft part of the hull that allows the mainsheet tackle to connect to the boat.

VHF radio

Marine VHF radio is a worldwide system of two-way radio transceivers on ships and watercraft used for bidirectional voice communication from ship-to-ship, ship-to-shore (for example with harbormasters), and in certain circumstances ship-to-aircraft.

Windex

A light balanced weathervane fixed on the mast to assist with wind direction finding.

Special Thanks

To everyone who assisted and donated to make this incredible journey a success including to name a few...

The Safety Channel - Emma, Peter, Rupert, Dave, Roger G, Roger O G,

Others who assisted before and during the journey Jeffski, Terry the Wand, Ron, Jeremy, Aussie Jeff, John Jono, James A (for the oars), Roger W (Weatherman), Gary S (Eastbourne's special genius), Ellie, the Jevington Eight Bells gang, Aaron at Simpson Marine, George my son.

People who assisted along the way-

Donald, harbour master at Helmsdale (thanks for the honest appraisal and advice getting me round Duncansby Head). Richard and Regula for all the food and fun evening at Keiss. Emmalyne at the Sinclair Arms for packets of Monster Munch. James, Gordon and Kettie (for the invaluable but unintelligible advice). The Dutch Lady and her husband for the water, Keiss. Karen and her walking friend from the volunteer coastguards at Duncansby head (for pointing me towards Ivor Thomas). Ivor for showing me and working out a tidal plan to get me through the Pentland Firth safely. Kevin (Donald's friend who helped me get off the beach at the Bay of Sannick) before departing along the Pentland Firth. The waitress at Popeyes Upperdeck and the Go West Sailing team. Anne and Sue with Finn the spaniel and Jack the flat coat lab for helping pull the boat across the sands at Sandside Bay, Dounreay. Betty, John, Matt and Brenda for feeding me the finest freshly caught BBQ'd Scottish fish. Rosie, Alan and James owner of Sango Sands Campsite for the free pitch. The man in the laundry room wielding a torch (for not bashing me on the head for frightening his wife). Andrew, John and Murray the three fishermen from Loch Eribol fish farm (who showed me the late-night drinking haunts of Durness). Andy, John his wife Cathay and the Cambridge University Scuba Diving Society; CUUEG (for putting me up in their dive lodge and rescuing me from death by midges). Jim, owner of Clachtoll campsite (providing a free pitch and hot showers on an inclement evening). Eric at Melvaig (who rescued the MOD27 from being washed off the slipway outside his sea front cottage in an unusually high tide). Gary the Gairloch Plummer and the Gairloch Sailing Club for use of the showers. Gairloch Museum for letting me use their address for my parcels of warm weather gear sent by Rooster. Rooster Sailing (for providing so much free equipment at a dark time of my trip). Andy for sending me his own personalised replacement windex. Max at Southeastsailboats.co.uk (for the replacement control lines and Harken blocks). Cobie for sponsoring a hotel room in Gairloch (a life saver from the terrible weather). Simon Ogden at Performance Sailcraft (for supplying a replacement mainsheet block and new sail). Biddy a drinking friend from The Eight Bells, Jevington for the £100 (which I used to buy a Personal Locater Beacon later in the trip). The Kayaker in Skye (who directed me to Leopards Bothy). The two lovely ladies who made coffee and fed me biscuits at Dun BanBay, Doune (instead of calling the Police to report an uninvited intruder). Paul at Porthnadoran (who befriended me and shared some emotional moments about his late wife in his caravan). The owner of the Porthnadoran Campsite, Arisaig (for the free pitch). Joe at Tobermory (allowed me to pull the MOD27 onto one of his floating pontoons. Tobermory YHA for a comfortable bed, Anja and the other lady who shared the room with me. Ian site manager at Sheilings Holiday Park (for use of his bullet proof marquee overnight). Josh and Craigy fish (for the entertainment and drunken advice navigating my way past Scarba and the Corryvreckan Whirlpool in the Western Isles). Duncan and Moira at Carsaig (who after a wary start became the most endearing and welcoming people, providing tea, cake and bought me a hot meal in theTayallich Inn, plus supplied a free bed in one of their caravans for the night). Dennis the transatlantic sailor at Carsaig (who helped me plot a route with his charts around the Mull of Kintyre. I should have heeded his warning to wait a day). The Land Lady of the Argyll Inn, Southend, Scotland for feeding me and supplying a free bottle of sparkling water. The cleaner of the Dunaverty Public Toilet (for keeping under the urinals so clean and the hand dryer serviced). The Irish Captain of Stena line Ferries for taking my VHF call and pointing out he was nowhere near running me down. Simon at No.4 B&B, Portpatrick (for the free accommodation and emotional tolerance). Portpatrick RNLI (for allowing me to park the MOD27 next to the lifeboat on their pontoon). Belfast Coastguard (for making reassuring noises during my crossing of the Irish Sea to the Isle of Man). Donald, the training officer at Manx SC, Ramsey on the Isle of Man (for making positive vibes prior to and during my crossing to the Isle of Man). Donald's dad, David (for providing a bed and way too much good whisky at night). Keith, Commodore of Manx SC and so many of the members who turned out to welcome me ashore. Afric, Donalds wife (for her in depth explanation about the historical origins of the parliament on the island). Jenny at Port St.Mary (for her extraordinarily warm hospitality, food and lodgings and her piloting skills into the harbour and relaying news to the coastguard when my communications failed). Tony, Coxswain at the Holyhead Lifeboat Station and all the crew (for free bed and generous donation of £30 to pay for my food and beer, collected from a whip round from the crew). Diana at Whistling Sands, who touched my soul with her heart-rending story of her husband's struggle with Parkinsons). Bear Grylls (who through one of his shows gave me the confidence and technique to quench my thirst in the absence of water). Peter Dickens from Eastbourne (who connected me to Wendy in Aberaeron). Wendy in Aberaeron (who introduced me to Nick Commodore of The Aberaeron Yacht Club and invited me to attend the Commodores reception coincidentally being held the evening I landed). Wendy again for chauffeuring, chaperoning me to The Commodores Reception and providing board and lodgings for the night and one of the finest cooked breakfasts, compliments of her friends Harbourmaster Cafe the following morning). The Aberaeron Yacht Club members for donating their raffle prize pot to my Prostate Cancer UK just giving page. Roger "Fish" and Gail in Fishguard (who gave all the help a single-handed circumnavigator could want for. Great chilli, chat and B&B. The lobster loading in the morning was a particular highlight I'll cherish. Piers of Solva for his telephone advice on passing through Ramsey Island at St David's head. Paul who met me on the beach at 5am with bacon butties and a cappuccino at Monorbier. Uncle Francis (My Godfather who recruited his daughter and buffed up the Bentley in anticipation of my arrival in Devon, only for me to miss him due to sailing 100 miles past him by road into Cornwall). Amanda and Julie Seaweed my first contacts in Crackington Haven, Julie for sharing her beautiful cottage and introducing me to Pete and Helen who hosted drinks at their place. Also, Robbie, and Phil (who rescued the MOD27 being sucked out through the haven entrance whilst I was unloading). The owner of the house on the front of Crackington Haven, where I used the front garden as a changing room and the outside shower to hose down on arrival. Denzil and Hannah collecting me from St. Ives (rehydrating me after a long day at sea with little or no water, providing 5-star overnight treatment and entertainment). Tim, Bec's and their two dogs – Stanley and Jess (providing me with their spare room in their holiday cottage at Mousehole). Nick for collecting me from Mousehole when the weather closed in helping me fix the sail and putting me and Emma up in his house in Mounts Bay. Tresanton Beach Hotel where I parked the MOD27 on their slipway overnight at St. Mawes. Dan, Ben, John, Mike, Kieran, Jena and Tom some of whom bought me beer and welcomed me into St. Mawes Sailing Club. Tim and Bernadette of Salcombe, who escorted me across the bar with Ester in their Lasers and Tiger a small vintage motor launch. Providing luxurious food and lodgings after a testing day for all. Sorry about the shower head Tim! Jon Emmett and the Weymouth Olympic Sailing Centre venturing out into 38 knot winds and escorting me into the harbour. Jon for providing a bed for sponsoring a double diner and putting me up for longer than either of us expected. Moat sails for repairing overnight free of charge my badly damaged sail batten pockets and rips in the luff. Thanks for the free T-shirt. I'm still wearing it now. To the Captain and crew of HMS Sutherland for ceasing fire after being alerted to my presence in the Lulworth firing range. Lymington Sailing Club for preparing a welcoming party I unwittingly sailed straight past. Island Sailing Club, Cowes for allowing me to park on their visitor pontoon and drink in the bar overnight. My old mate Nick and his Met Police sailing mates for plying me with too much drink and a bed for the night in Cowes. The Colonel (a founder member of the FAFF Gang) from Portsmouth for his advice early on in the journey to try and run at 70%. Nick from Stokes Bay sorry about the amnesia had I remembered I would have called in. Becky and Tim on Hayling Island for taking a photo when my hands wouldn't stop shaking. Steve and Sarah for rescuing me from the beach at Hayling and looking after me for days until the weather finally offered a window to make the final dash back to Eastbourne.

Everyone who came out to meet me on my final leg home from Hayling to Eastbourne. Especially Mick and Gary from Eastbourne Sovereign Sailing Club who escorted me home in Legacy, Jason the kite surfer and all the other small craft who braved the seas.

Big thanks to everyone who followed on Facebook and all of the messages of support and anyone I might have overlooked or forgotten.

Finally, thanks to my Mum and Dad for encouraging me to get into sailing.

DAY 31 HELMSDALE P8

DONALD SUTHERLAND P10

DAY 32 KEISS P15

RICHARD & REGULA P15

WILD CAMPING KEISS

DAY 33 DUNCANSBY HEAD

DAY 34 IVOR THOMAS P32

KEVIN-PENTLAND FIRTH P34

DUNNET HEAD P35

GO WEST SAILING P38

DAY 35 DOUNREAY NUCLEAR REACTOR P42

ANNE BENNET & SUE RUSSEL

SANDSIDE BAY - FINN THE DOG

ALAN & ROSIE SANGO SANDS P55

DAY 36 SANGO SANDS

JOHN, ANDREW & MURRAY P60

DAY 39 CAPE WRATH

ANDY JENNINGS & DIVERS OF CUUEG P64

OLDSHORE MORE NR KINLOCHBERVIE

JIM - CLACHTOL P 72

DAY 43 MELVAIG - ERICS

ERICS HOUSE MELVAIG P74

LEOPARD MANS BOTHY P85

DAY 46 - LOCALSH ISLE OF SKYE

INSIDE THE BOTHY ISLE OF SKYE

DAY 47- PAUL PORTNADORAN P93

DAY 49 - TOBERMORY - P100

DAY 50 - IAN SHEILINGS HOLIDAY PARK

CRAIGY FISH N JOSH CRAIGNURE INN - P108

DAY 51 - CARSAIG P114

DUNCAN P116

DENNIS - CARSAIG

ROUTE THROUGH WESTERN SCOTLAND

DAY 52 - MADNESS AT THE MULL OF KINTYRE

DAY 52 - SOUTHEND PUBLIC GENTS - P132

DAY 52 - MULL OF KINTYRE ROUTE

DAY 55 DONALD & DAVID P149

DAY 53 SIMON NO 4 PORTPATRICK P139

KEITH POOLE MANX SC COMMODORE P149

P150 ROGER GLASS SAFETY CHANNEL

DAY 56 -JEN KNEALE PORT ST. MARY

PORT ST. MARY

DAY 57 - IRISH SEA CROSSING P158

DAY 58 - TONY PRICE COXSWAIN HOLYHEAD RNLI

DAY 59- WHISTLING SANDS P170

WHISTLING SANDS P172

DAY 60 - WENDY PRICE (FRONT RIGHT) ABERAERON

COMMODORES RECEPTION DINER ABERAERON

DAY 61 - ROGER FISH & GAIL P184

NEWPORT P184

DAY 62 - PAUL HINKS P190

ARRIVING SUNSET - MANORBIER

DAY 63 DEPARTING SUNRISE MANORBIER

DAY 63 BRISTOL CROSSING, LUNDY

CORNWALL CRACKINGTON HAVEN

JULIE SEAWEED, ROBBIE & PHIL P203

CRACKINGTON HAVEN OPEN AIR LAUNDRETTE

DAY 64 - DENZIL MAY ST. IVES P209

DAY 65 LANDS END ROUNDING IN SUNSHINE

DAY 65 MOUSEHOLE

BECY & TIM GREEN, STANLEY & JESS P218

NICK & WENDY STOTTEN MOUNTS BAY P221

DAY 67 LIZARD POINT

LIZARD POINT P224